Snow White
with the Red Hair

4

SHOJO BEAT EDITION

STORY AND ART BY
Sorata Akiduki

TRANSLATION **Caleb Cook**
TOUCH-UP ART & LETTERING **Brandon Bovia**
DESIGN **Alice Lewis**
EDITOR **Rae First, Karla Clark**

Akagami no Shirayukihime by Sorata Akiduki
© Sorata Akiduki 2010
All rights reserved.
First published in Japan in 2010 by HAKUSENSHA, Inc., Tokyo.
English language translation rights arranged with HAKUSENSHA, Inc., Tokyo.

The stories, characters and incidents mentioned
in this publication are entirely fictional.

Printed in Italy

Published by VIZ Media, LLC
P.O. Box 77010
San Francisco, CA 94107

10 9 8 7 6 5 4 3 2
First printing, November 2019
Second printing, January 2022

PARENTAL ADVISORY
SNOW WHITE WITH THE RED HAIR is
rated T for Teen and is recommended
for ages 13 and up for mild language.

viz.com

shojobeat.com

Sorata Akiduki was born on March 21 and is an accomplished shojo manga author. She made her debut in January 2002 with a one-shot titled "Utopia." Her previous works include *Vahlia no Hanamuko* (Vahlia's Bridegroom), *Seishun Kouryakubon* (Youth Strategy Guide) and *Natsu Yasumi Zero Zero Nichime* (00 Days of Summer Vacation). *Snow White with the Red Hair* began serialization in August 2006 in *LaLa DX* in Japan and has since moved to *LaLa*.

THE STORY

Shirayuki was born with beautiful hair as red as apples, but when her rare hair earns her unwanted attention from the notorious prince Raj, she's forced to flee her home. A young man named Zen helps her in the forest of the neighboring kingdom, Clarines, and it turns out he is that kingdom's second prince! Shirayuki decides to accompany Zen back to Wistal, the capital city of Clarines.

Shirayuki has met all manner of people since becoming a court herbalist, and her relationship with Zen continues to grow.

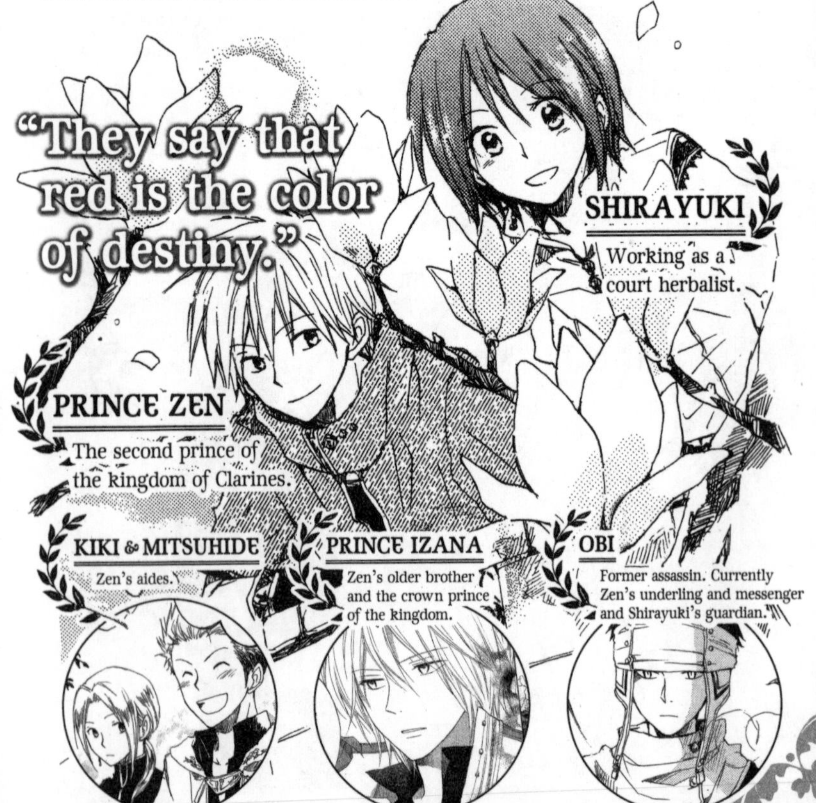
"They say that red is the color of destiny."
SHIRAYUKI
Working as a court herbalist.
PRINCE ZEN
The second prince of the kingdom of Clarines.
KIKI & MITSUHIDE
Zen's aides.
PRINCE IZANA
Zen's older brother and the crown prince of the kingdom.
OBI
Former assassin. Currently Zen's underling and messenger and Shirayuki's guardian.

Snow White with the Red Hair

Sorata Akiduki

4

Red Riding Hood Version
My lady...
Erm, I mean, "Red Riding Hood."
Where's the hood though?
My hair's red, so I didn't think it mattered...?

One day, a girl named Kihal travels from her home—an island within the kingdom—to the royal palace. She seeks protection for a species of bird integral to the lives of her and her people—birds being hunted for sport and profit by the local lord. Zen soon sees the birds' value and wonders if they might be used as a means of communication for the kingdom.

MY PLEASURE.
FLY NOW, POPO.
SHIRAYUKI AWAITS TO THE WEST.
FWEEE
...

As part of a trial to prove the birds' utility, Shirayuki travels to Kokoku to await Kihal's bird, Popo. Viscount Brecker is determined to sabotage the trial, however, and he locks Shirayuki inside the watchtower!

...MEANS NOTHING TO ME!!

Snow White with the Red Hair

VOLUME 4
TABLE of CONTENTS

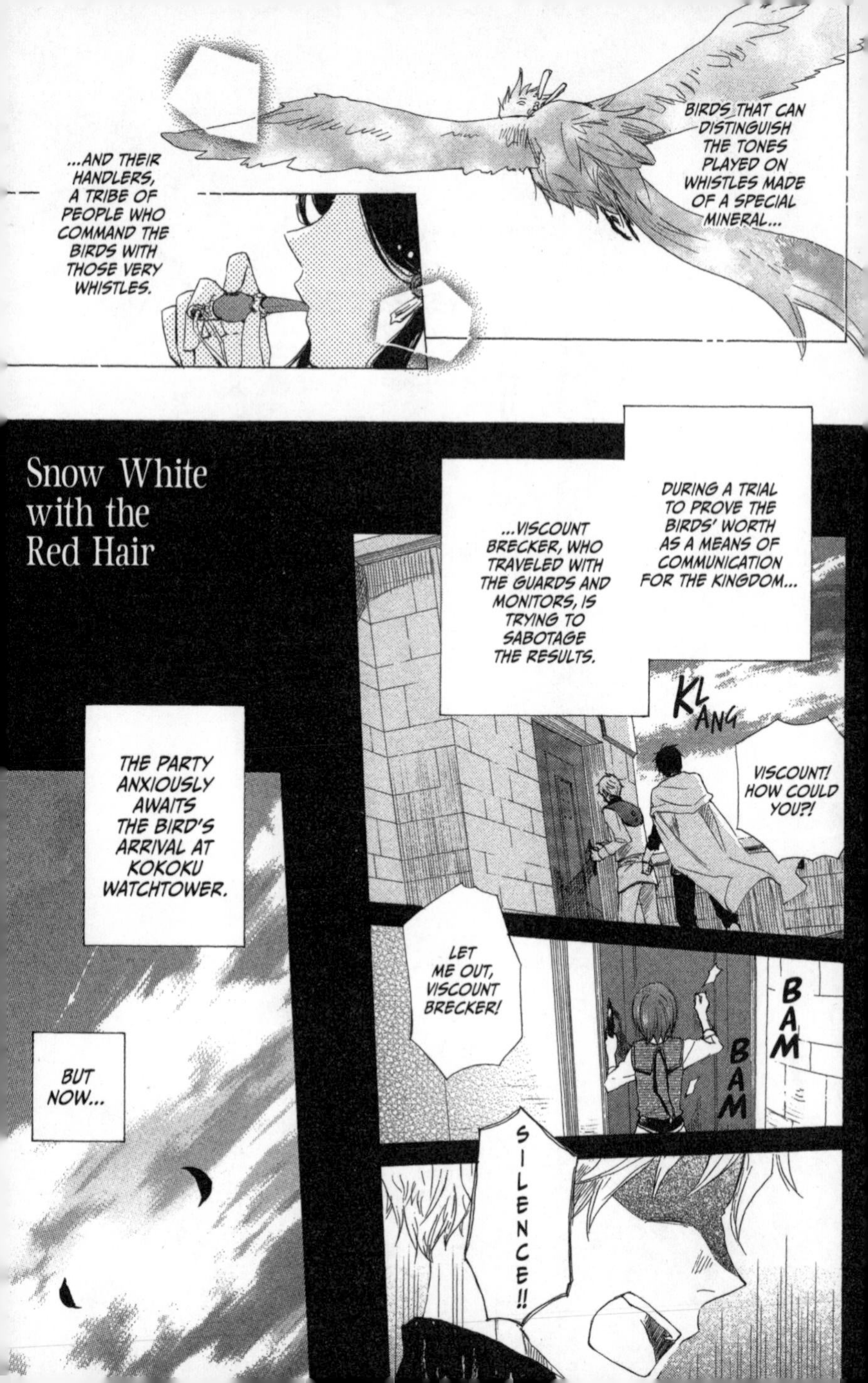
BIRDS THAT CAN DISTINGUISH THE TONES PLAYED ON WHISTLES MADE OF A SPECIAL MINERAL...
...AND THEIR HANDLERS, A TRIBE OF PEOPLE WHO COMMAND THE BIRDS WITH THOSE VERY WHISTLES.
DURING A TRIAL TO PROVE THE BIRDS' WORTH AS A MEANS OF COMMUNICATION FOR THE KINGDOM...
...VISCOUNT BRECKER, WHO TRAVELED WITH THE GUARDS AND MONITORS, IS TRYING TO SABOTAGE THE RESULTS.
Snow White with the Red Hair
KLANG
VISCOUNT! HOW COULD YOU?!
LET ME OUT, VISCOUNT BRECKER!
BAM
BAM
SILENCE!!
THE PARTY ANXIOUSLY AWAITS THE BIRD'S ARRIVAL AT KOKOKU WATCHTOWER.
BUT NOW...

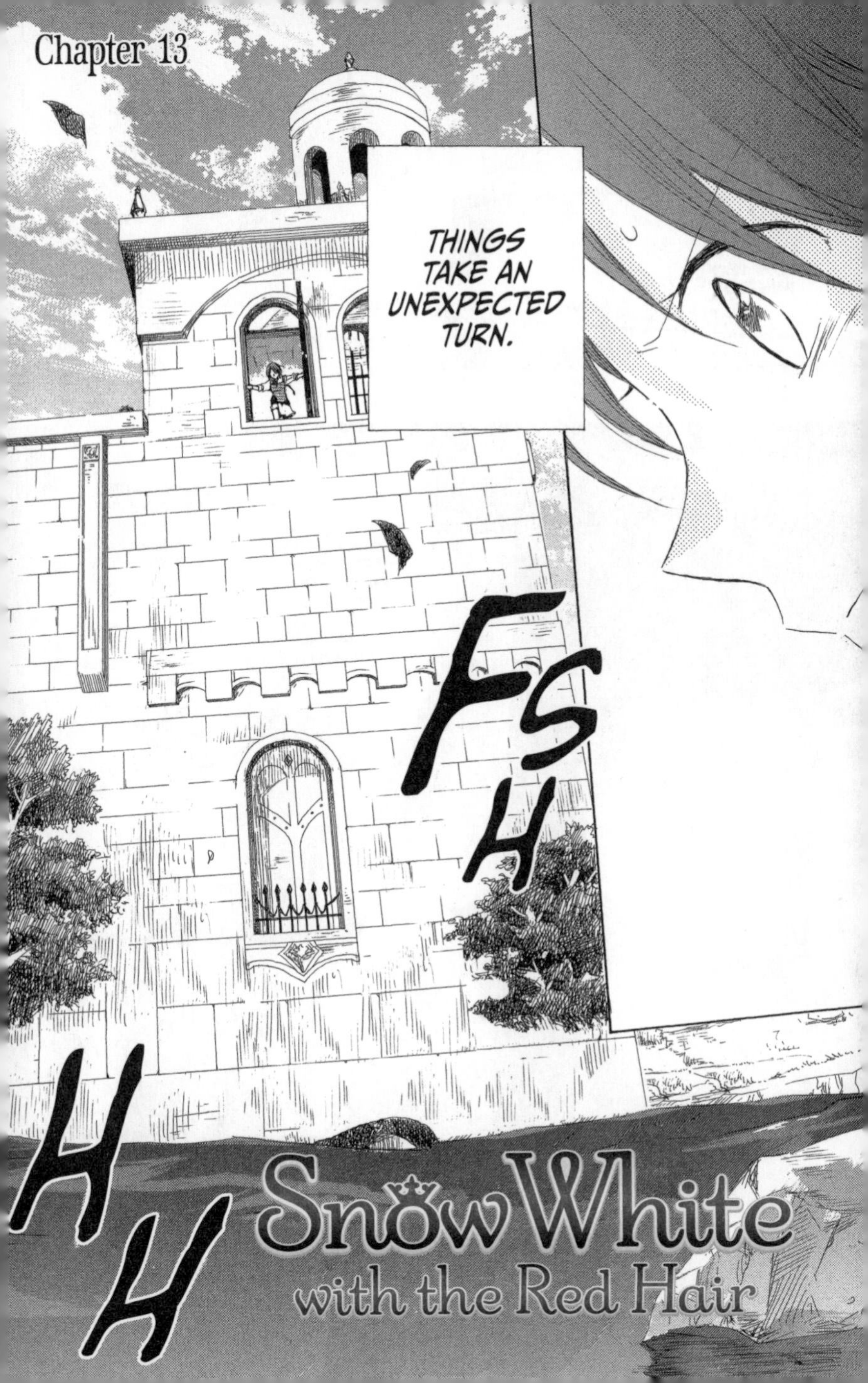
Chapter 13
THINGS TAKE AN UNEXPECTED TURN.
FSH
HH
Snow White with the Red Hair

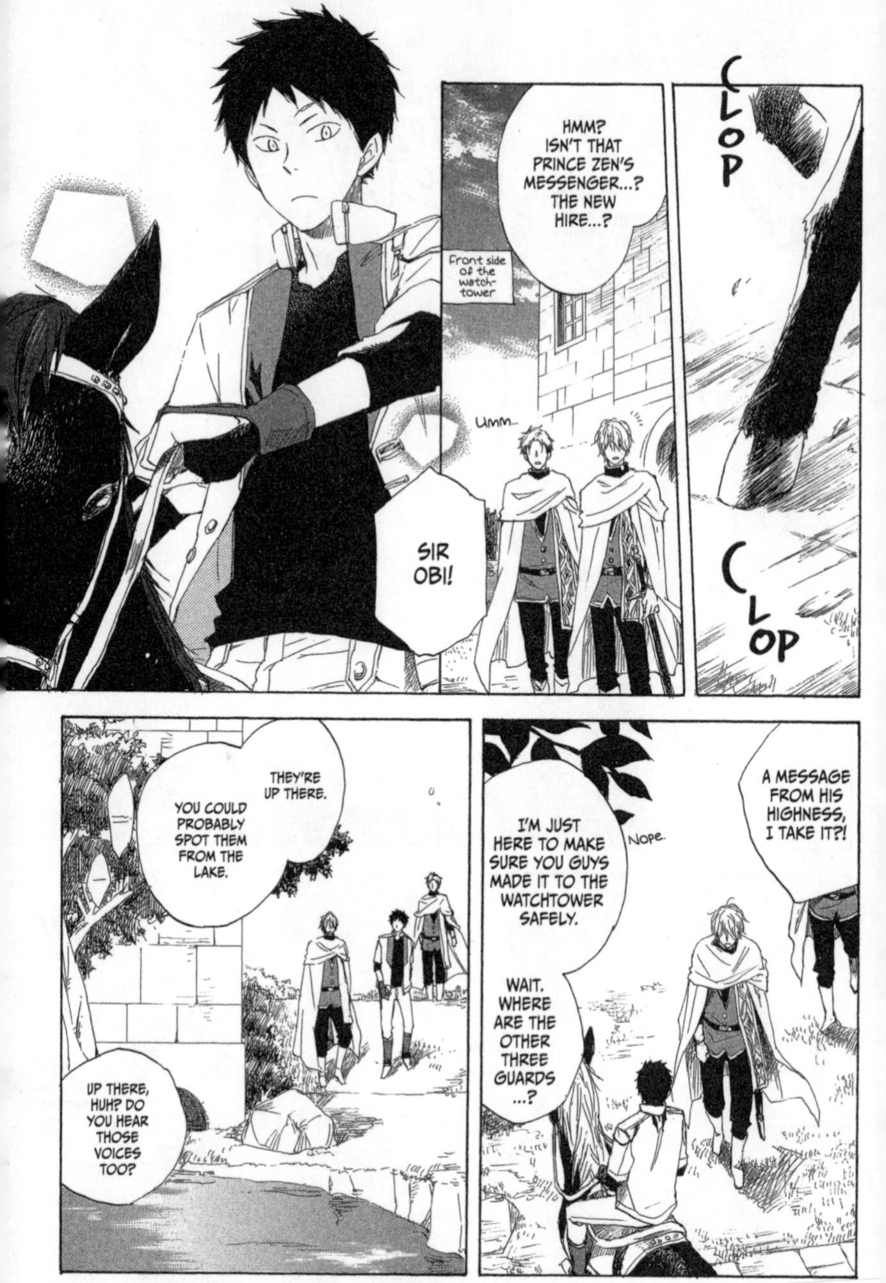
CLOP
CLOP
HMM? ISN'T THAT PRINCE ZEN'S MESSENGER...? THE NEW HIRE...?
Front side of the watch-tower
Umm...
SIR OBI!
A MESSAGE FROM HIS HIGHNESS, I TAKE IT?!
Nope.
I'M JUST HERE TO MAKE SURE YOU GUYS MADE IT TO THE WATCHTOWER SAFELY.
WAIT. WHERE ARE THE OTHER THREE GUARDS ...?
THEY'RE UP THERE.
YOU COULD PROBABLY SPOT THEM FROM THE LAKE.
UP THERE, HUH? DO YOU HEAR THOSE VOICES TOO?

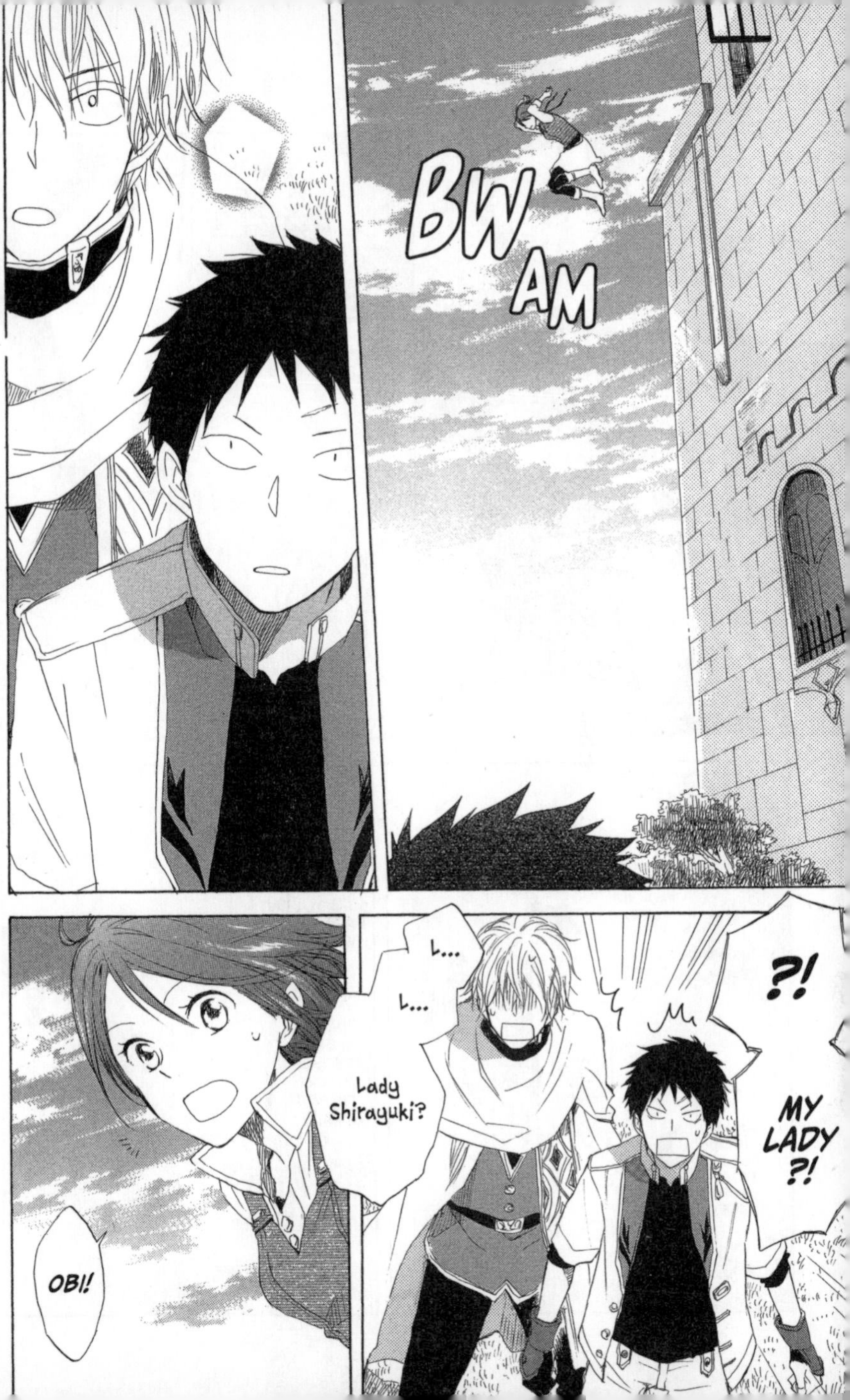
BWAM
?!
MY LADY ?!
L...
L...
Lady Shirayuki?
OBI!

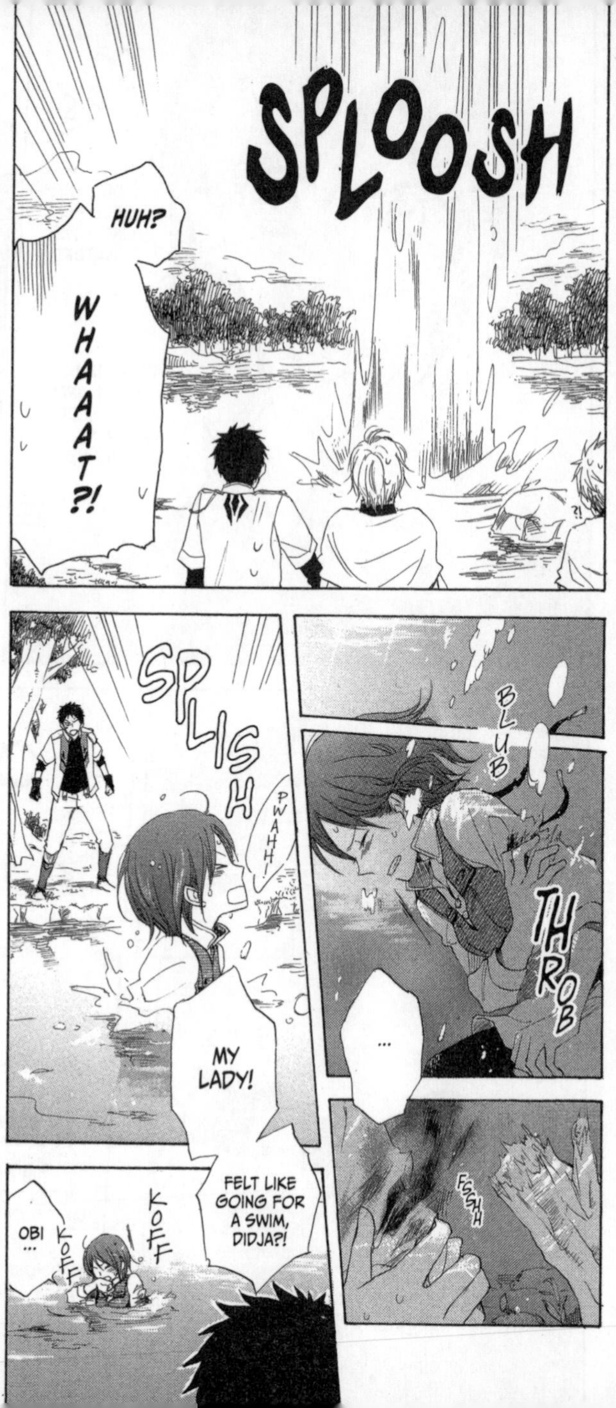
SPLOOSH
HUH?
WHAAAAT?!
?!
BLUB
THROB
...
FSSHH
SPLISH
PWAHH!
MY LADY!
FELT LIKE GOING FOR A SWIM, DIDJA?!
KOFF
KOFF
OBI...

GREETINGS

Happy New Year!

Volume 4 releases in Japan on January 4, 2010, so I included a preemptive New Year's message even though it's still 2009 at the moment. Please excuse me for that.

Volume 4... I sketched out a first draft of the cover featuring Obi, and lo and behold, it got approved!

Despite the fact that he didn't even have a name in volume 1.

This book is solely *Snow White with the Red Hair* again. No old one-shots.

Hope you enjoy it!

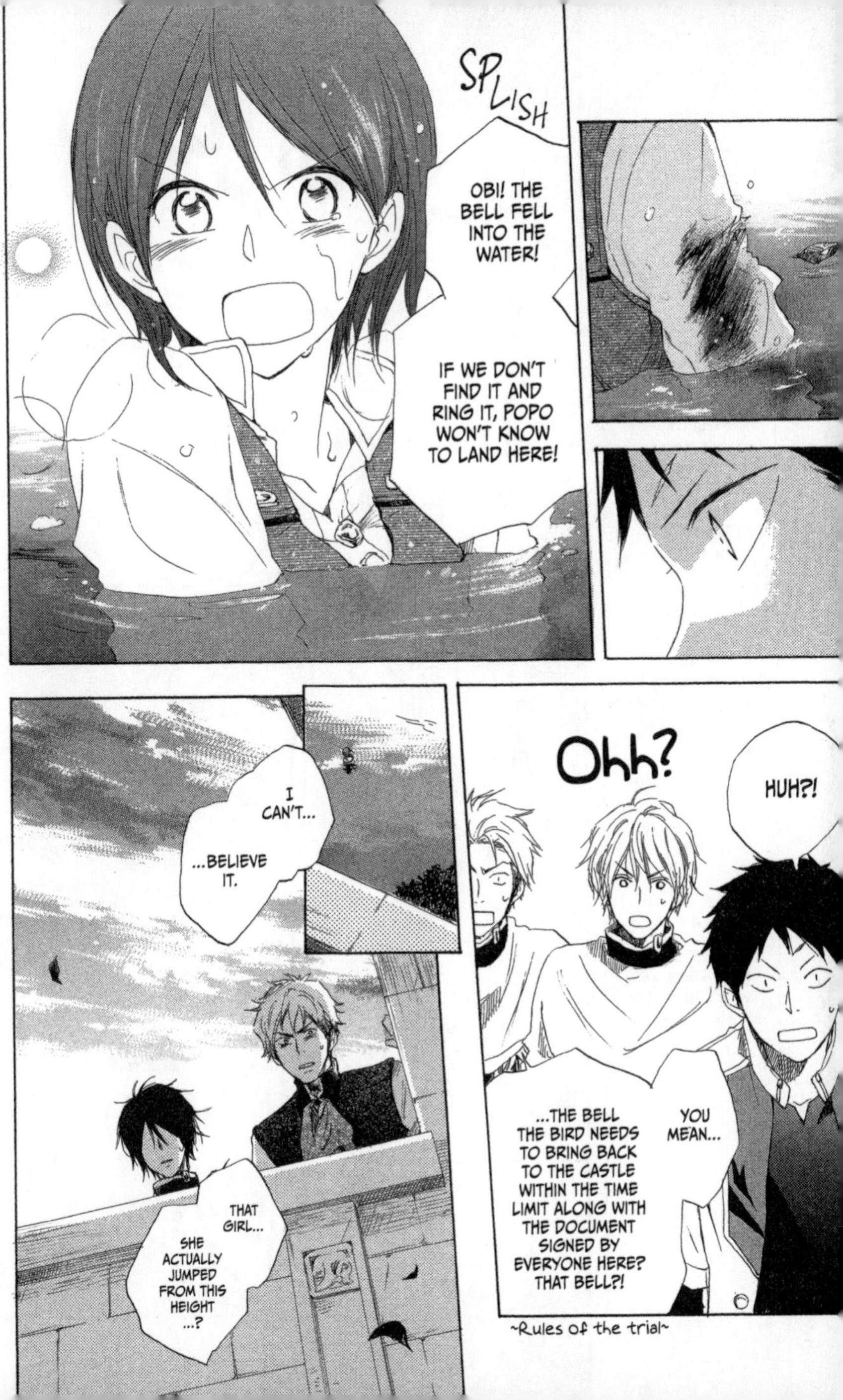
SPLISH
OBI! THE BELL FELL INTO THE WATER!
IF WE DON'T FIND IT AND RING IT, POPO WON'T KNOW TO LAND HERE!
HUH?!
Ohh?
YOU MEAN...
...THE BELL THE BIRD NEEDS TO BRING BACK TO THE CASTLE WITHIN THE TIME LIMIT ALONG WITH THE DOCUMENT SIGNED BY EVERYONE HERE? THAT BELL?!
~Rules of the trial~
I CAN'T...
...BELIEVE IT.
THAT GIRL...
SHE ACTUALLY JUMPED FROM THIS HEIGHT ...?

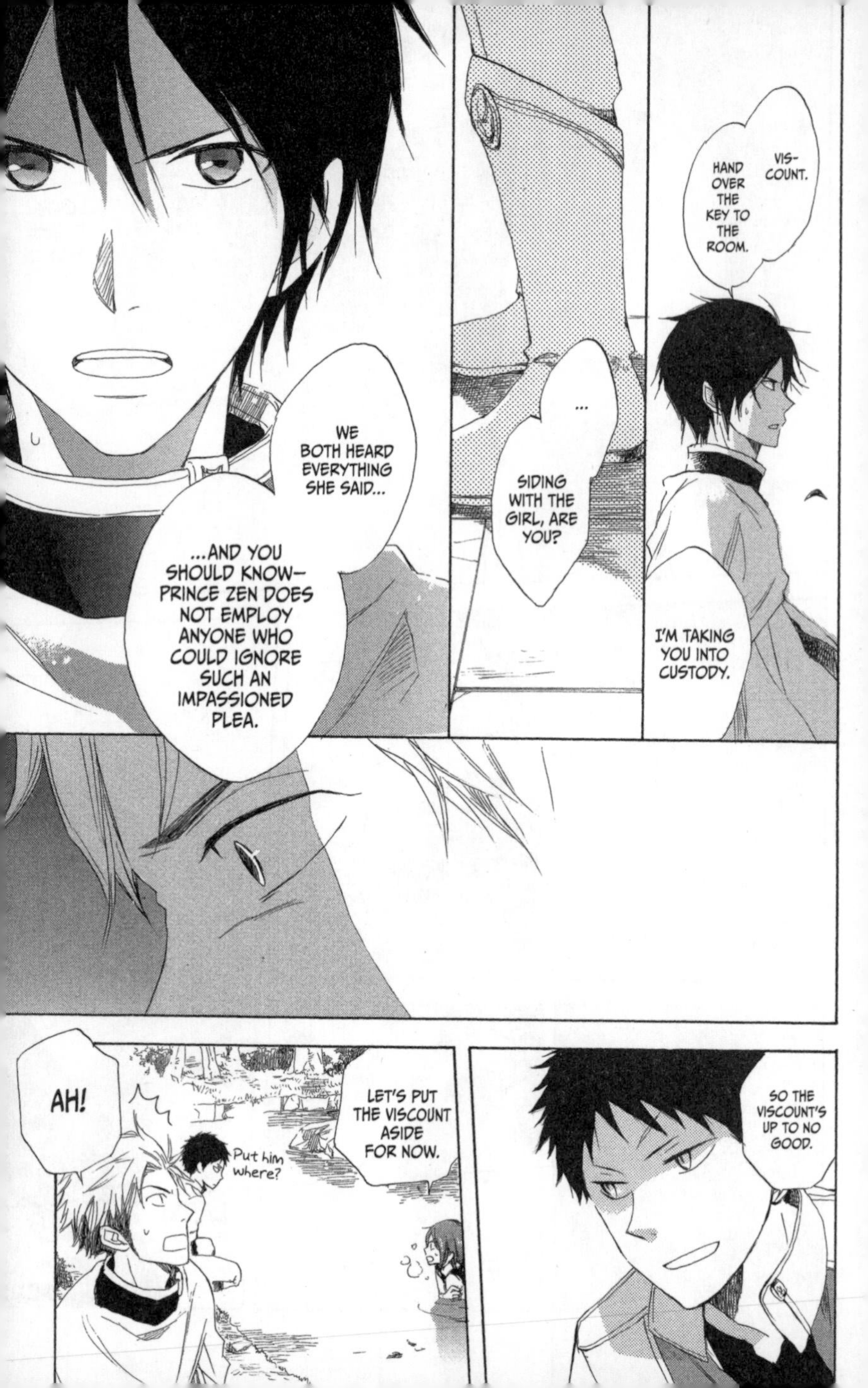
VIS-COUNT.
HAND OVER THE KEY TO THE ROOM.
I'M TAKING YOU INTO CUSTODY.
...
SIDING WITH THE GIRL, ARE YOU?
WE BOTH HEARD EVERYTHING SHE SAID...
...AND YOU SHOULD KNOW—PRINCE ZEN DOES NOT EMPLOY ANYONE WHO COULD IGNORE SUCH AN IMPASSIONED PLEA.
SO THE VISCOUNT'S UP TO NO GOOD.
LET'S PUT THE VISCOUNT ASIDE FOR NOW.
AH!
Put him where?

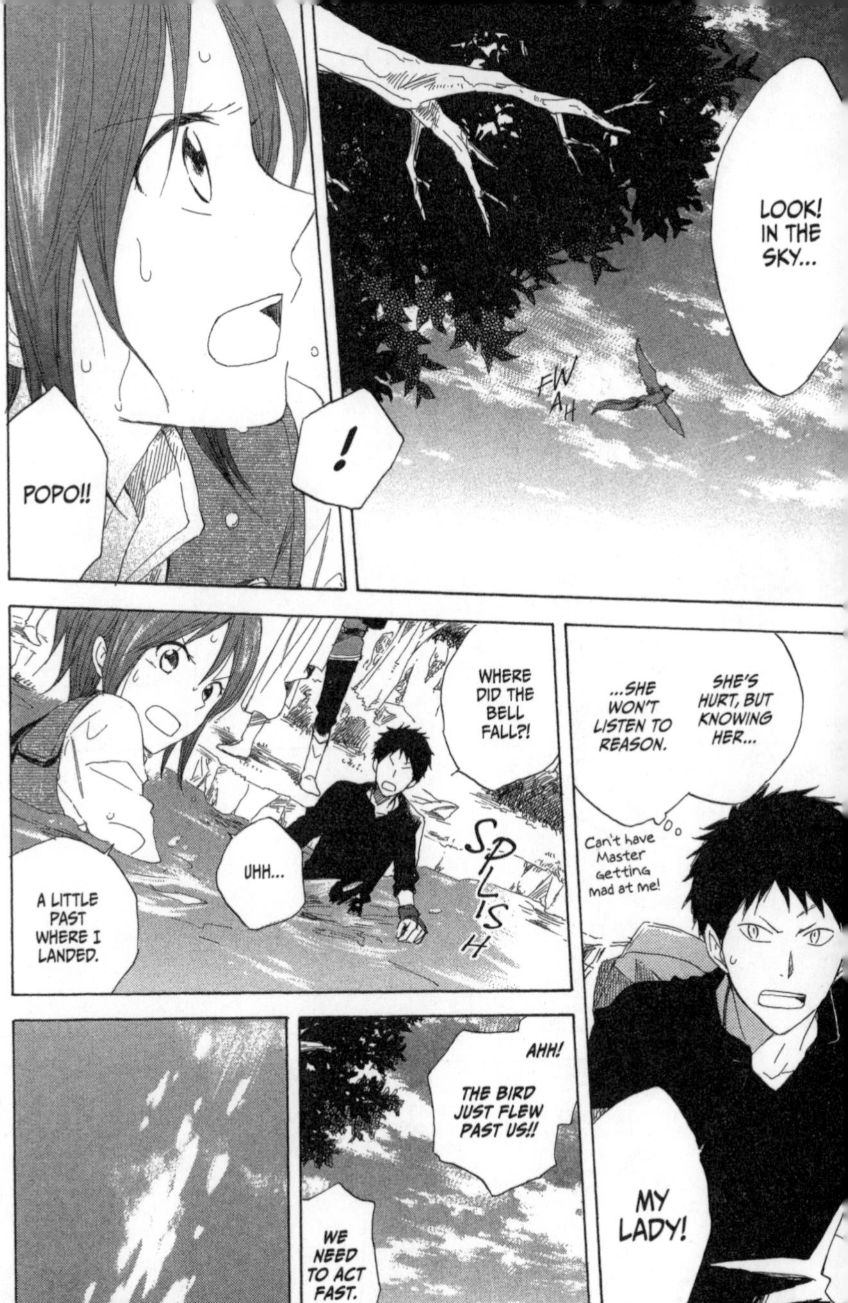
LOOK! IN THE SKY...
FWAH
!
POPO!!
SHE'S HURT, BUT KNOWING HER...
...SHE WON'T LISTEN TO REASON.
Can't have Master getting mad at me!
MY LADY!
WHERE DID THE BELL FALL?!
SPLISH
UHH...
A LITTLE PAST WHERE I LANDED.
AHH!
THE BIRD JUST FLEW PAST US!!
WE NEED TO ACT FAST.

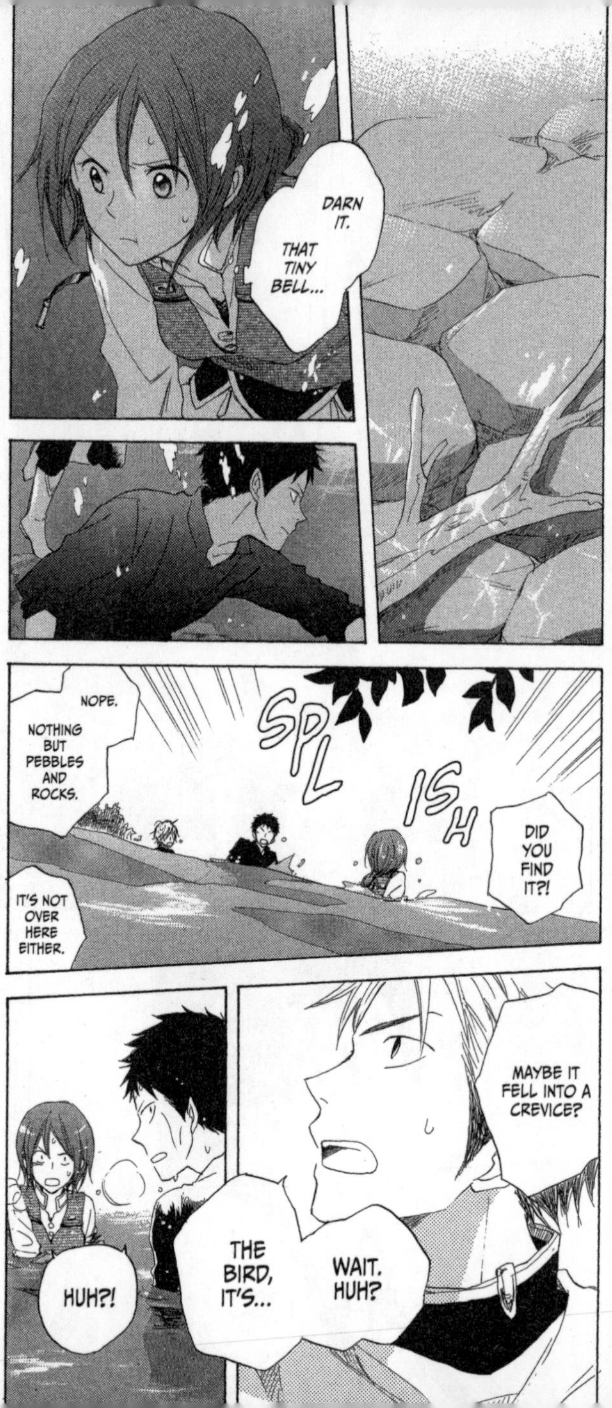
DARN IT.
THAT TINY BELL...
DID YOU FIND IT?!
SPLISH
NOPE.
NOTHING BUT PEBBLES AND ROCKS.
IT'S NOT OVER HERE EITHER.
MAYBE IT FELL INTO A CREVICE?
WAIT. HUH?
THE BIRD, IT'S...
HUH?!

Chapter 17 has a part where the characters talk about likes and dislikes, so I figured I might as well include some of that info here.

Like their tastes in food and other things.

Why? Because I've got 12 of these quarter-page spaces to fill up...

I happen to like udon. Much respect for all noodles, in fact!

I also can't go without salted beef tongue and candied sweet potatoes.

YUM!

In terms of activities, I love long car trips where I get to be the passenger.

I'm not a big fan of arcades.

2

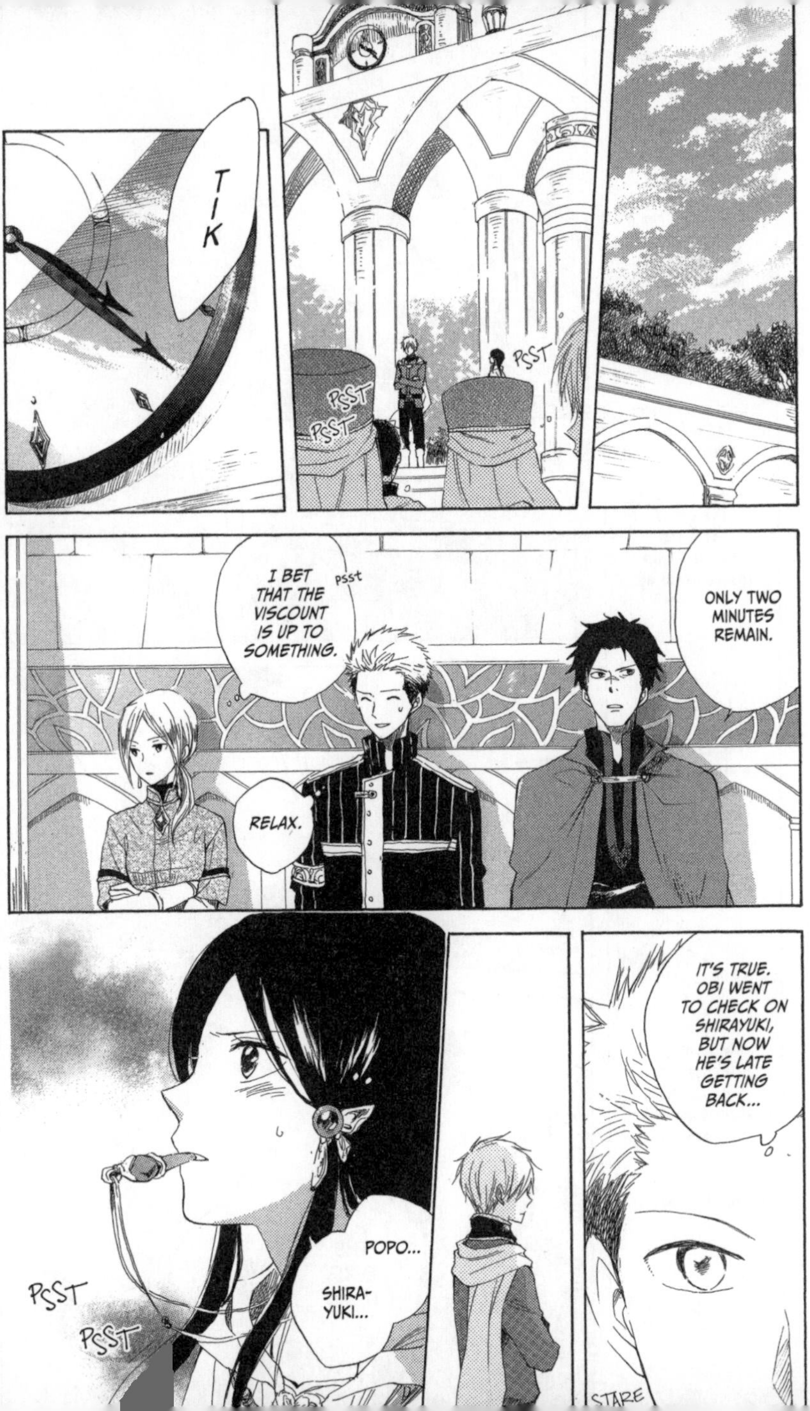
PSST
PSST
PSST
TIK
ONLY TWO MINUTES REMAIN.
I BET THAT THE VISCOUNT IS UP TO SOMETHING.
psst
RELAX.
IT'S TRUE. OBI WENT TO CHECK ON SHIRAYUKI, BUT NOW HE'S LATE GETTING BACK...
STARE
POPO...
SHIRA-YUKI...
PSST
PSST

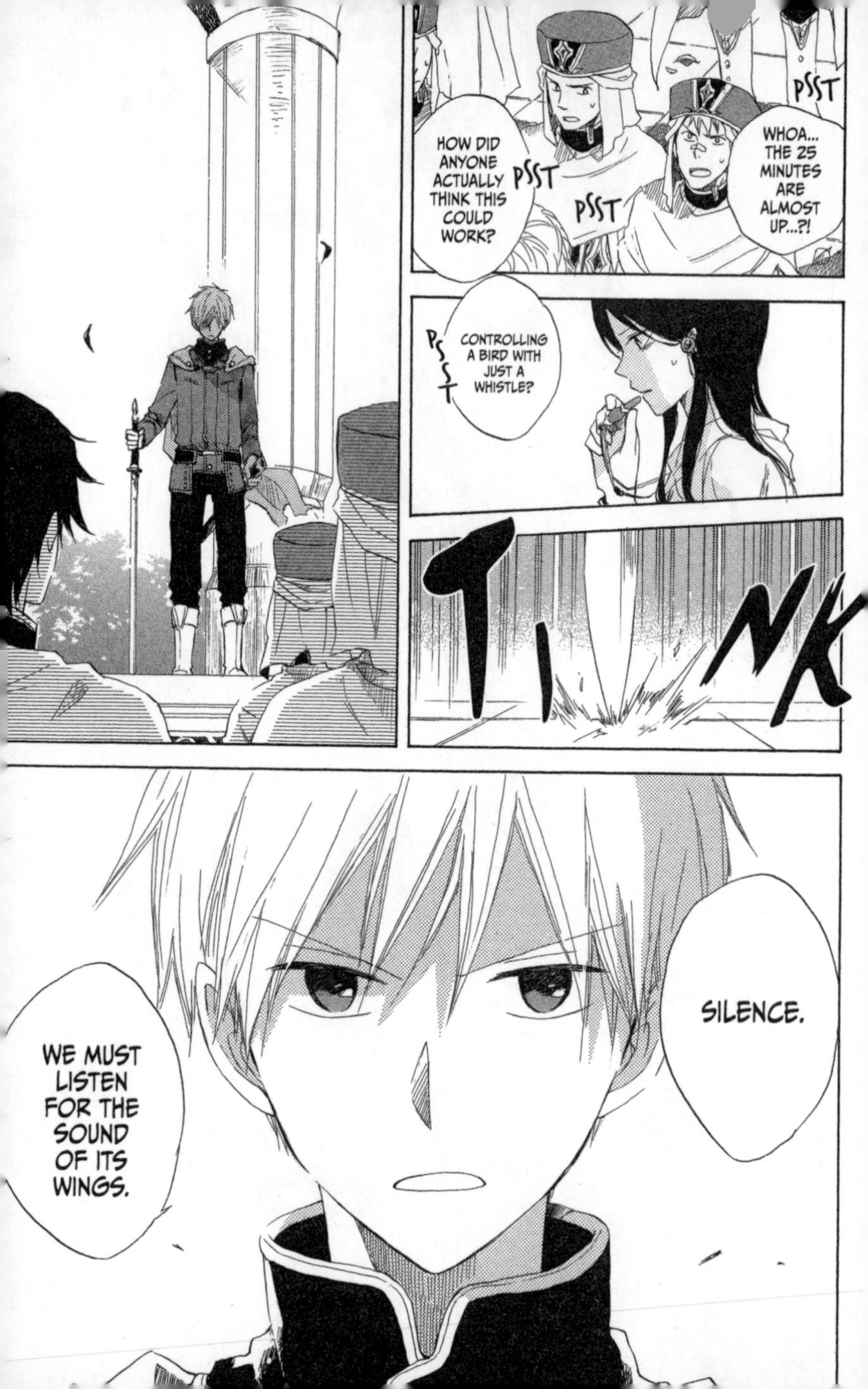
PSST
WHOA... THE 25 MINUTES ARE ALMOST UP...?!
PSST
PSST
HOW DID ANYONE ACTUALLY THINK THIS COULD WORK?
CONTROLLING A BIRD WITH JUST A WHISTLE?
PSST
TINK
SILENCE.
WE MUST LISTEN FOR THE SOUND OF ITS WINGS.

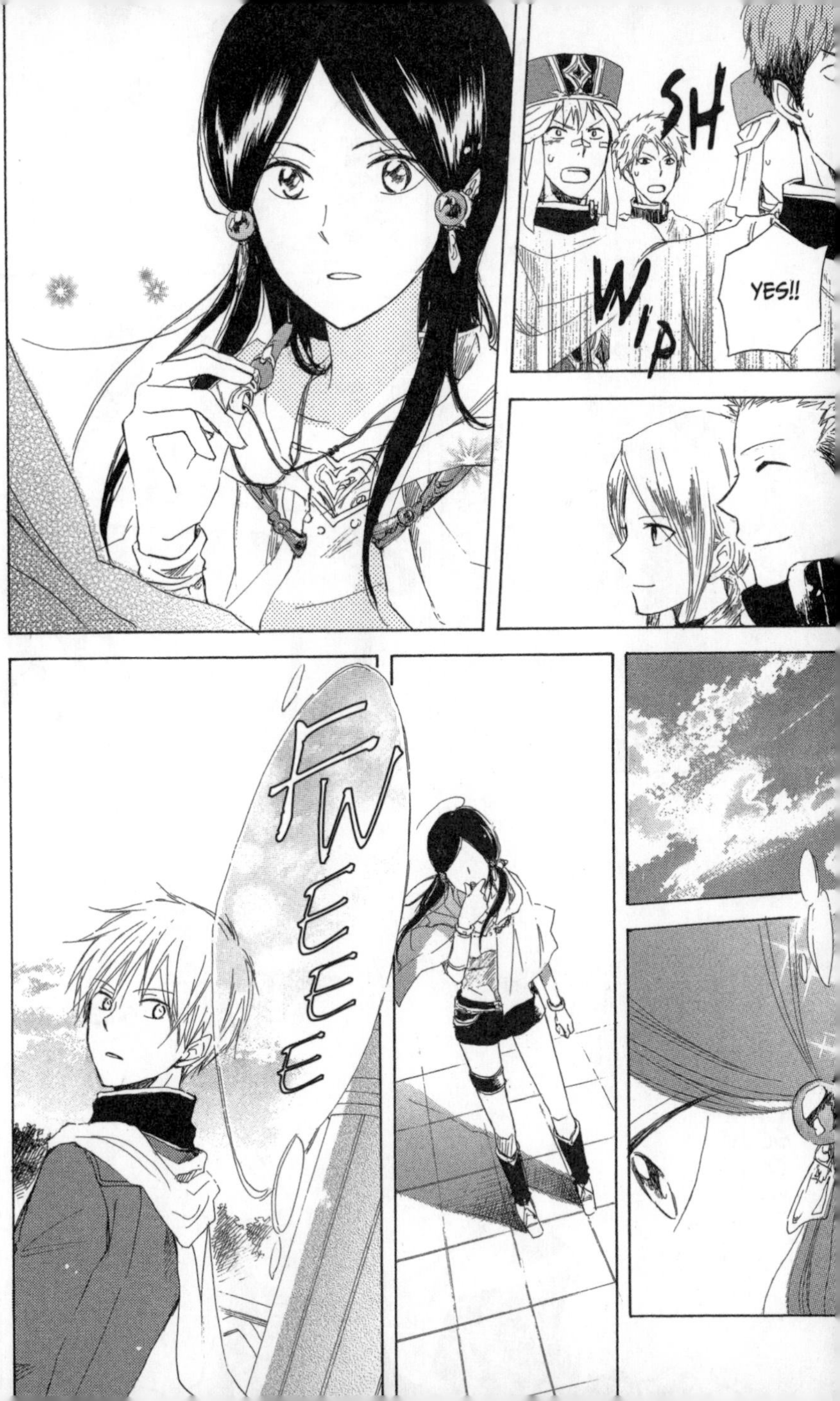
YES!!
SH
WIP
FWEEEE

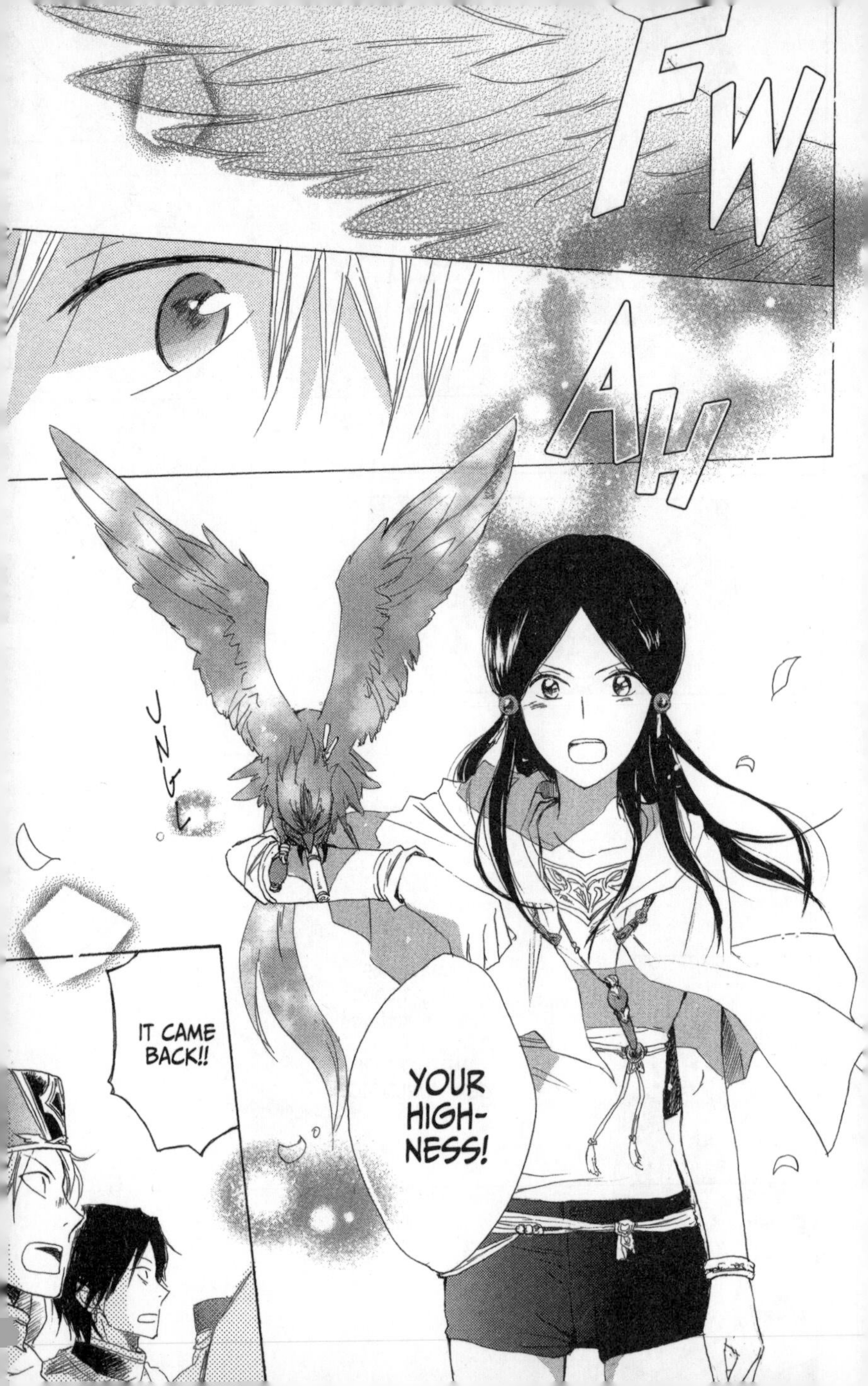
FW
AH
JNGL
YOUR HIGH-NESS!
IT CAME BACK!!

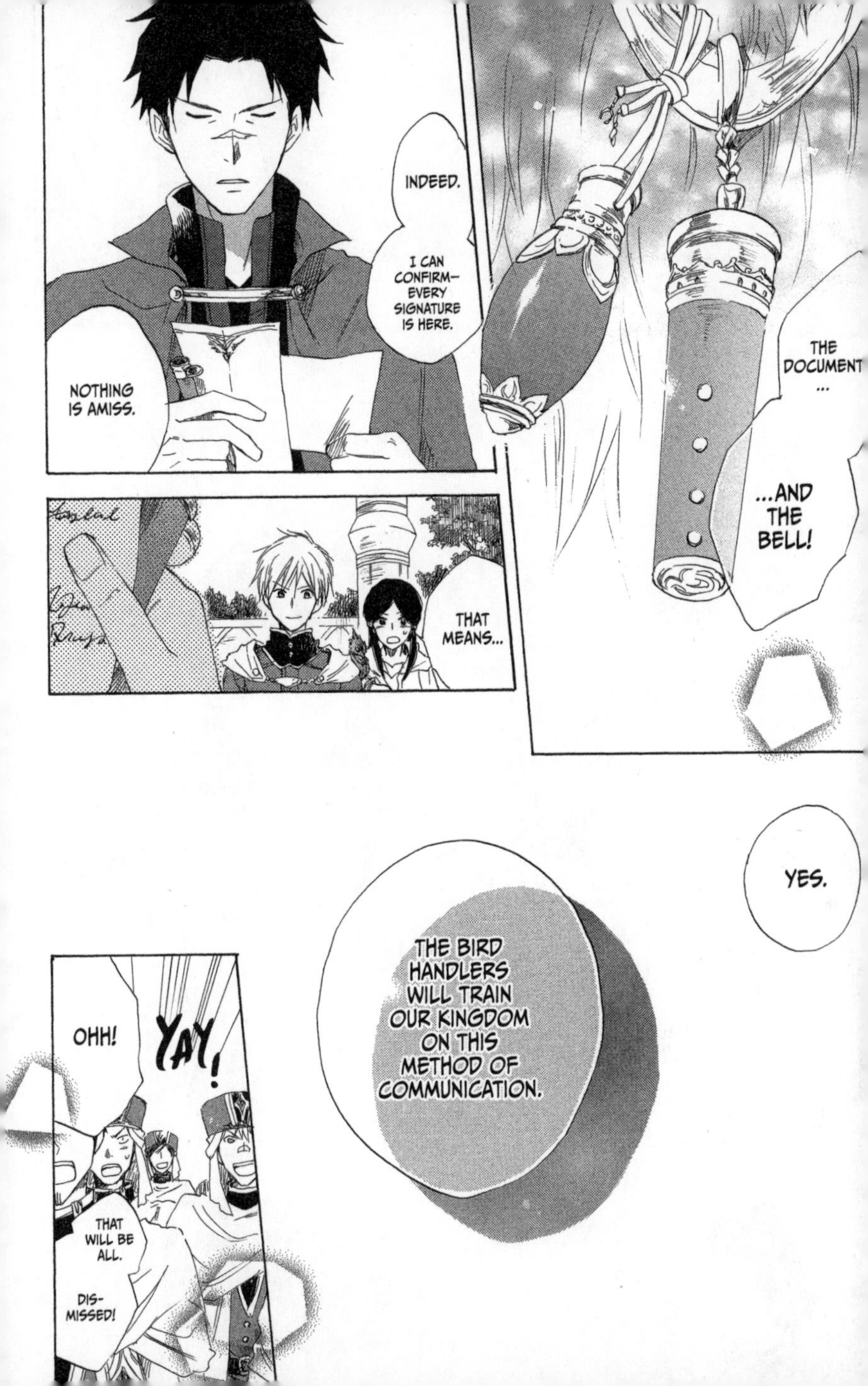
THE DOCUMENT...
...AND THE BELL!
INDEED.
I CAN CONFIRM—EVERY SIGNATURE IS HERE.
NOTHING IS AMISS.
THAT MEANS...
YES.
THE BIRD HANDLERS WILL TRAIN OUR KINGDOM ON THIS METHOD OF COMMUNICATION.
YAY!
OHH!
THAT WILL BE ALL.
DIS-MISSED!

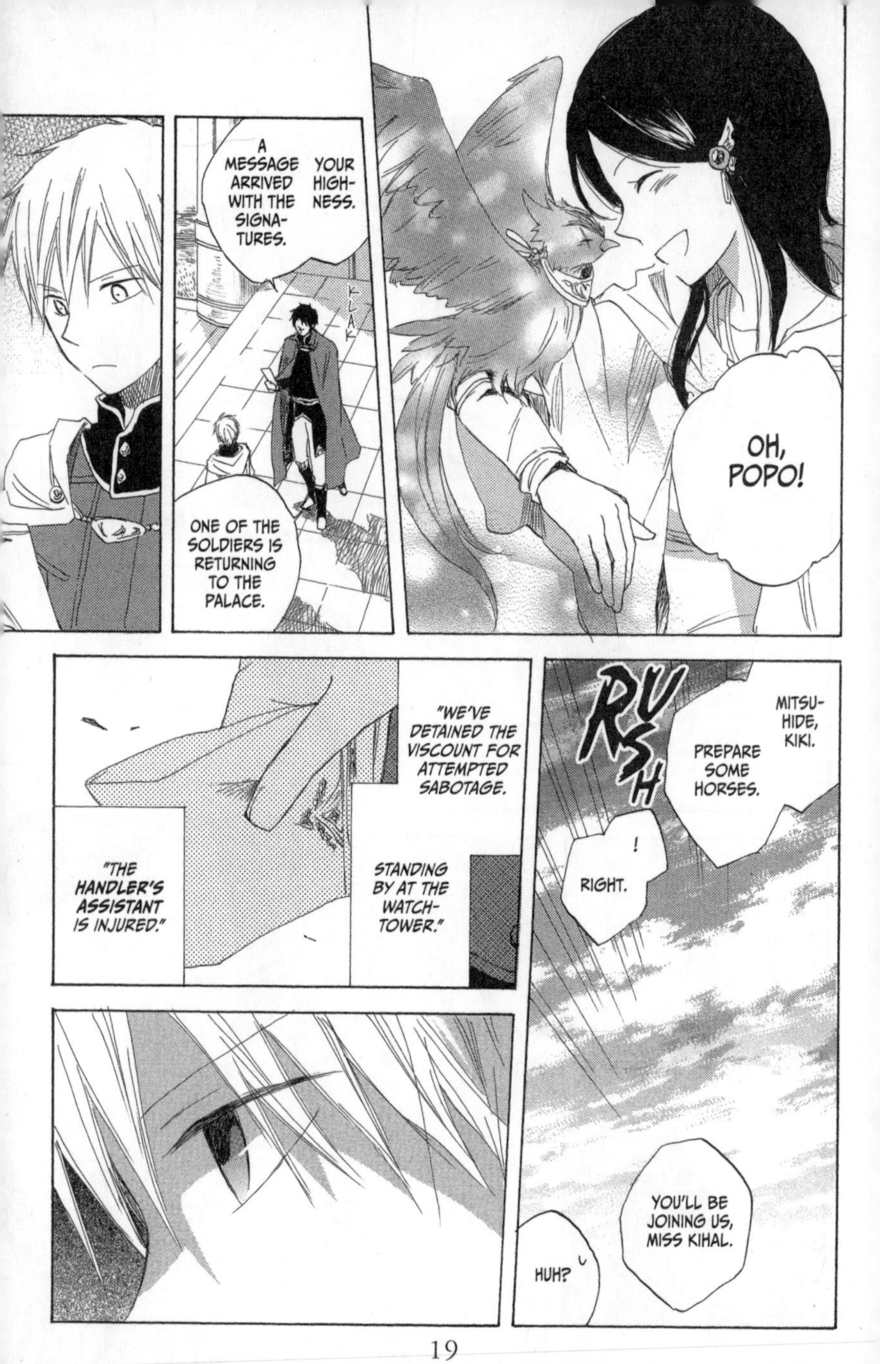
OH, POPO!
YOUR HIGHNESS.
A MESSAGE ARRIVED WITH THE SIGNATURES.
KLAK
ONE OF THE SOLDIERS IS RETURNING TO THE PALACE.
RUSH
MITSUHIDE, KIKI.
PREPARE SOME HORSES.
!
RIGHT.
YOU'LL BE JOINING US, MISS KIHAL.
HUH?
"WE'VE DETAINED THE VISCOUNT FOR ATTEMPTED SABOTAGE.
STANDING BY AT THE WATCHTOWER."
"THE HANDLER'S ASSISTANT IS INJURED."

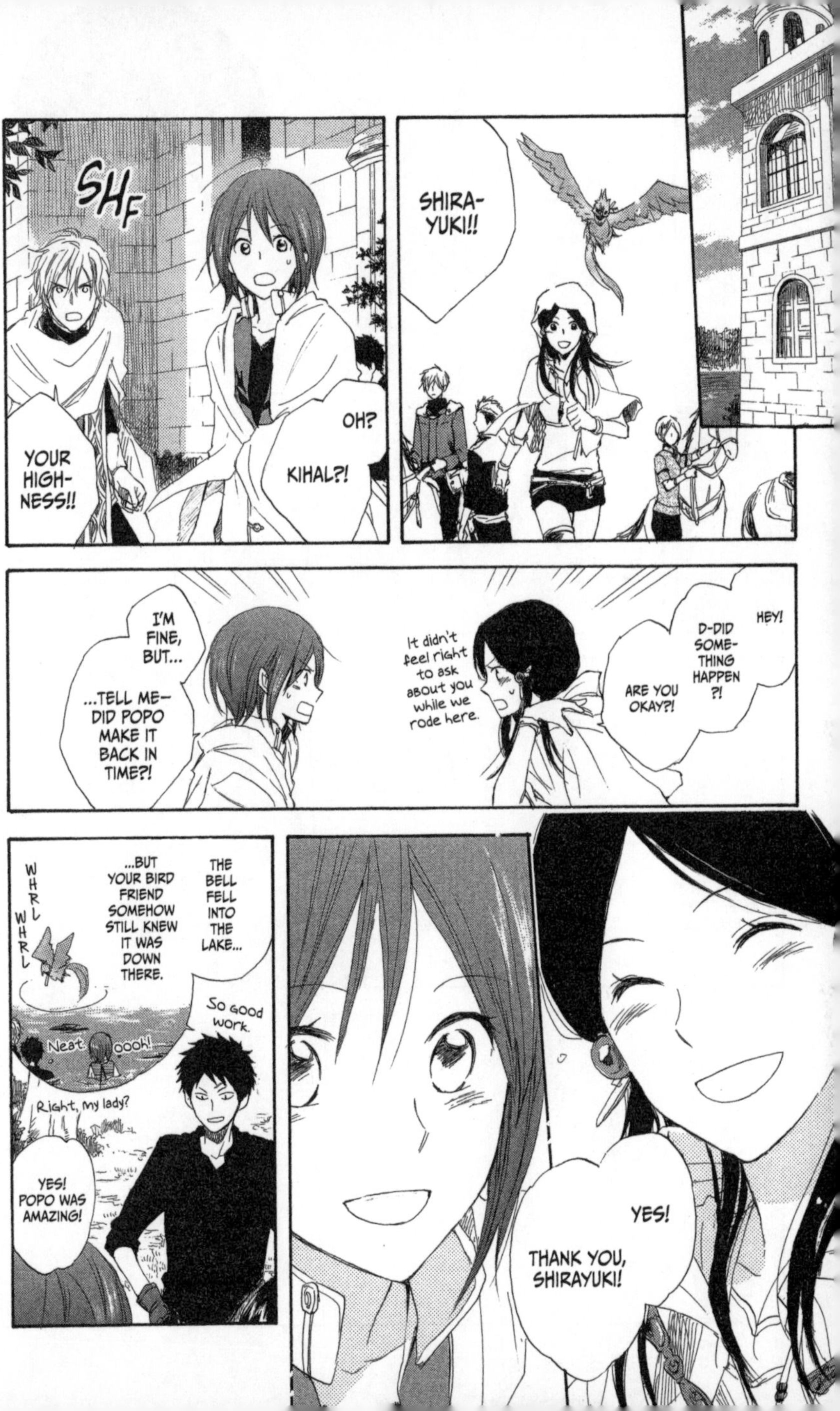
SHIRA-YUKI!!
OH?
KIHAL?!
SHF
YOUR HIGH-NESS!!
HEY!
D-DID SOME-THING HAPPEN ?!
ARE YOU OKAY?!
It didn't feel right to ask about you while we rode here.
I'M FINE, BUT...
...TELL ME— DID POPO MAKE IT BACK IN TIME?!
YES!
THANK YOU, SHIRAYUKI!
THE BELL FELL INTO THE LAKE...
...BUT YOUR BIRD FRIEND SOMEHOW STILL KNEW IT WAS DOWN THERE.
WHRL WHRL
So good work.
Neat.
oooh!
Right, my lady?
YES! POPO WAS AMAZING!

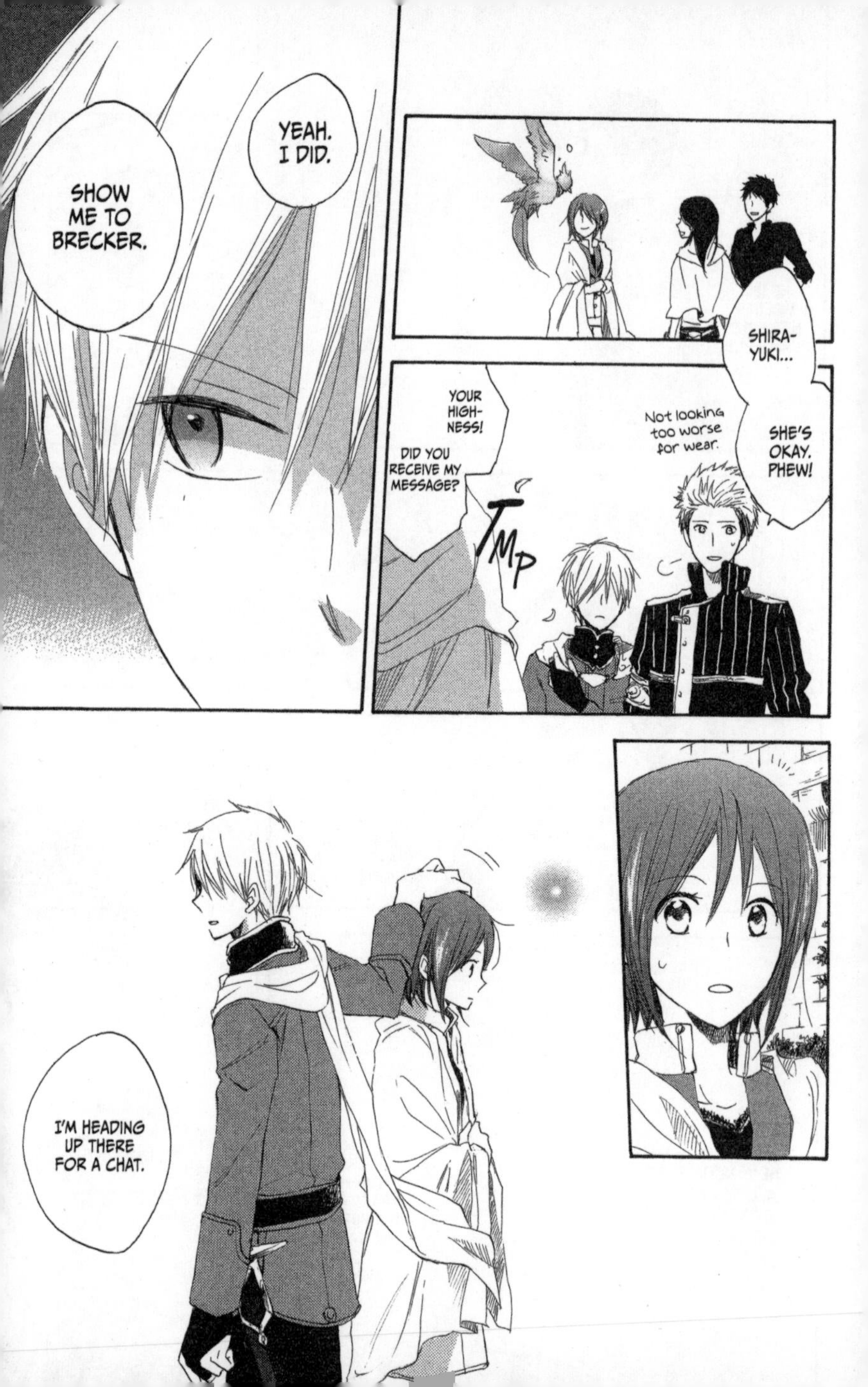
SHIRA-YUKI...
SHE'S OKAY. PHEW!
Not looking too worse for wear.
YOUR HIGHNESS!
DID YOU RECEIVE MY MESSAGE?
TMP
YEAH. I DID.
SHOW ME TO BRECKER.
I'M HEADING UP THERE FOR A CHAT.

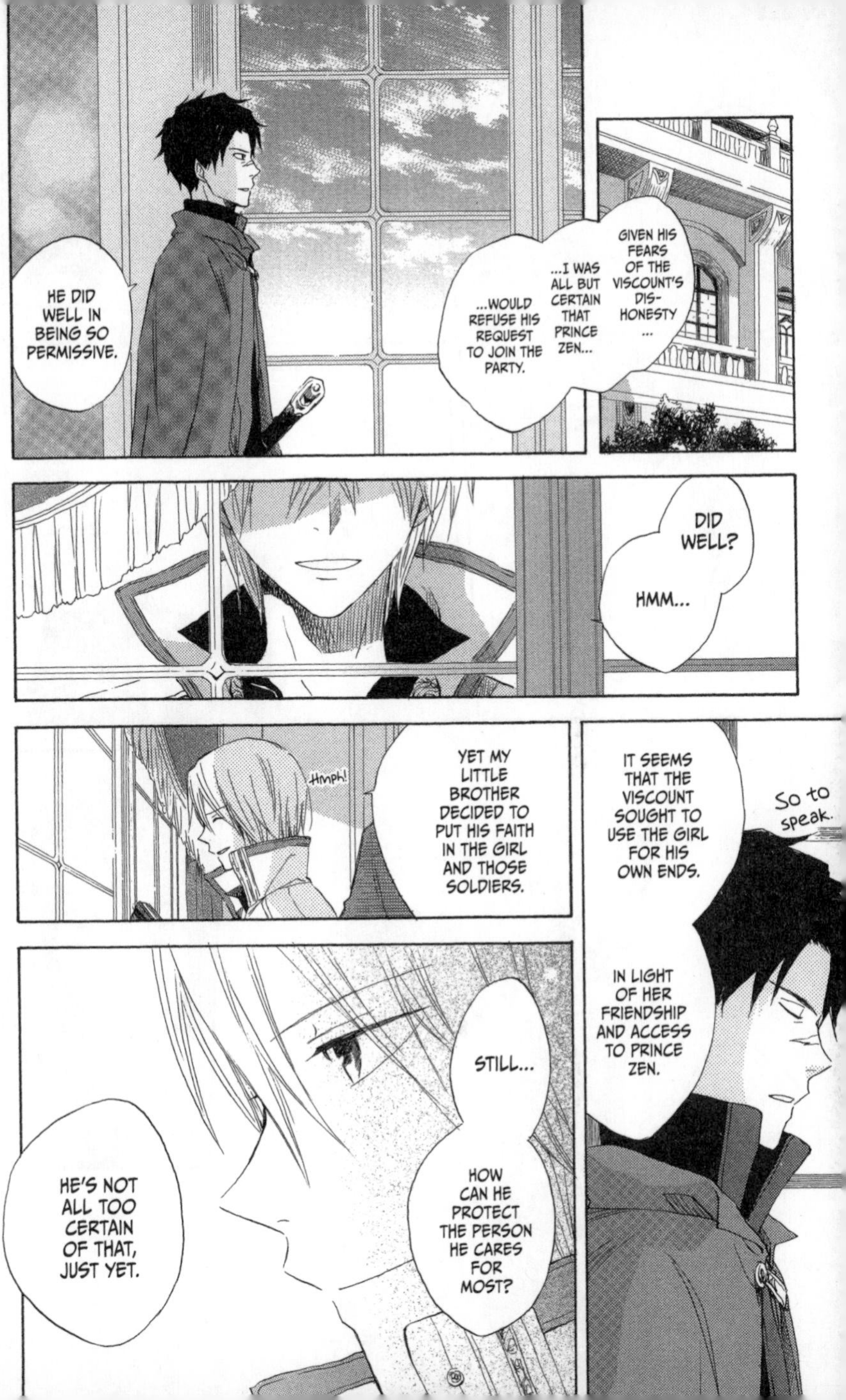
GIVEN HIS FEARS OF THE VISCOUNT'S DIS-HONESTY ...
...I WAS ALL BUT CERTAIN THAT PRINCE ZEN...
...WOULD REFUSE HIS REQUEST TO JOIN THE PARTY.
HE DID WELL IN BEING SO PERMISSIVE.
DID WELL?
HMM...
So to speak.
IT SEEMS THAT THE VISCOUNT SOUGHT TO USE THE GIRL FOR HIS OWN ENDS.
IN LIGHT OF HER FRIENDSHIP AND ACCESS TO PRINCE ZEN.
Hmph!
YET MY LITTLE BROTHER DECIDED TO PUT HIS FAITH IN THE GIRL AND THOSE SOLDIERS.
STILL...
HOW CAN HE PROTECT THE PERSON HE CARES FOR MOST?
HE'S NOT ALL TOO CERTAIN OF THAT, JUST YET.

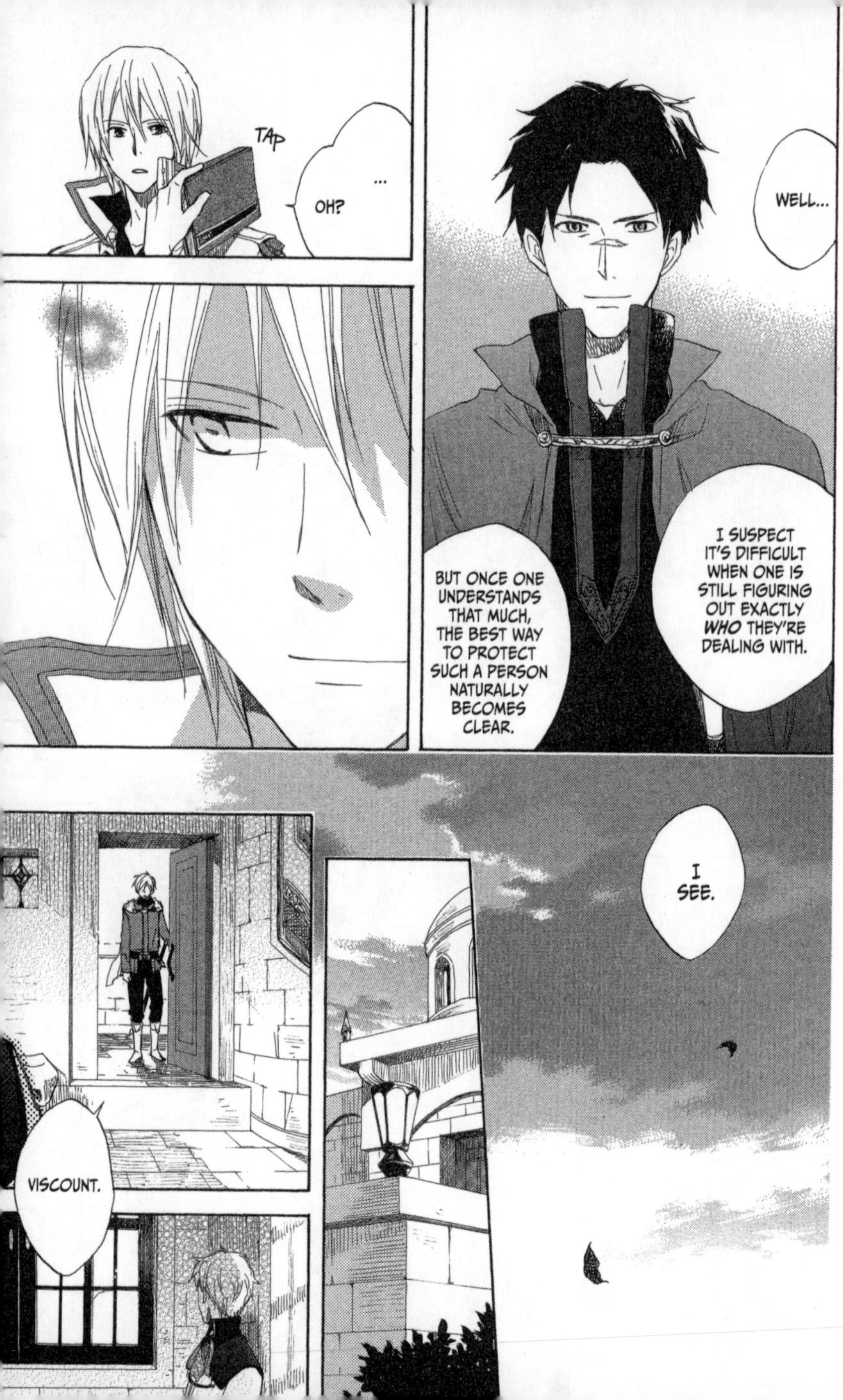
WELL...
I SUSPECT IT'S DIFFICULT WHEN ONE IS STILL FIGURING OUT EXACTLY *WHO* THEY'RE DEALING WITH.
BUT ONCE ONE UNDERSTANDS THAT MUCH, THE BEST WAY TO PROTECT SUCH A PERSON NATURALLY BECOMES CLEAR.
...
OH?
TAP
I SEE.
VISCOUNT.

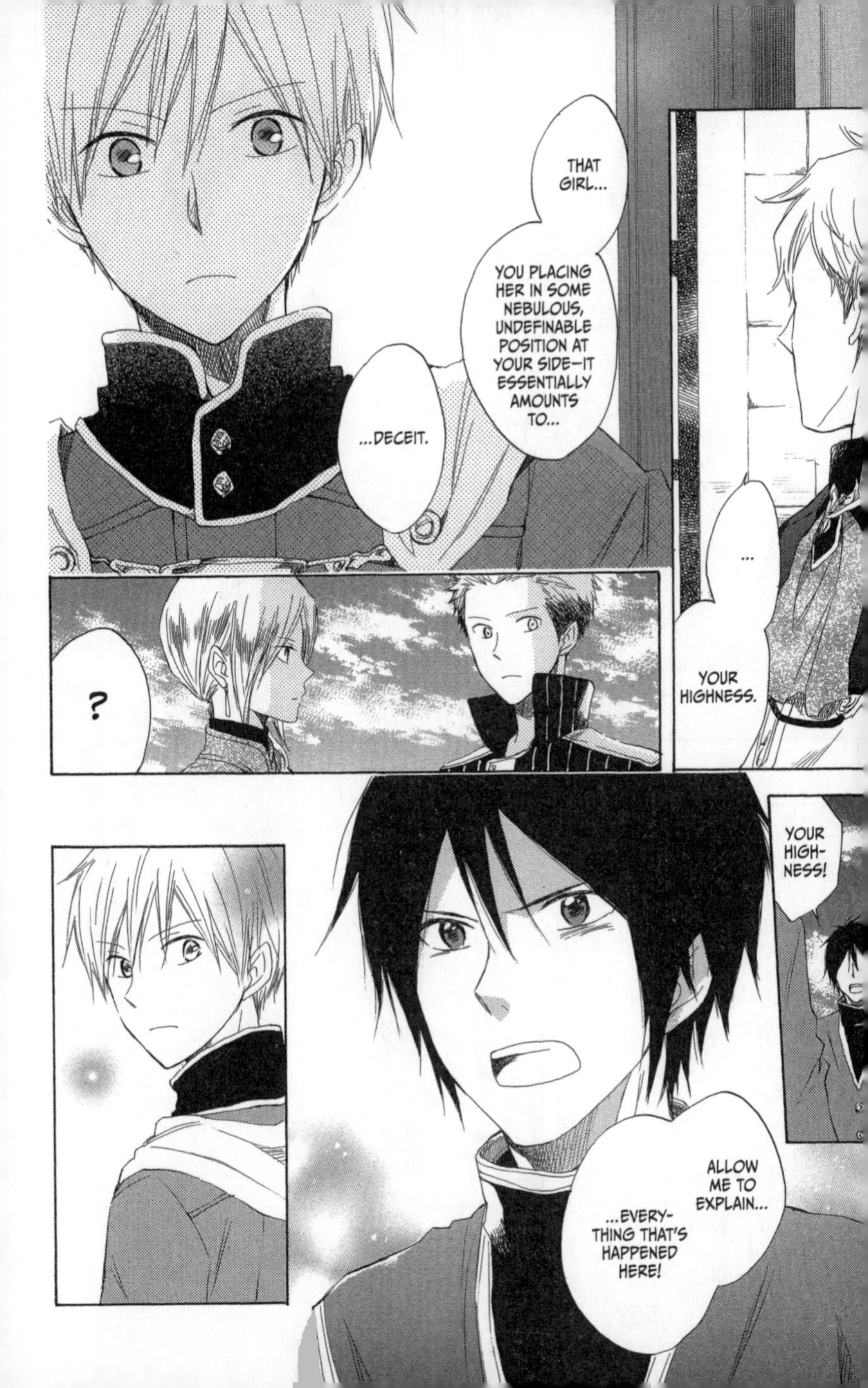
THAT GIRL...
YOU PLACING HER IN SOME NEBULOUS, UNDEFINABLE POSITION AT YOUR SIDE—IT ESSENTIALLY AMOUNTS TO...
...DECEIT.
...
YOUR HIGHNESS.
?
YOUR HIGH-NESS!
ALLOW ME TO EXPLAIN...
...EVERY-THING THAT'S HAPPENED HERE!

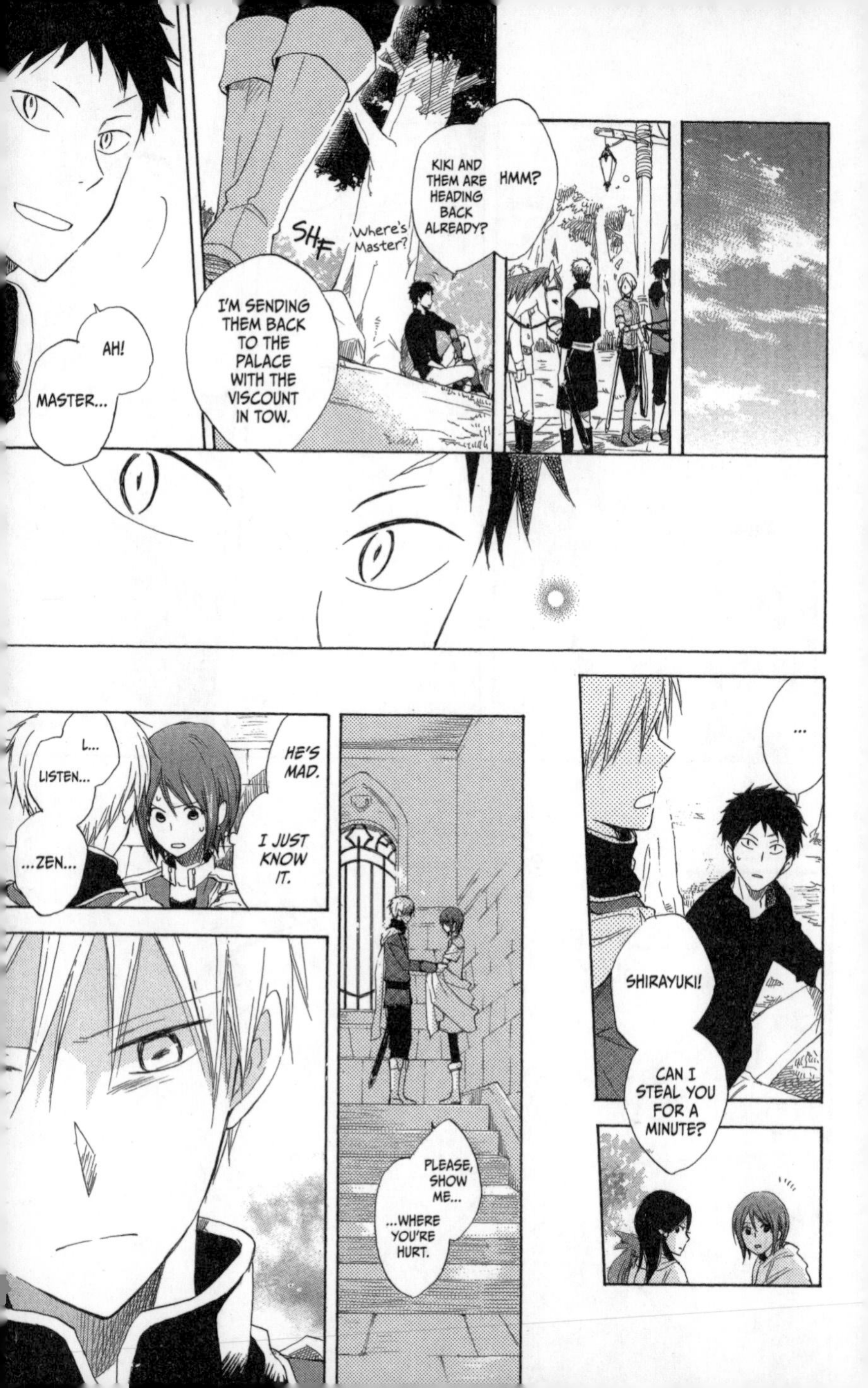
HMM?
KIKI AND THEM ARE HEADING BACK ALREADY?
SHF
Where's Master?
I'M SENDING THEM BACK TO THE PALACE WITH THE VISCOUNT IN TOW.
AH!
MASTER...
...
SHIRAYUKI!
CAN I STEAL YOU FOR A MINUTE?
PLEASE, SHOW ME...
...WHERE YOU'RE HURT.
HE'S MAD.
I JUST KNOW IT.
L...
LISTEN...
...ZEN...

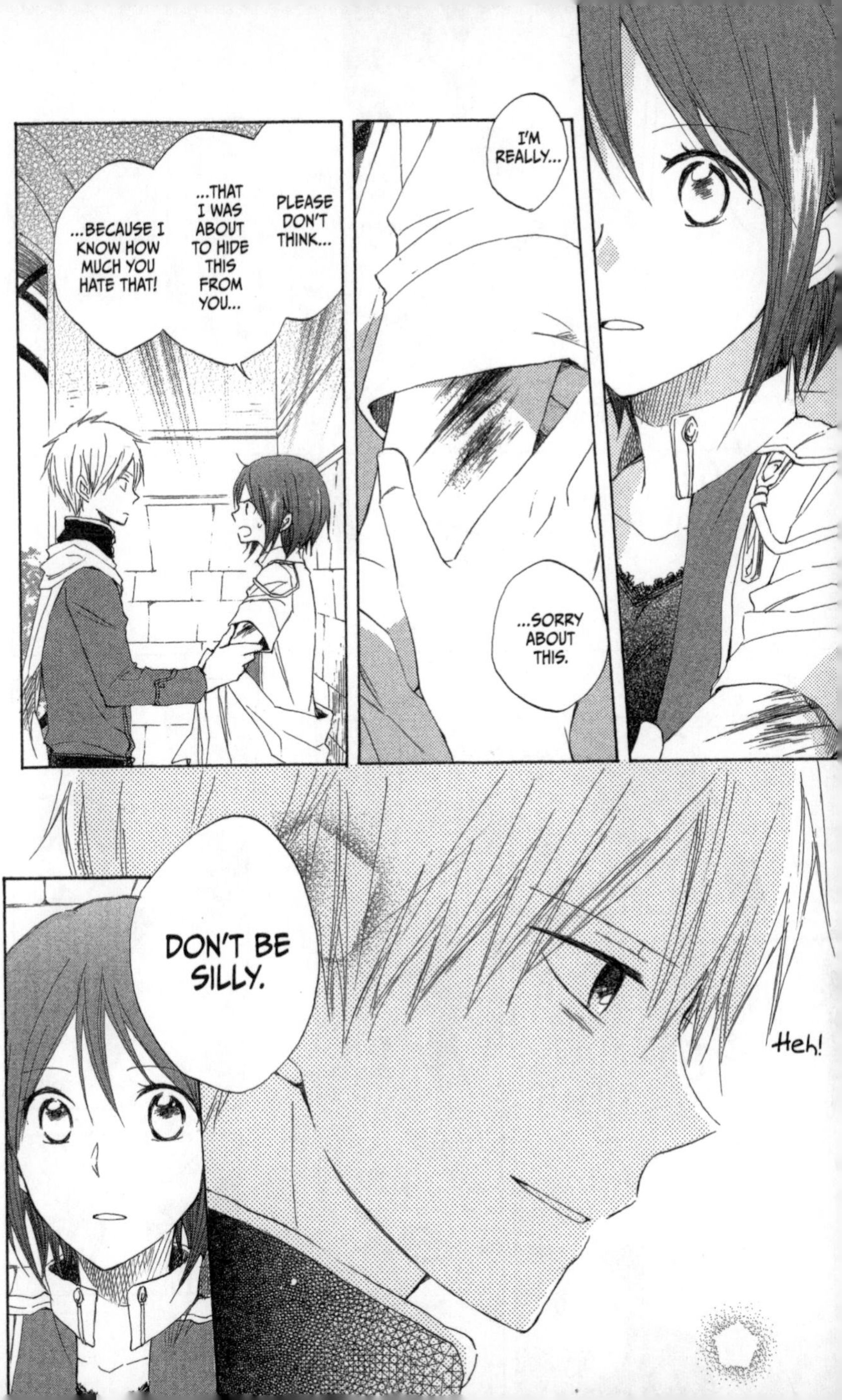
I'M REALLY...
...SORRY ABOUT THIS.
PLEASE DON'T THINK...
...THAT I WAS ABOUT TO HIDE THIS FROM YOU...
...BECAUSE I KNOW HOW MUCH YOU HATE THAT!
Heh!
DON'T BE SILLY.

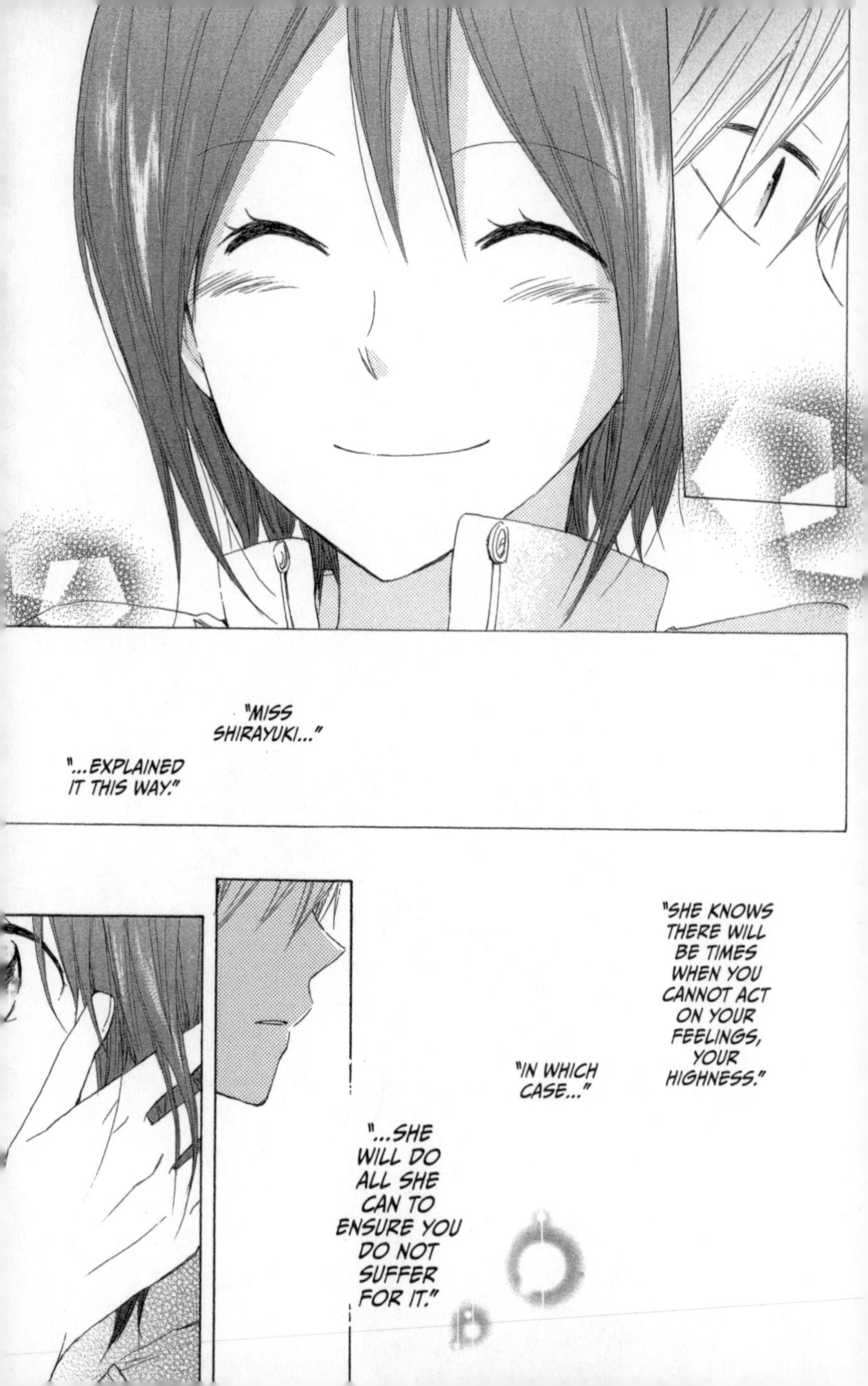
"MISS SHIRAYUKI..."
"...EXPLAINED IT THIS WAY."
"SHE KNOWS THERE WILL BE TIMES WHEN YOU CANNOT ACT ON YOUR FEELINGS, YOUR HIGHNESS."
"IN WHICH CASE..."
"...SHE WILL DO ALL SHE CAN TO ENSURE YOU DO NOT SUFFER FOR IT."

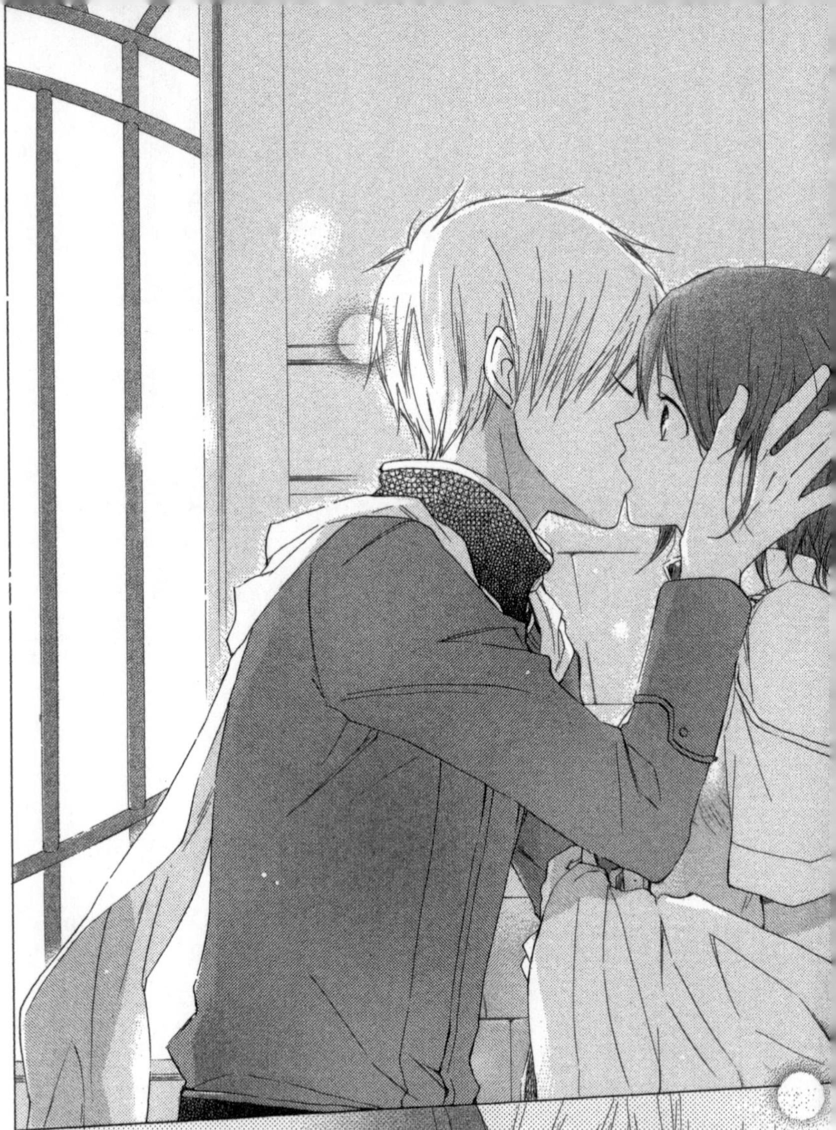
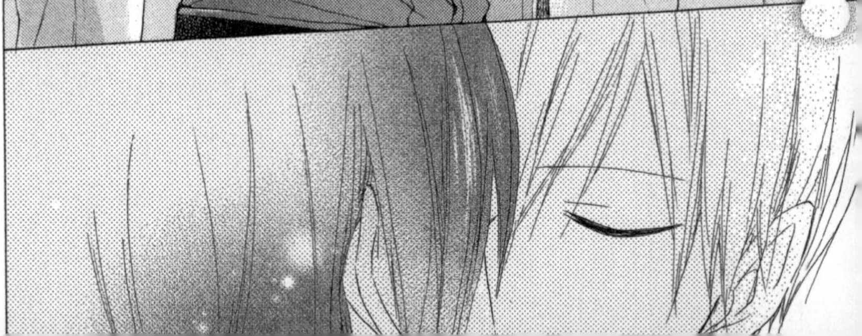

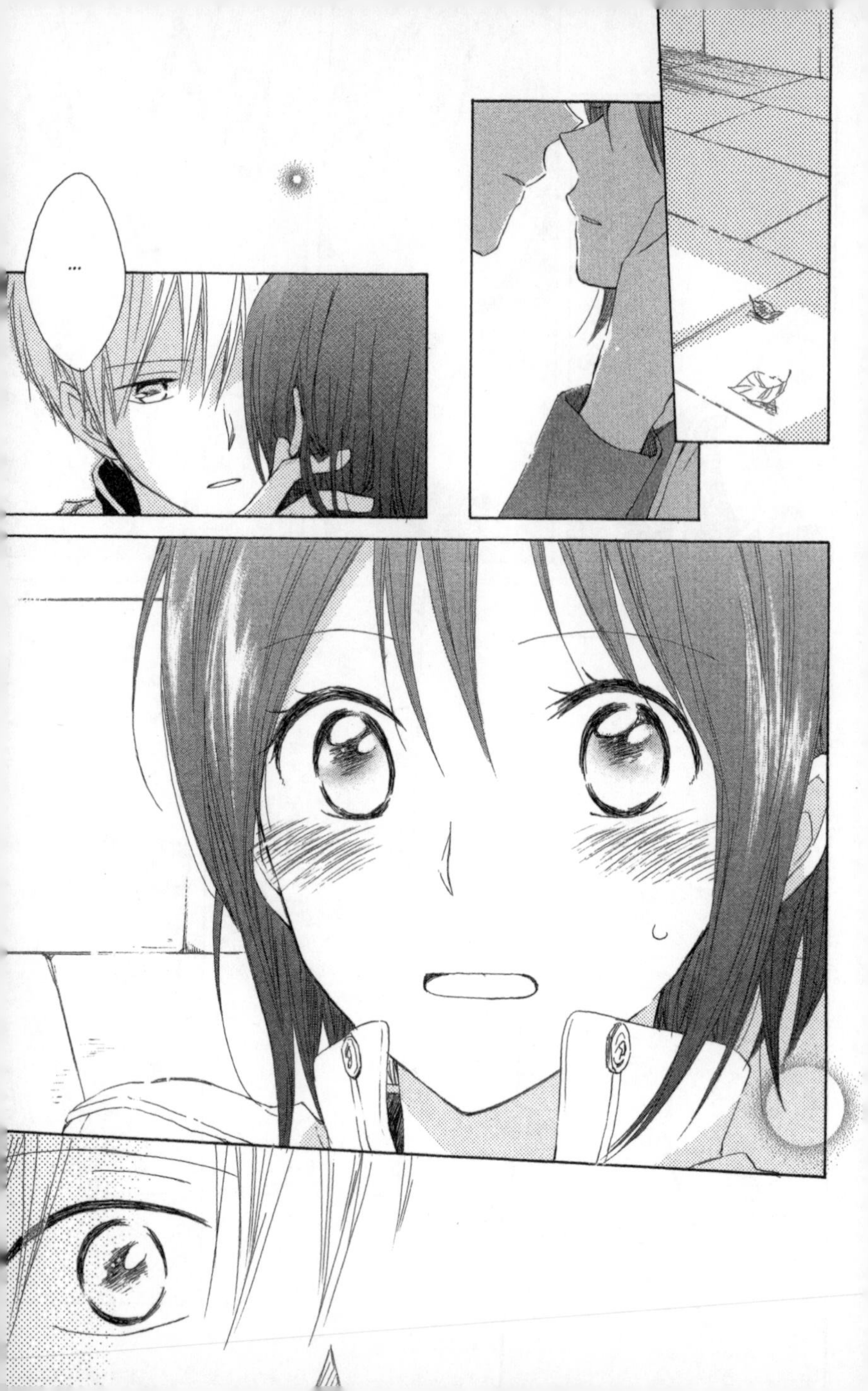
...

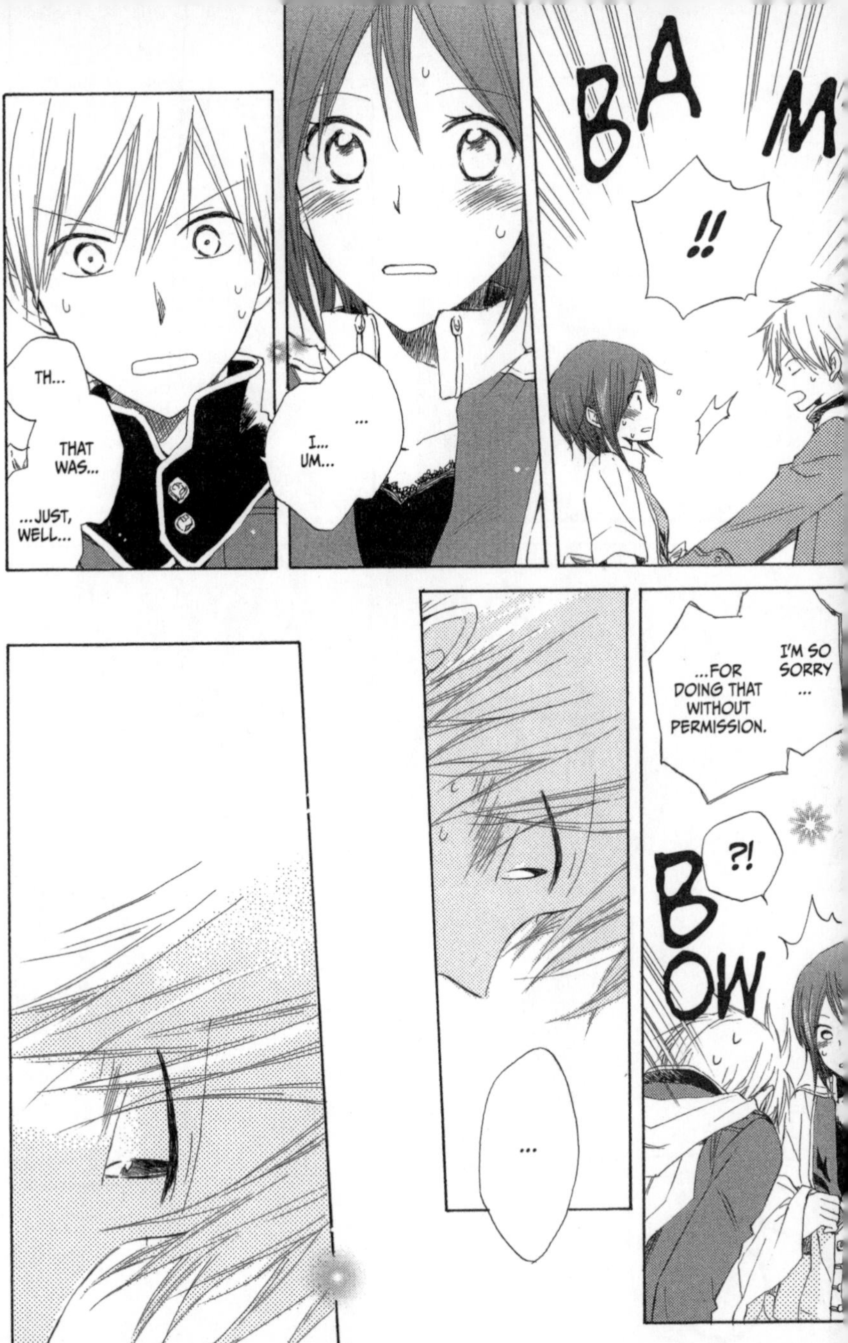
BAM
!!
...
I... UM...
TH...
THAT WAS...
...JUST, WELL...
I'M SO SORRY ...
...FOR DOING THAT WITHOUT PERMISSION.
BOW
?!
...

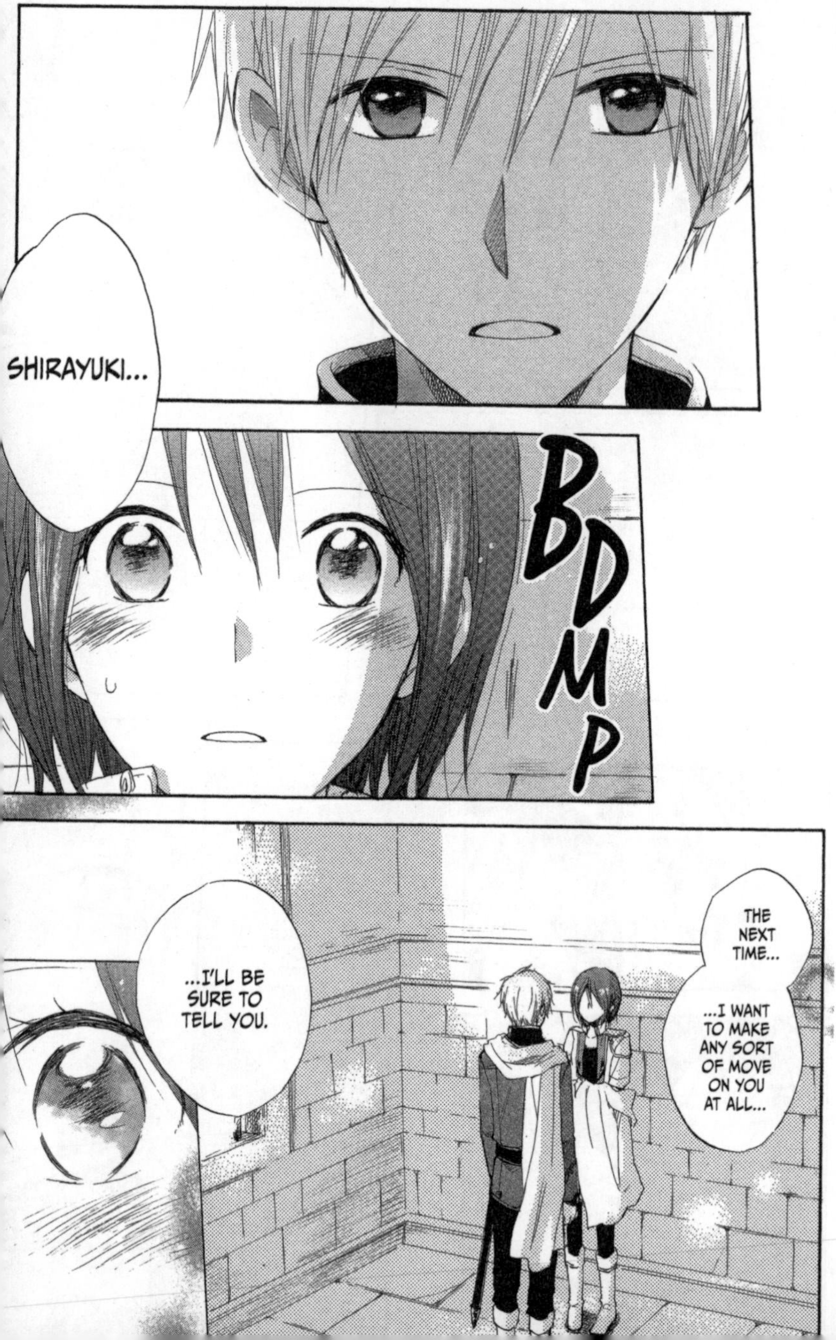
SHIRAYUKI...
BDMP
THE NEXT TIME...
...I WANT TO MAKE ANY SORT OF MOVE ON YOU AT ALL...
...I'LL BE SURE TO TELL YOU.

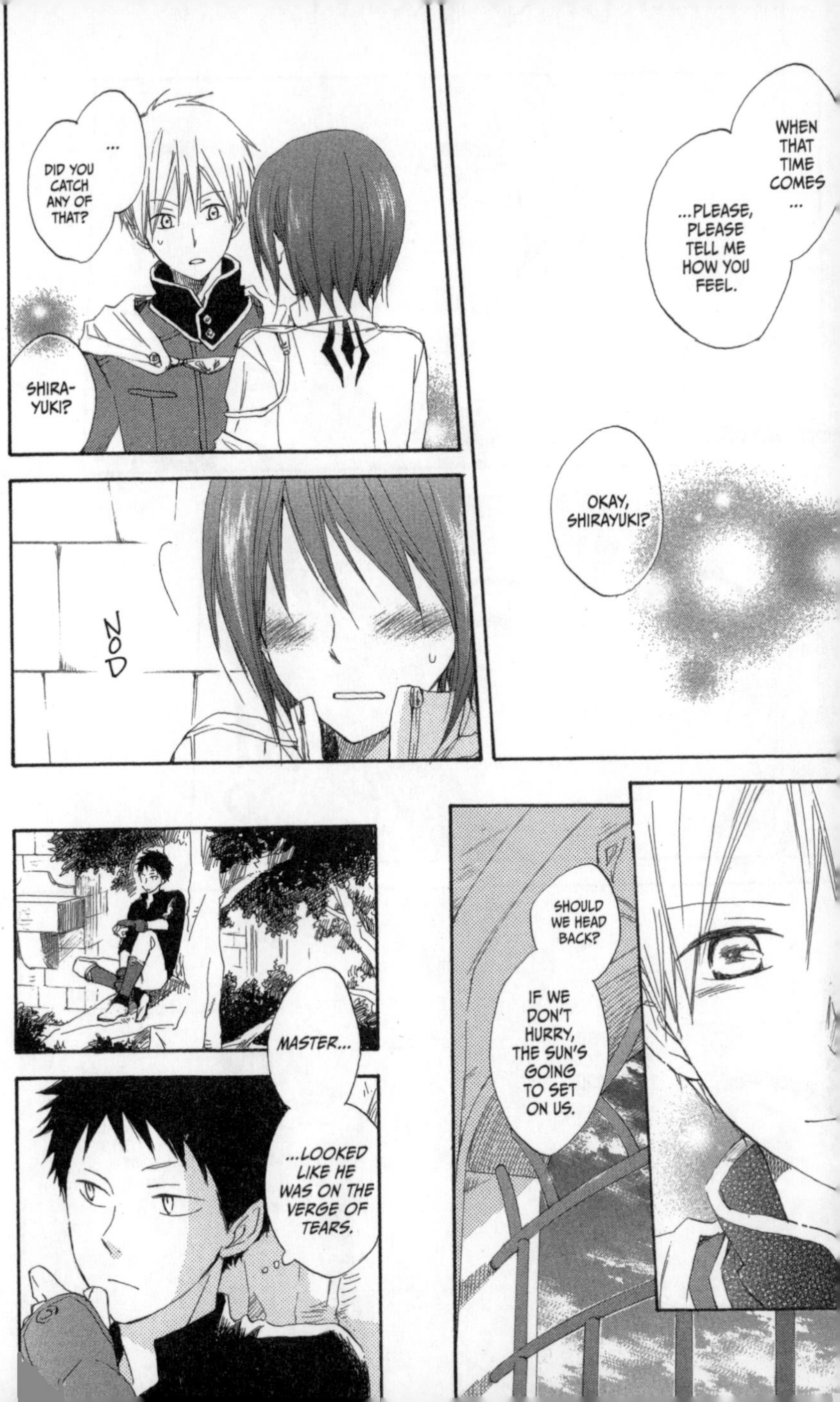
WHEN THAT TIME COMES...
...PLEASE, PLEASE TELL ME HOW YOU FEEL.
OKAY, SHIRAYUKI?
...
DID YOU CATCH ANY OF THAT?
SHIRA-YUKI?
NOD
SHOULD WE HEAD BACK?
IF WE DON'T HURRY, THE SUN'S GOING TO SET ON US.
MASTER...
...LOOKED LIKE HE WAS ON THE VERGE OF TEARS.

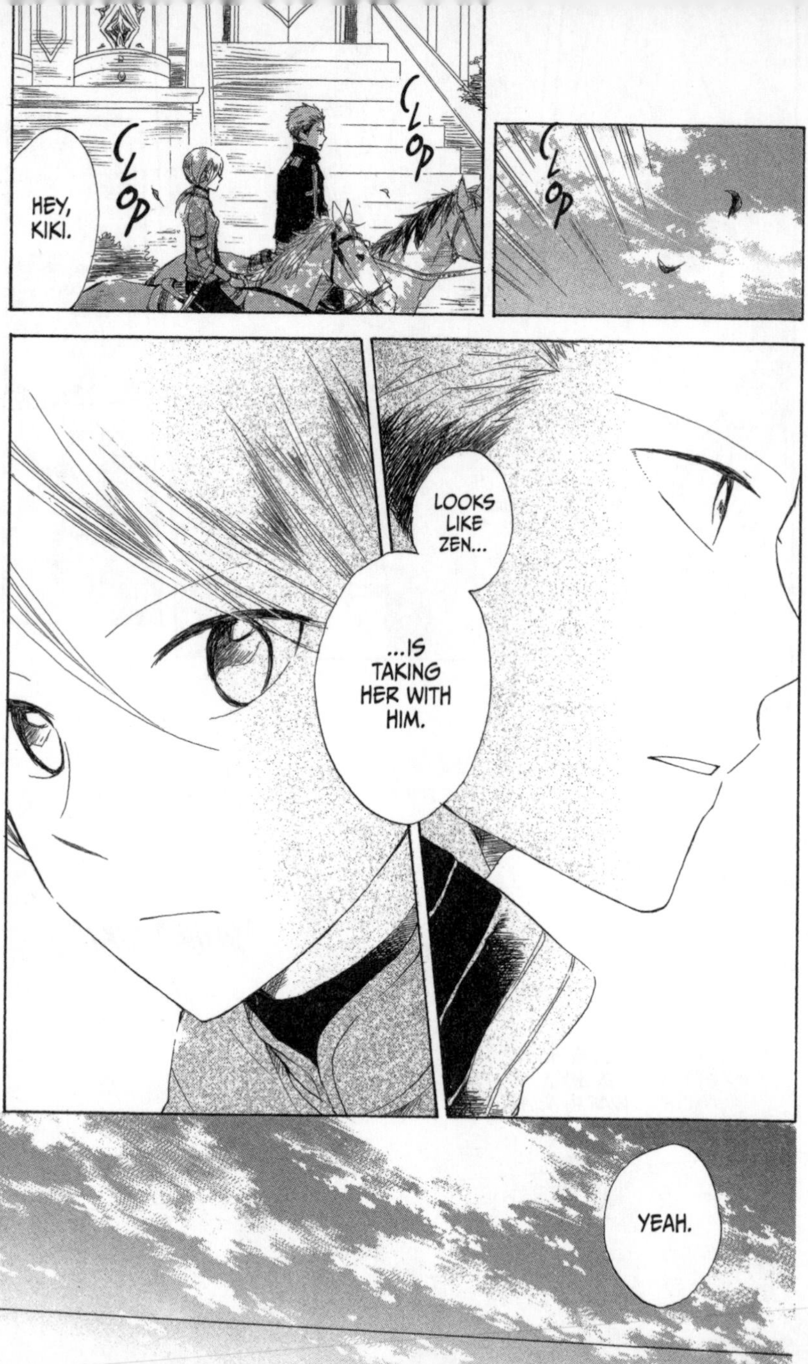
CLOP
CLOP
CLOP
HEY, KIKI.
LOOKS LIKE ZEN...
...IS TAKING HER WITH HIM.
YEAH.

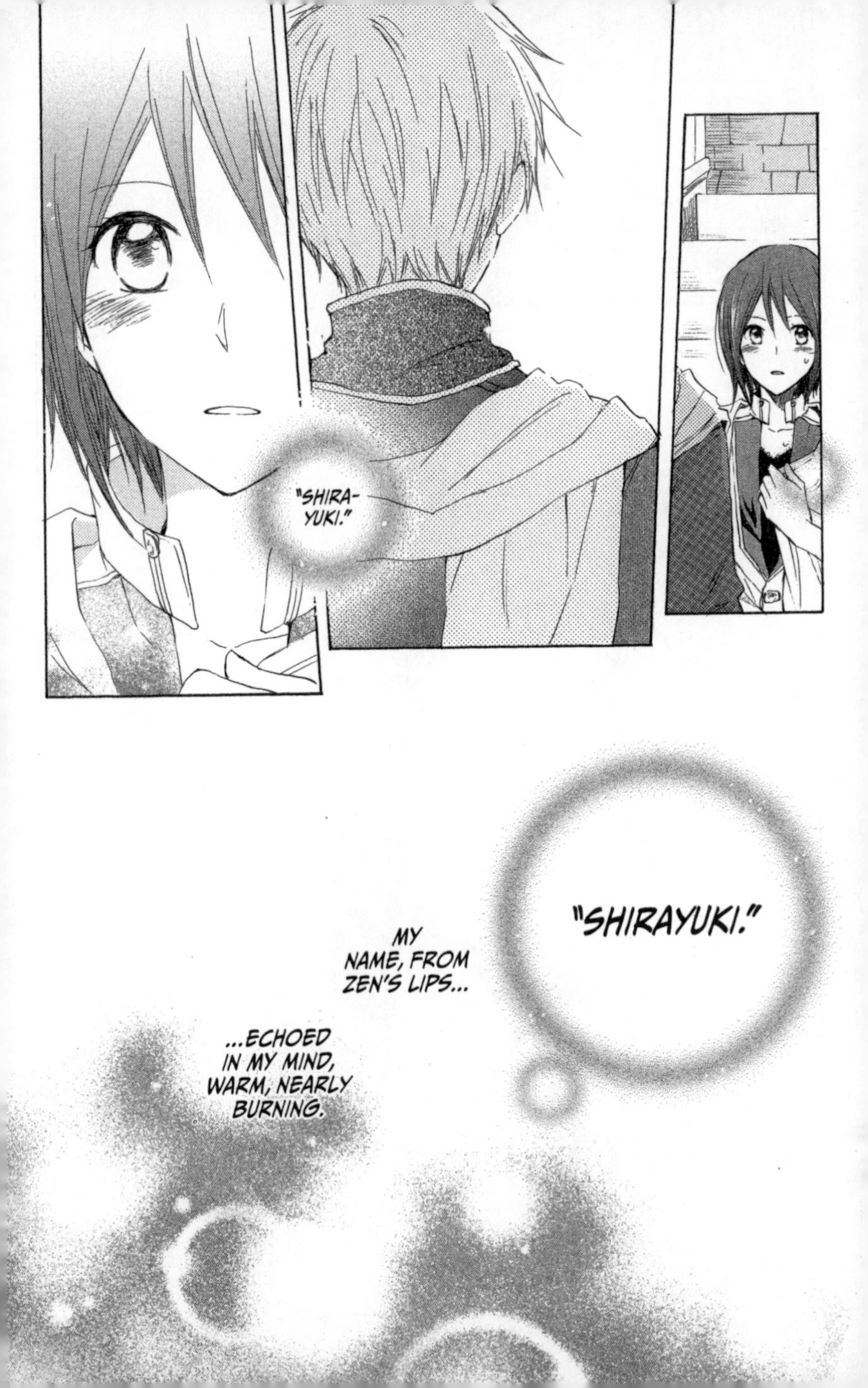
"SHIRA-YUKI."
"SHIRAYUKI."
MY NAME, FROM ZEN'S LIPS...
...ECHOED IN MY MIND, WARM, NEARLY BURNING.

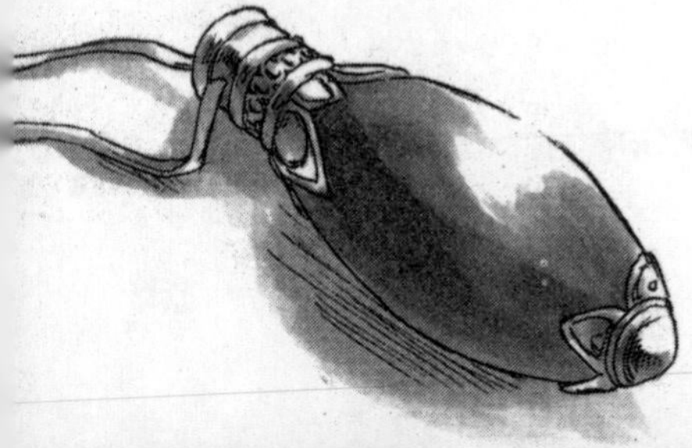

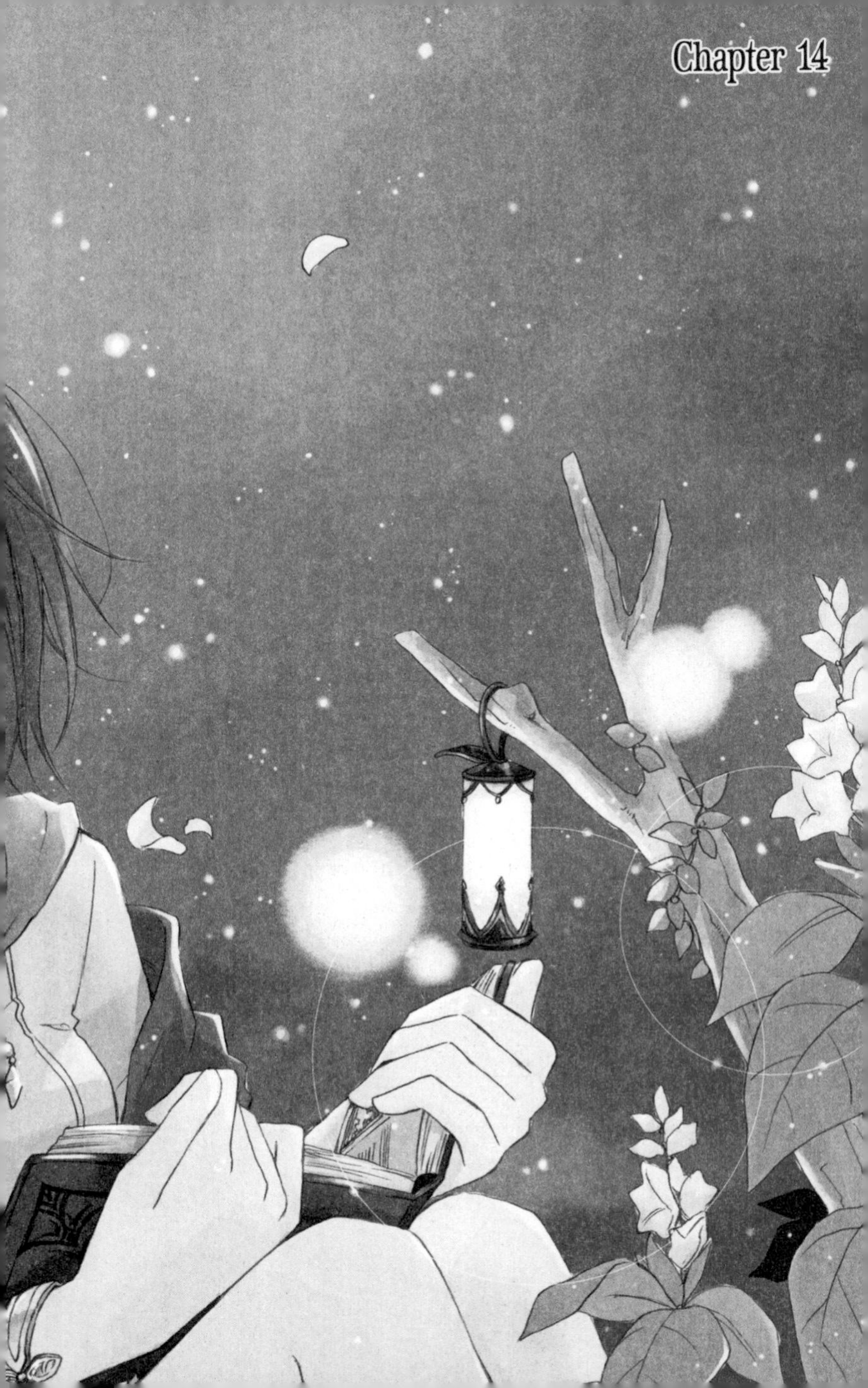
Chapter 14

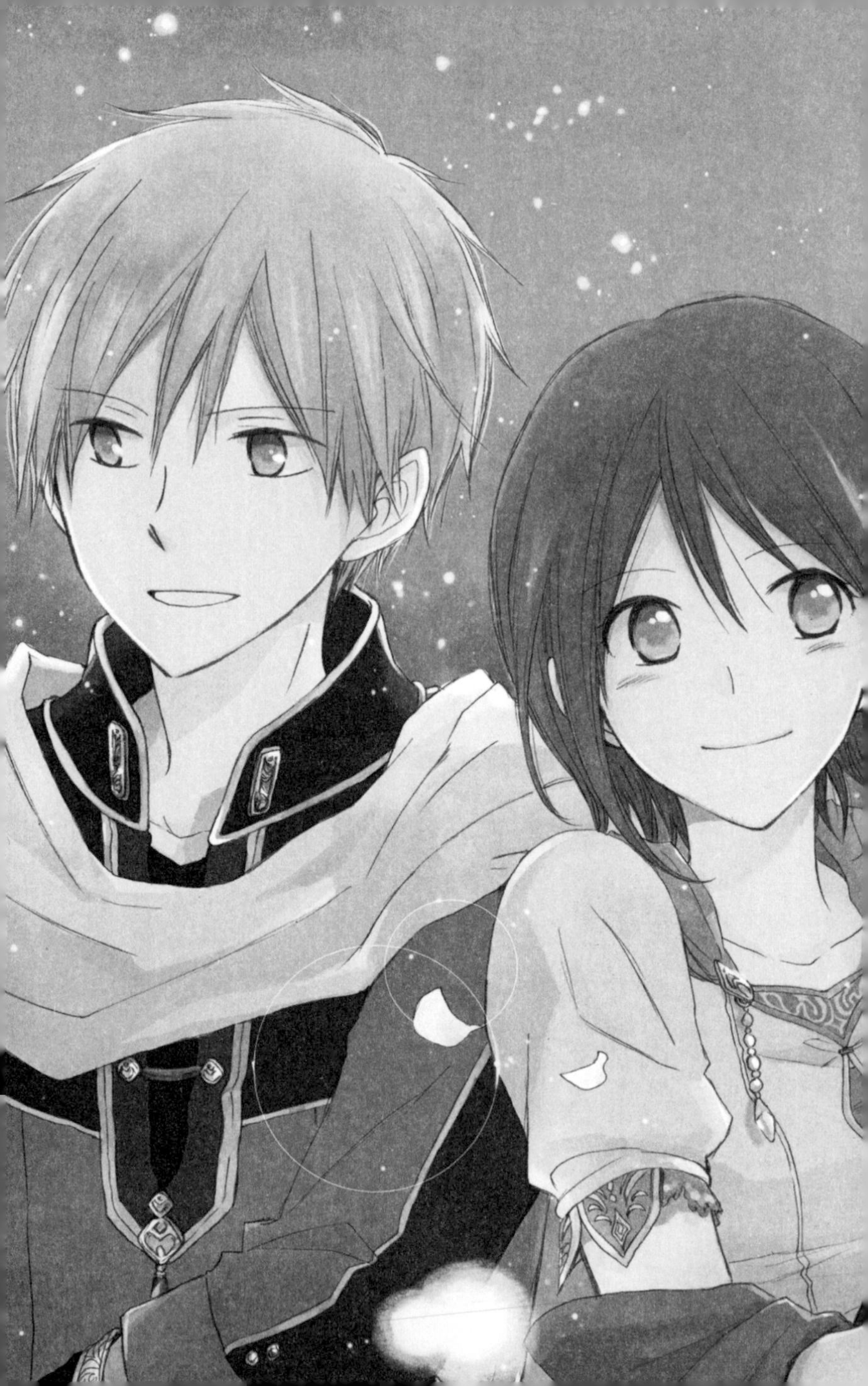

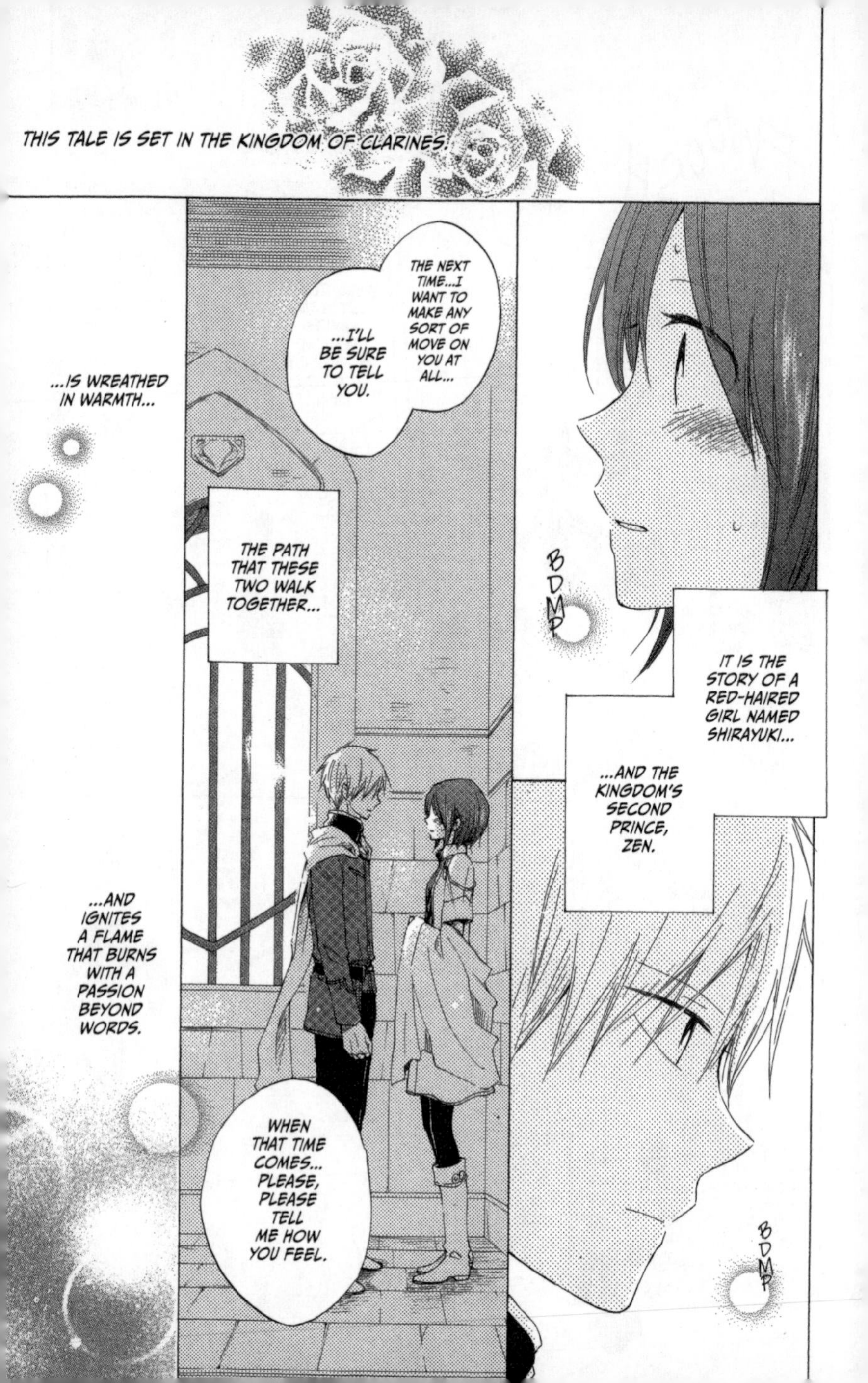
THIS TALE IS SET IN THE KINGDOM OF CLARINES.
BDMP
IT IS THE STORY OF A RED-HAIRED GIRL NAMED SHIRAYUKI...
...AND THE KINGDOM'S SECOND PRINCE, ZEN.
BDMP
THE NEXT TIME...I WANT TO MAKE ANY SORT OF MOVE ON YOU AT ALL...
...I'LL BE SURE TO TELL YOU.
THE PATH THAT THESE TWO WALK TOGETHER...
WHEN THAT TIME COMES... PLEASE, PLEASE TELL ME HOW YOU FEEL.
...IS WREATHED IN WARMTH...
...AND IGNITES A FLAME THAT BURNS WITH A PASSION BEYOND WORDS.

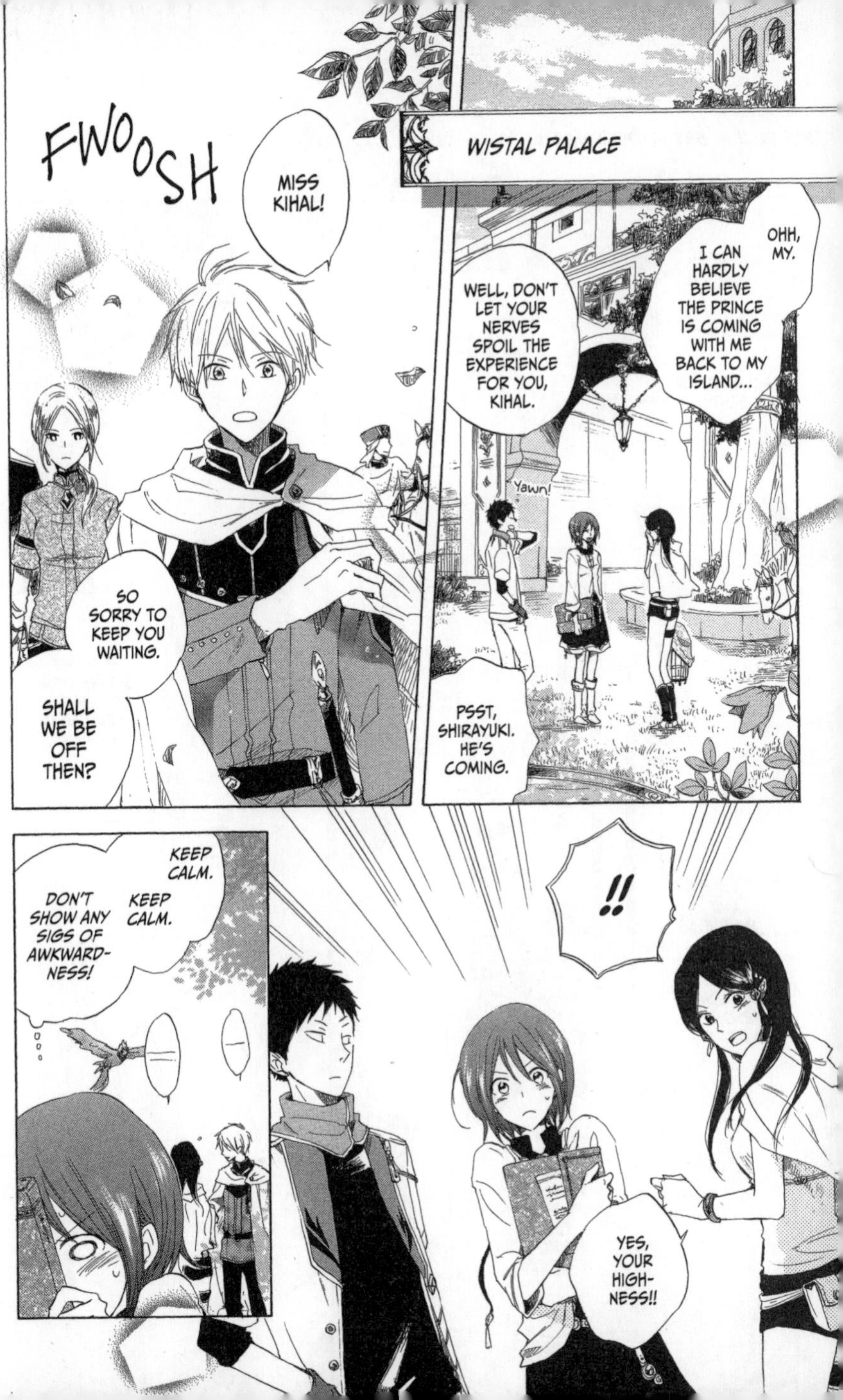
WISTAL PALACE
OHH, MY. I CAN HARDLY BELIEVE THE PRINCE IS COMING WITH ME BACK TO MY ISLAND...
WELL, DON'T LET YOUR NERVES SPOIL THE EXPERIENCE FOR YOU, KIHAL.
Yawn!
PSST, SHIRAYUKI. HE'S COMING.
FWOOSH
MISS KIHAL!
SO SORRY TO KEEP YOU WAITING.
SHALL WE BE OFF THEN?
!!
YES, YOUR HIGH-NESS!!
—
—
KEEP CALM.
KEEP CALM.
DON'T SHOW ANY SIGS OF AWKWARD-NESS!

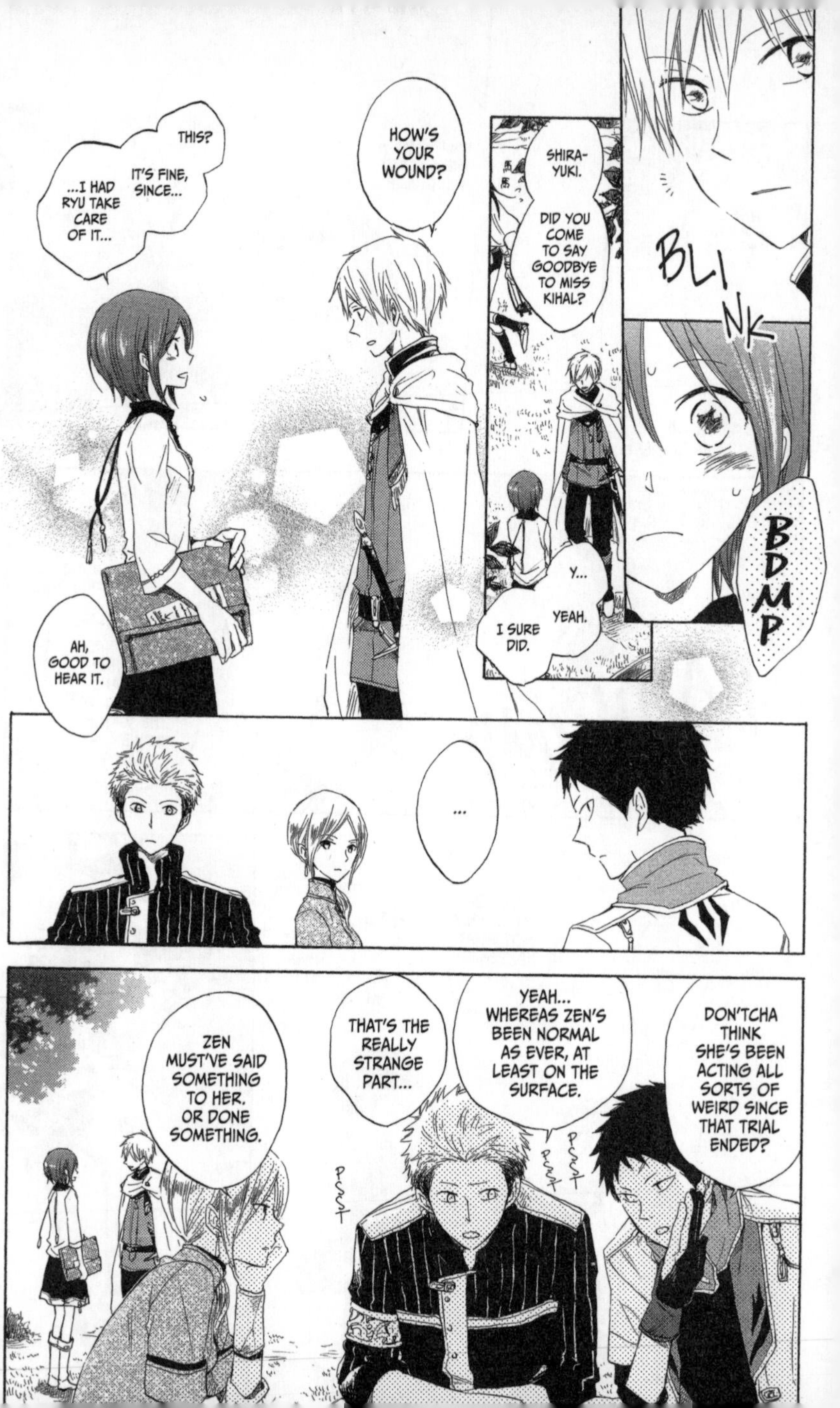
BLINK
BDMP
SHIRA-YUKI.
DID YOU COME TO SAY GOODBYE TO MISS KIHAL?
Y... YEAH. I SURE DID.
HOW'S YOUR WOUND?
THIS? IT'S FINE, SINCE... ...I HAD RYU TAKE CARE OF IT...
AH, GOOD TO HEAR IT.
...
DON'TCHA THINK SHE'S BEEN ACTING ALL SORTS OF WEIRD SINCE THAT TRIAL ENDED?
YEAH... WHEREAS ZEN'S BEEN NORMAL AS EVER, AT LEAST ON THE SURFACE.
PSST PSST
THAT'S THE REALLY STRANGE PART...
ZEN MUST'VE SAID SOMETHING TO HER. OR DONE SOMETHING.
PSST

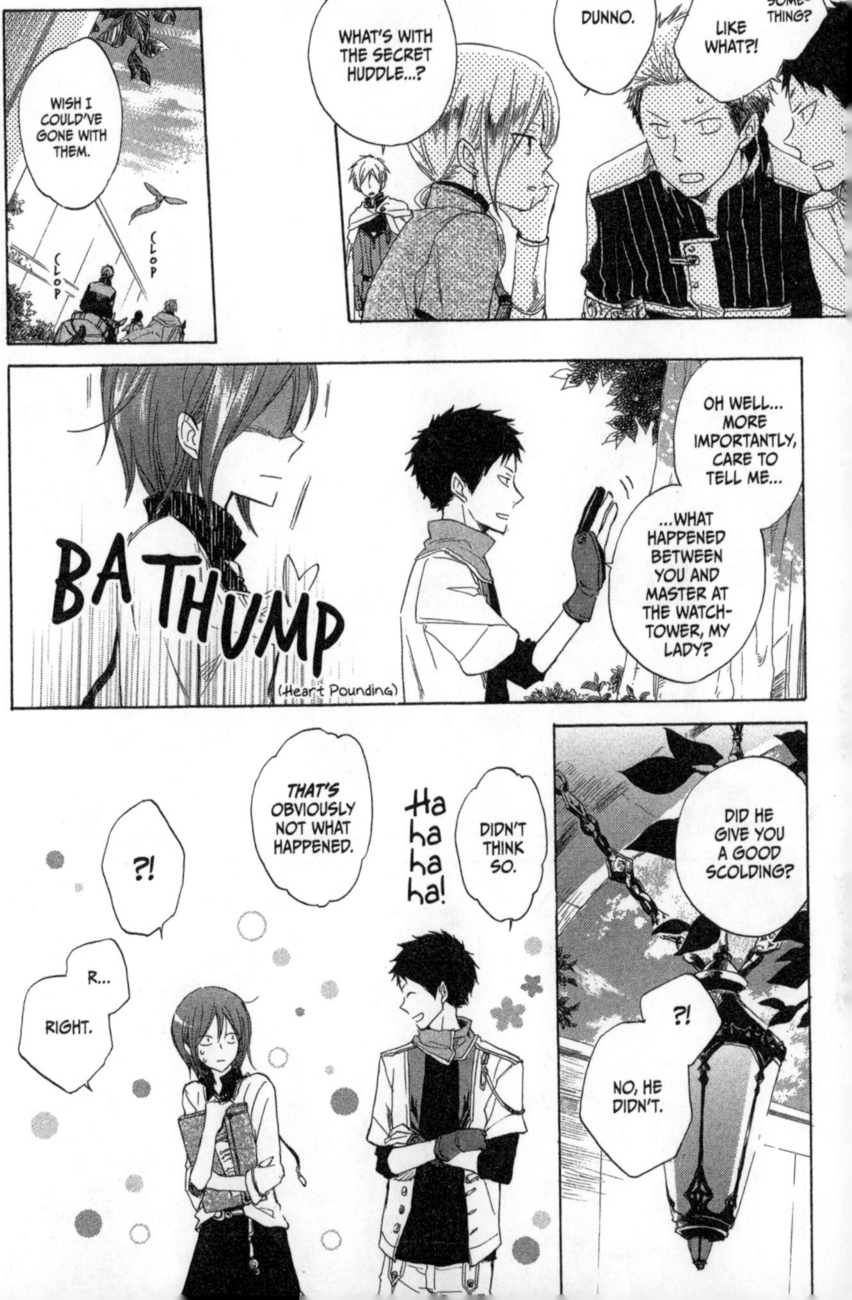
SOME-THING?
LIKE WHAT?!
DUNNO.
WHAT'S WITH THE SECRET HUDDLE...?
WISH I COULD'VE GONE WITH THEM.
CLOP
CLOP
OH WELL... MORE IMPORTANTLY, CARE TO TELL ME...
...WHAT HAPPENED BETWEEN YOU AND MASTER AT THE WATCH-TOWER, MY LADY?
BA THUMP
(Heart Pounding)
DID HE GIVE YOU A GOOD SCOLDING?
?!
NO, HE DIDN'T.
DIDN'T THINK SO.
Ha ha ha ha!
THAT'S OBVIOUSLY NOT WHAT HAPPENED.
?!
R... RIGHT.

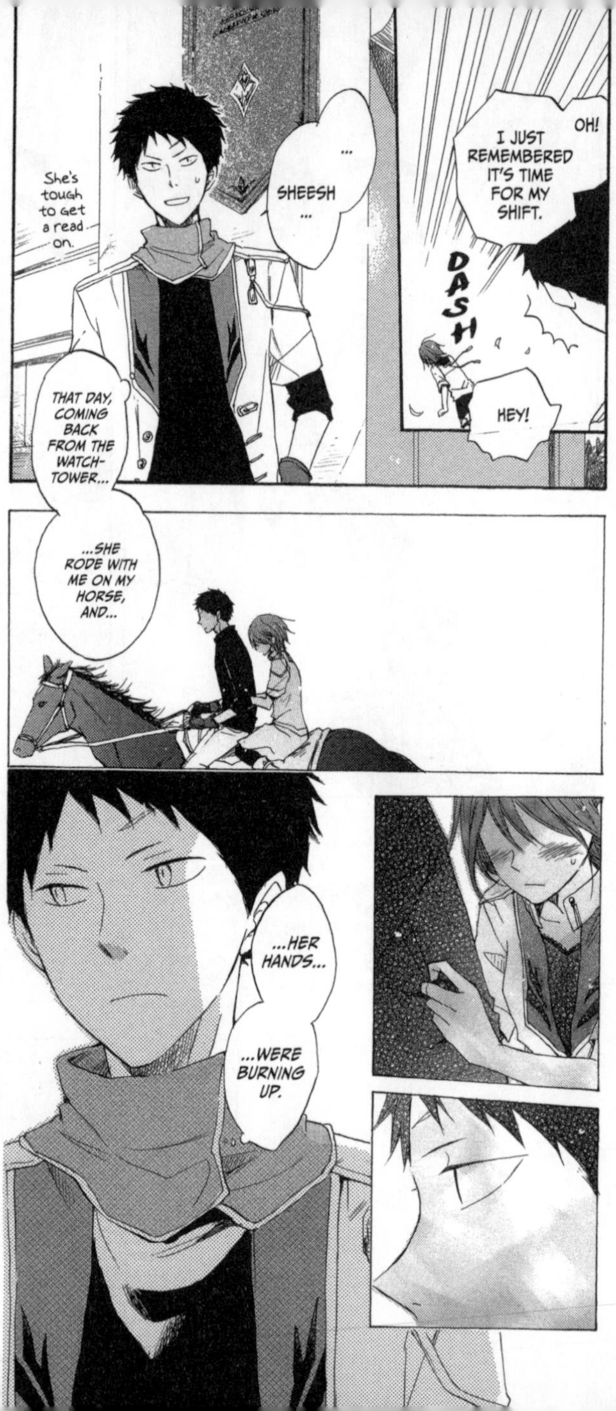
OH!
I JUST REMEMBERED IT'S TIME FOR MY SHIFT.
DASH
HEY!
...
SHEESH ...
She's tough to get a read on.
THAT DAY, COMING BACK FROM THE WATCH-TOWER...
...SHE RODE WITH ME ON MY HORSE, AND...
...HER HANDS...
...WERE BURNING UP.

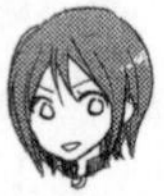

Shirayuki

Likes

-Especially chewy breads
-Jam (making it)
-Mornings

Can't Handle

-Seaweed
-The arts (as a patron)

She's early to bed and early to rise. She sleeps like a log.

The type to get right to work after waking up.

Zen is basically the total opposite.

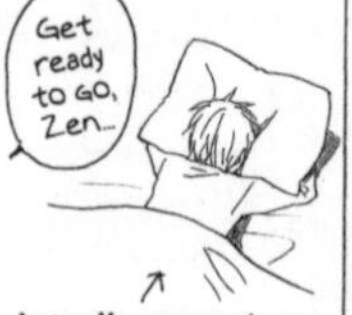
Get ready to GO, Zen...

Actually awake, but...

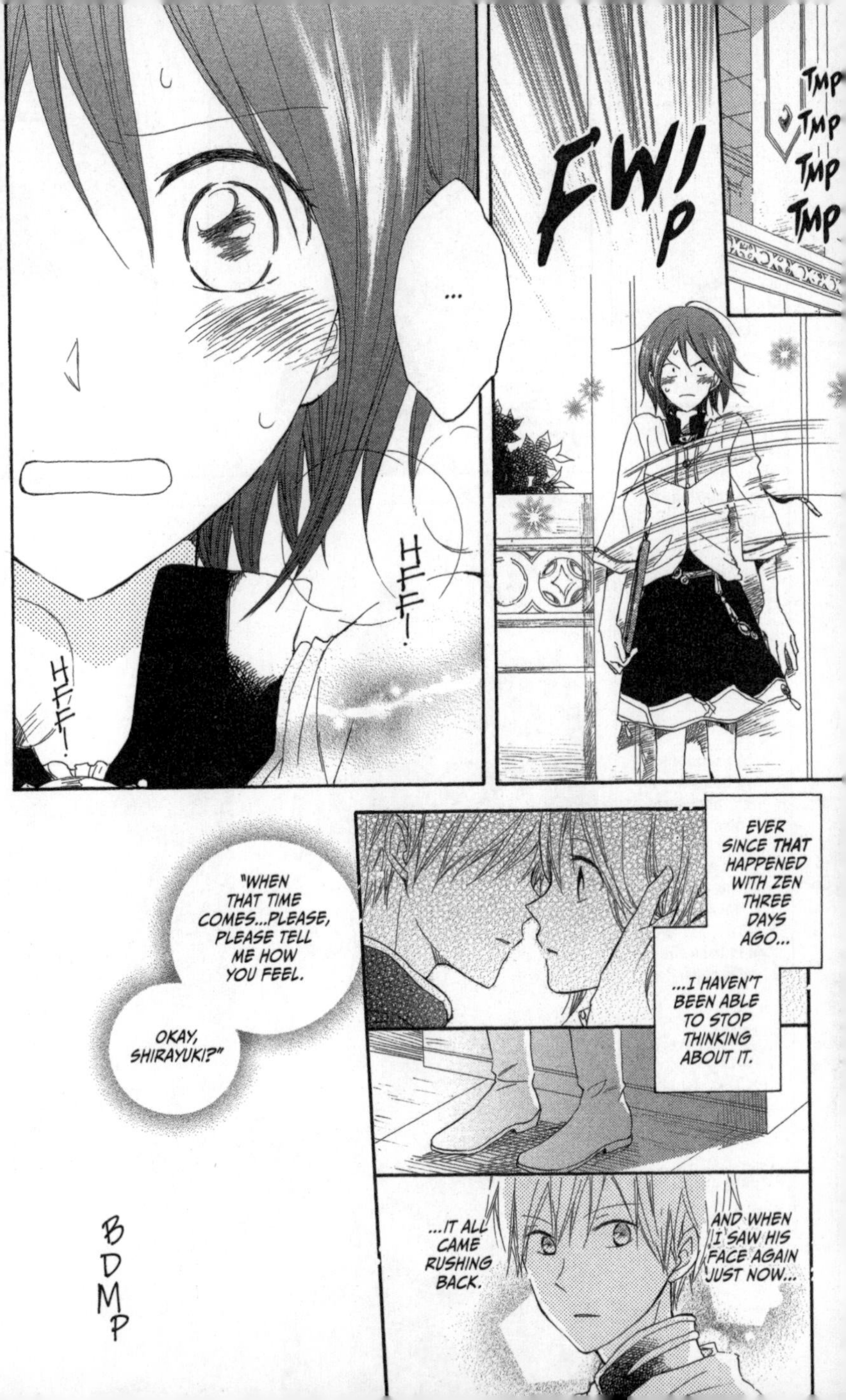
TMP TMP TMP TMP
FWIP
...
HUFF
HUFF
EVER SINCE THAT HAPPENED WITH ZEN THREE DAYS AGO...
"WHEN THAT TIME COMES...PLEASE, PLEASE TELL ME HOW YOU FEEL.
OKAY, SHIRAYUKI?"
...I HAVEN'T BEEN ABLE TO STOP THINKING ABOUT IT.
AND WHEN I SAW HIS FACE AGAIN JUST NOW...
...IT ALL CAME RUSHING BACK.
BDMP

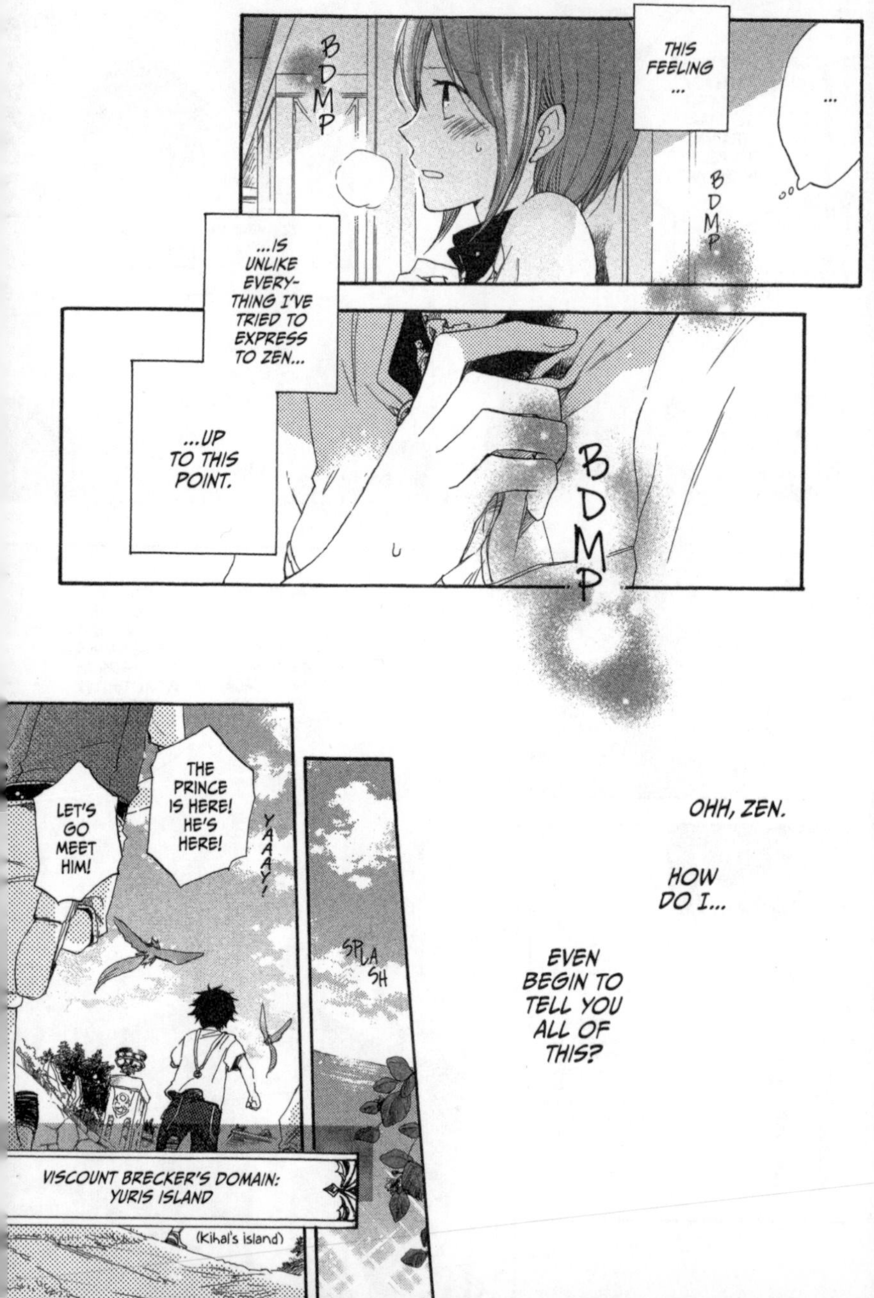
...
THIS FEELING...
BDMP
BDMP
...IS UNLIKE EVERY-THING I'VE TRIED TO EXPRESS TO ZEN...
...UP TO THIS POINT.
BDMP
OHH, ZEN.
HOW DO I...
EVEN BEGIN TO TELL YOU ALL OF THIS?
SPLASH
THE PRINCE IS HERE! HE'S HERE!
YAAAY!
LET'S GO MEET HIM!
VISCOUNT BRECKER'S DOMAIN: YURIS ISLAND
(Kihal's island)

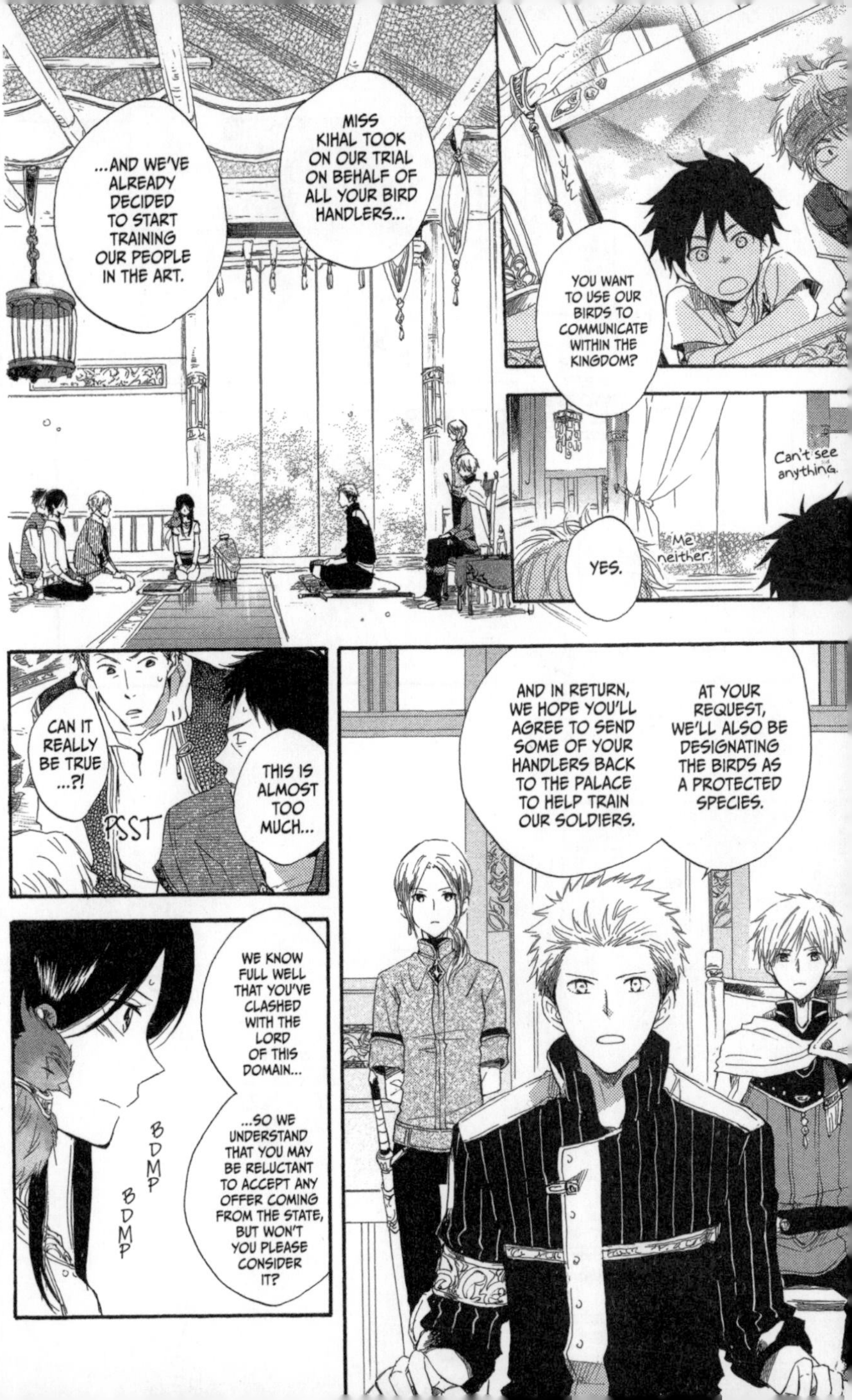
YOU WANT TO USE OUR BIRDS TO COMMUNICATE WITHIN THE KINGDOM?
Can't see anything.
Me neither.
YES.
MISS KIHAL TOOK ON OUR TRIAL ON BEHALF OF ALL YOUR BIRD HANDLERS...
...AND WE'VE ALREADY DECIDED TO START TRAINING OUR PEOPLE IN THE ART.
AT YOUR REQUEST, WE'LL ALSO BE DESIGNATING THE BIRDS AS A PROTECTED SPECIES.
AND IN RETURN, WE HOPE YOU'LL AGREE TO SEND SOME OF YOUR HANDLERS BACK TO THE PALACE TO HELP TRAIN OUR SOLDIERS.
CAN IT REALLY BE TRUE ...?!
PSST
THIS IS ALMOST TOO MUCH...
WE KNOW FULL WELL THAT YOU'VE CLASHED WITH THE LORD OF THIS DOMAIN...
...SO WE UNDERSTAND THAT YOU MAY BE RELUCTANT TO ACCEPT ANY OFFER COMING FROM THE STATE, BUT WON'T YOU PLEASE CONSIDER IT?
BDMP
BDMP

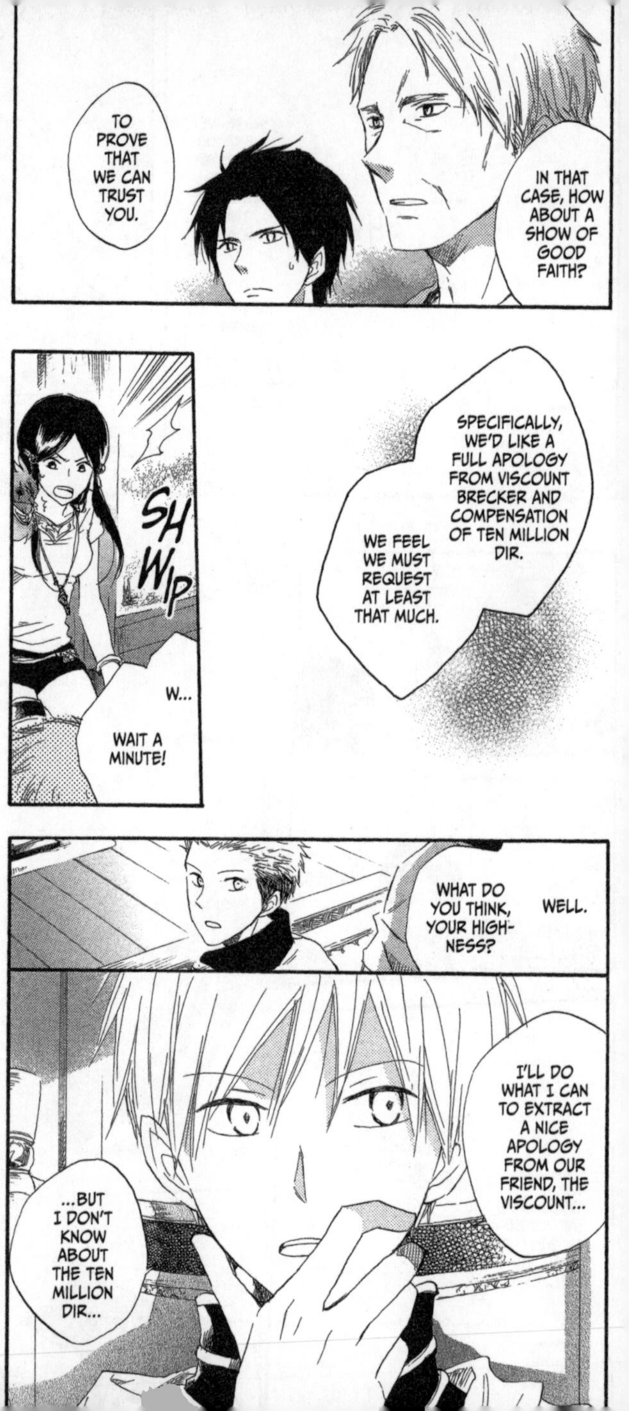
IN THAT CASE, HOW ABOUT A SHOW OF GOOD FAITH?
TO PROVE THAT WE CAN TRUST YOU.
SPECIFICALLY, WE'D LIKE A FULL APOLOGY FROM VISCOUNT BRECKER AND COMPENSATION OF TEN MILLION DIR.
WE FEEL WE MUST REQUEST AT LEAST THAT MUCH.
SHWIP
W...
WAIT A MINUTE!
WELL.
WHAT DO YOU THINK, YOUR HIGHNESS?
I'LL DO WHAT I CAN TO EXTRACT A NICE APOLOGY FROM OUR FRIEND, THE VISCOUNT...
...BUT I DON'T KNOW ABOUT THE TEN MILLION DIR...

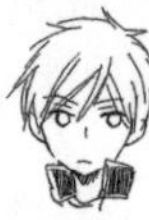

Zen

Likes

-Pies
-Tarts
-Reading
-Red things, silver things

Can't Handle

-Perfume

He also hates being alone during the day, so he tends to walk around the palace chatting up the guards.

He's fine being alone at night, though.

4

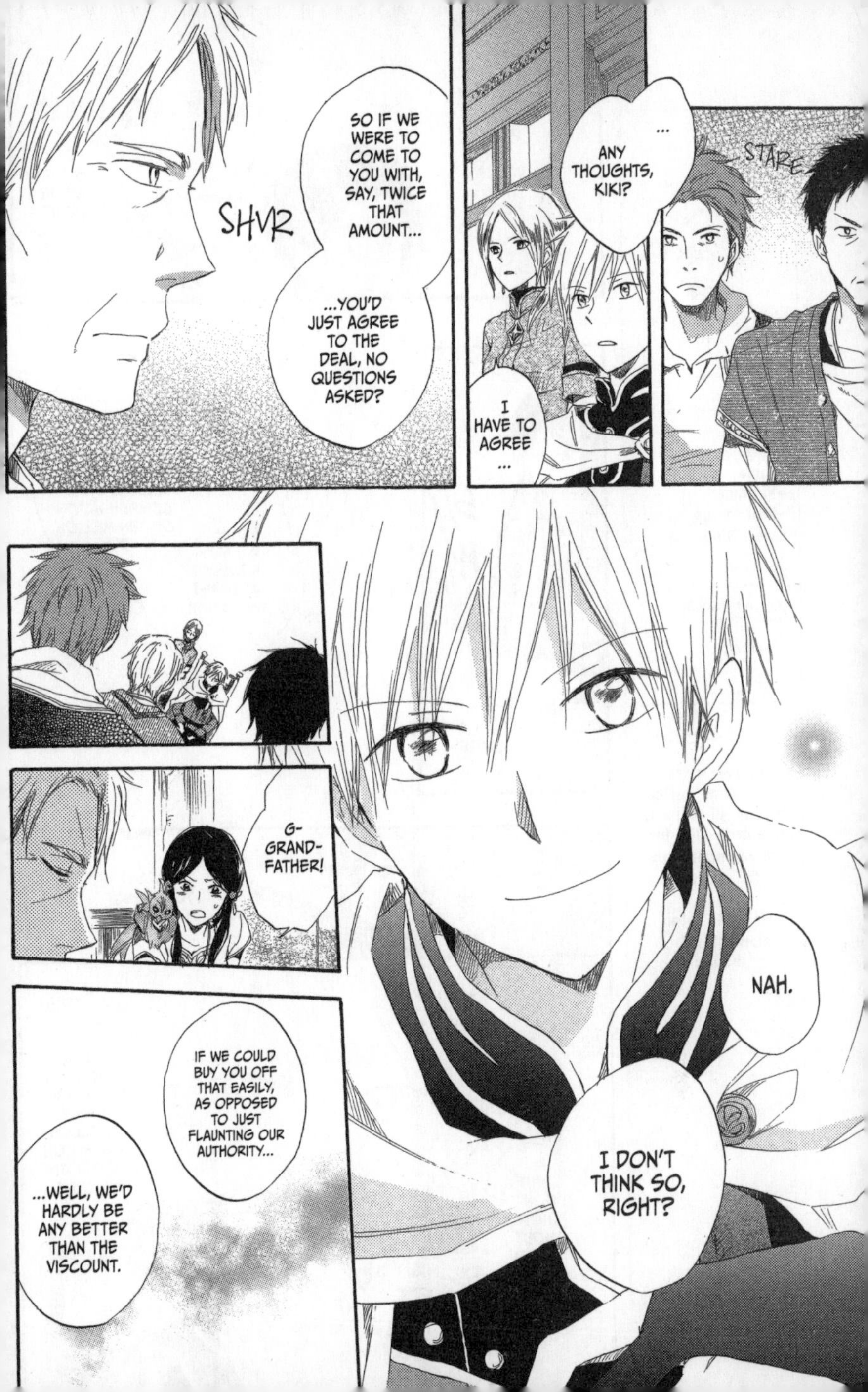
STARE
...
ANY THOUGHTS, KIKI?
I HAVE TO AGREE ...
SO IF WE WERE TO COME TO YOU WITH, SAY, TWICE THAT AMOUNT...
...YOU'D JUST AGREE TO THE DEAL, NO QUESTIONS ASKED?
SHVR
NAH.
I DON'T THINK SO, RIGHT?
G-GRAND-FATHER!
IF WE COULD BUY YOU OFF THAT EASILY, AS OPPOSED TO JUST FLAUNTING OUR AUTHORITY...
...WELL, WE'D HARDLY BE ANY BETTER THAN THE VISCOUNT.

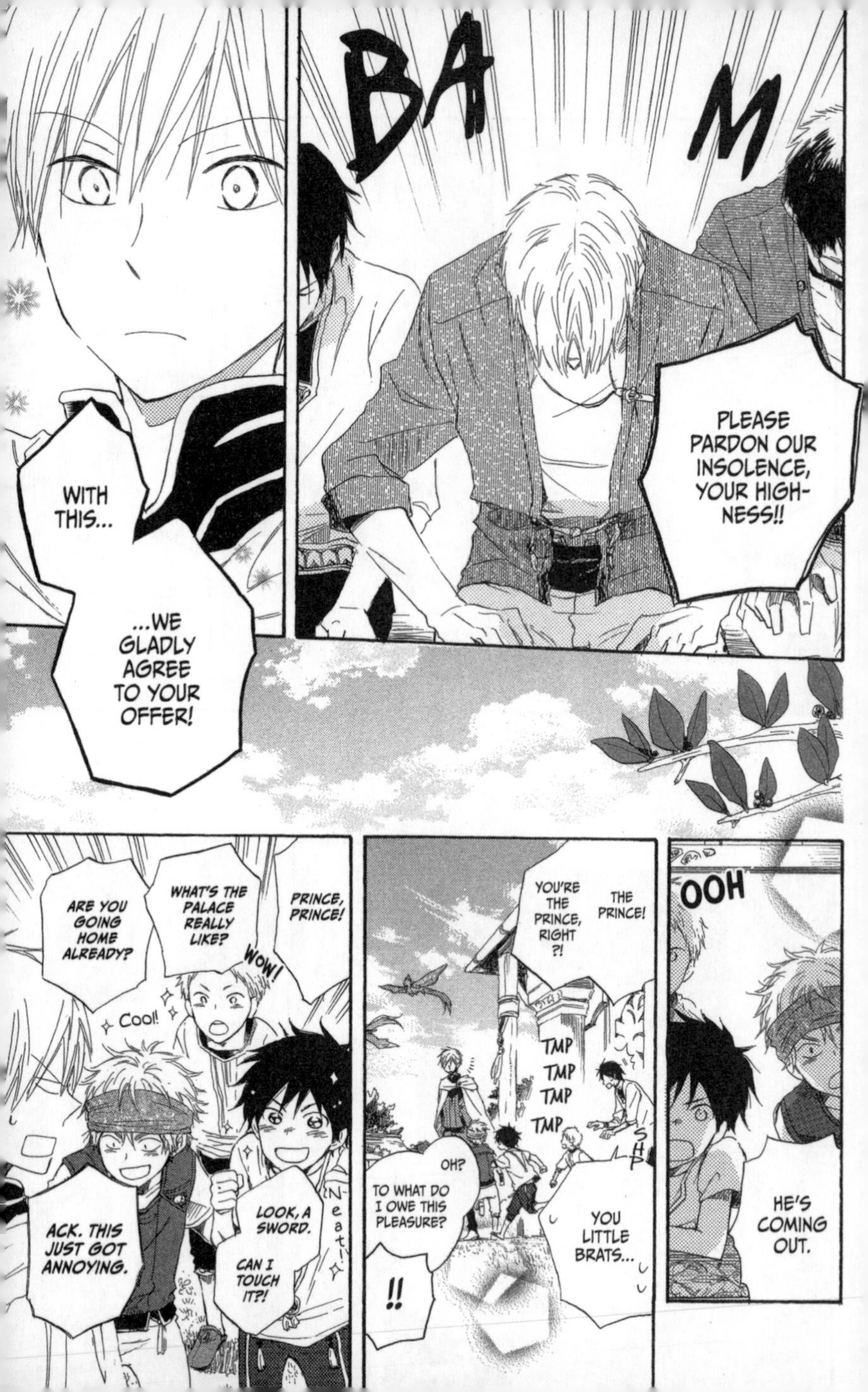
BAM
PLEASE PARDON OUR INSOLENCE, YOUR HIGHNESS!!
WITH THIS...
...WE GLADLY AGREE TO YOUR OFFER!
OOH
HE'S COMING OUT.
THE PRINCE!
YOU'RE THE PRINCE, RIGHT?!
TMP
TMP
TMP
TMP
SHP
YOU LITTLE BRATS...
OH?
TO WHAT DO I OWE THIS PLEASURE?
!!
PRINCE, PRINCE!
WHAT'S THE PALACE REALLY LIKE?
WOW!
ARE YOU GOING HOME ALREADY?
Cool!
LOOK, A SWORD.
CAN I TOUCH IT?!
Neat!
ACK. THIS JUST GOT ANNOYING.

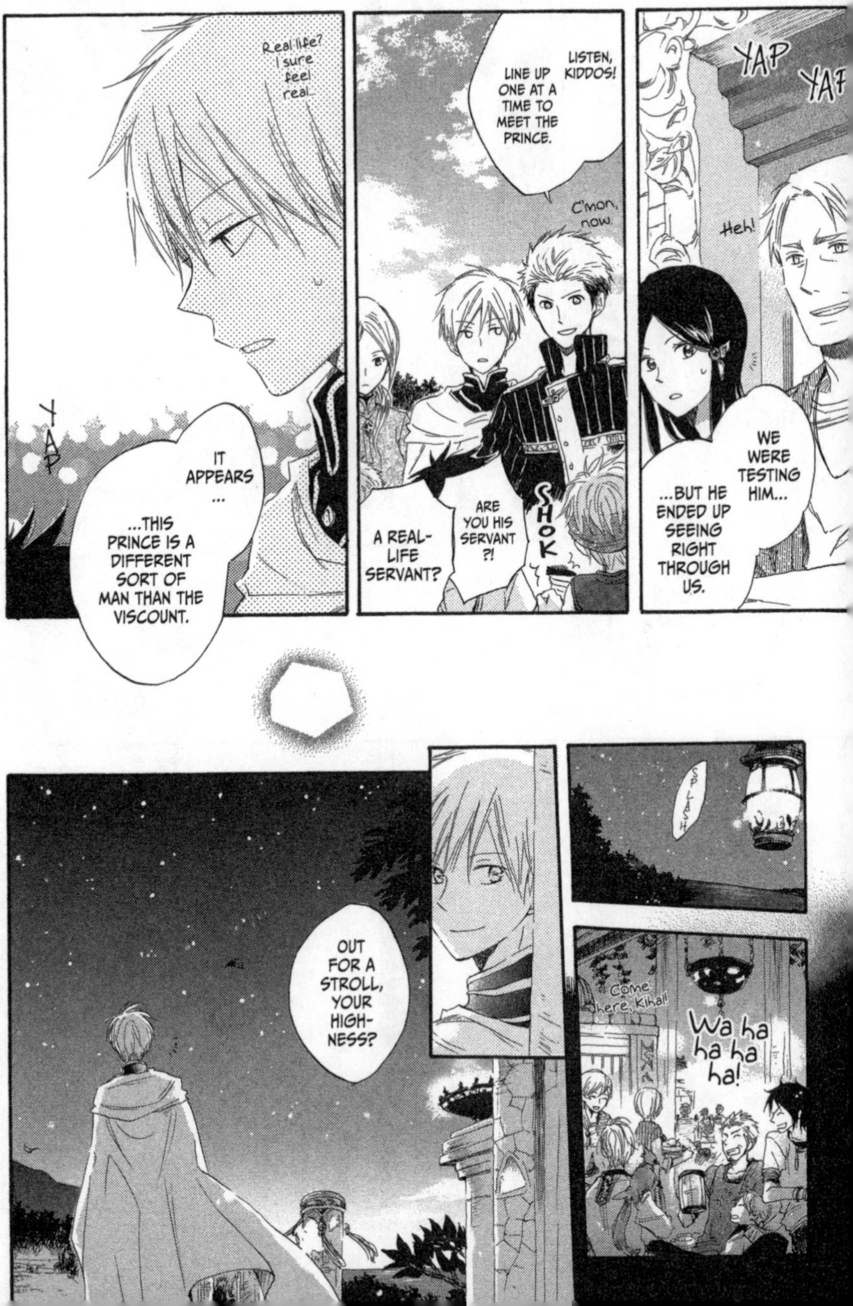
YAP YAP
Heh!
WE WERE TESTING HIM...
...BUT HE ENDED UP SEEING RIGHT THROUGH US.
LISTEN, KIDDOS!
LINE UP ONE AT A TIME TO MEET THE PRINCE.
C'mon, now.
ARE YOU HIS SERVANT?!
SHOK
A REAL-LIFE SERVANT?
Real-life? I sure feel real...
YAP
IT APPEARS...
...THIS PRINCE IS A DIFFERENT SORT OF MAN THAN THE VISCOUNT.
SPLASH
Come here, Kihal!
Wa ha ha ha ha!
OUT FOR A STROLL, YOUR HIGHNESS?

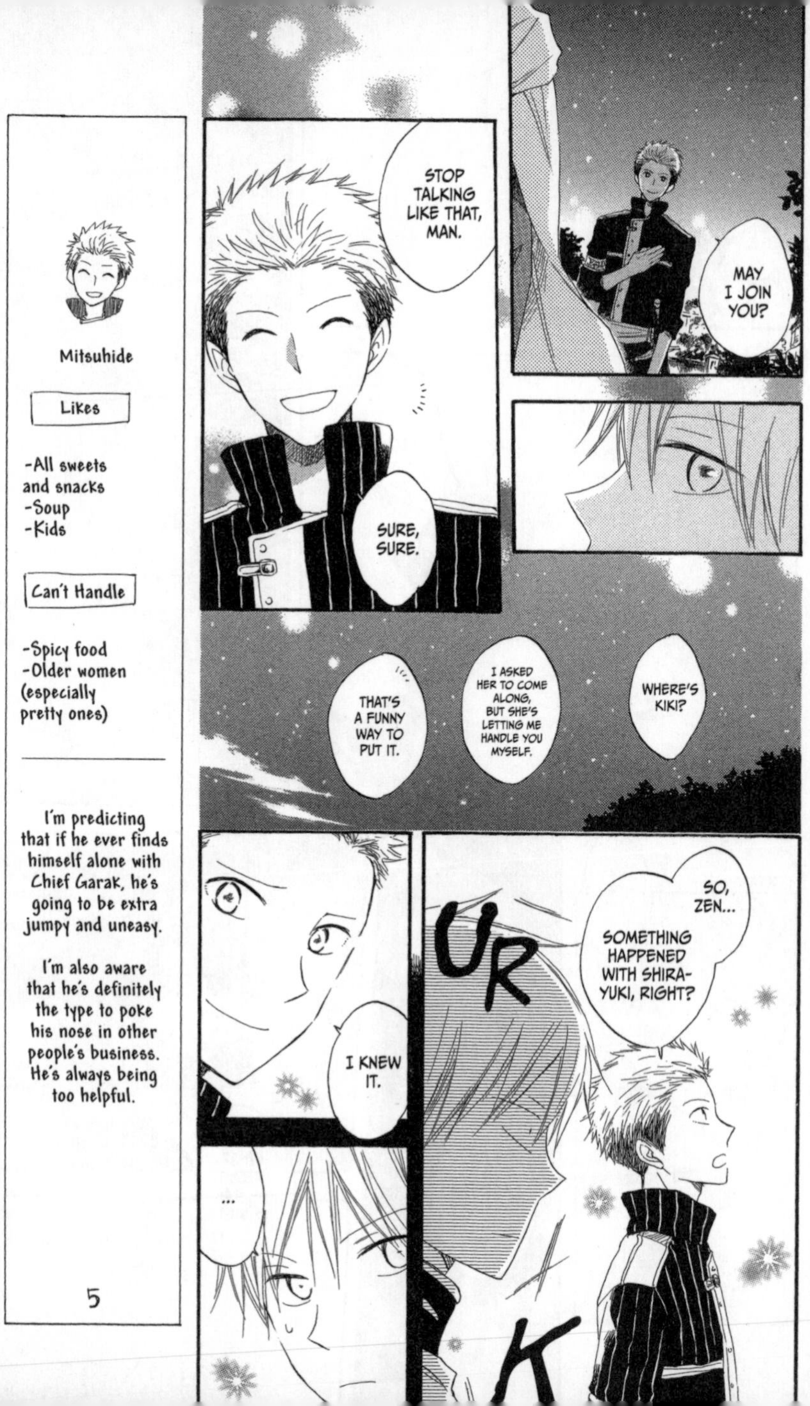
MAY I JOIN YOU?
STOP TALKING LIKE THAT, MAN.
SURE, SURE.
WHERE'S KIKI?
I ASKED HER TO COME ALONG, BUT SHE'S LETTING ME HANDLE YOU MYSELF.
THAT'S A FUNNY WAY TO PUT IT.
SO, ZEN...
SOMETHING HAPPENED WITH SHIRA-YUKI, RIGHT?
URK
I KNEW IT.
...

Mitsuhide

Likes

-All sweets and snacks
-Soup
-Kids

Can't Handle

-Spicy food
-Older women (especially pretty ones)

I'm predicting that if he ever finds himself alone with Chief Garak, he's going to be extra jumpy and uneasy.

I'm also aware that he's definitely the type to poke his nose in other people's business. He's always being too helpful.

5

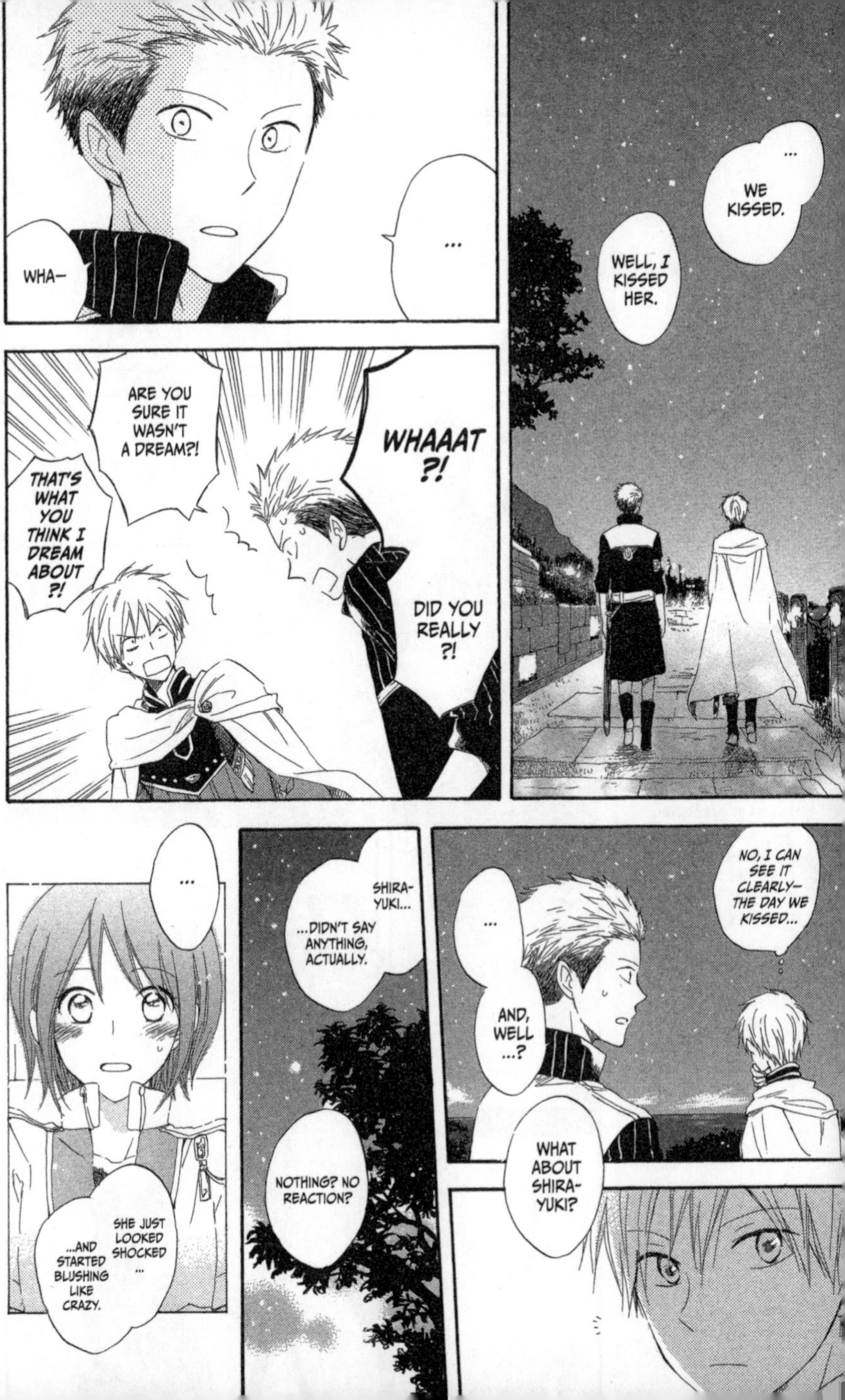
...
WE KISSED.
WELL, I KISSED HER.
...
WHA—
WHAAAT ?!
DID YOU REALLY ?!
ARE YOU SURE IT WASN'T A DREAM?!
THAT'S WHAT YOU THINK I DREAM ABOUT ?!
NO, I CAN SEE IT CLEARLY— THE DAY WE KISSED...
...
AND, WELL ...?
WHAT ABOUT SHIRA-YUKI?
SHIRA-YUKI...
...DIDN'T SAY ANYTHING, ACTUALLY.
NOTHING? NO REACTION?
...
SHE JUST LOOKED SHOCKED ...
...AND STARTED BLUSHING LIKE CRAZY.

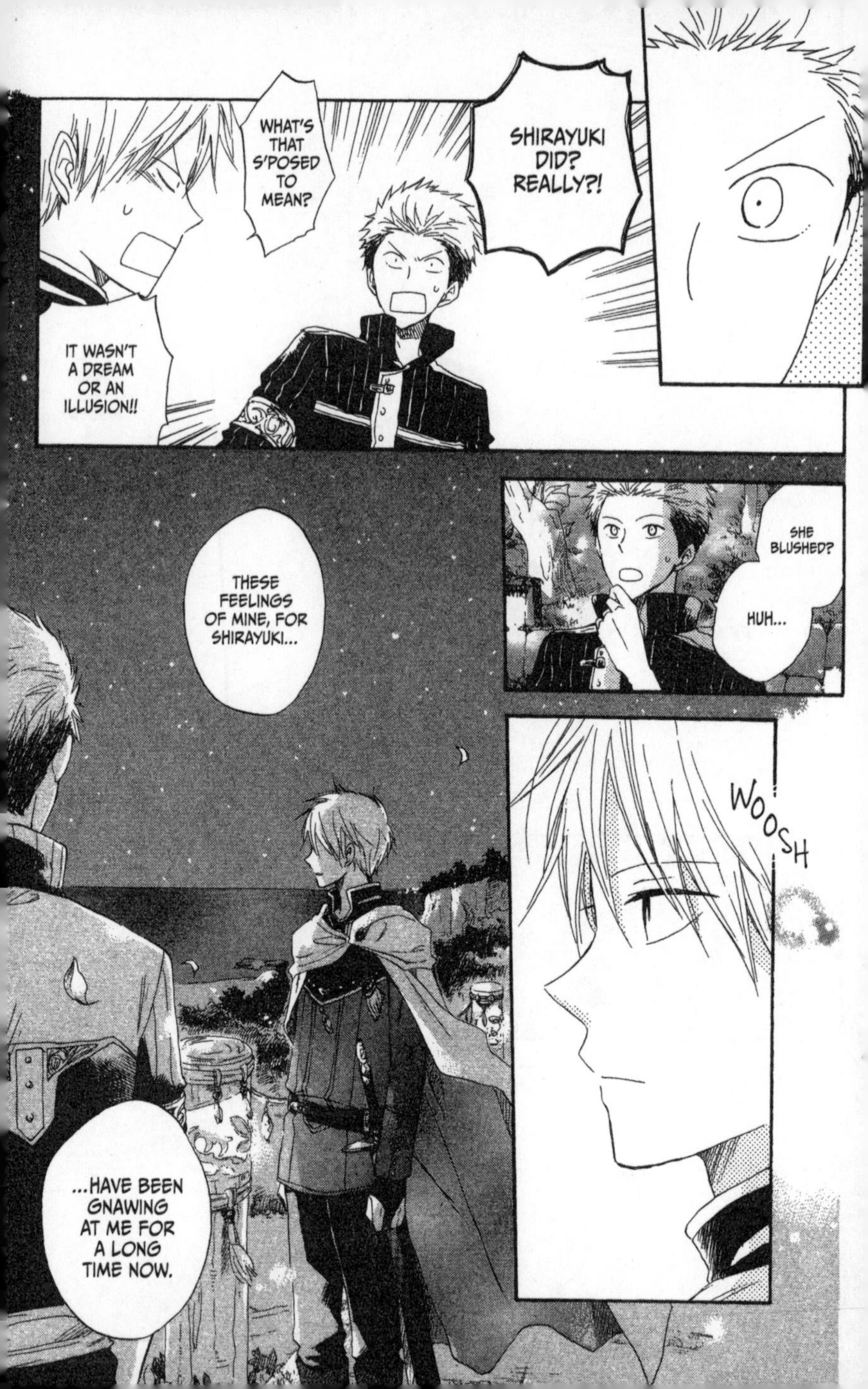
SHIRAYUKI DID? REALLY?!
WHAT'S THAT S'POSED TO MEAN?
IT WASN'T A DREAM OR AN ILLUSION!!
SHE BLUSHED?
HUH...
WOOSH
THESE FEELINGS OF MINE, FOR SHIRAYUKI...
...HAVE BEEN GNAWING AT ME FOR A LONG TIME NOW.

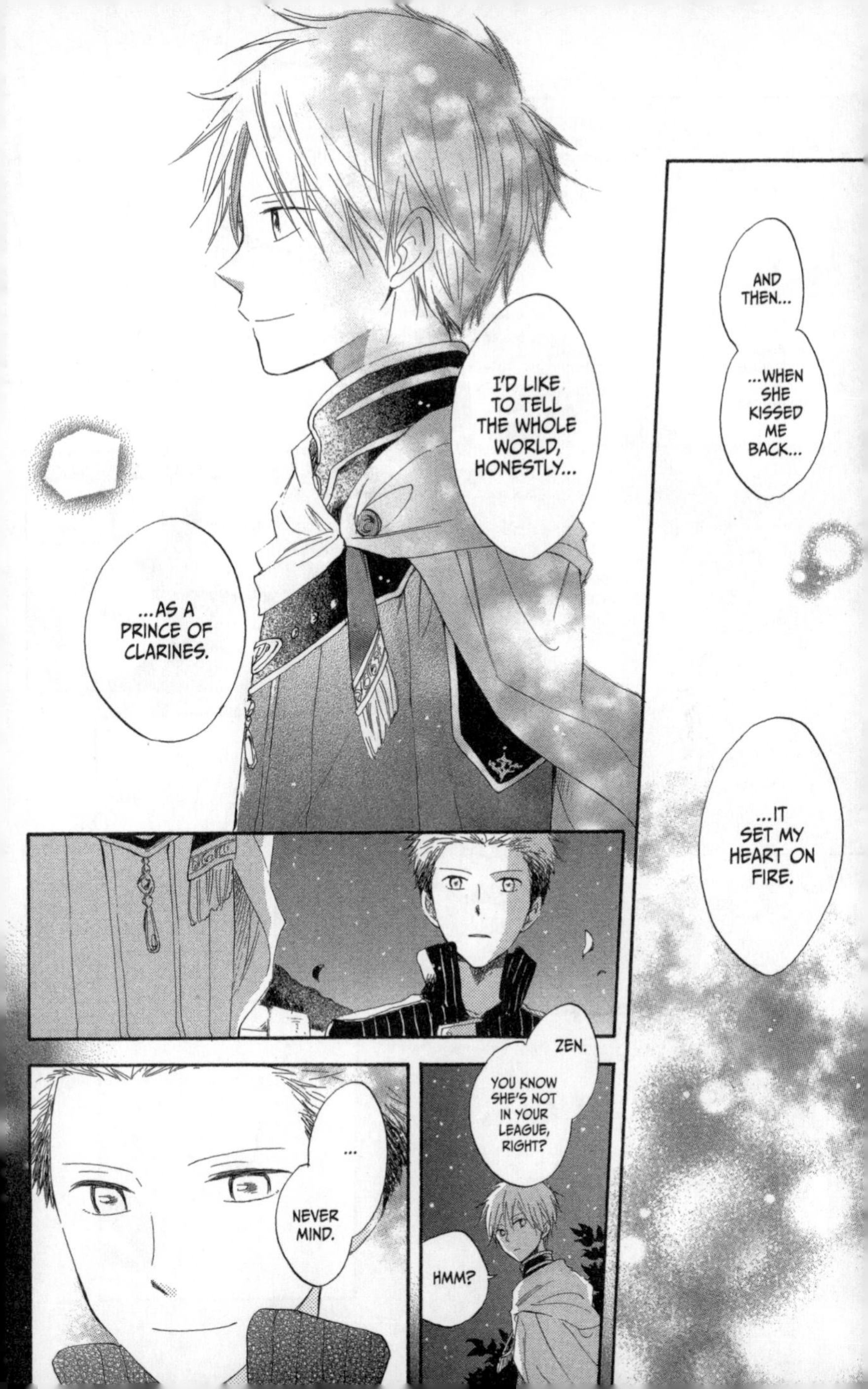

AND THEN...
...WHEN SHE KISSED ME BACK...
...IT SET MY HEART ON FIRE.
I'D LIKE TO TELL THE WHOLE WORLD, HONESTLY...
...AS A PRINCE OF CLARINES.
ZEN.
YOU KNOW SHE'S NOT IN YOUR LEAGUE, RIGHT?
HMM?
...
NEVER MIND.

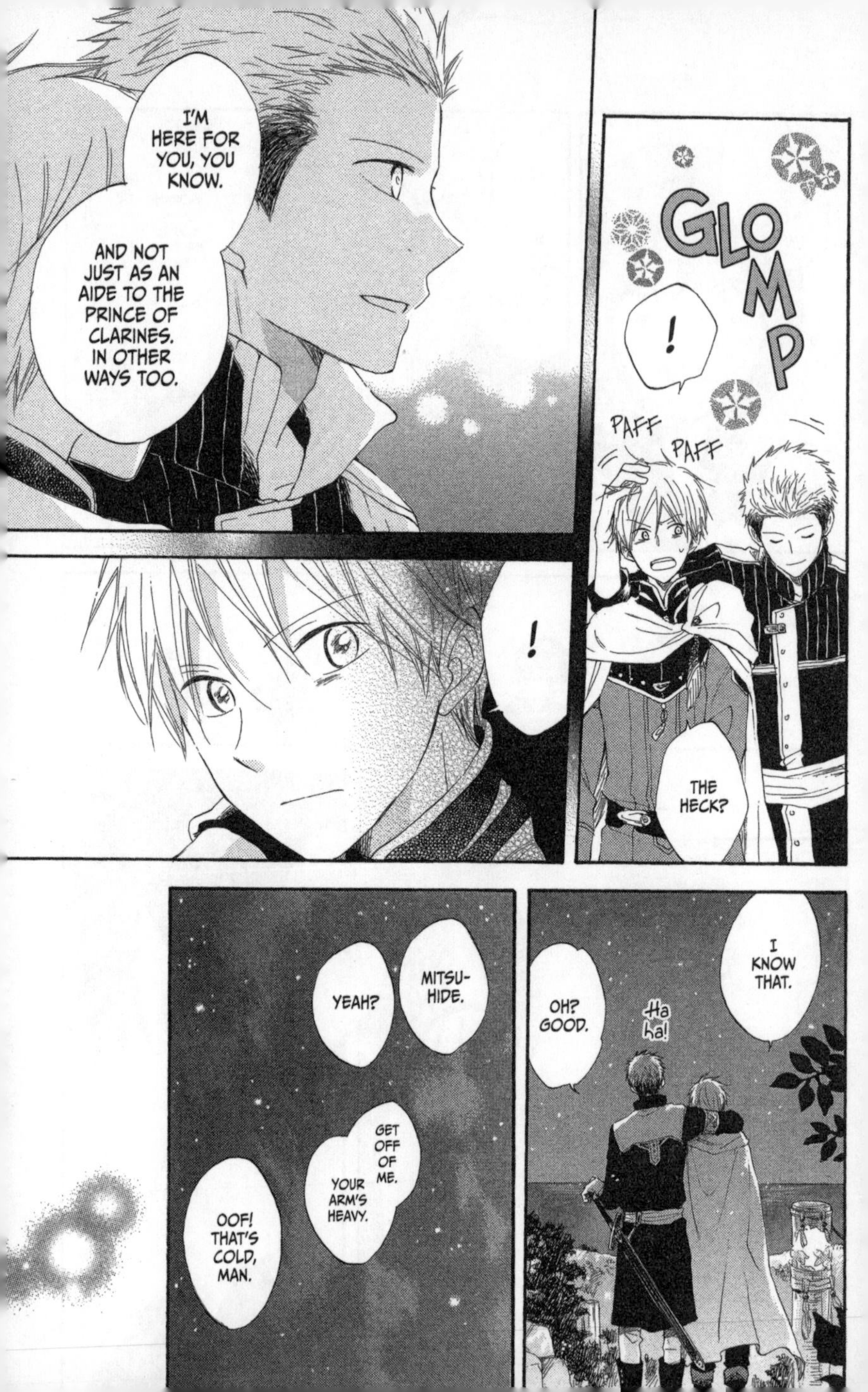
GLOMP
!
PAFF
PAFF
THE HECK?
I'M HERE FOR YOU, YOU KNOW.
AND NOT JUST AS AN AIDE TO THE PRINCE OF CLARINES. IN OTHER WAYS TOO.
!
I KNOW THAT.
Ha ha!
OH? GOOD.
MITSU-HIDE.
YEAH?
GET OFF OF ME.
YOUR ARM'S HEAVY.
OOF! THAT'S COLD, MAN.

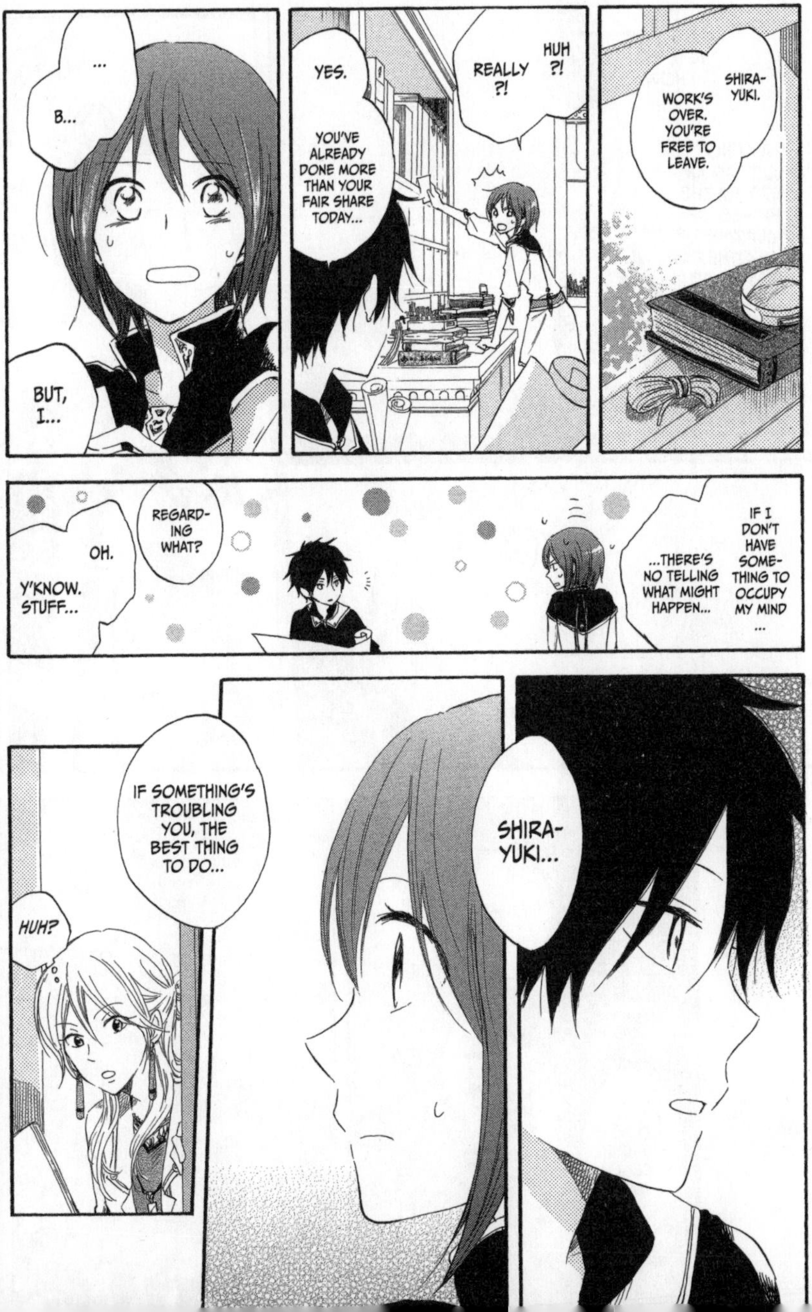
SHIRA-YUKI.
WORK'S OVER. YOU'RE FREE TO LEAVE.
HUH ?!
REALLY ?!
YES.
YOU'VE ALREADY DONE MORE THAN YOUR FAIR SHARE TODAY...
...
B...
BUT, I...
IF I DON'T HAVE SOME-THING TO OCCUPY MY MIND ...
...THERE'S NO TELLING WHAT MIGHT HAPPEN...
REGARD-ING WHAT?
OH.
Y'KNOW. STUFF...
SHIRA-YUKI...
IF SOMETHING'S TROUBLING YOU, THE BEST THING TO DO...
HUH?

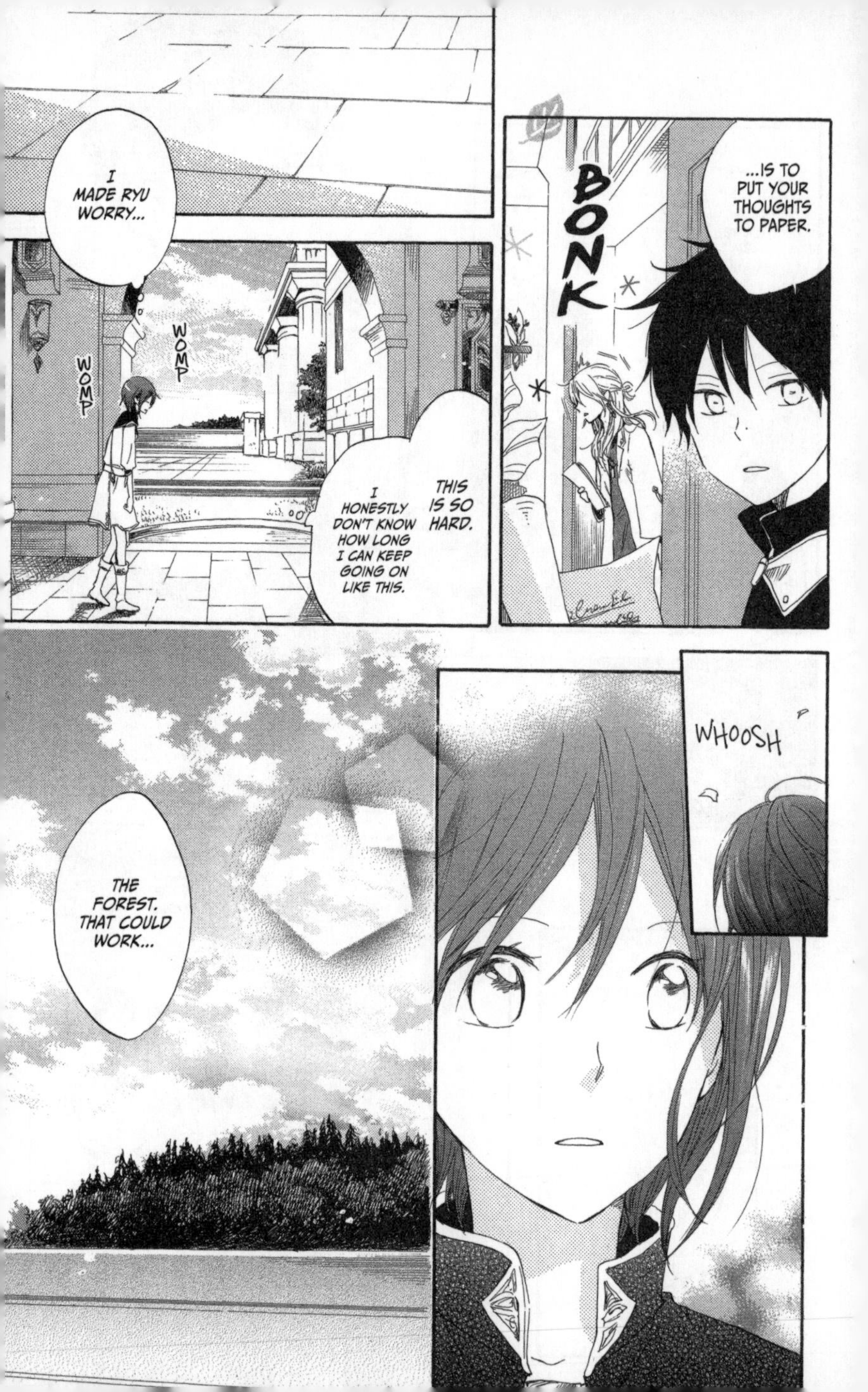
...IS TO PUT YOUR THOUGHTS TO PAPER.
BONK
I MADE RYU WORRY...
WOMP
WOMP
THIS IS SO HARD.
I HONESTLY DON'T KNOW HOW LONG I CAN KEEP GOING ON LIKE THIS.
WHOOSH
THE FOREST. THAT COULD WORK...

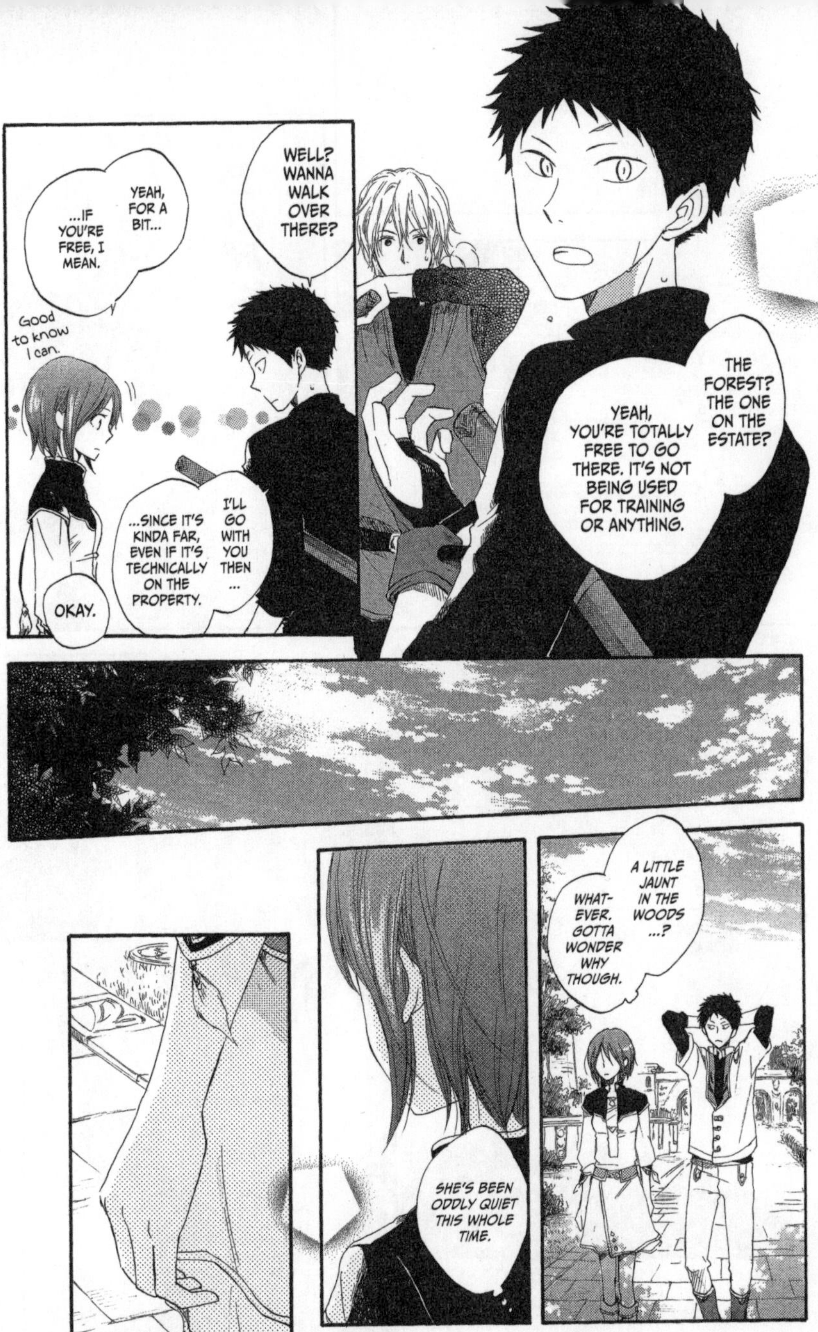
THE FOREST? THE ONE ON THE ESTATE?
YEAH, YOU'RE TOTALLY FREE TO GO THERE. IT'S NOT BEING USED FOR TRAINING OR ANYTHING.
WELL? WANNA WALK OVER THERE?
YEAH, FOR A BIT...
...IF YOU'RE FREE, I MEAN.
Good to know I can.
I'LL GO WITH YOU THEN...
...SINCE IT'S KINDA FAR, EVEN IF IT'S TECHNICALLY ON THE PROPERTY.
OKAY.
A LITTLE JAUNT IN THE WOODS...?
WHATEVER. GOTTA WONDER WHY THOUGH.
SHE'S BEEN ODDLY QUIET THIS WHOLE TIME.

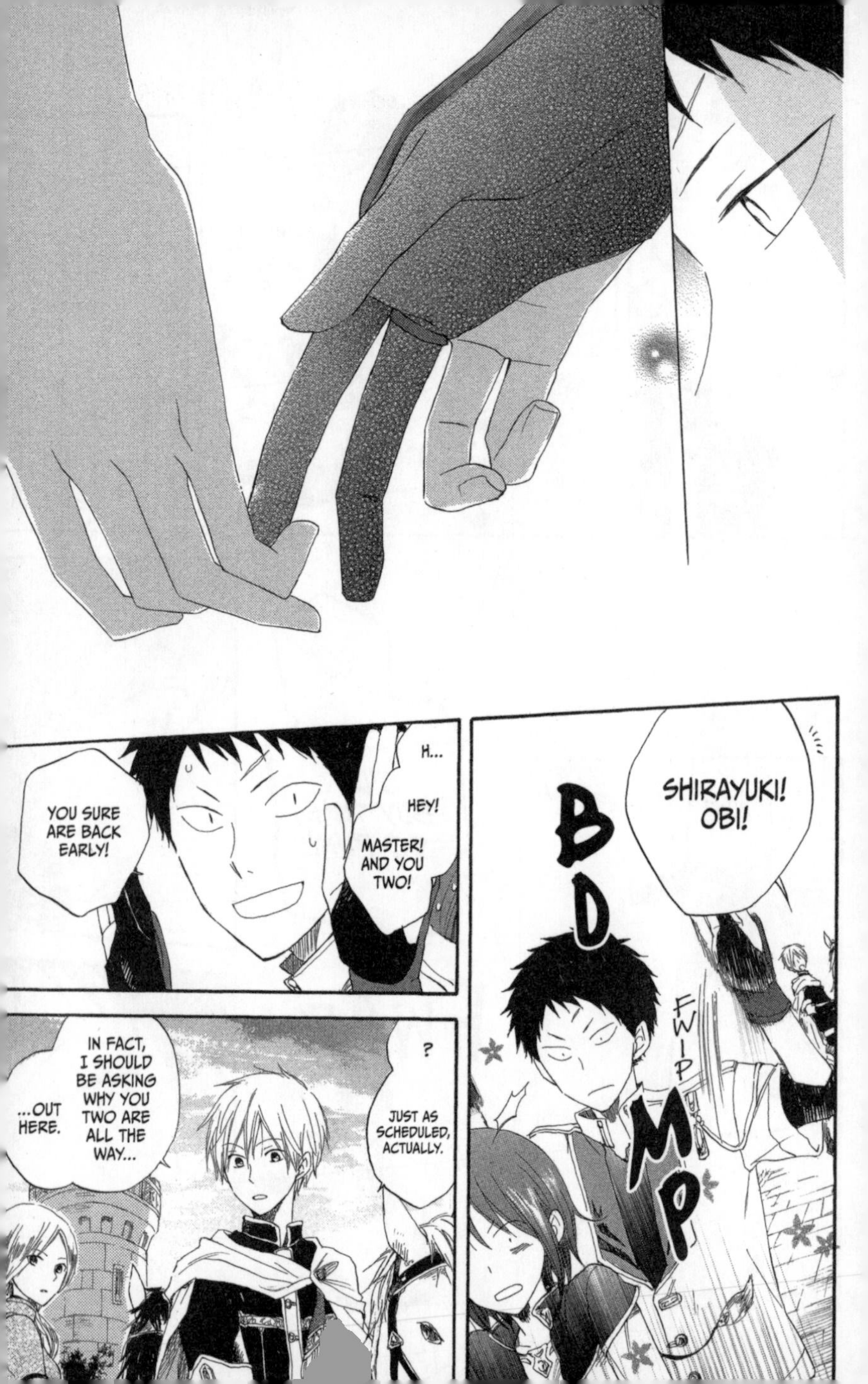
SHIRAYUKI! OBI!
FWIP
BDMP
H...
HEY!
MASTER! AND YOU TWO!
YOU SURE ARE BACK EARLY!
?
JUST AS SCHEDULED, ACTUALLY.
IN FACT, I SHOULD BE ASKING WHY YOU TWO ARE ALL THE WAY...
...OUT HERE.

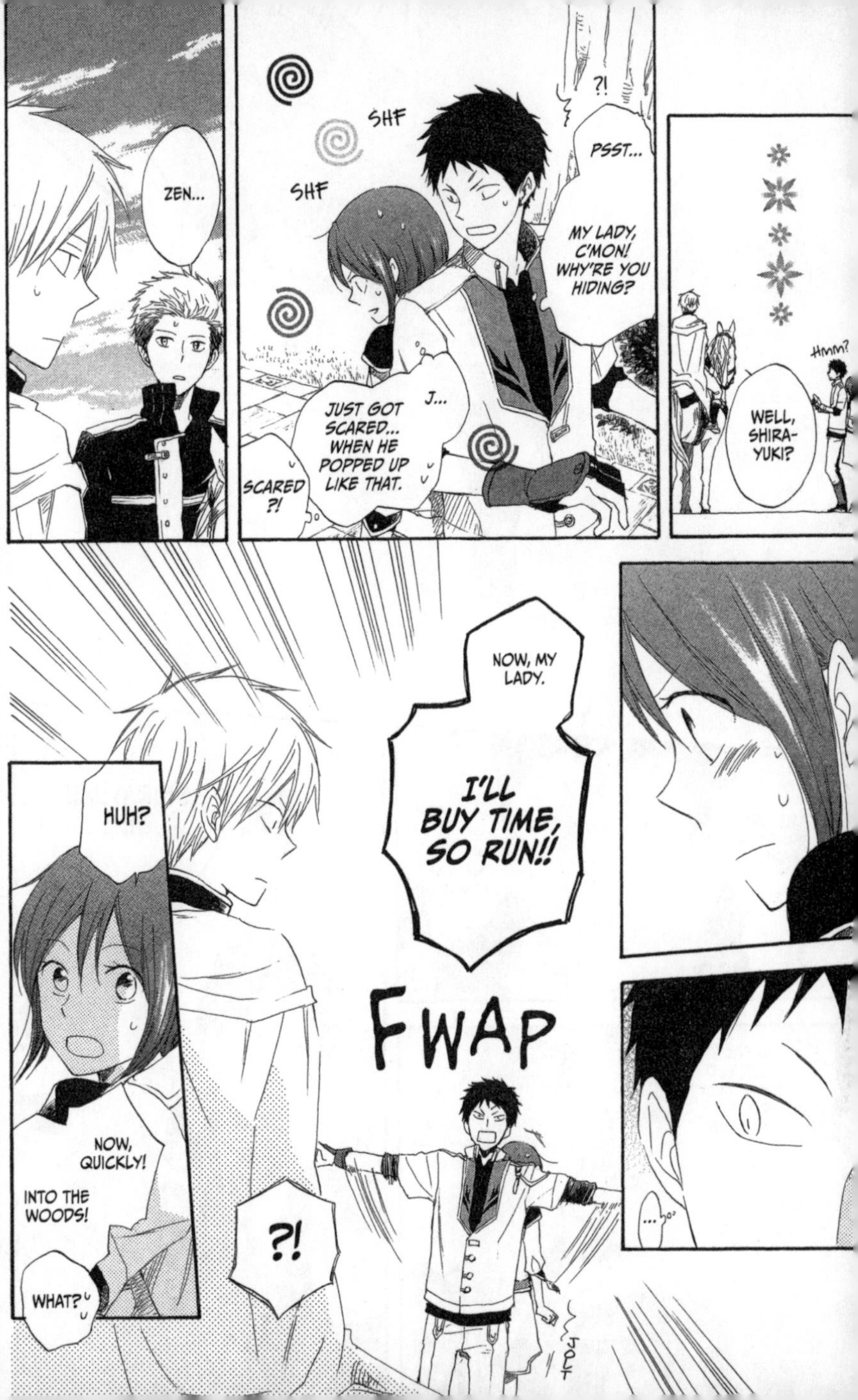
HMM?
WELL, SHIRAYUKI?
?!
PSST...
MY LADY, C'MON! WHY'RE YOU HIDING?
SHF
SHF
J...
JUST GOT SCARED... WHEN HE POPPED UP LIKE THAT.
SCARED?!
ZEN...
...
NOW, MY LADY.
I'LL BUY TIME, SO RUN!!
FWAP
HUH?
?!
JOLT
NOW, QUICKLY!
INTO THE WOODS!
WHAT?

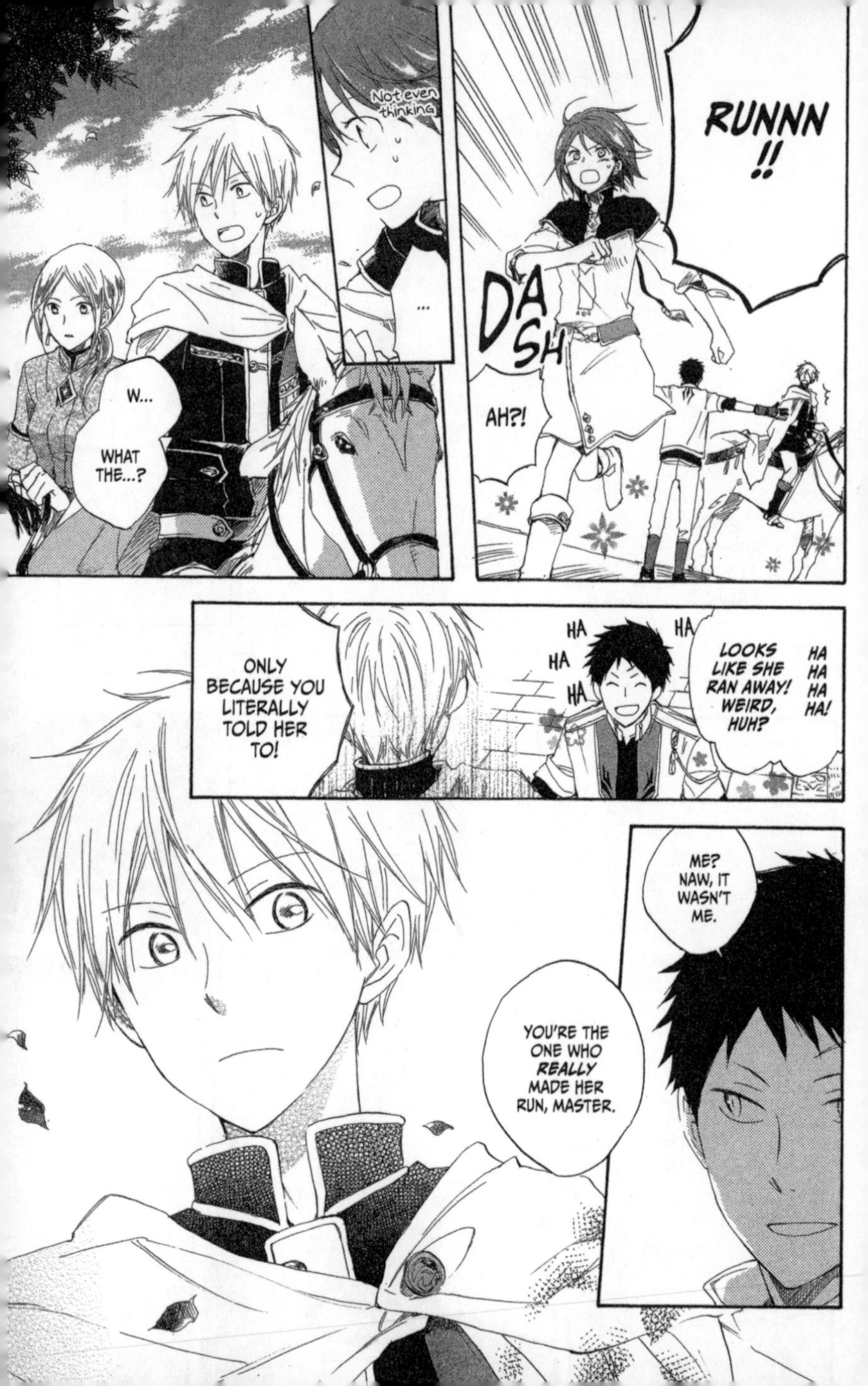
RUNNN !!
DASH
AH?!
Not even thinking
...
W...
WHAT THE...?
HA
HA
HA
HA
LOOKS LIKE SHE RAN AWAY! WEIRD, HUH?
HA HA HA HA!
ONLY BECAUSE YOU LITERALLY TOLD HER TO!
ME? NAW, IT WASN'T ME.
YOU'RE THE ONE WHO *REALLY* MADE HER RUN, MASTER.

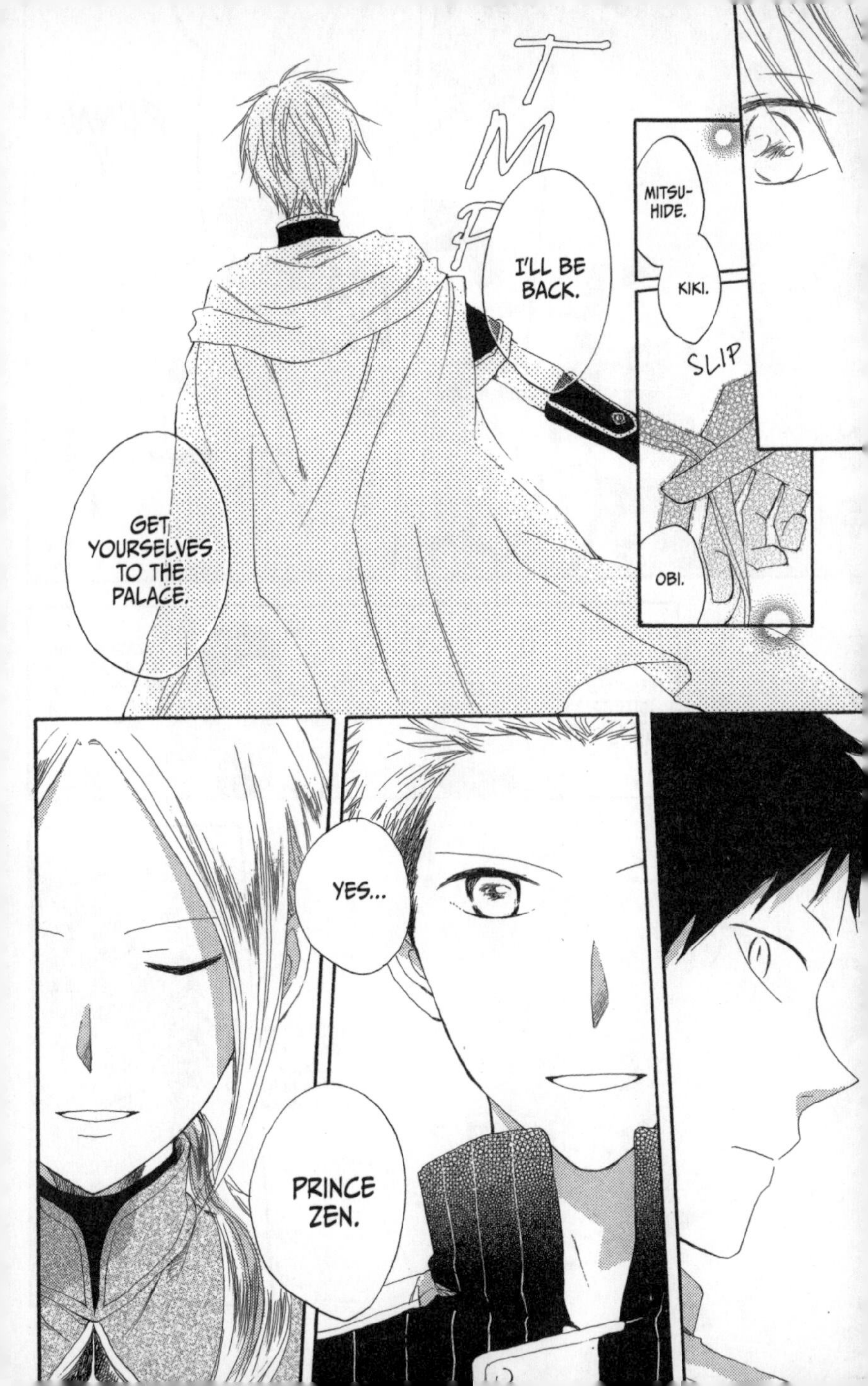
MITSU-HIDE.
KIKI.
SLIP
OBI.
TMP
I'LL BE BACK.
GET YOURSELVES TO THE PALACE.
YES...
PRINCE ZEN.

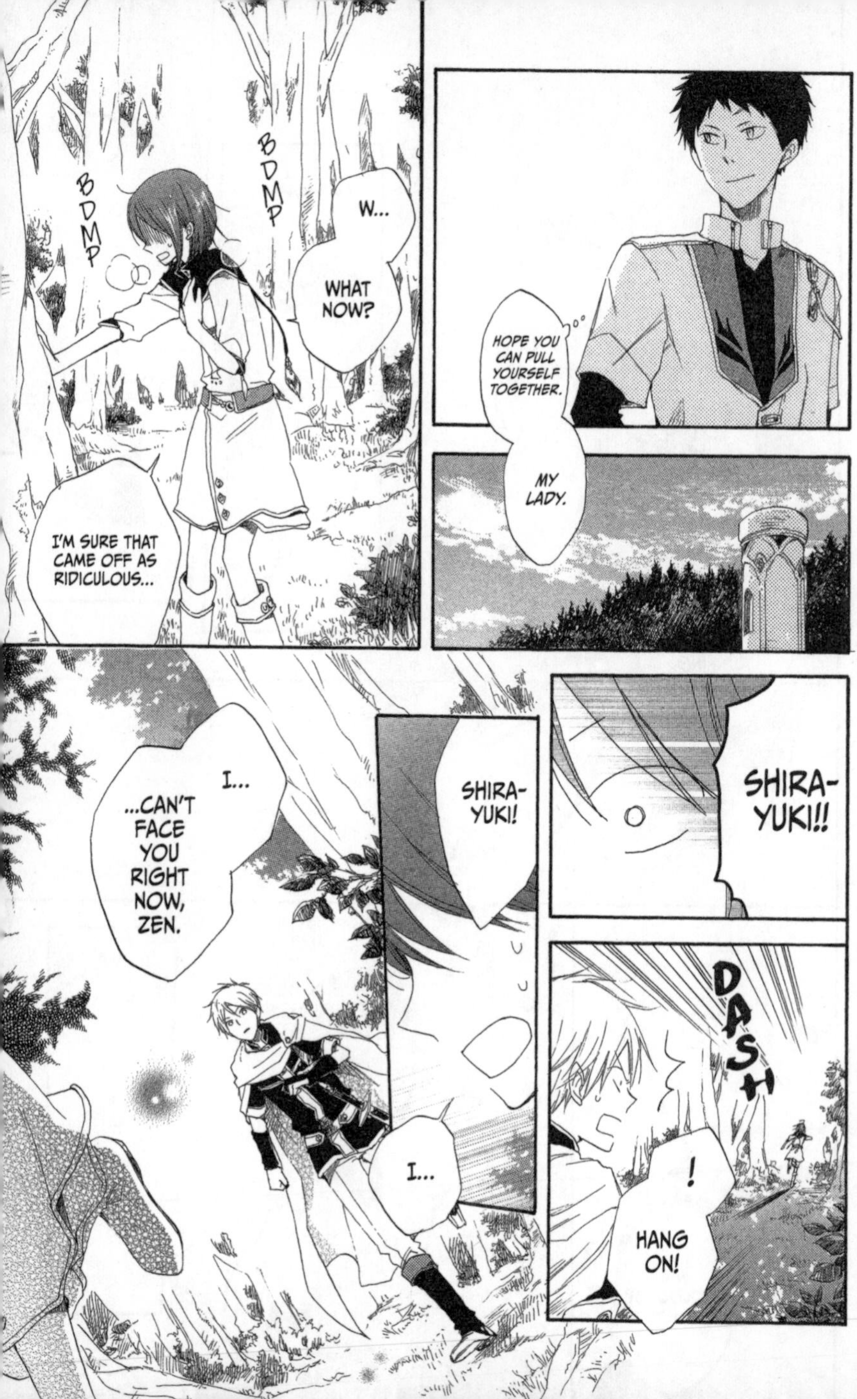
HOPE YOU CAN PULL YOURSELF TOGETHER.
MY LADY.
BDMP
BDMP
W...
WHAT NOW?
I'M SURE THAT CAME OFF AS RIDICULOUS...
SHIRA-YUKI!!
DASH
!
HANG ON!
SHIRA-YUKI!
I...
I...
...CAN'T FACE YOU RIGHT NOW, ZEN.

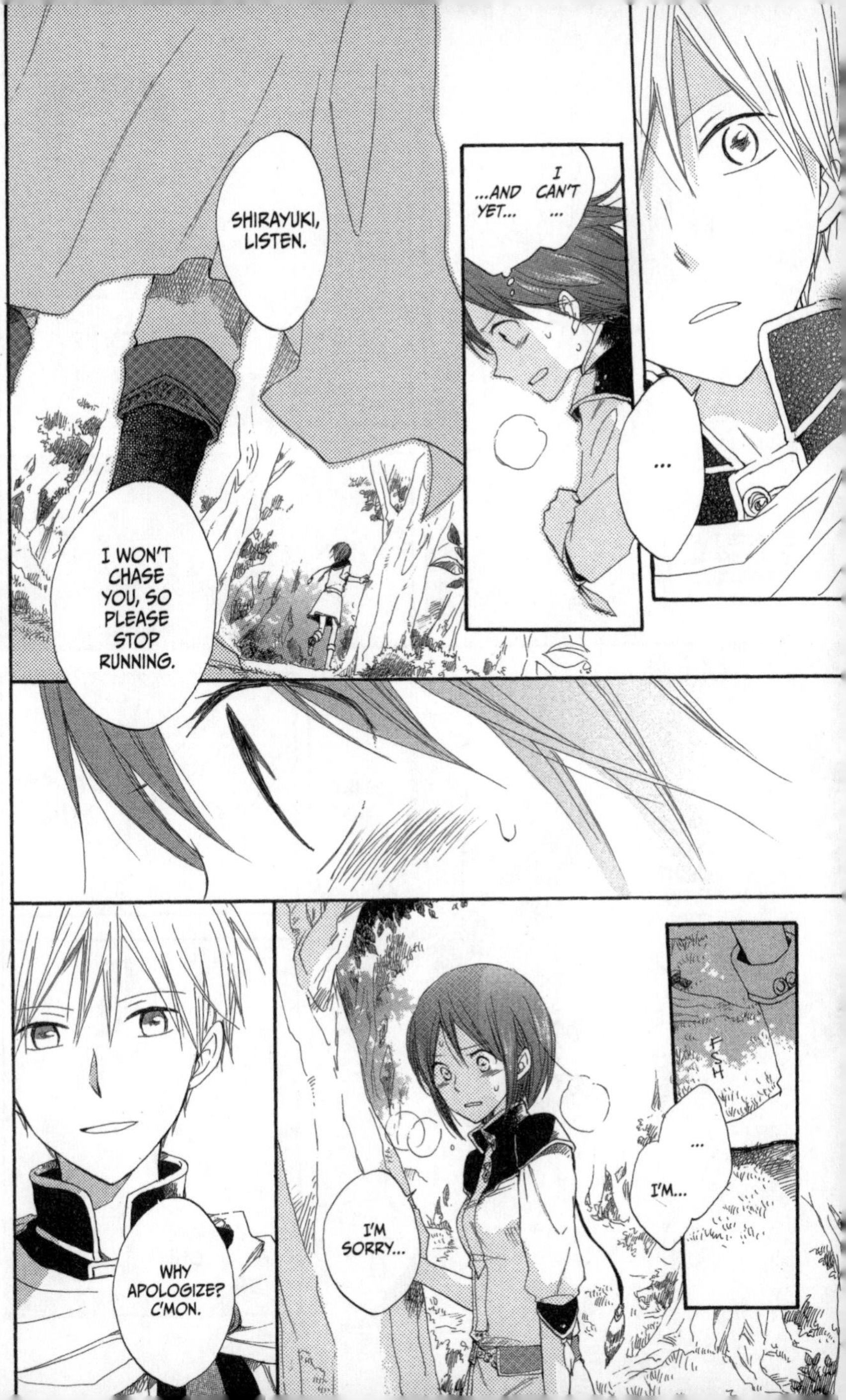
...
I CAN'T ... ...AND YET...
SHIRAYUKI, LISTEN.
I WON'T CHASE YOU, SO PLEASE STOP RUNNING.
FSH
... I'M...
I'M SORRY...
WHY APOLOGIZE? C'MON.

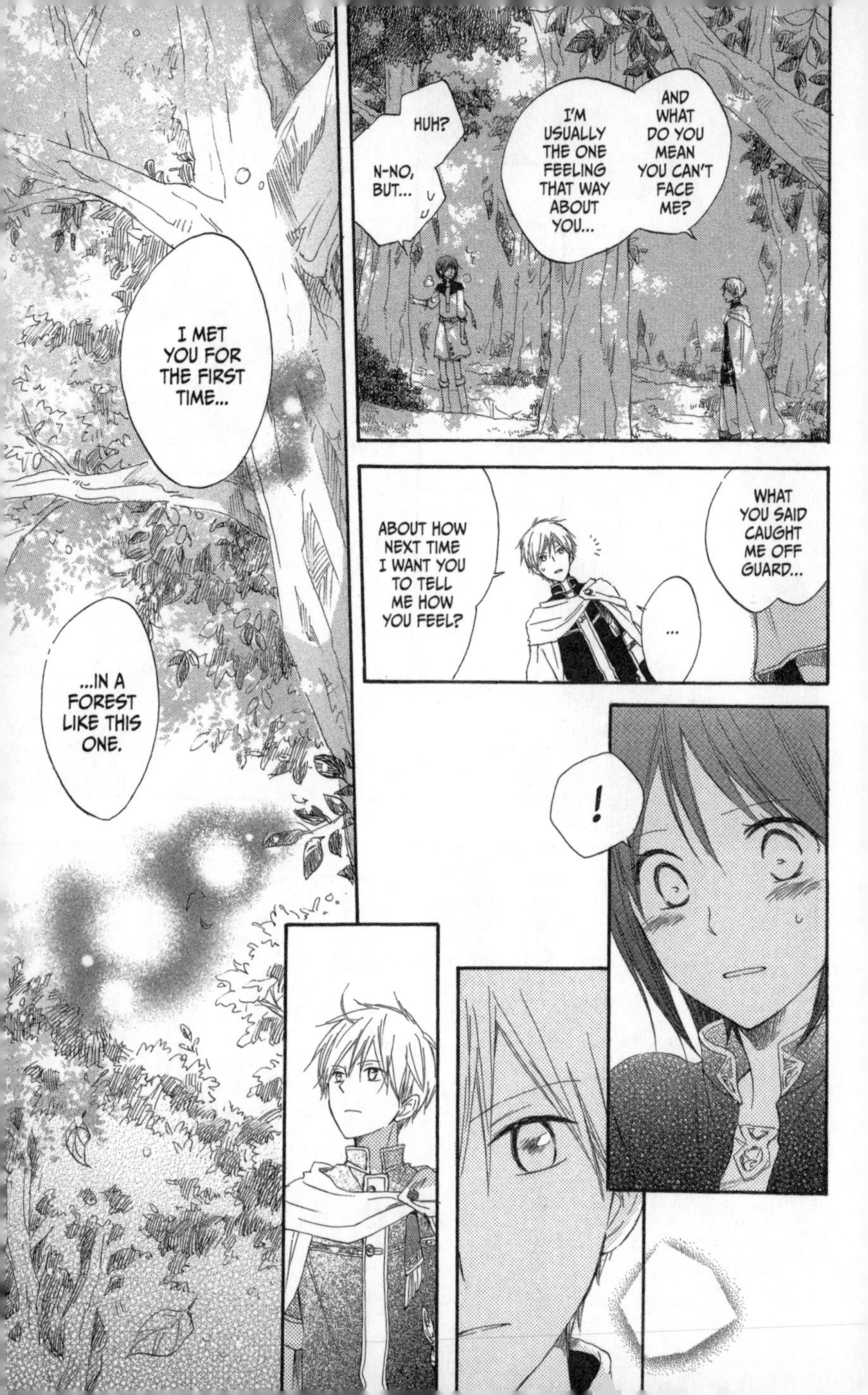
AND WHAT DO YOU MEAN YOU CAN'T FACE ME?
I'M USUALLY THE ONE FEELING THAT WAY ABOUT YOU...
HUH?
N-NO, BUT...
WHAT YOU SAID CAUGHT ME OFF GUARD...
...
ABOUT HOW NEXT TIME I WANT YOU TO TELL ME HOW YOU FEEL?
!
I MET YOU FOR THE FIRST TIME...
...IN A FOREST LIKE THIS ONE.

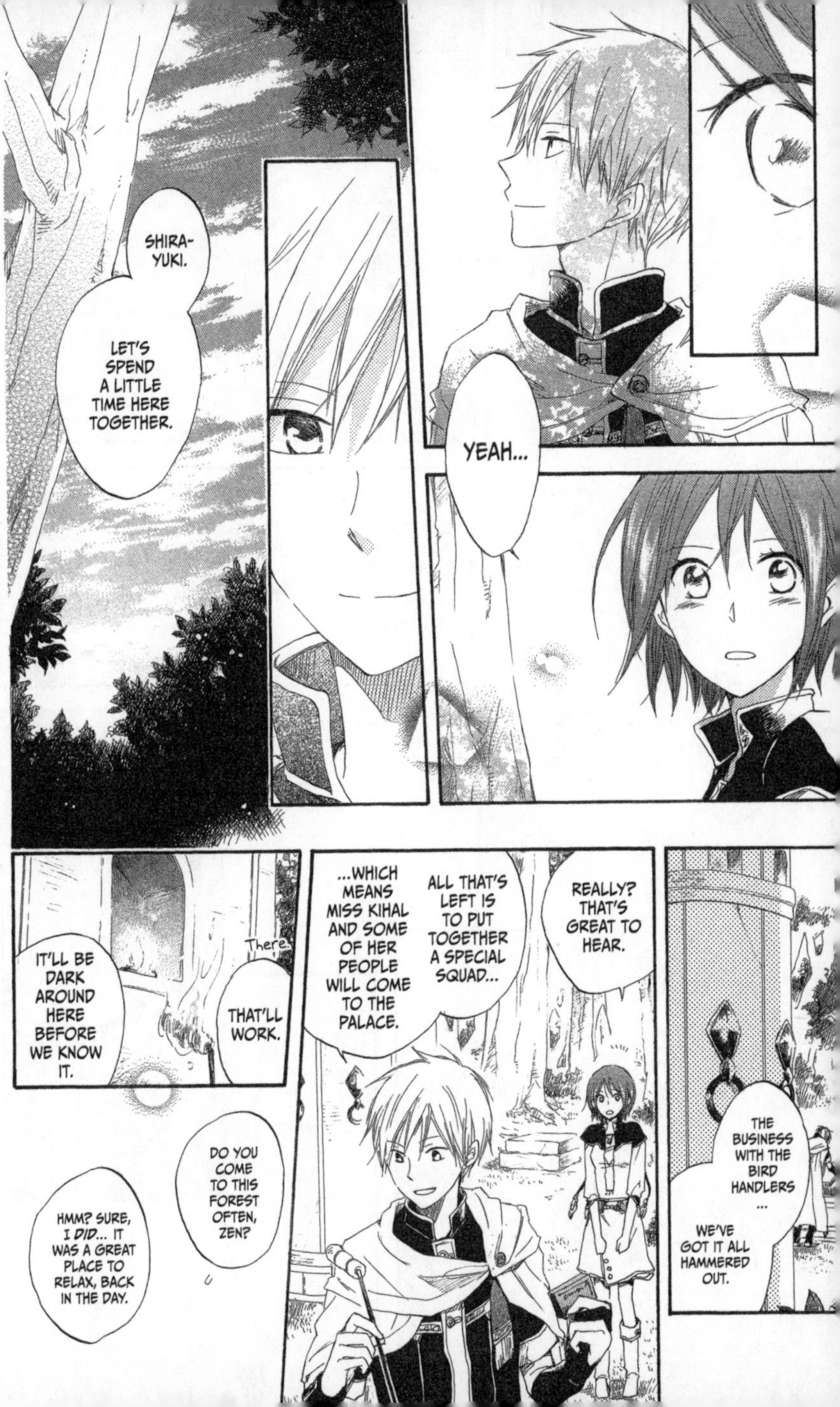
SHIRA-YUKI.
LET'S SPEND A LITTLE TIME HERE TOGETHER.
YEAH...
THE BUSINESS WITH THE BIRD HANDLERS...
WE'VE GOT IT ALL HAMMERED OUT.
REALLY? THAT'S GREAT TO HEAR.
ALL THAT'S LEFT IS TO PUT TOGETHER A SPECIAL SQUAD...
...WHICH MEANS MISS KIHAL AND SOME OF HER PEOPLE WILL COME TO THE PALACE.
DO YOU COME TO THIS FOREST OFTEN, ZEN?
HMM? SURE, I DID... IT WAS A GREAT PLACE TO RELAX, BACK IN THE DAY.
There.
THAT'LL WORK.
IT'LL BE DARK AROUND HERE BEFORE WE KNOW IT.

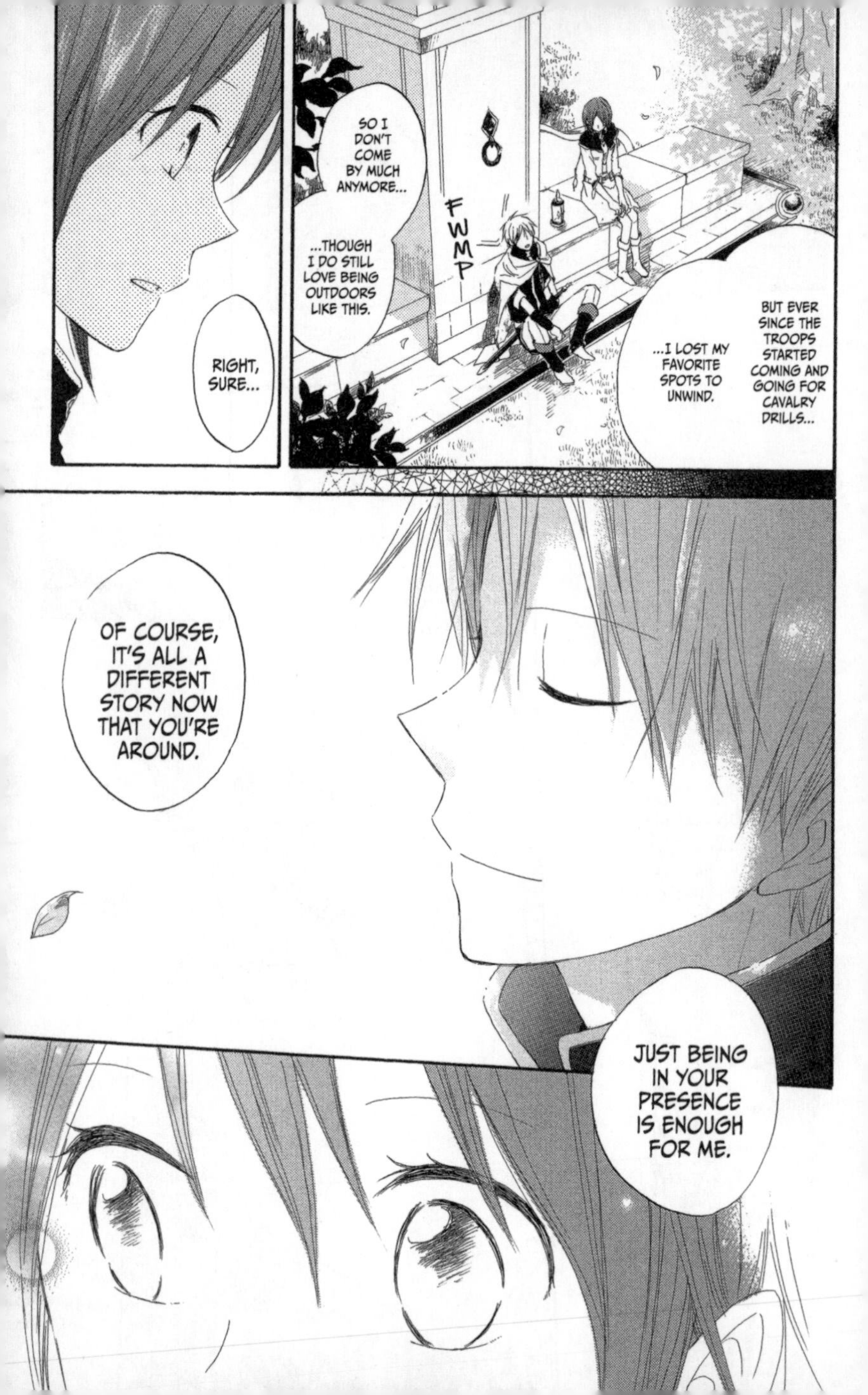
BUT EVER SINCE THE TROOPS STARTED COMING AND GOING FOR CAVALRY DRILLS...
...I LOST MY FAVORITE SPOTS TO UNWIND.
SO I DON'T COME BY MUCH ANYMORE...
FWMP
...THOUGH I DO STILL LOVE BEING OUTDOORS LIKE THIS.
RIGHT, SURE...
OF COURSE, IT'S ALL A DIFFERENT STORY NOW THAT YOU'RE AROUND.
JUST BEING IN YOUR PRESENCE IS ENOUGH FOR ME.

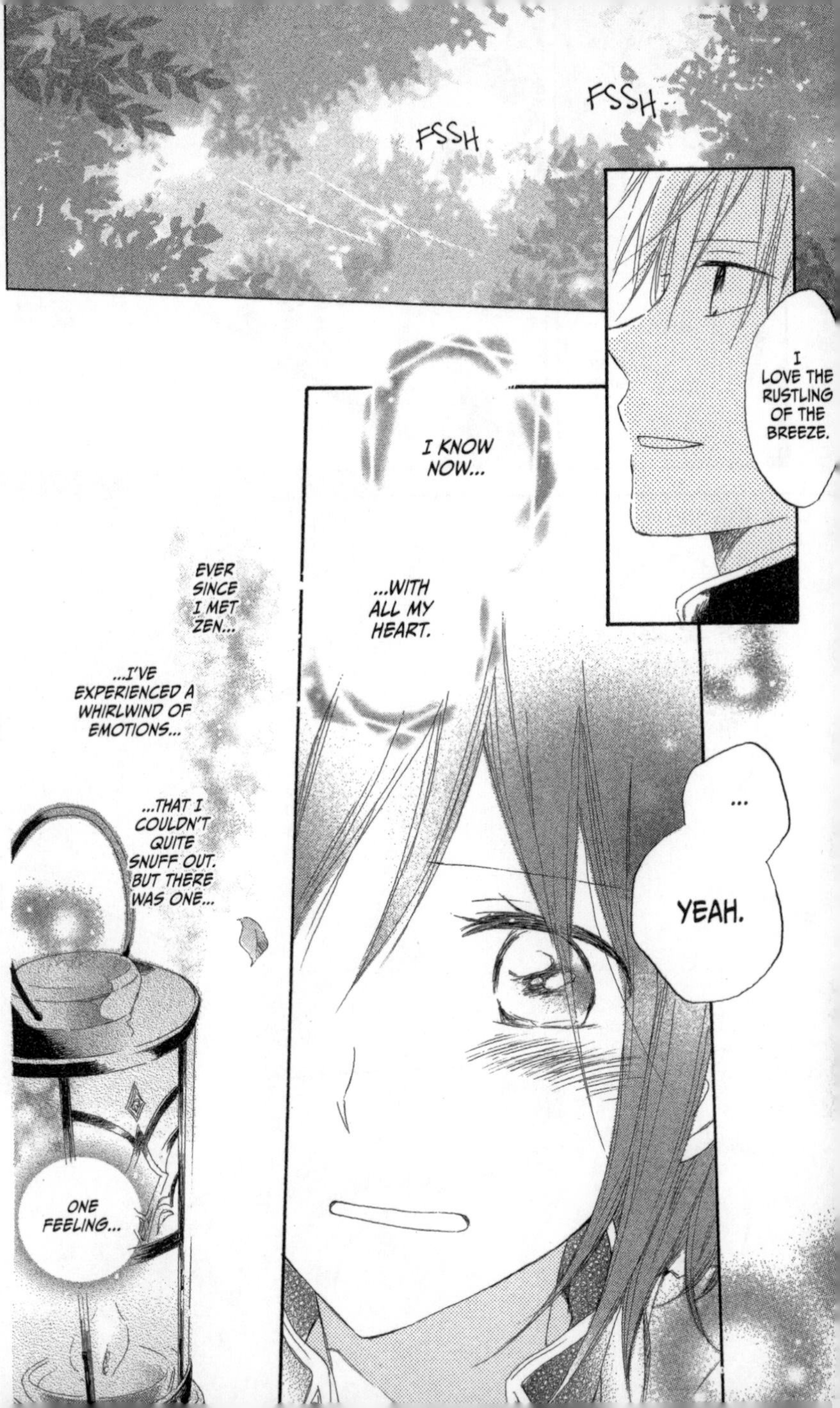
FSSH
FSSH
I LOVE THE RUSTLING OF THE BREEZE.
...
YEAH.
EVER SINCE I MET ZEN...
...I'VE EXPERIENCED A WHIRLWIND OF EMOTIONS...
...THAT I COULDN'T QUITE SNUFF OUT. BUT THERE WAS ONE...
ONE FEELING...
I KNOW NOW...
...WITH ALL MY HEART.

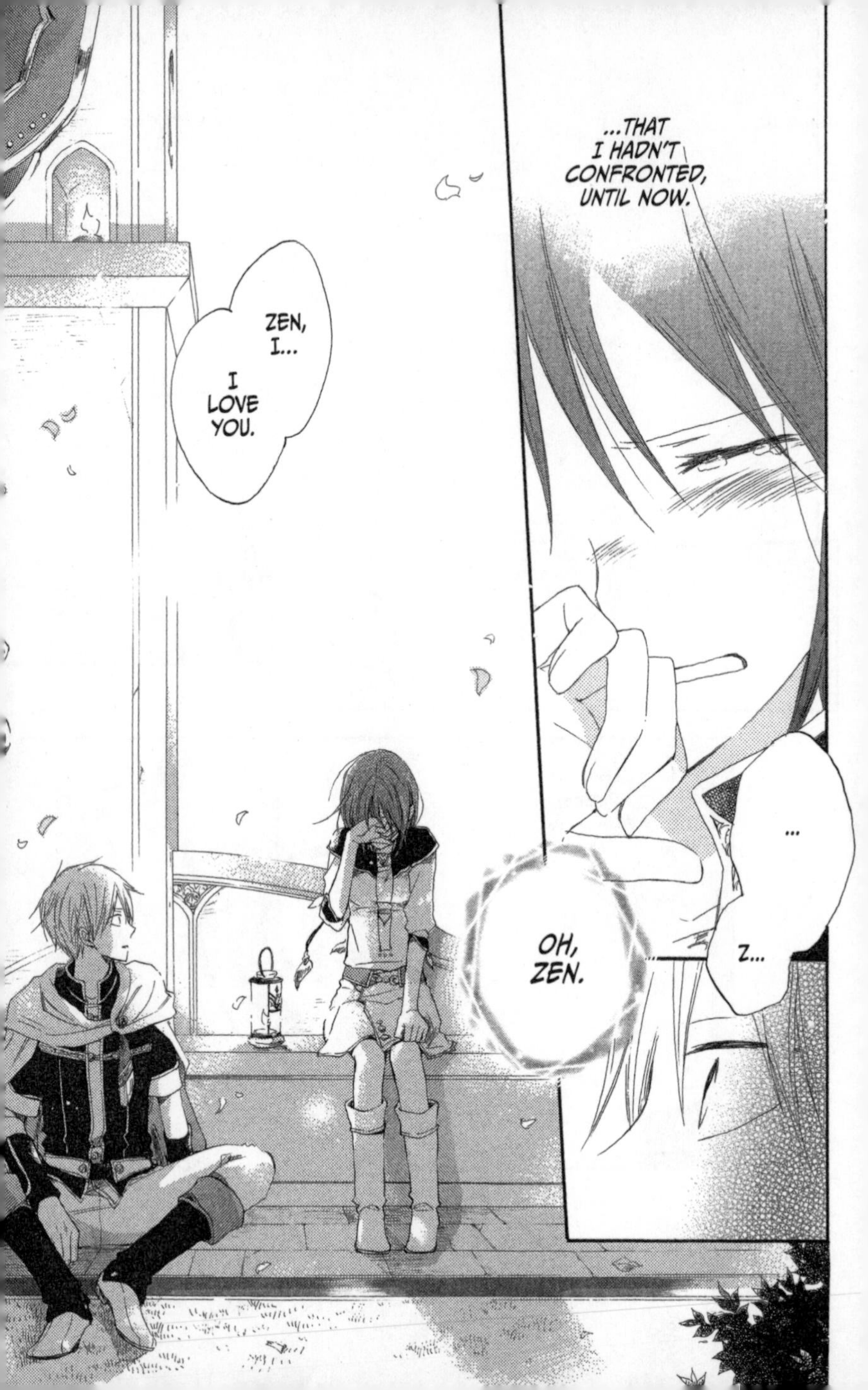
...THAT I HADN'T CONFRONTED, UNTIL NOW.
... Z...
OH, ZEN.
ZEN, I... I LOVE YOU.

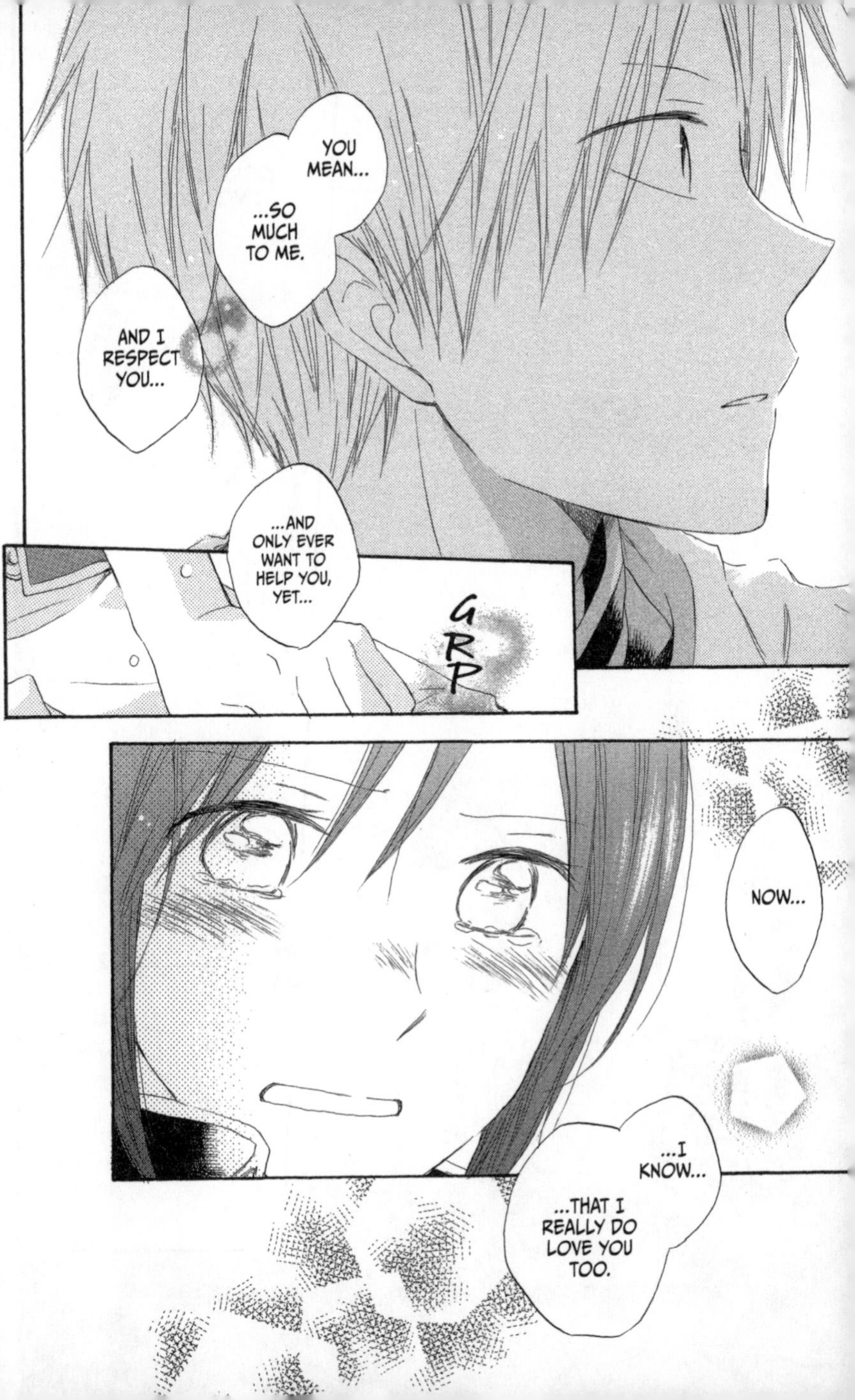
YOU MEAN...
...SO MUCH TO ME.
AND I RESPECT YOU...
...AND ONLY EVER WANT TO HELP YOU, YET...
GRP
NOW...
...I KNOW...
...THAT I REALLY DO LOVE YOU TOO.

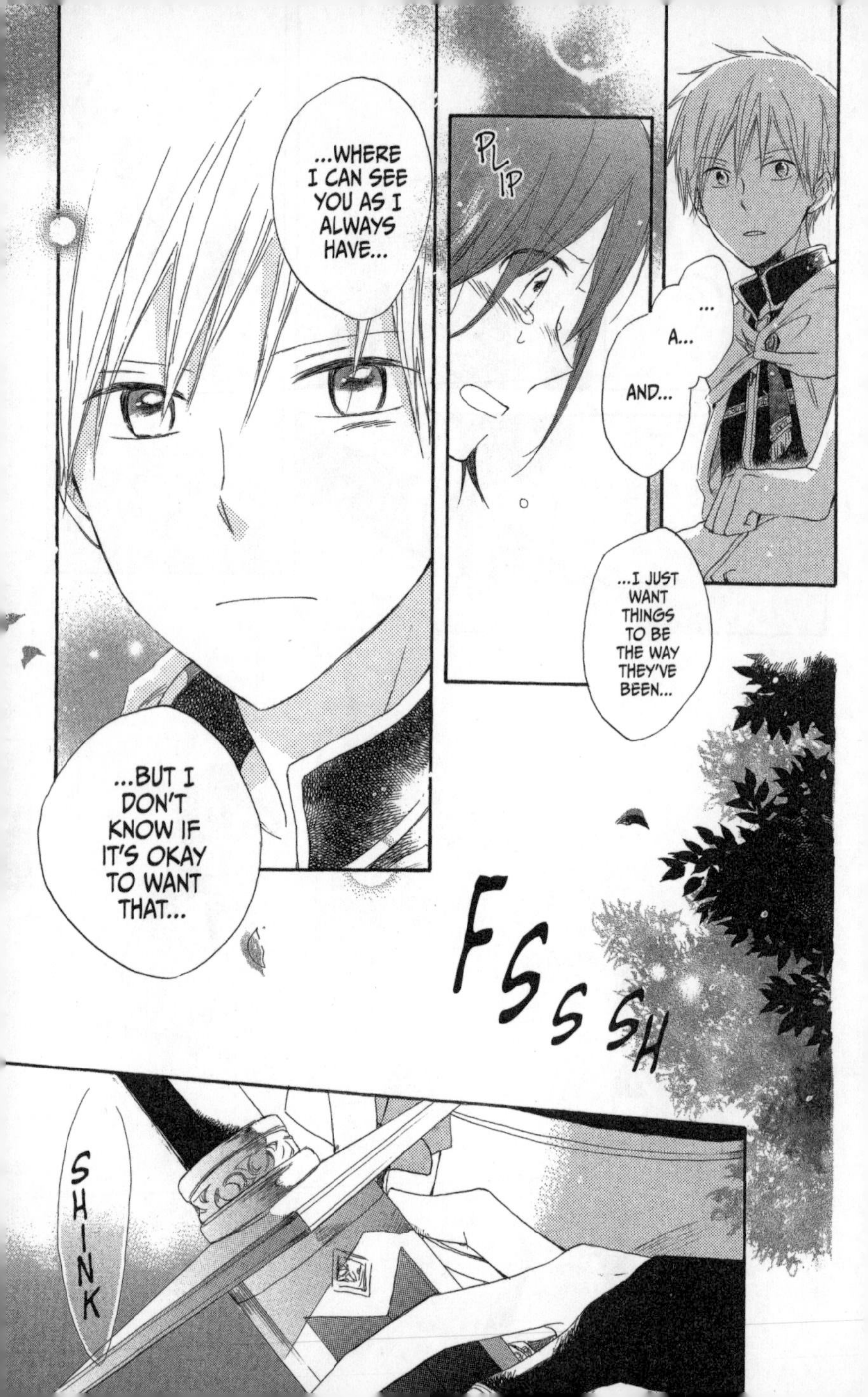
... A... AND...
PLIP
...I JUST WANT THINGS TO BE THE WAY THEY'VE BEEN...
...WHERE I CAN SEE YOU AS I ALWAYS HAVE...
...BUT I DON'T KNOW IF IT'S OKAY TO WANT THAT...
FSSSH
SHINK

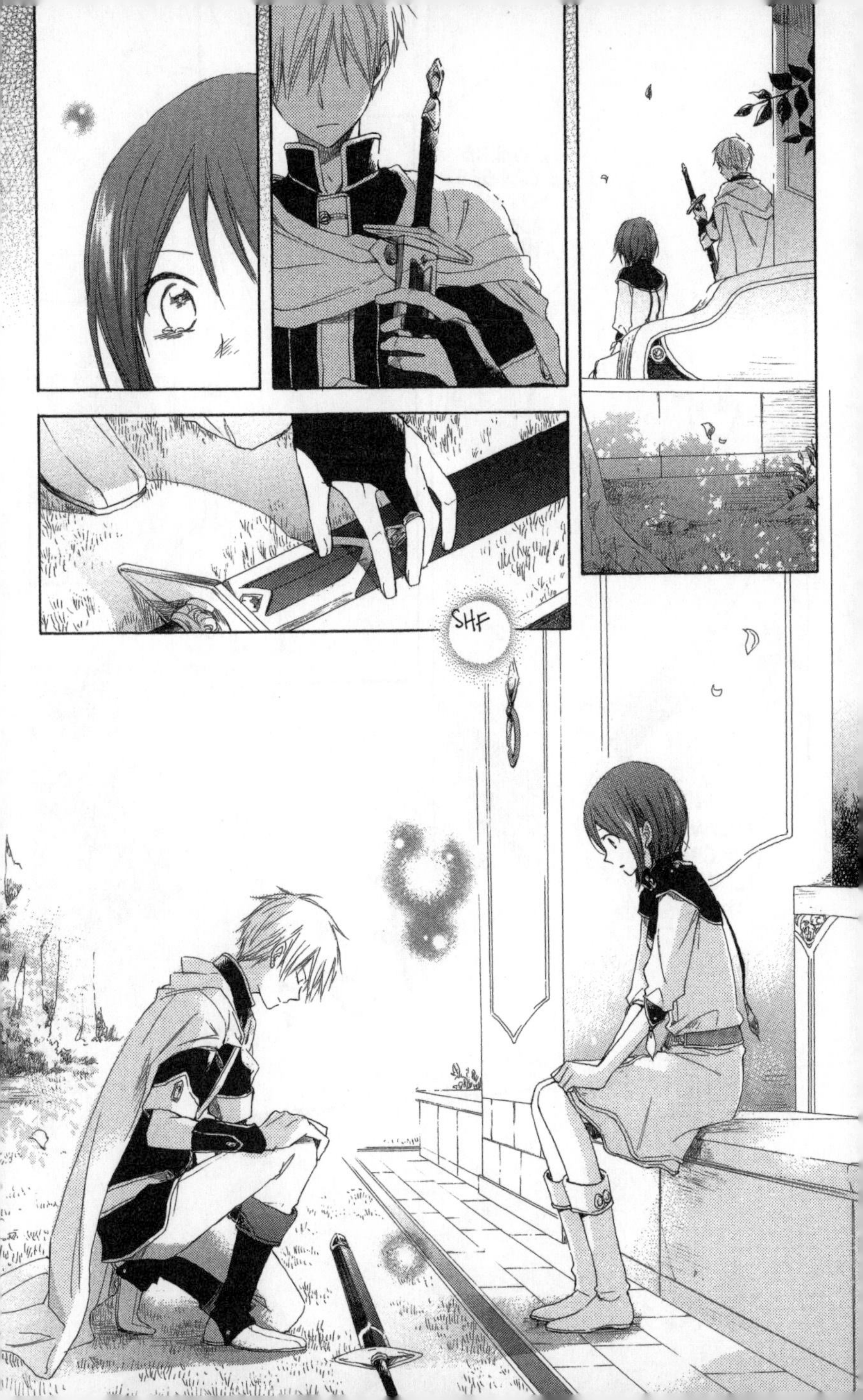
SHF

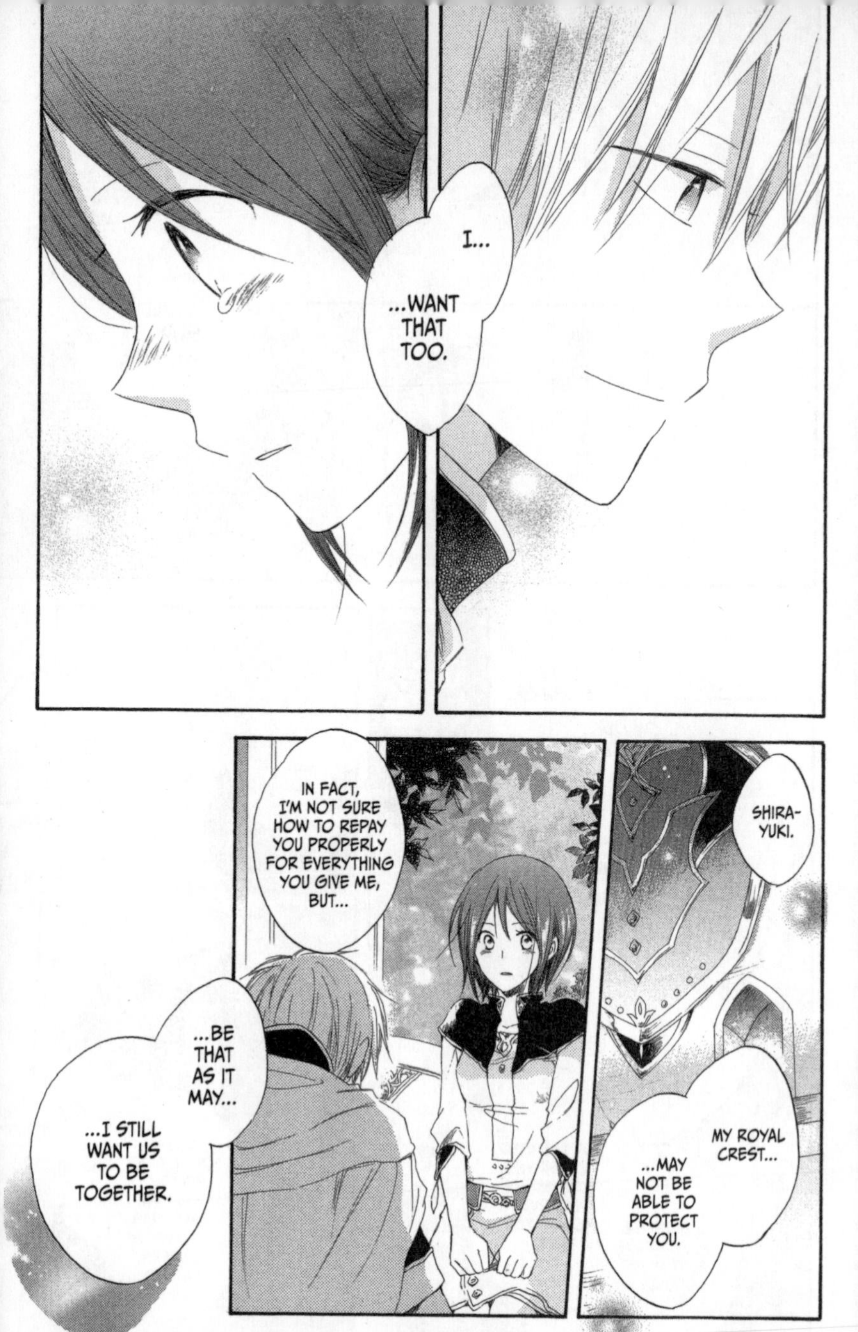
I...
...WANT THAT TOO.
SHIRA-YUKI.
MY ROYAL CREST...
...MAY NOT BE ABLE TO PROTECT YOU.
IN FACT, I'M NOT SURE HOW TO REPAY YOU PROPERLY FOR EVERYTHING YOU GIVE ME, BUT...
...BE THAT AS IT MAY...
...I STILL WANT US TO BE TOGETHER.

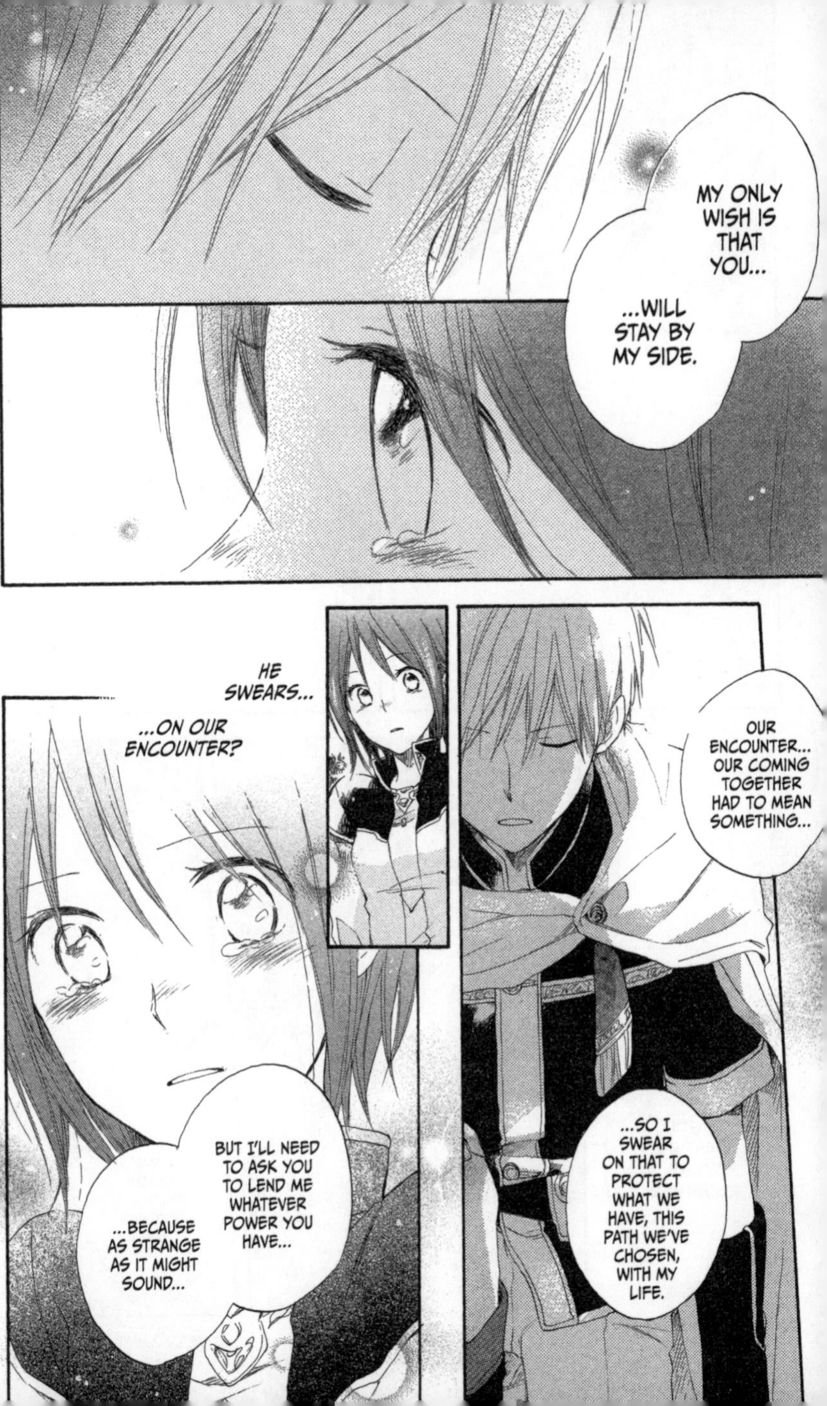
MY ONLY WISH IS THAT YOU...
...WILL STAY BY MY SIDE.
OUR ENCOUNTER... OUR COMING TOGETHER HAD TO MEAN SOMETHING...
...SO I SWEAR ON THAT TO PROTECT WHAT WE HAVE, THIS PATH WE'VE CHOSEN, WITH MY LIFE.
HE SWEARS...
...ON OUR ENCOUNTER?
BUT I'LL NEED TO ASK YOU TO LEND ME WHATEVER POWER YOU HAVE...
...BECAUSE AS STRANGE AS IT MIGHT SOUND...

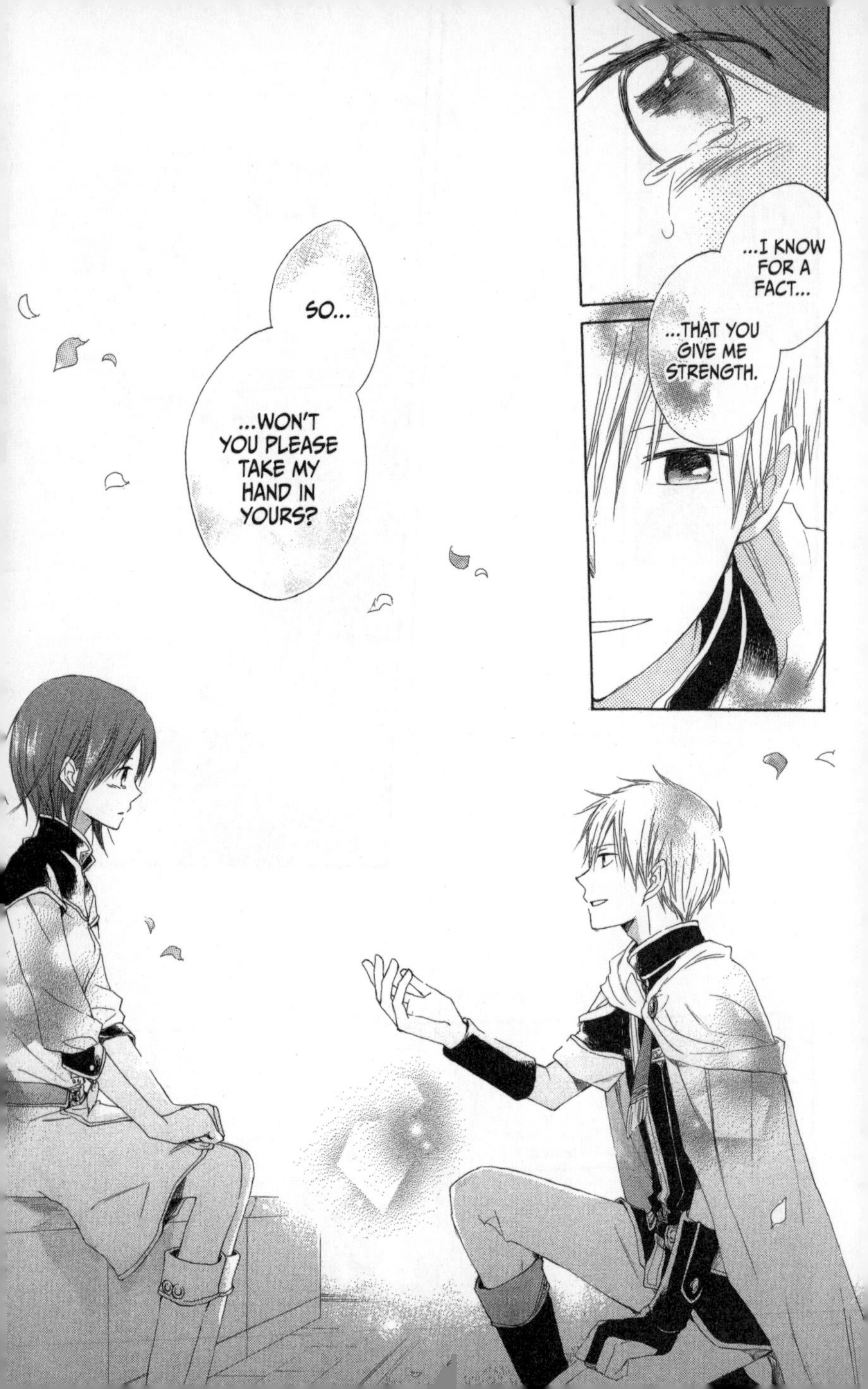
...I KNOW FOR A FACT...
...THAT YOU GIVE ME STRENGTH.
SO...
...WON'T YOU PLEASE TAKE MY HAND IN YOURS?

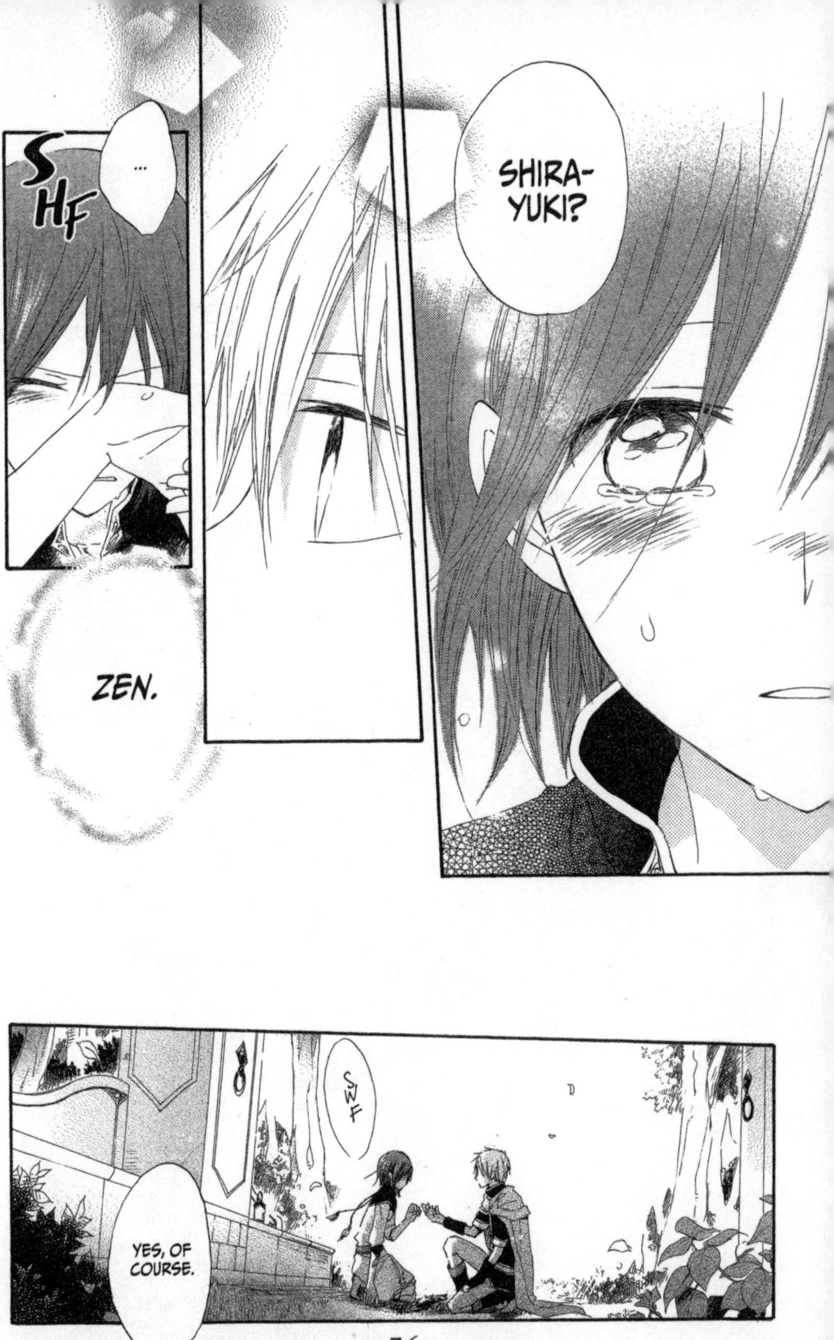
SHIRA-YUKI?
SHF
...
ZEN.
SWF
YES, OF COURSE.

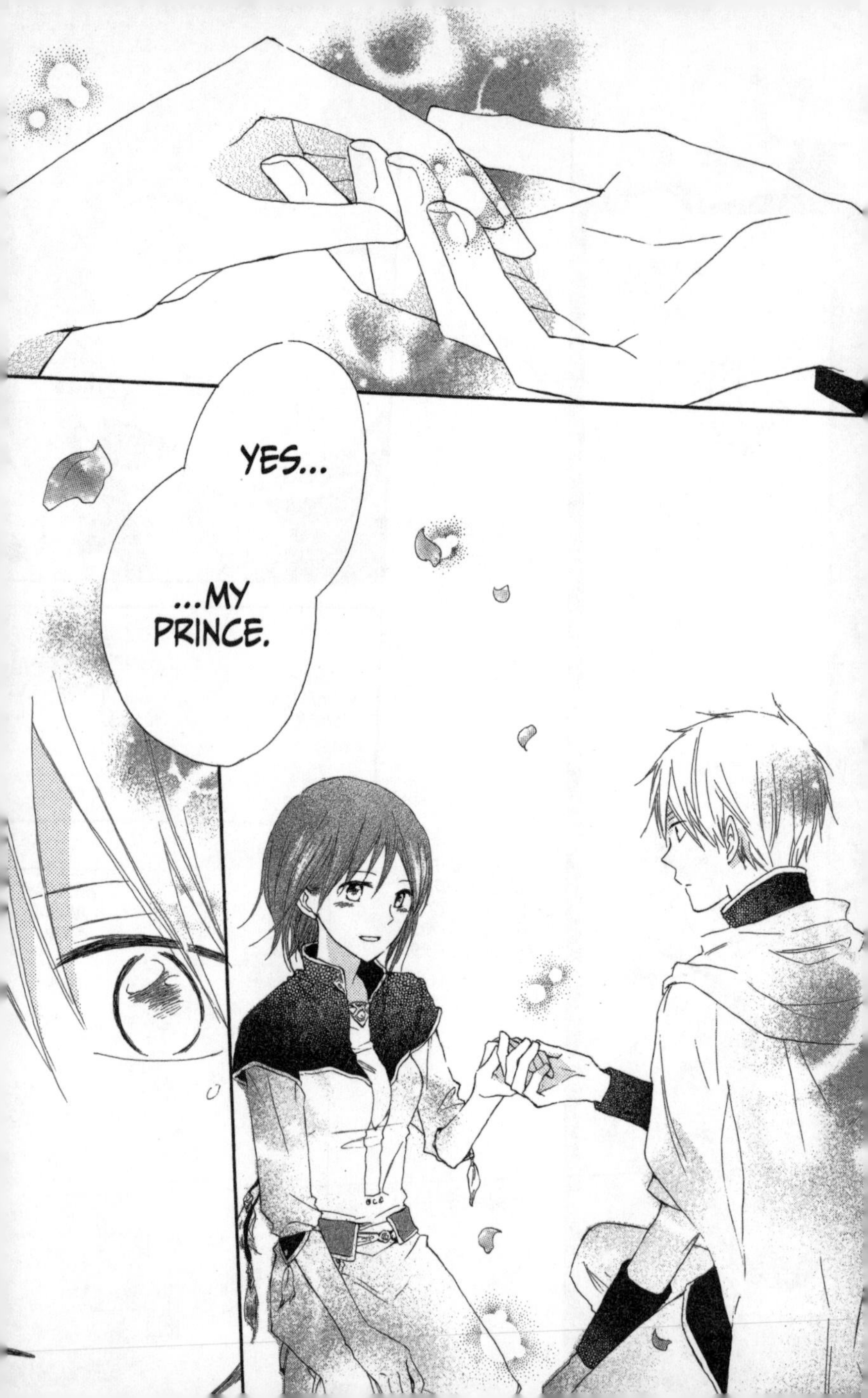
YES...
...MY PRINCE.

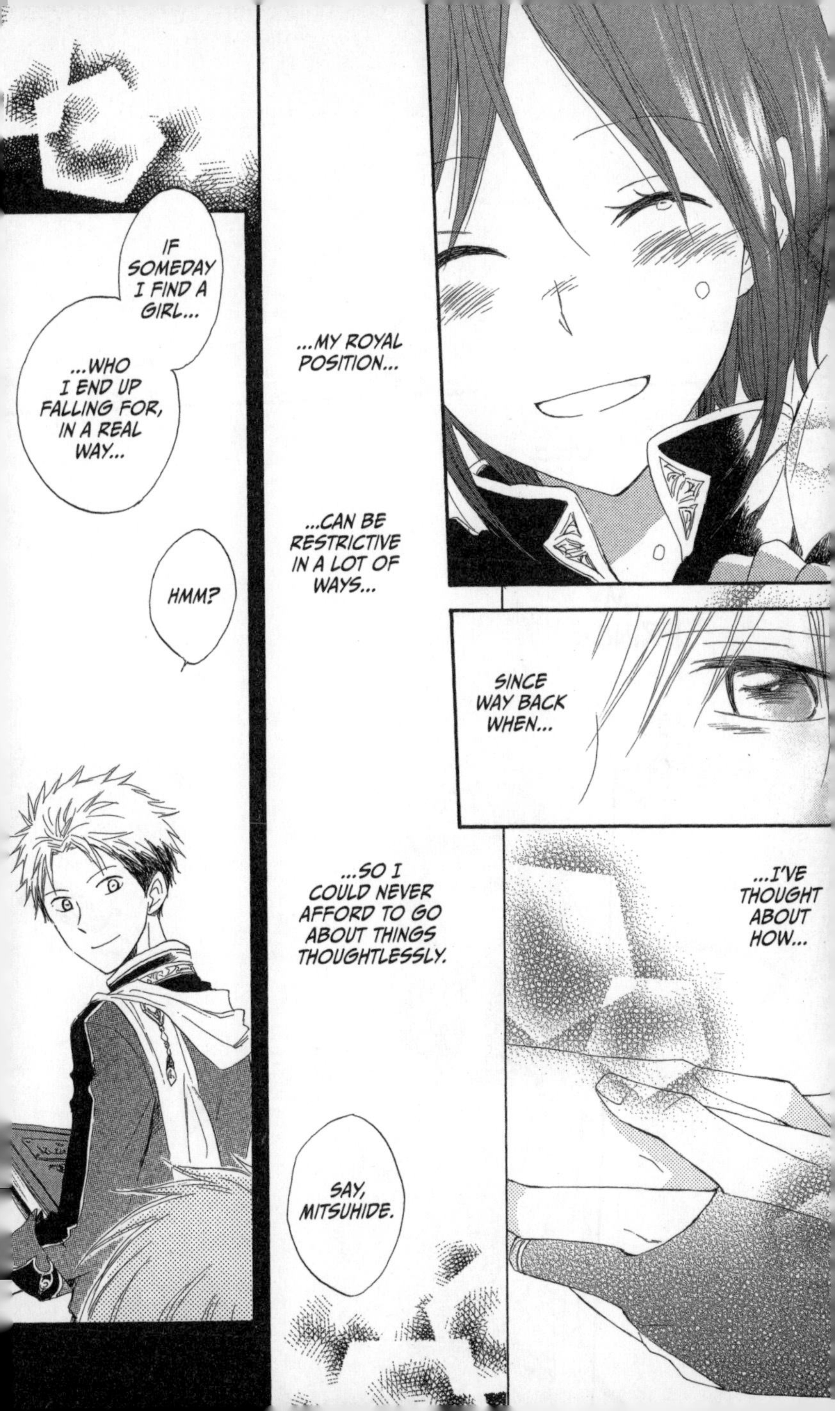
SINCE WAY BACK WHEN...
...I'VE THOUGHT ABOUT HOW...
...MY ROYAL POSITION...
...CAN BE RESTRICTIVE IN A LOT OF WAYS...
...SO I COULD NEVER AFFORD TO GO ABOUT THINGS THOUGHTLESSLY.
SAY, MITSUHIDE.
IF SOMEDAY I FIND A GIRL...
...WHO I END UP FALLING FOR, IN A REAL WAY...
HMM?

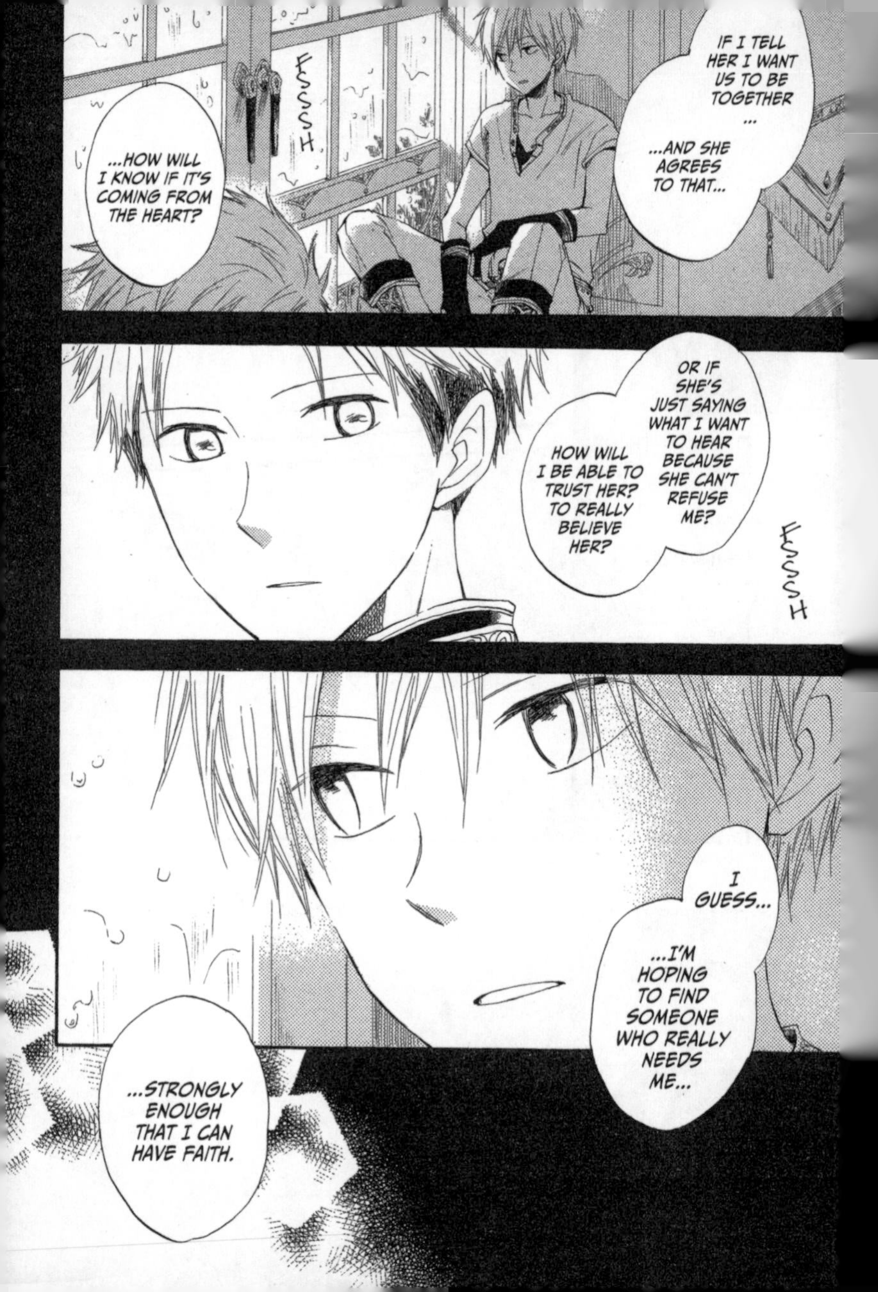
IF I TELL HER I WANT US TO BE TOGETHER ...
...AND SHE AGREES TO THAT...
FSSSH
...HOW WILL I KNOW IF IT'S COMING FROM THE HEART?
FSSSH
OR IF SHE'S JUST SAYING WHAT I WANT TO HEAR BECAUSE SHE CAN'T REFUSE ME?
HOW WILL I BE ABLE TO TRUST HER? TO REALLY BELIEVE HER?
I GUESS...
...I'M HOPING TO FIND SOMEONE WHO REALLY NEEDS ME...
...STRONGLY ENOUGH THAT I CAN HAVE FAITH.

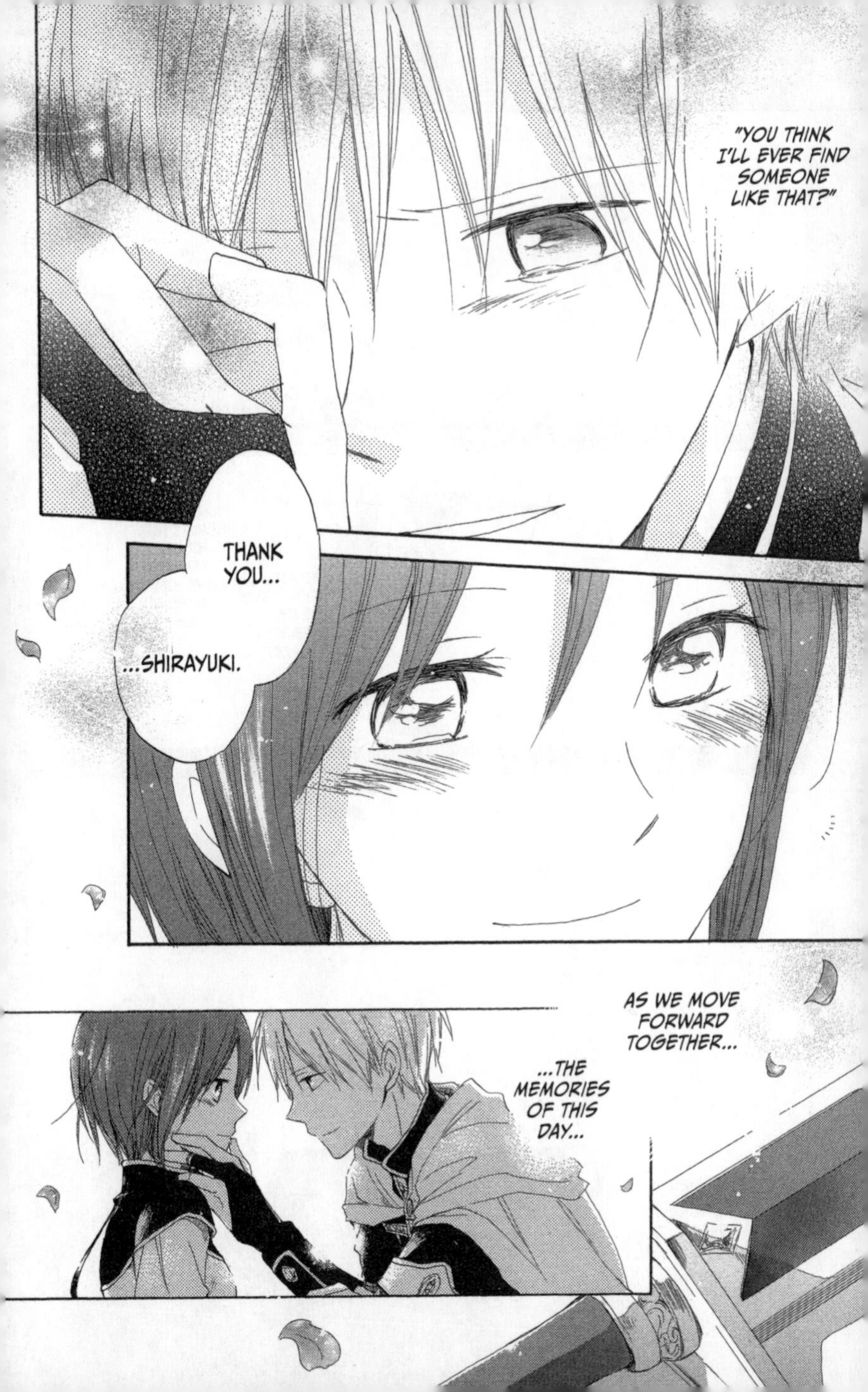
"YOU THINK I'LL EVER FIND SOMEONE LIKE THAT?"
THANK YOU...
...SHIRAYUKI.
AS WE MOVE FORWARD TOGETHER...
...THE MEMORIES OF THIS DAY...

...ARE SURE TO
FILL ME WITH
COURAGE TIME
AFTER TIME.

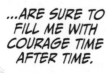

Excerpt from an ad featuring Zen.

This is the rough sketch.

And the
finished version!

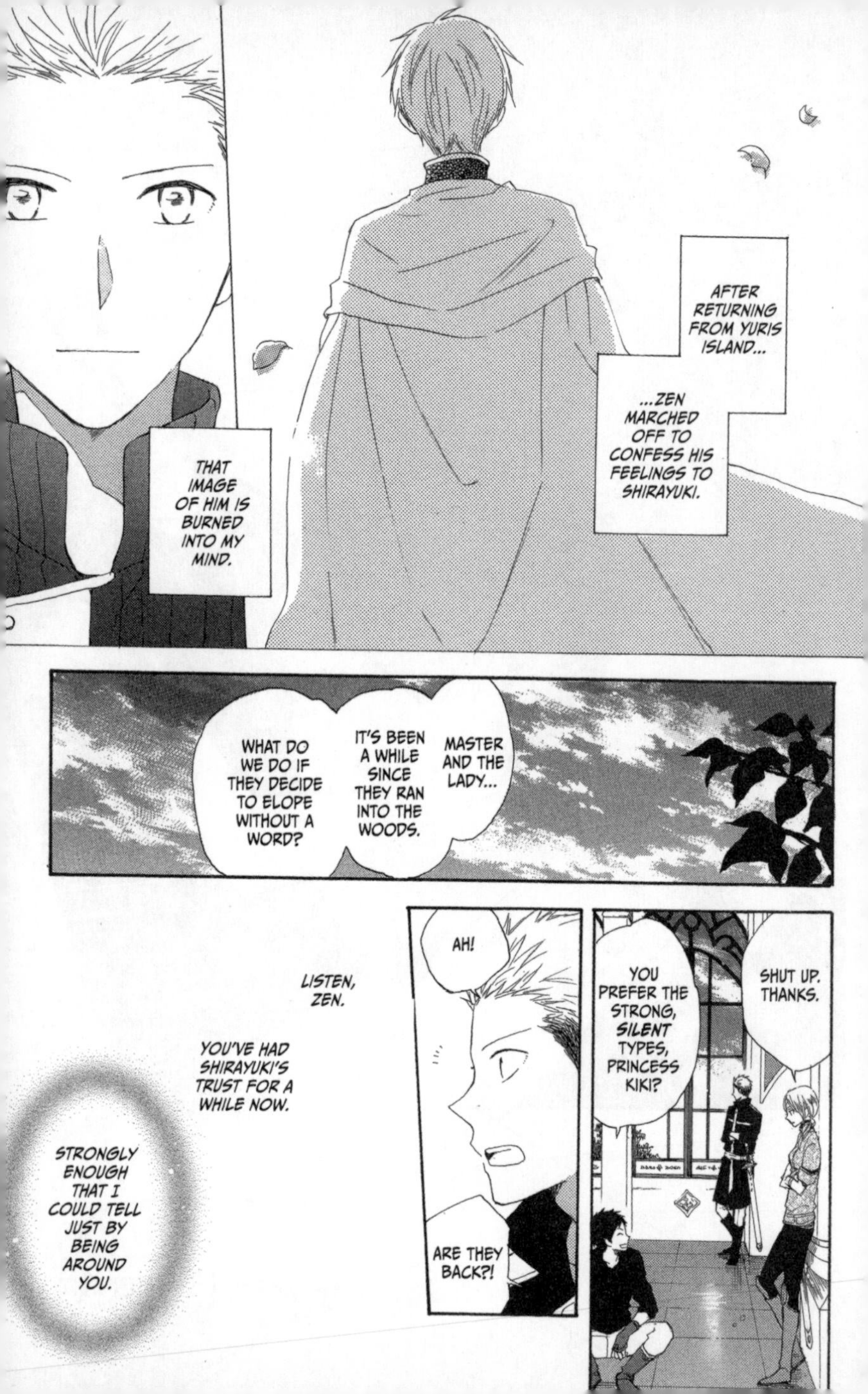
AFTER RETURNING FROM YURIS ISLAND...
...ZEN MARCHED OFF TO CONFESS HIS FEELINGS TO SHIRAYUKI.
THAT IMAGE OF HIM IS BURNED INTO MY MIND.
MASTER AND THE LADY...
IT'S BEEN A WHILE SINCE THEY RAN INTO THE WOODS.
WHAT DO WE DO IF THEY DECIDE TO ELOPE WITHOUT A WORD?
SHUT UP. THANKS.
YOU PREFER THE STRONG, SILENT TYPES, PRINCESS KIKI?
AH!
ARE THEY BACK?!
LISTEN, ZEN.
YOU'VE HAD SHIRAYUKI'S TRUST FOR A WHILE NOW.
STRONGLY ENOUGH THAT I COULD TELL JUST BY BEING AROUND YOU.

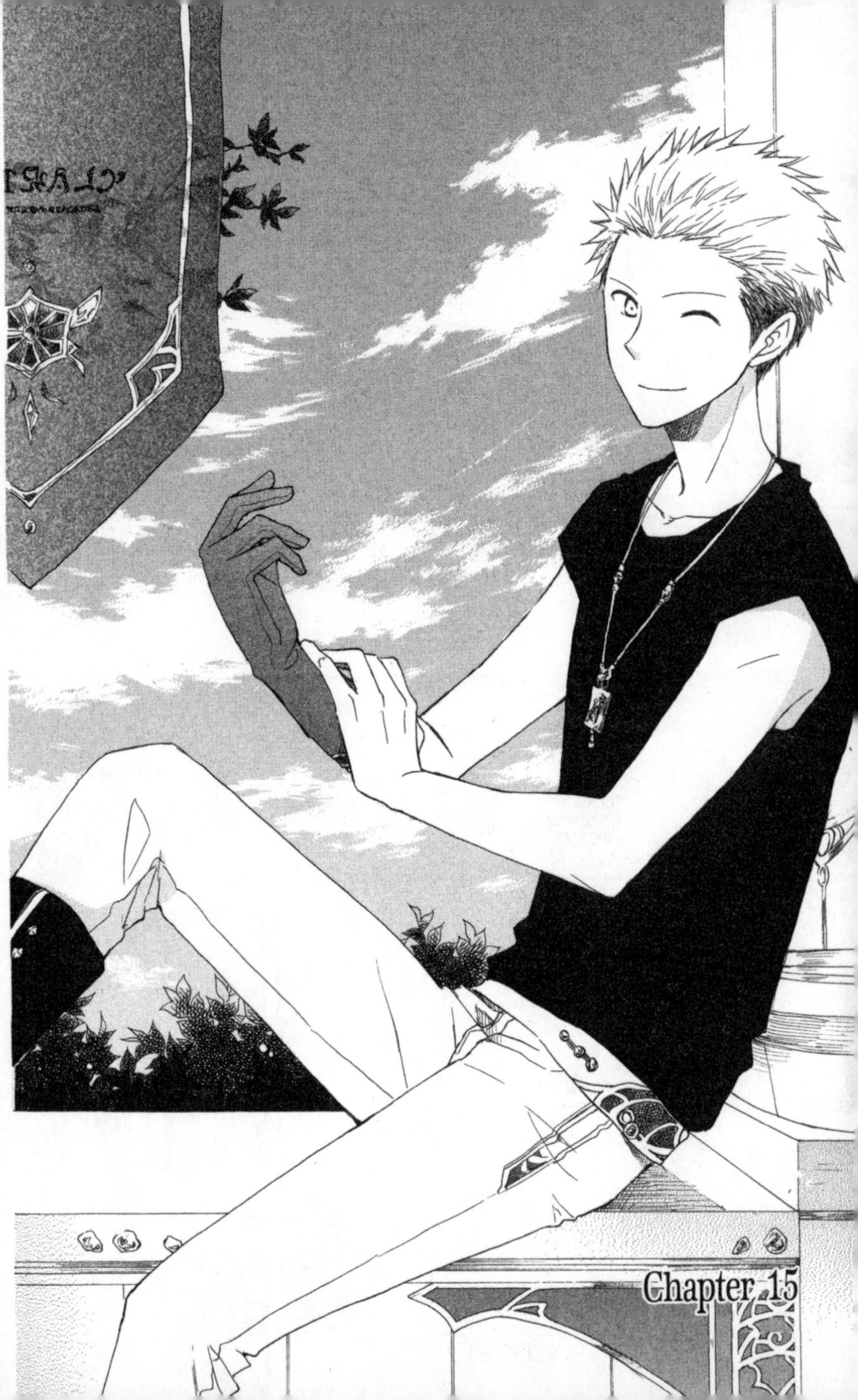
Chapter 15

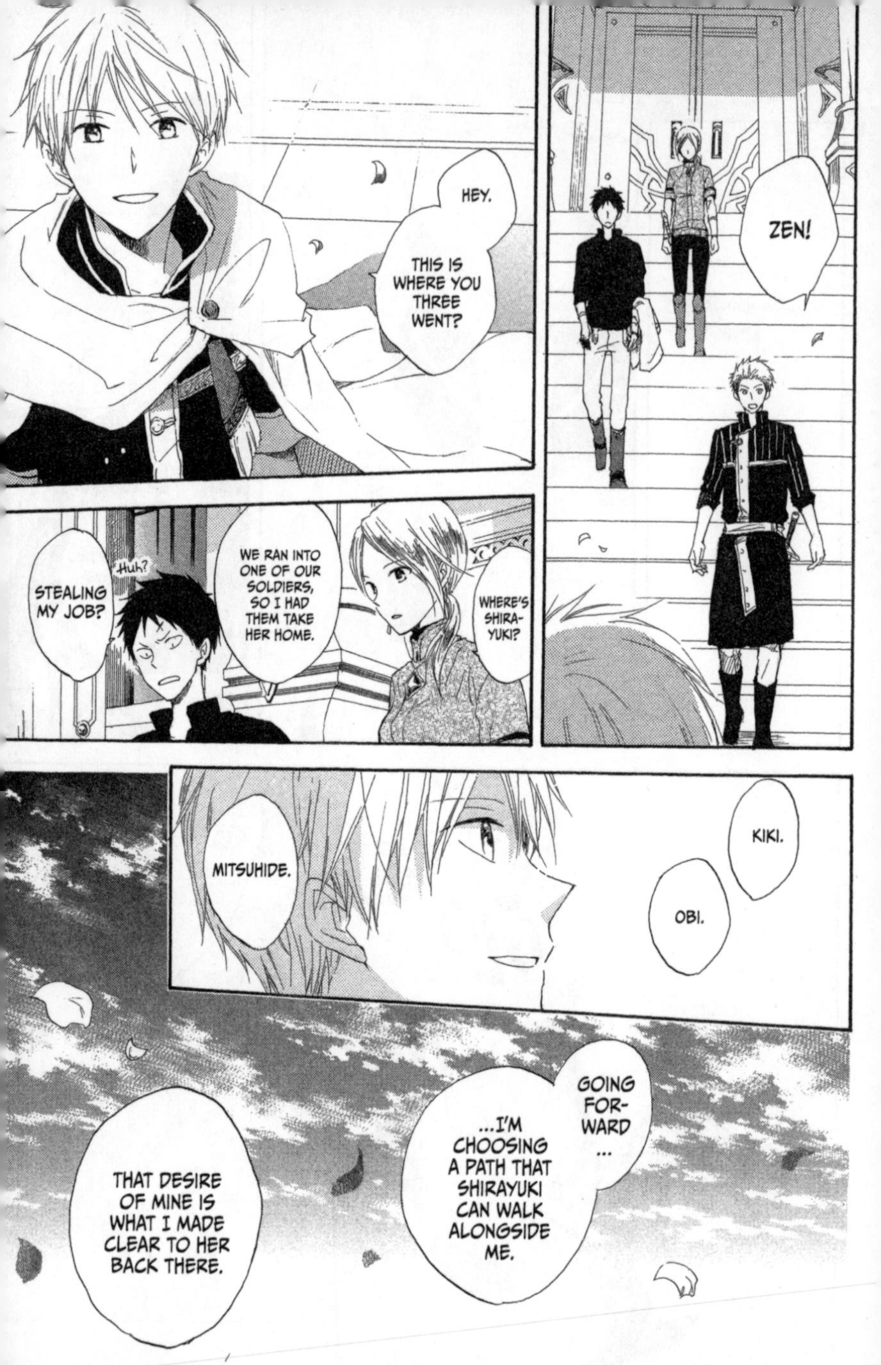
ZEN!
HEY.
THIS IS WHERE YOU THREE WENT?
WHERE'S SHIRA-YUKI?
WE RAN INTO ONE OF OUR SOLDIERS, SO I HAD THEM TAKE HER HOME.
Huh?
STEALING MY JOB?
KIKI.
OBI.
MITSUHIDE.
GOING FOR-WARD ...
...I'M CHOOSING A PATH THAT SHIRAYUKI CAN WALK ALONGSIDE ME.
THAT DESIRE OF MINE IS WHAT I MADE CLEAR TO HER BACK THERE.

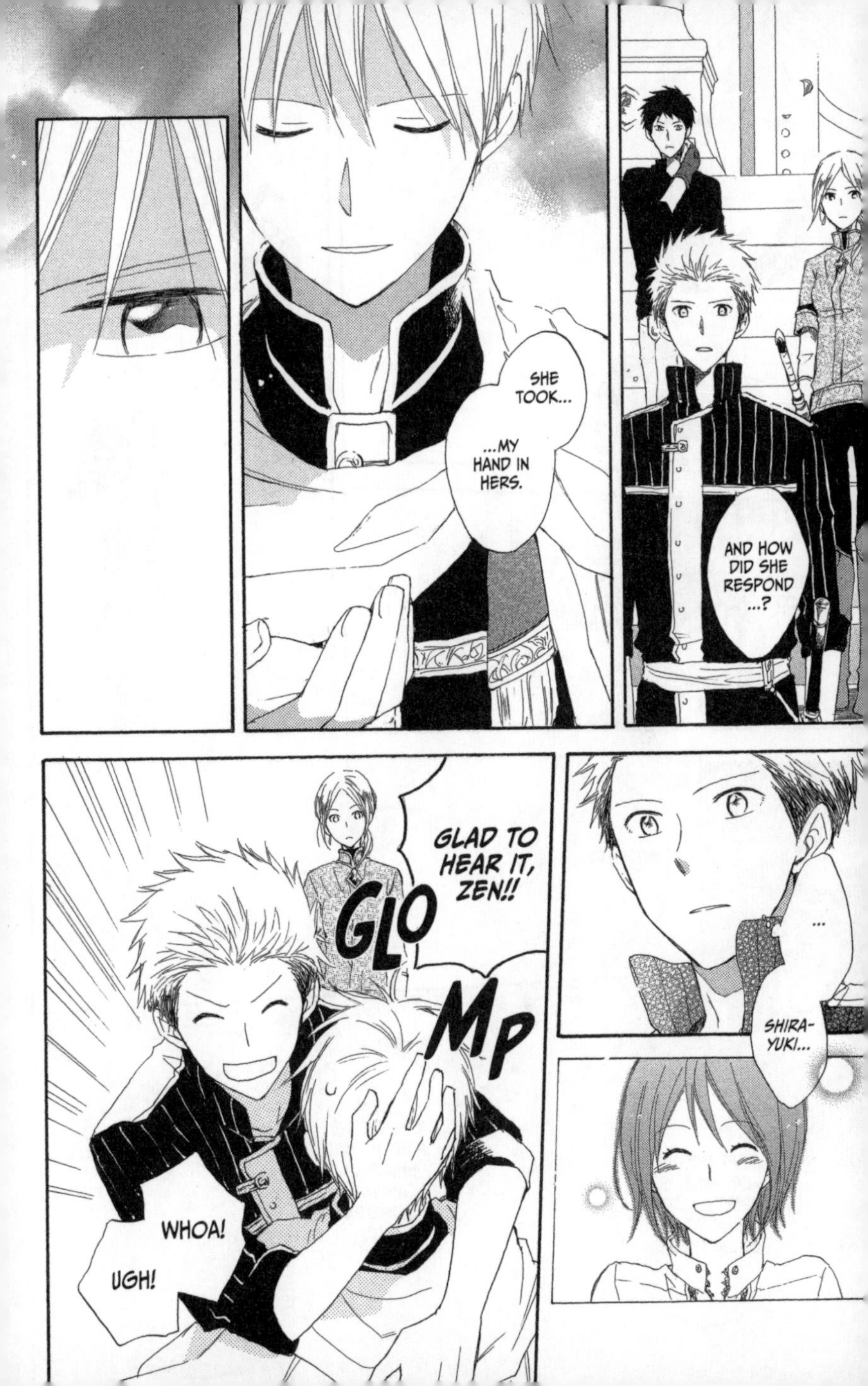
AND HOW DID SHE RESPOND ...?
SHE TOOK...
...MY HAND IN HERS.
...
SHIRA-YUKI...
GLAD TO HEAR IT, ZEN!!
GLOMP
WHOA!
UGH!

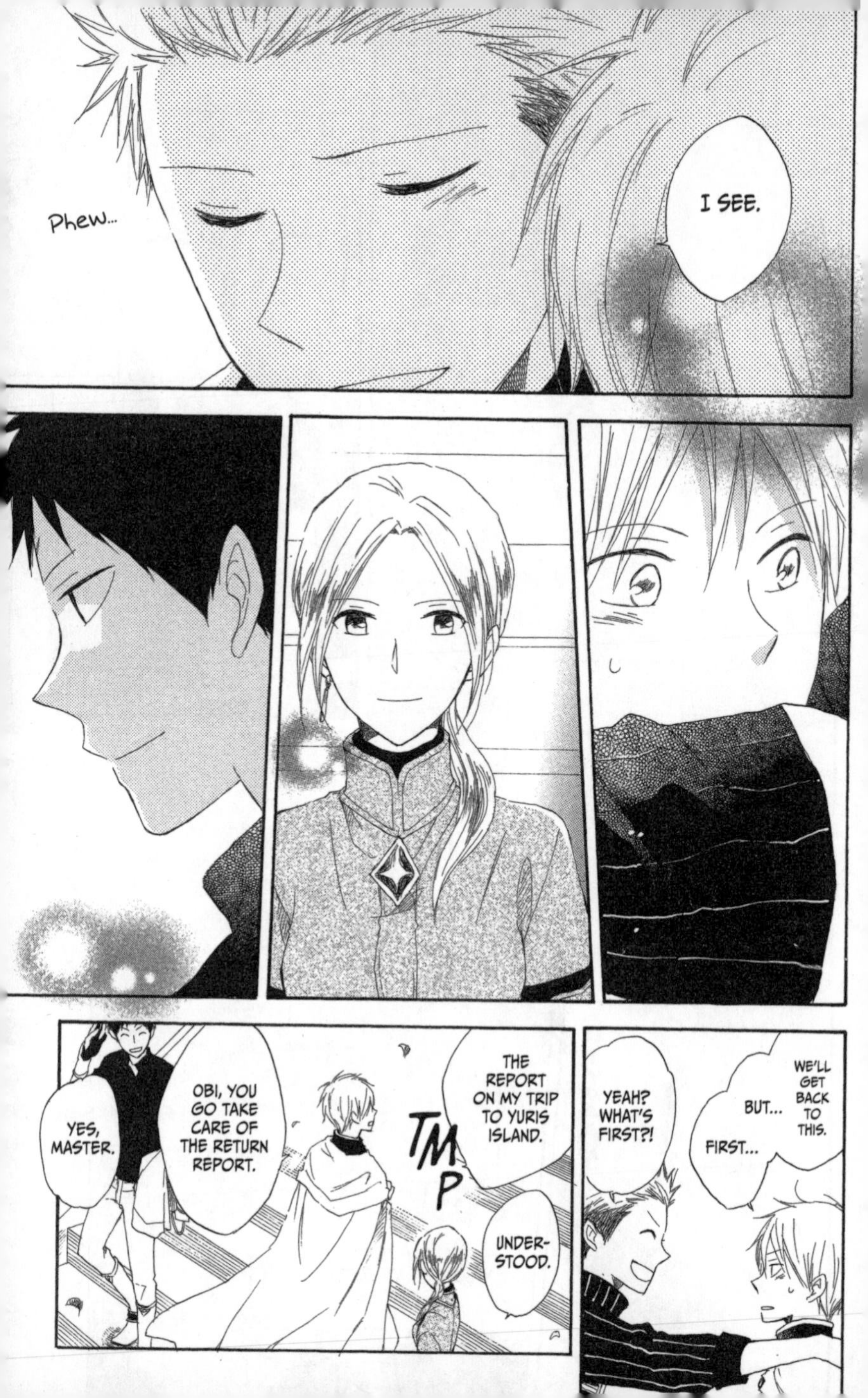
I SEE.
Phew...
WE'LL GET BACK TO THIS.
BUT... FIRST...
YEAH? WHAT'S FIRST?!
THE REPORT ON MY TRIP TO YURIS ISLAND.
TMP
UNDER-STOOD.
OBI, YOU GO TAKE CARE OF THE RETURN REPORT.
YES, MASTER.

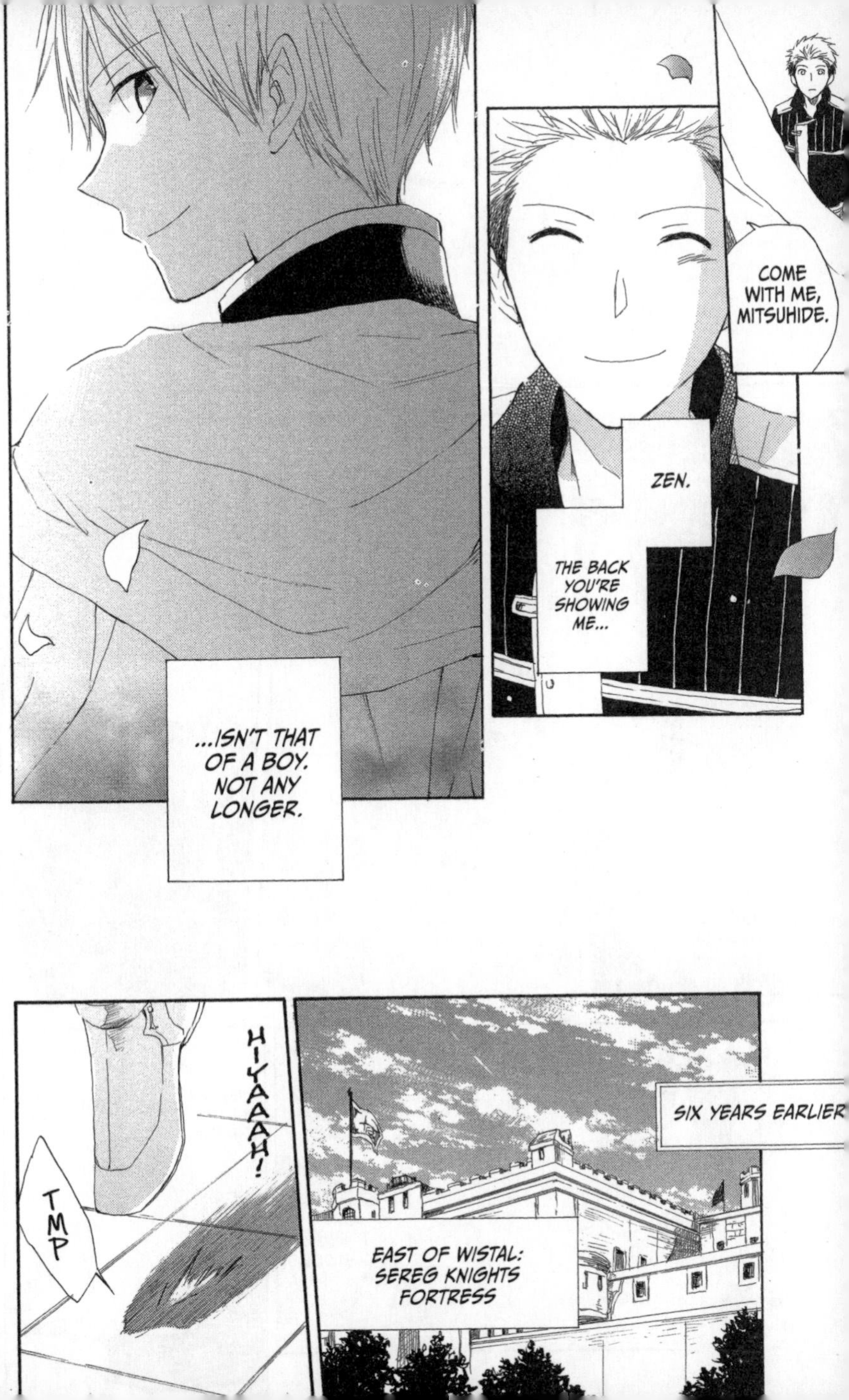
COME WITH ME, MITSUHIDE.
ZEN.
THE BACK YOU'RE SHOWING ME...
...ISN'T THAT OF A BOY. NOT ANY LONGER.
SIX YEARS EARLIER
EAST OF WISTAL: SEREG KNIGHTS FORTRESS
HIYAAAH!
TMP

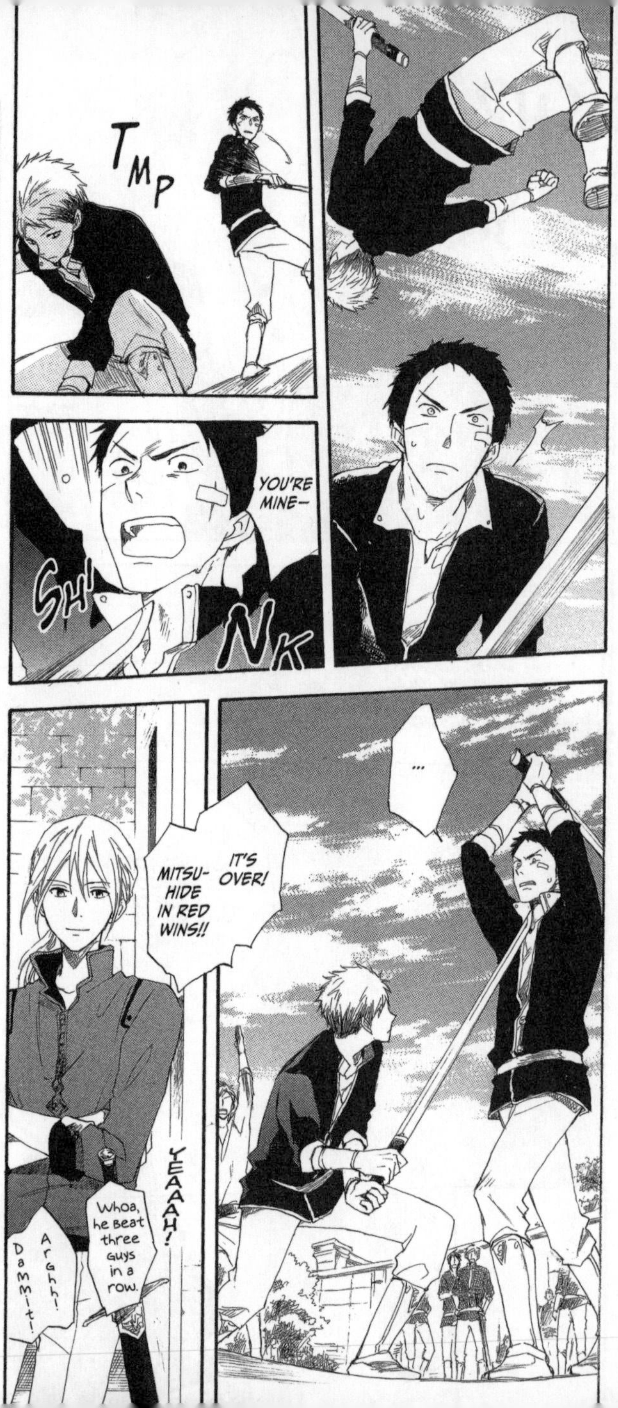
TMP
YOU'RE MINE—
SHINK
...
IT'S OVER! MITSU-HIDE IN RED WINS!!
YEAAAAH!
Whoa, he beat three guys in a row.
Arghh!
Dammit!

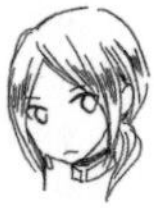

Kiki

Likes

- -Veggie salads
- -Marquis Haruka's personality
- -Card games (she's good)
- -The color green

Can't handle

- -Hot places
- -Viscount Brecker's personality

Quantity over quality when it comes to food.

Prefers loud and bustling places over the quiet of nature.

Never sleeps if other people are around.

6

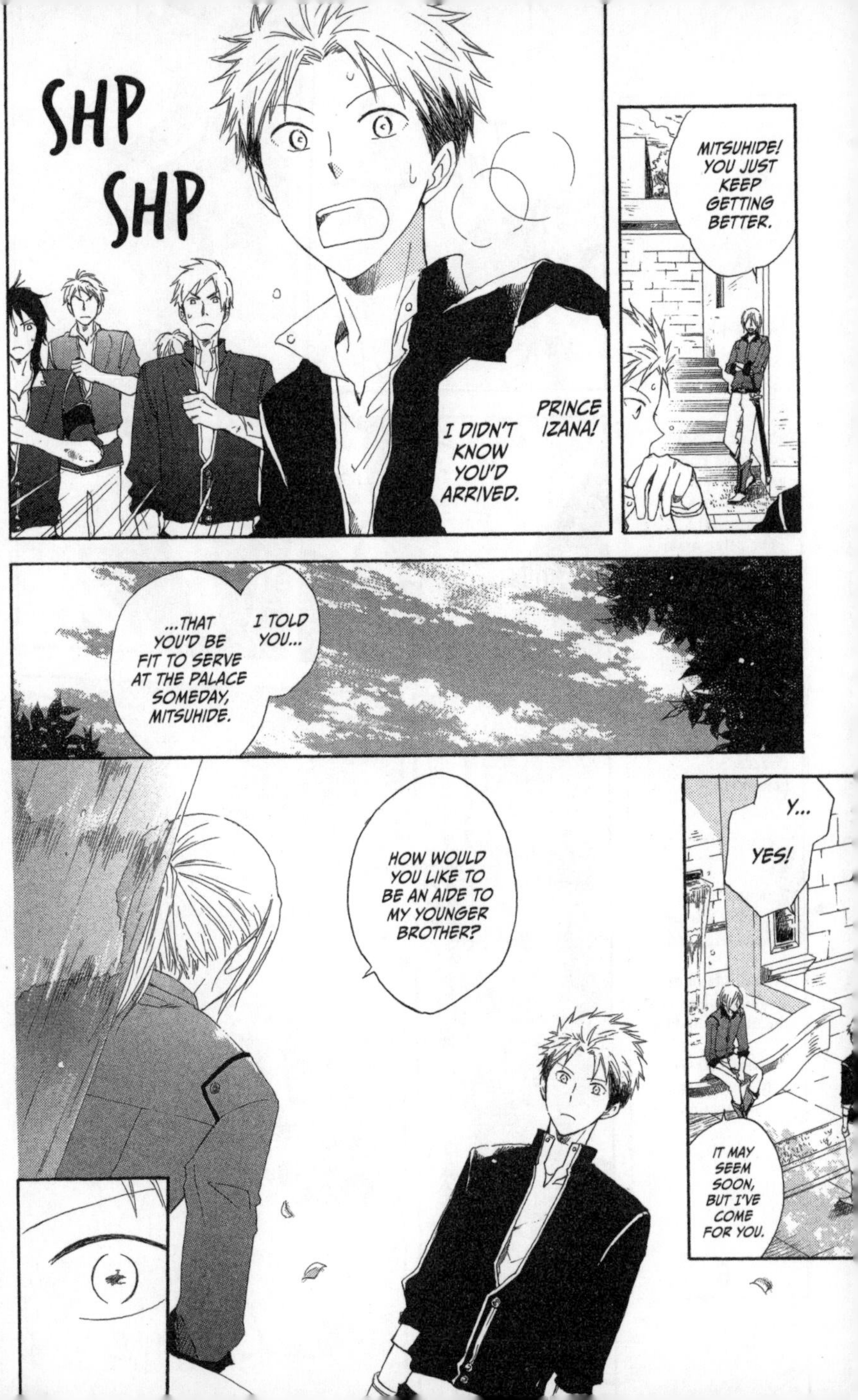
MITSUHIDE! YOU JUST KEEP GETTING BETTER.
SHP SHP
PRINCE IZANA!
I DIDN'T KNOW YOU'D ARRIVED.
I TOLD YOU...
...THAT YOU'D BE FIT TO SERVE AT THE PALACE SOMEDAY, MITSUHIDE.
Y...
YES!
IT MAY SEEM SOON, BUT I'VE COME FOR YOU.
HOW WOULD YOU LIKE TO BE AN AIDE TO MY YOUNGER BROTHER?

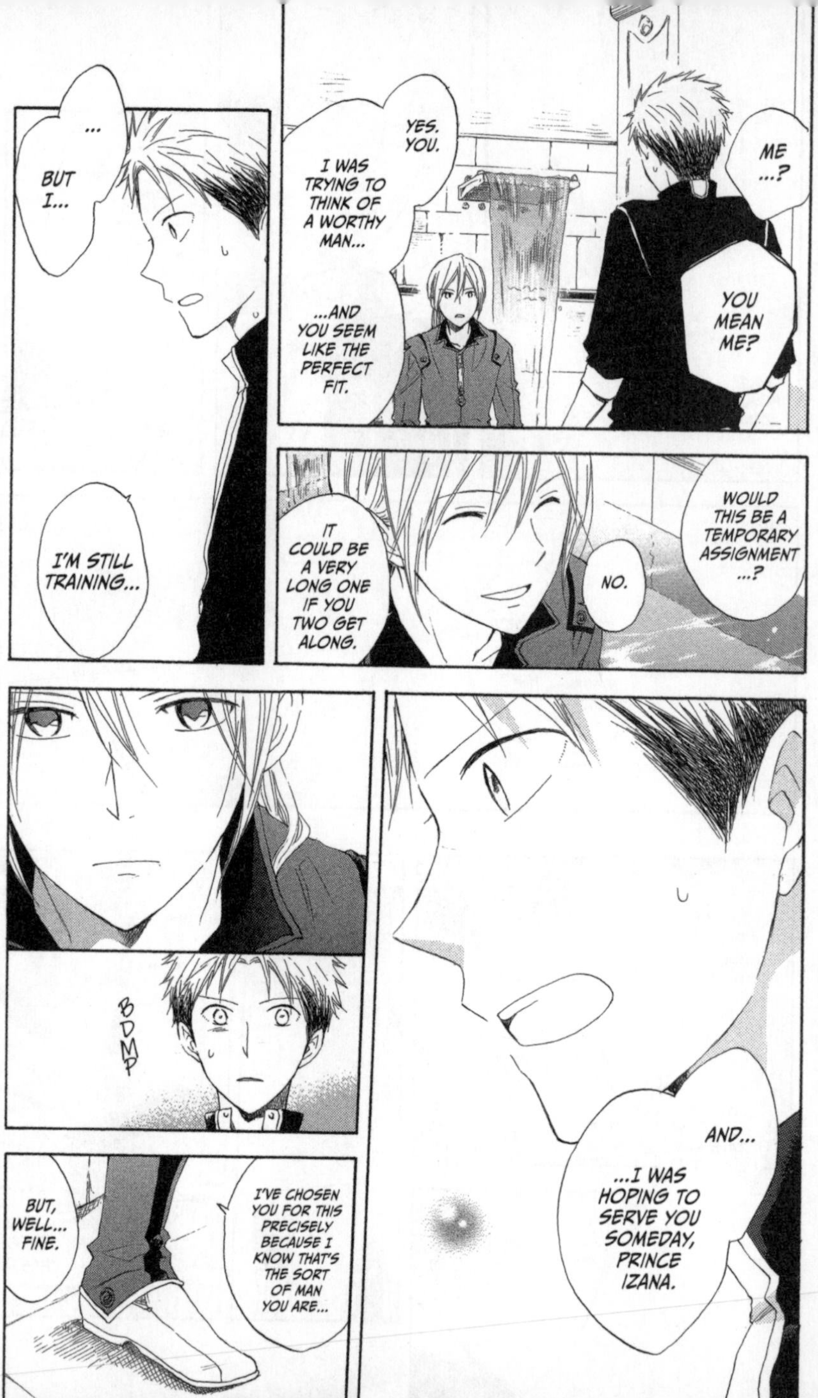
ME ...?
YOU MEAN ME?
YES. YOU.
I WAS TRYING TO THINK OF A WORTHY MAN...
...AND YOU SEEM LIKE THE PERFECT FIT.
WOULD THIS BE A TEMPORARY ASSIGNMENT ...?
NO.
IT COULD BE A VERY LONG ONE IF YOU TWO GET ALONG.
... BUT I...
I'M STILL TRAINING...
AND...
...I WAS HOPING TO SERVE YOU SOMEDAY, PRINCE IZANA.
BDMP
I'VE CHOSEN YOU FOR THIS PRECISELY BECAUSE I KNOW THAT'S THE SORT OF MAN YOU ARE...
BUT, WELL... FINE.

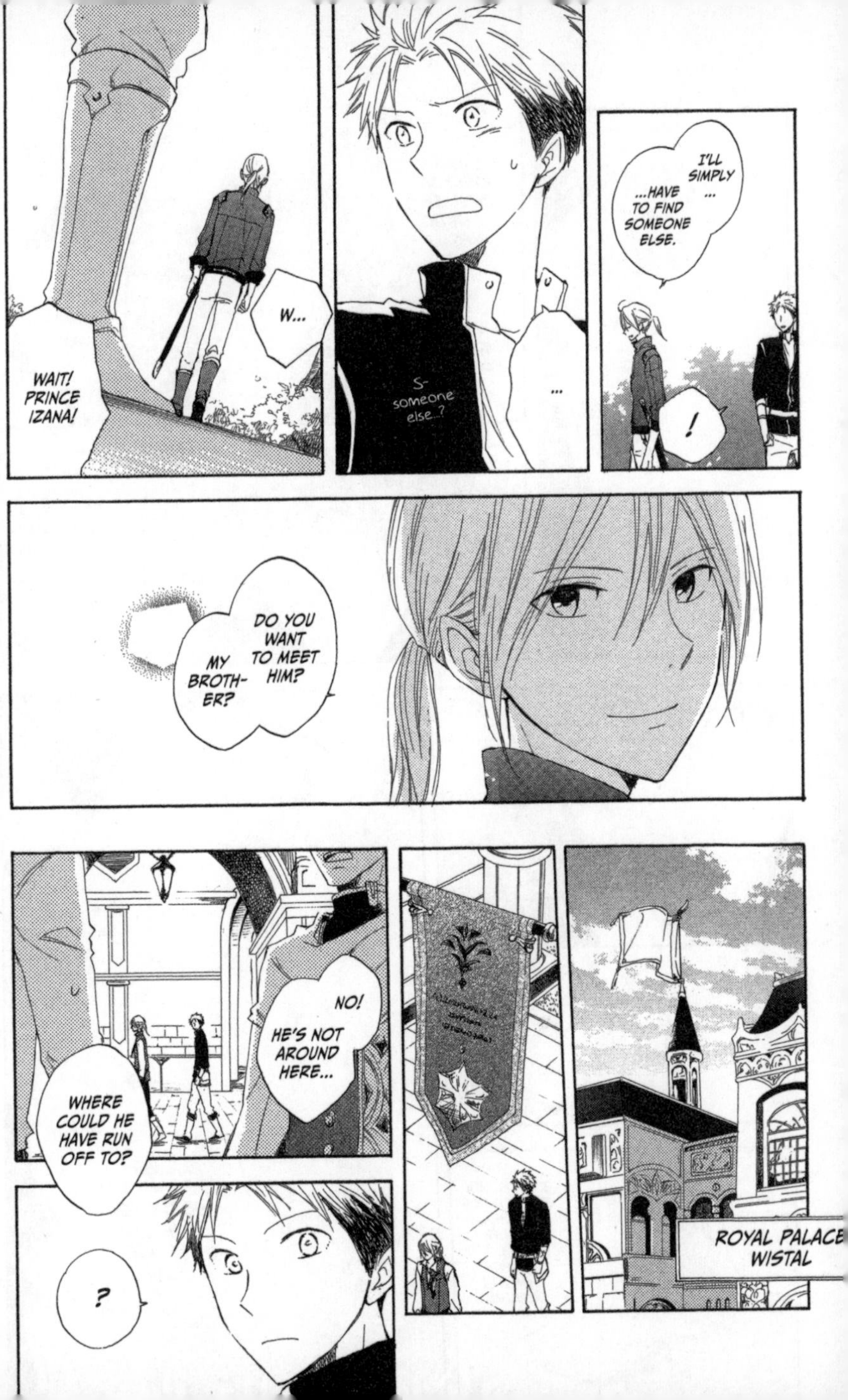
I'LL SIMPLY ... ...HAVE TO FIND SOMEONE ELSE.
!
...
S- someone else...?
W...
WAIT! PRINCE IZANA!
DO YOU WANT TO MEET HIM?
MY BROTHER?
ROYAL PALACE WISTAL
NO! HE'S NOT AROUND HERE...
WHERE COULD HE HAVE RUN OFF TO?
?

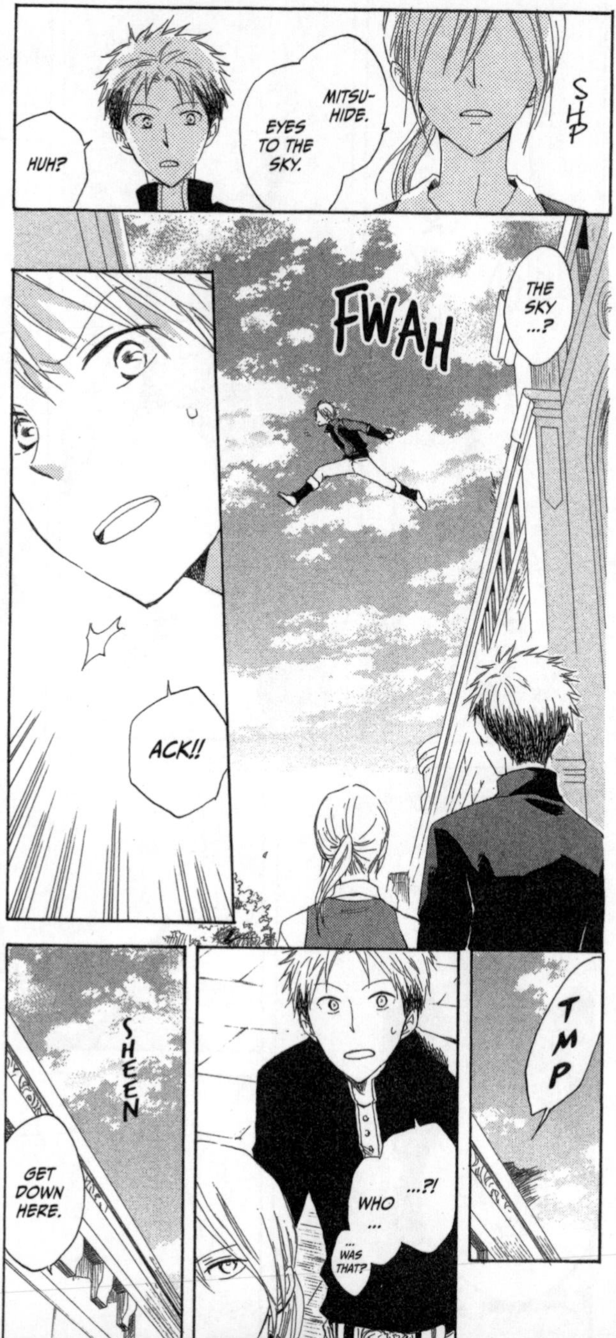
SHP
MITSU-HIDE.
EYES TO THE SKY.
HUH?
THE SKY ...?
FWAH
ACK!!
TMP
...?!
WHO ...
... WAS THAT?
SHEEN
GET DOWN HERE.

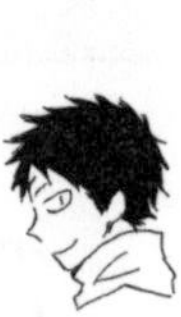

Obi

Likes

- Spicy food
- Booze (and bars)

Can't handle

- Jigsaw puzzles
- Puppies

Good at cooking. Probably has the most core life skills out of all the main characters. Shirayuki would be second.

He's bad at time-sensitive jobs that have to be done in silence with nobody else around.

He's a creature of the night.

7

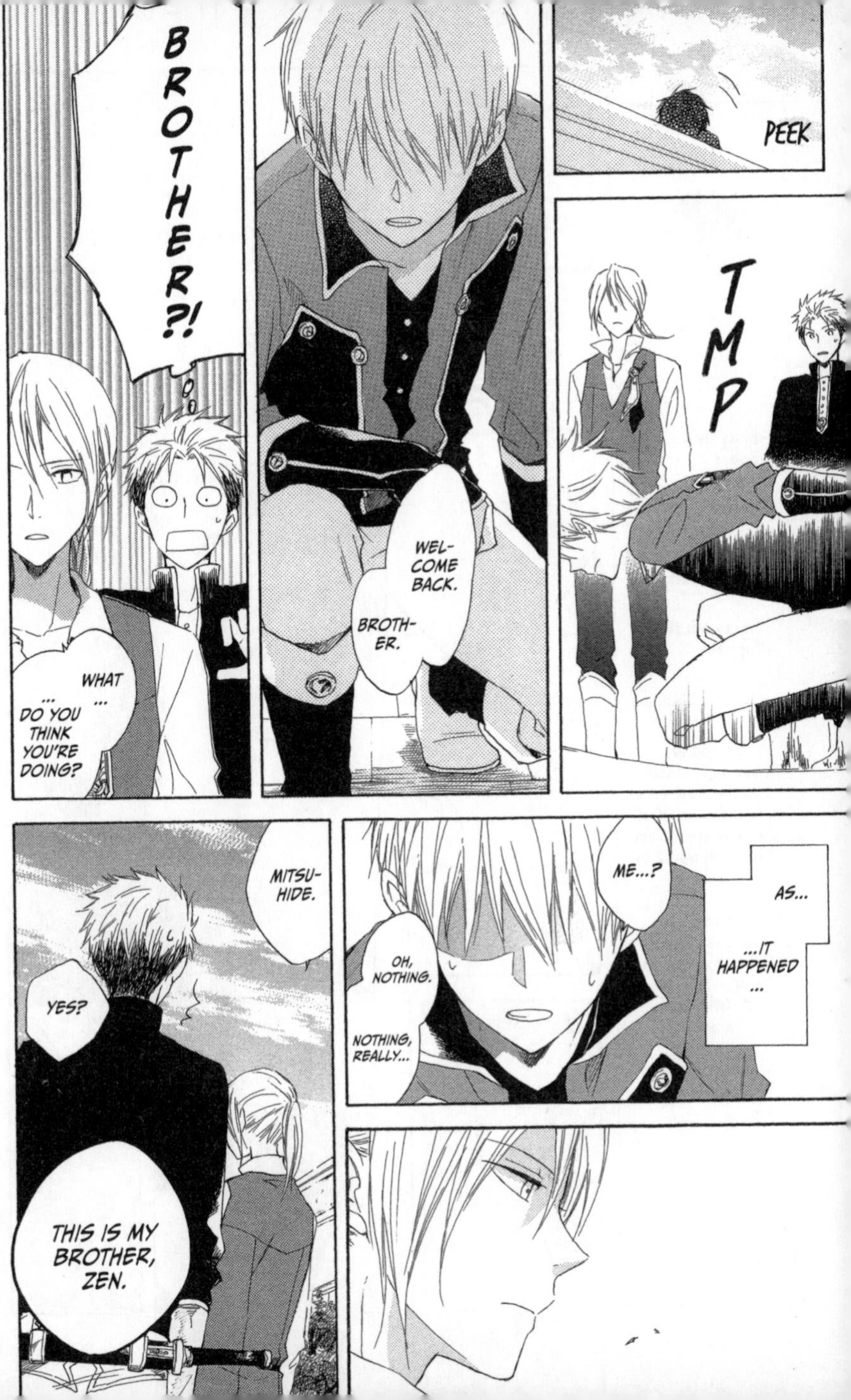
PEEK
TMP
WEL-COME BACK.
BROTH-ER.
BROTHER?!
WHAT ... ... DO YOU THINK YOU'RE DOING?
AS... ...IT HAPPENED ...
ME...?
OH, NOTHING.
NOTHING, REALLY...
MITSU-HIDE.
YES?
THIS IS MY BROTHER, ZEN.

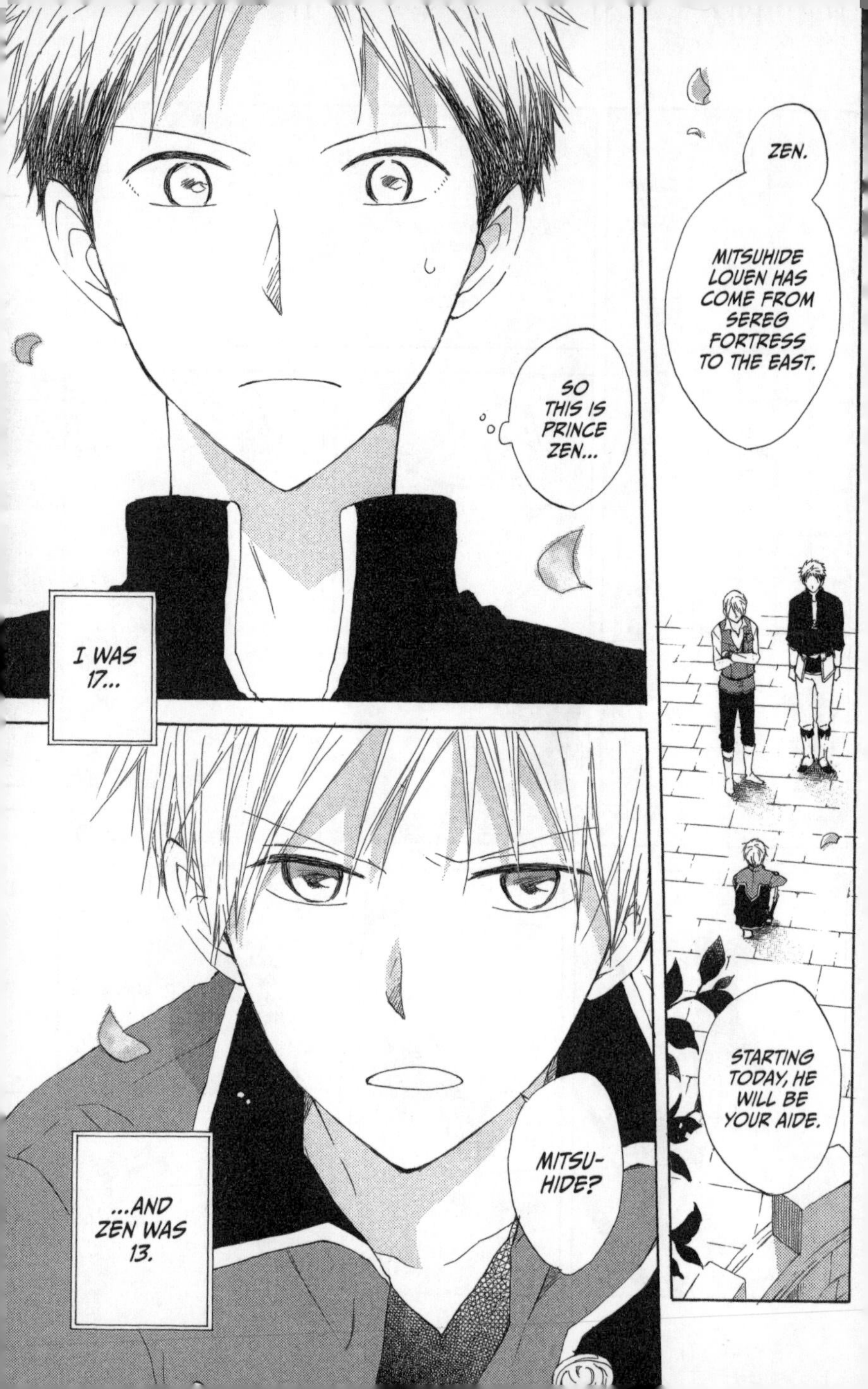
ZEN.
MITSUHIDE LOUEN HAS COME FROM SEREG FORTRESS TO THE EAST.
STARTING TODAY, HE WILL BE YOUR AIDE.
SO THIS IS PRINCE ZEN...
I WAS 17...
MITSU-HIDE?
...AND ZEN WAS 13.

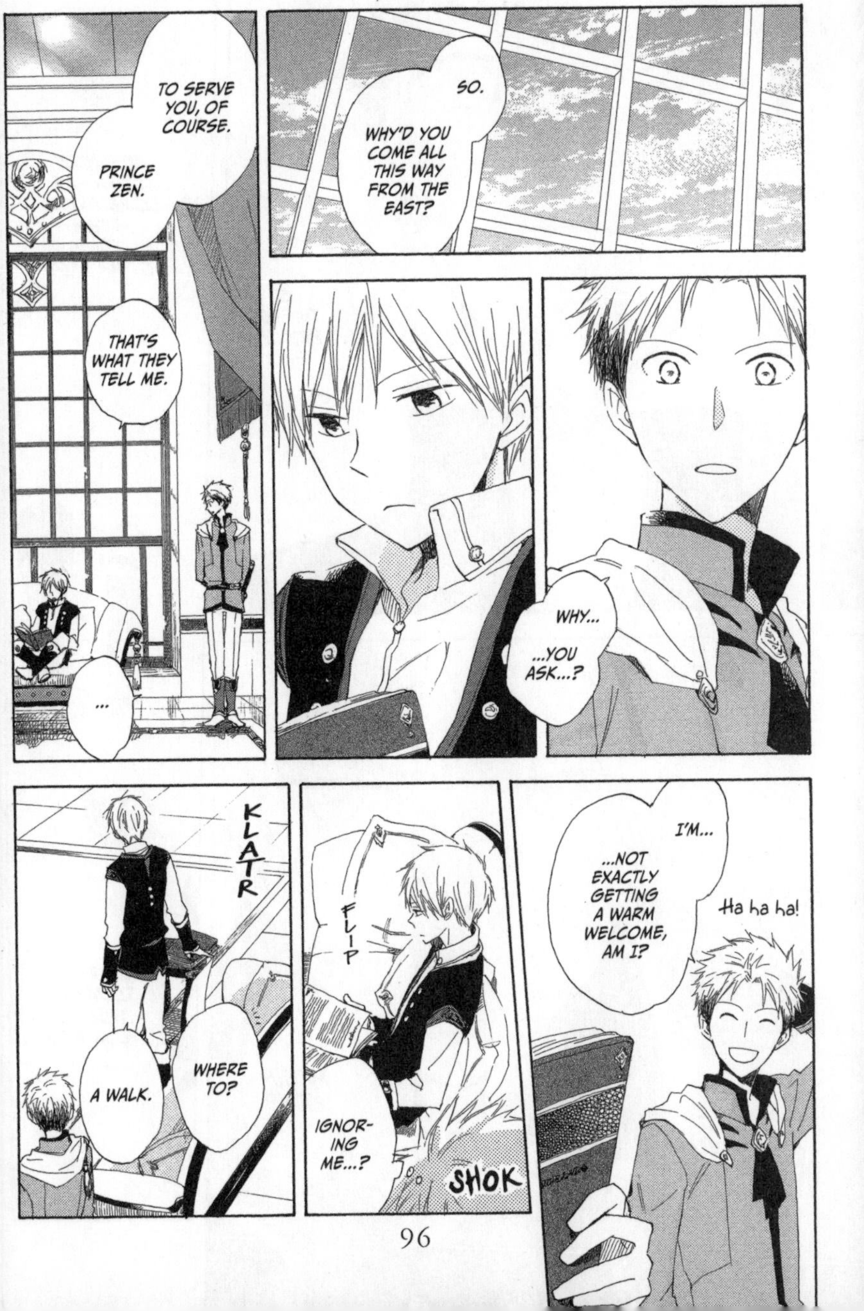
SO.
WHY'D YOU COME ALL THIS WAY FROM THE EAST?
WHY...
...YOU ASK...?
TO SERVE YOU, OF COURSE.
PRINCE ZEN.
THAT'S WHAT THEY TELL ME.
...
I'M...
...NOT EXACTLY GETTING A WARM WELCOME, AM I?
Ha ha ha!
FLIP
IGNOR-ING ME...?
SHOK
KLATR
WHERE TO?
A WALK.

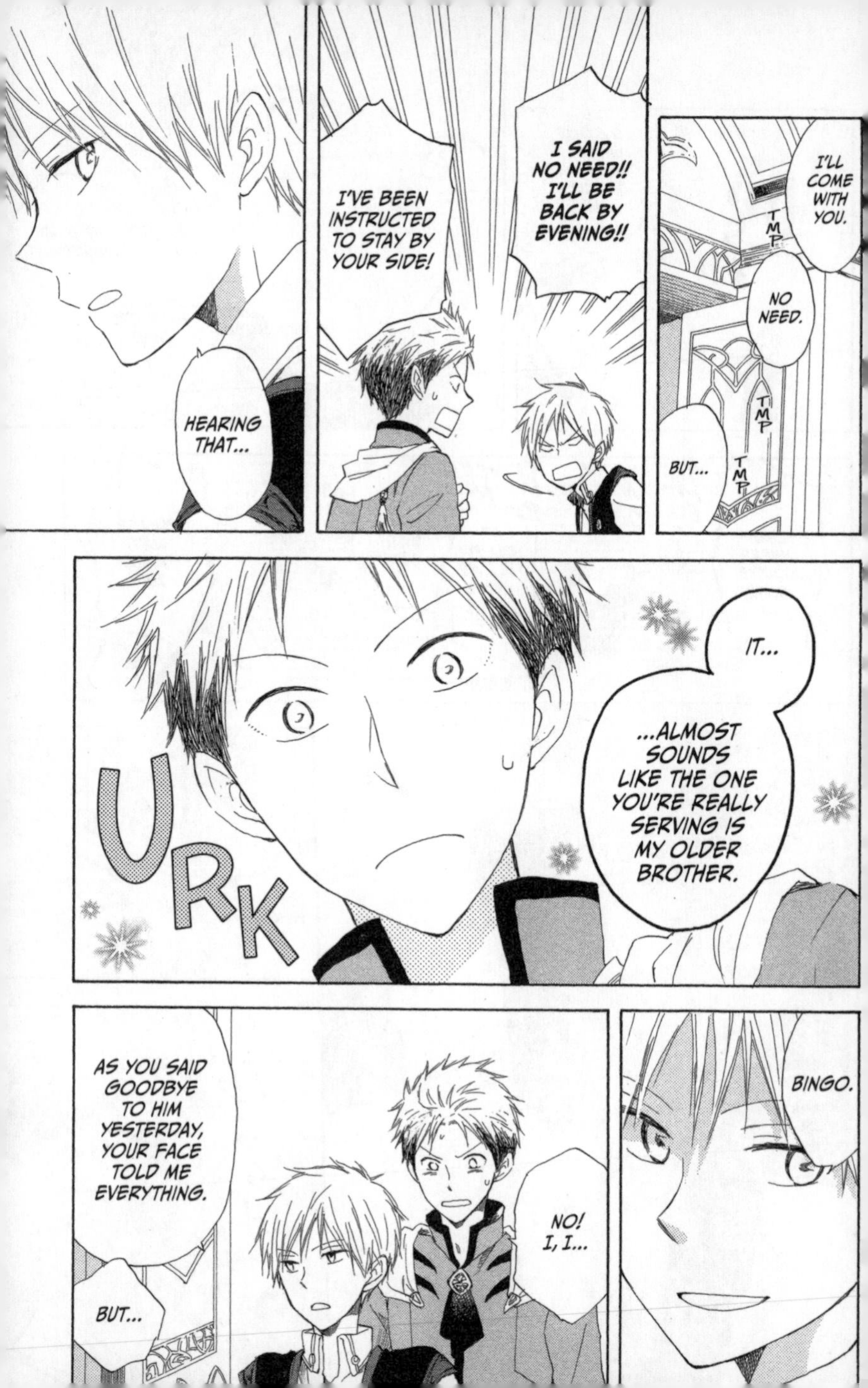
I'LL COME WITH YOU.
TMP
NO NEED.
TMP
TMP
BUT...
I SAID NO NEED!! I'LL BE BACK BY EVENING!!
I'VE BEEN INSTRUCTED TO STAY BY YOUR SIDE!
HEARING THAT...
IT...
...ALMOST SOUNDS LIKE THE ONE YOU'RE REALLY SERVING IS MY OLDER BROTHER.
URK
BINGO.
AS YOU SAID GOODBYE TO HIM YESTERDAY, YOUR FACE TOLD ME EVERYTHING.
NO! I, I...
BUT...

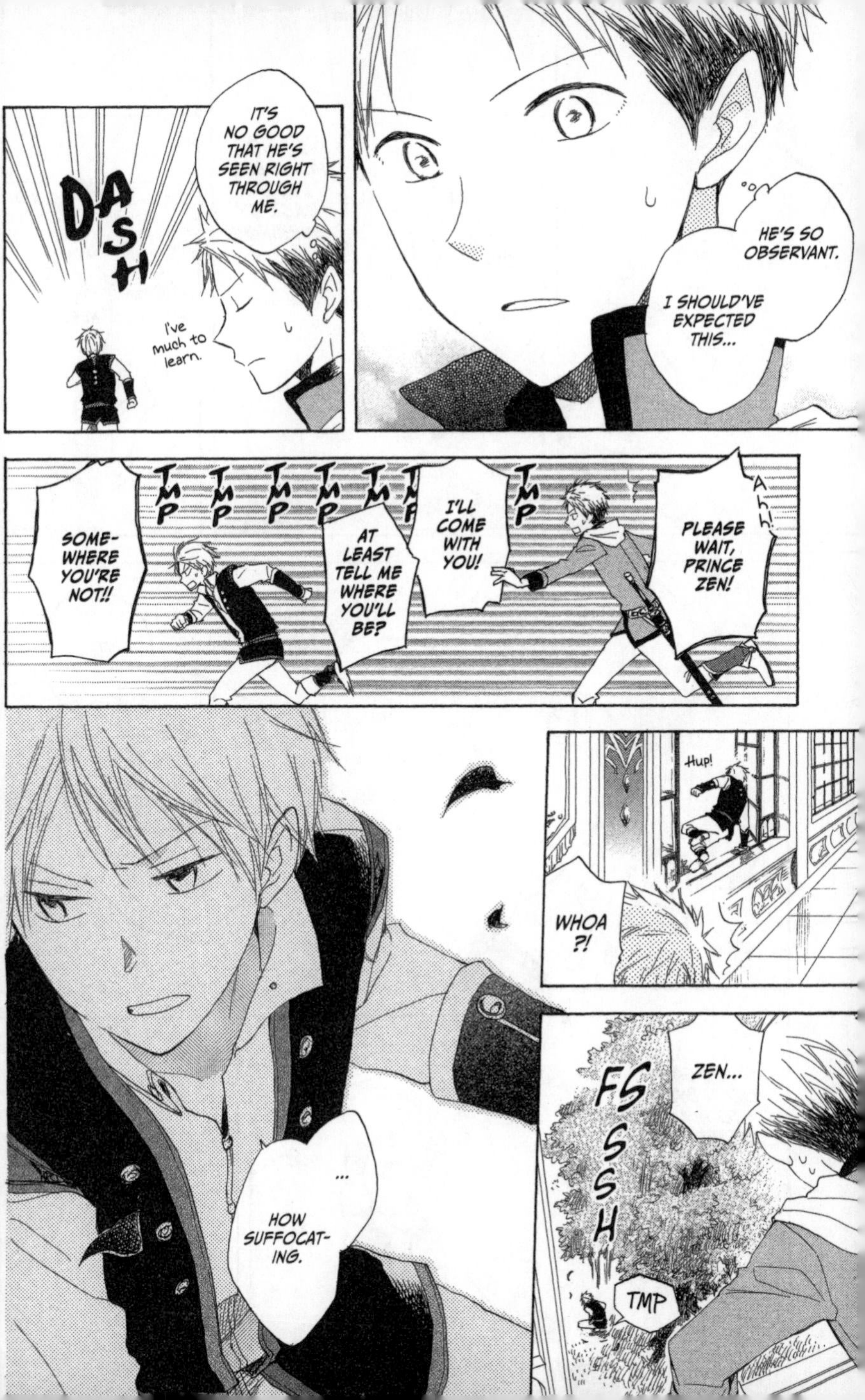
HE'S SO OBSERVANT.
I SHOULD'VE EXPECTED THIS...
IT'S NO GOOD THAT HE'S SEEN RIGHT THROUGH ME.
DASH
I've much to learn.
Ahh!
PLEASE WAIT, PRINCE ZEN!
TMP TMP TMP TMP TMP TMP TMP
I'LL COME WITH YOU!
AT LEAST TELL ME WHERE YOU'LL BE?
SOME-WHERE YOU'RE NOT!!
Hup!
WHOA ?!
ZEN...
FSSSH
TMP
...
HOW SUFFOCAT-ING.

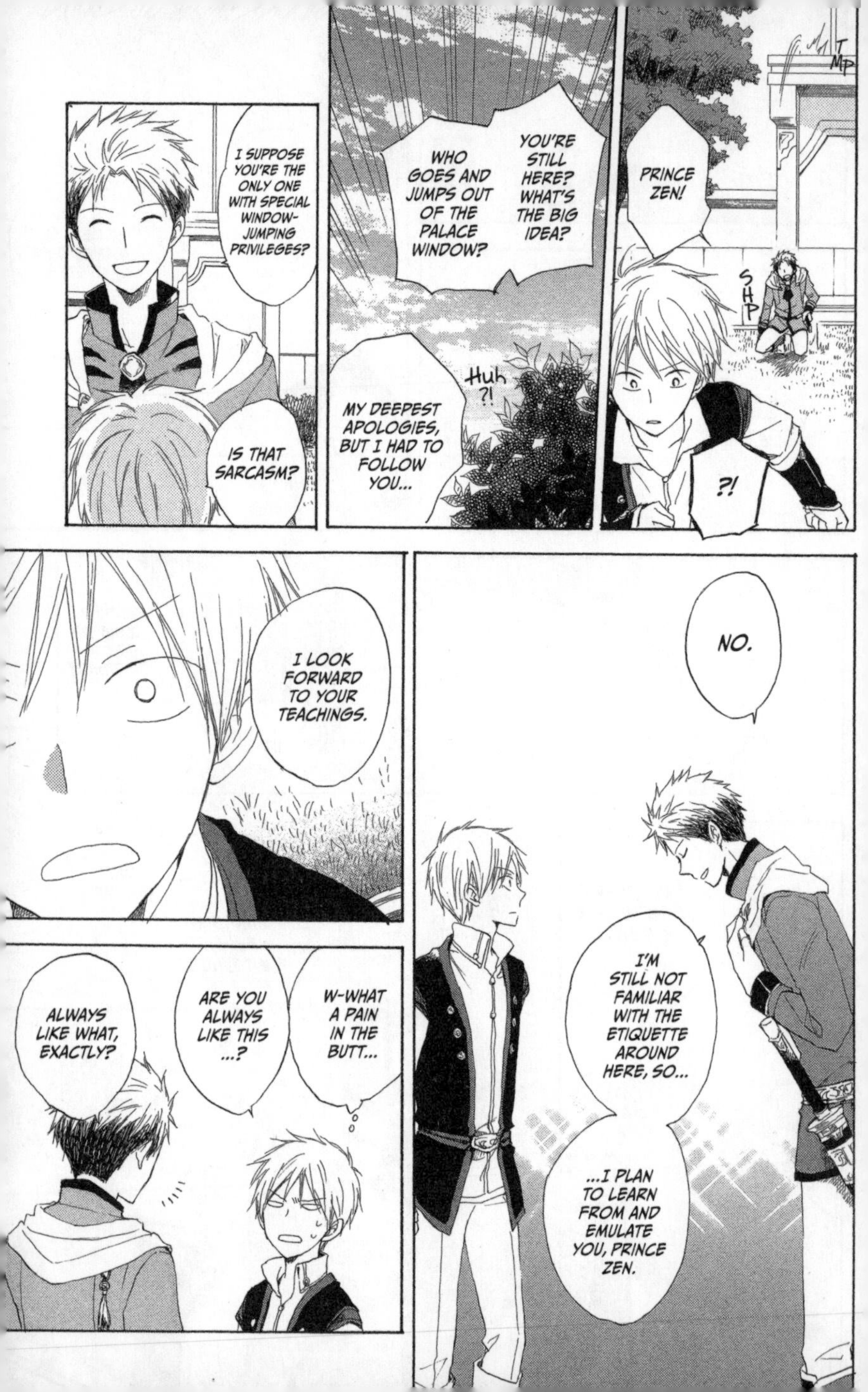
TMP
PRINCE ZEN!
SHP
?!
YOU'RE STILL HERE? WHAT'S THE BIG IDEA?
WHO GOES AND JUMPS OUT OF THE PALACE WINDOW?
Huh ?!
MY DEEPEST APOLOGIES, BUT I HAD TO FOLLOW YOU...
I SUPPOSE YOU'RE THE ONLY ONE WITH SPECIAL WINDOW-JUMPING PRIVILEGES?
IS THAT SARCASM?
NO.
I'M STILL NOT FAMILIAR WITH THE ETIQUETTE AROUND HERE, SO...
...I PLAN TO LEARN FROM AND EMULATE YOU, PRINCE ZEN.
I LOOK FORWARD TO YOUR TEACHINGS.
W-WHAT A PAIN IN THE BUTT...
ARE YOU ALWAYS LIKE THIS ...?
ALWAYS LIKE WHAT, EXACTLY?

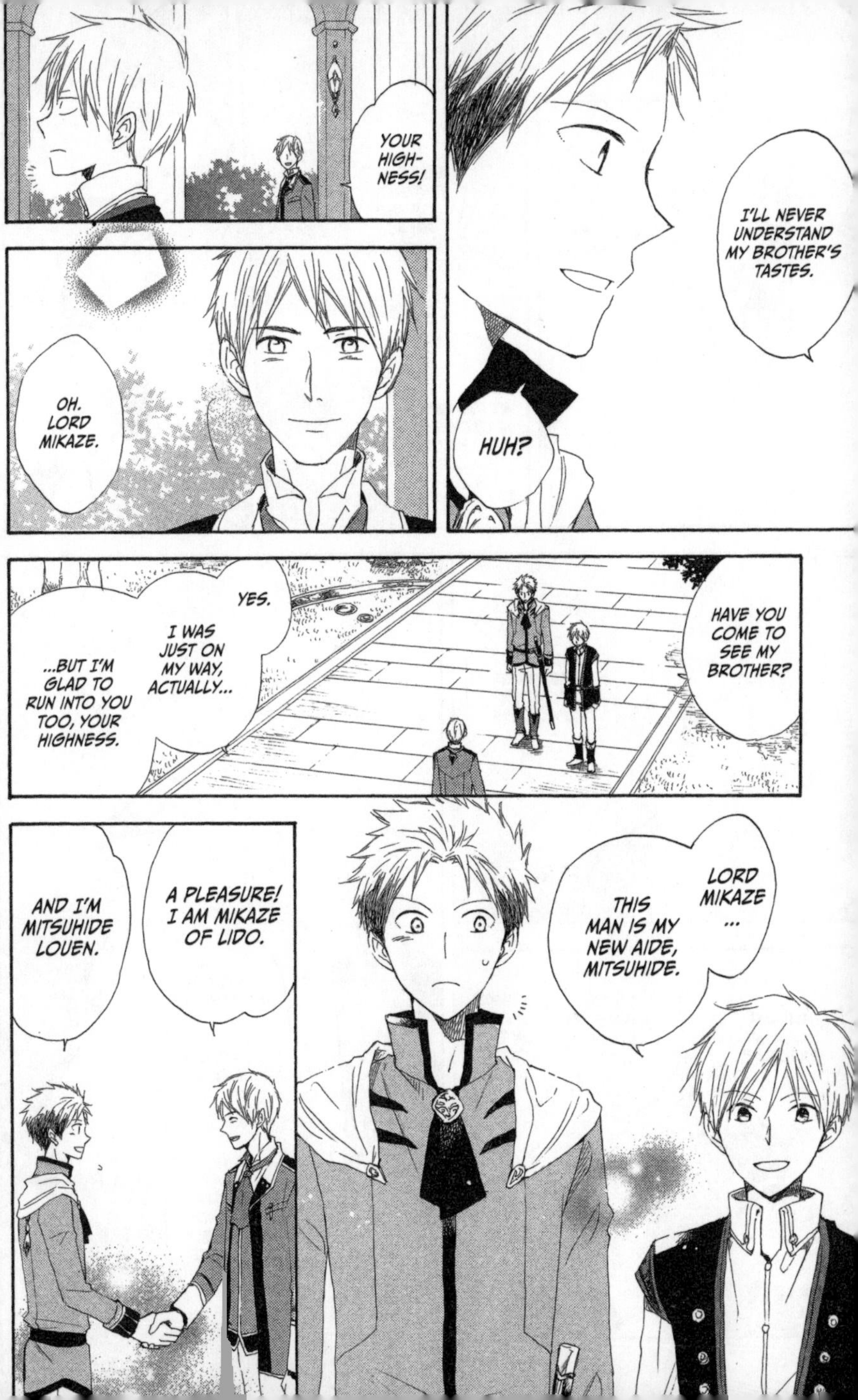
I'LL NEVER UNDERSTAND MY BROTHER'S TASTES.
HUH?
YOUR HIGHNESS!
OH. LORD MIKAZE.
HAVE YOU COME TO SEE MY BROTHER?
YES.
I WAS JUST ON MY WAY, ACTUALLY...
...BUT I'M GLAD TO RUN INTO YOU TOO, YOUR HIGHNESS.
LORD MIKAZE...
THIS MAN IS MY NEW AIDE, MITSUHIDE.
A PLEASURE! I AM MIKAZE OF LIDO.
AND I'M MITSUHIDE LOUEN.

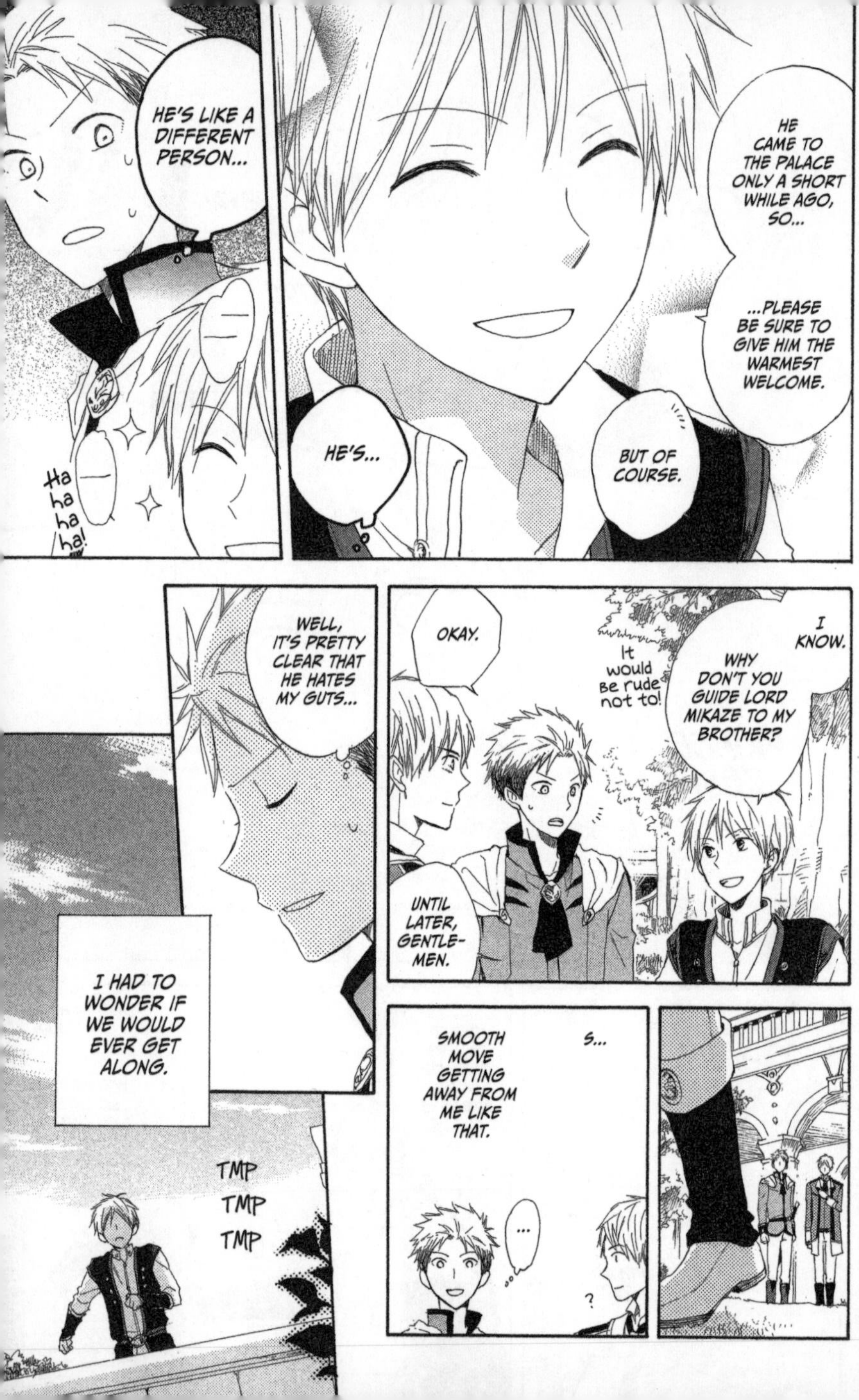
HE CAME TO THE PALACE ONLY A SHORT WHILE AGO, SO...
...PLEASE BE SURE TO GIVE HIM THE WARMEST WELCOME.
BUT OF COURSE.
HE'S...
HE'S LIKE A DIFFERENT PERSON...
Ha ha ha ha!
I KNOW.
WHY DON'T YOU GUIDE LORD MIKAZE TO MY BROTHER?
It would be rude not to!
OKAY.
UNTIL LATER, GENTLEMEN.
S...
SMOOTH MOVE GETTING AWAY FROM ME LIKE THAT.
...
?
WELL, IT'S PRETTY CLEAR THAT HE HATES MY GUTS...
I HAD TO WONDER IF WE WOULD EVER GET ALONG.
TMP
TMP
TMP

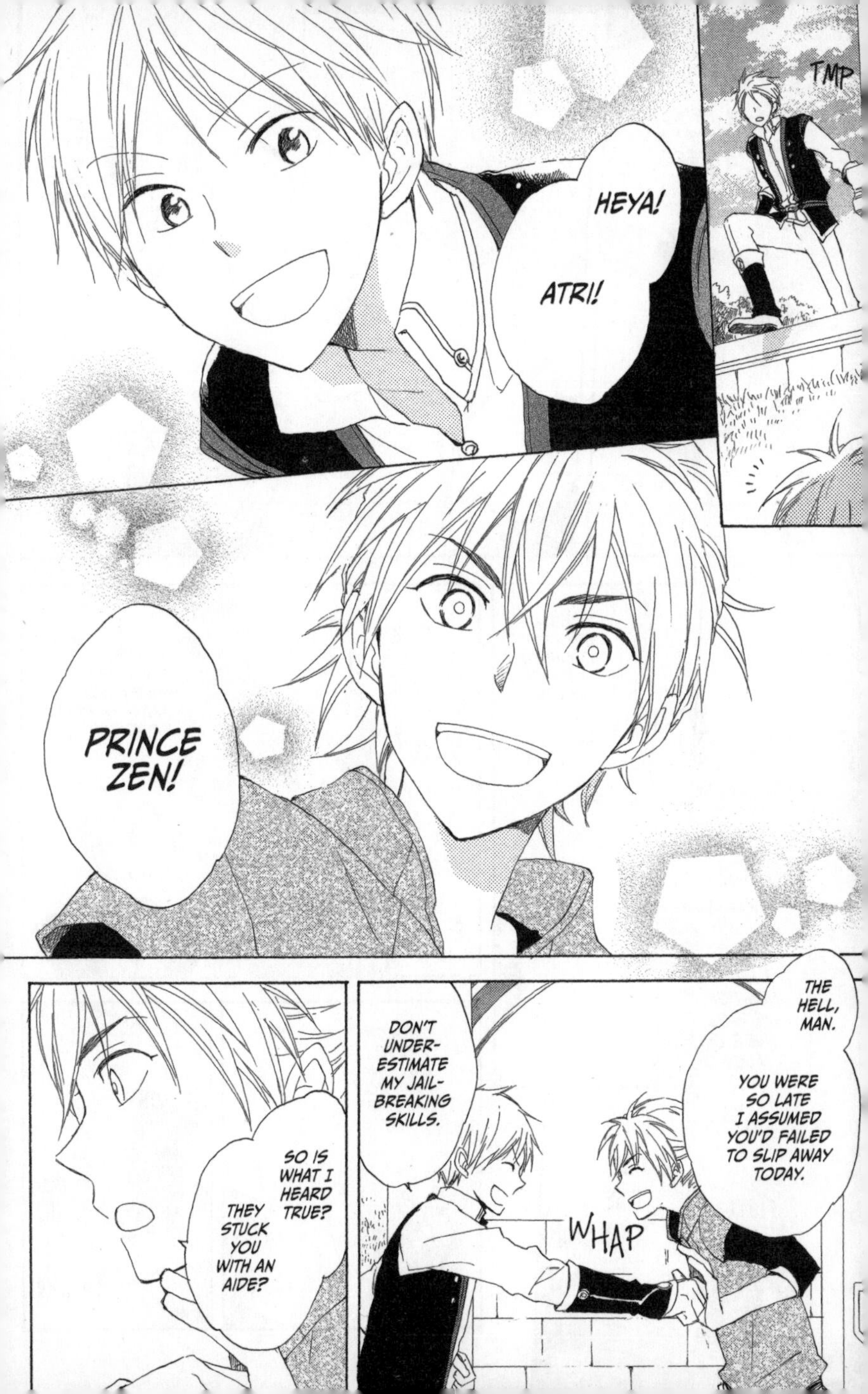
TMP
HEYA!
ATRI!
PRINCE ZEN!
THE HELL, MAN.
YOU WERE SO LATE I ASSUMED YOU'D FAILED TO SLIP AWAY TODAY.
DON'T UNDER-ESTIMATE MY JAIL-BREAKING SKILLS.
WHAP
SO IS WHAT I HEARD TRUE?
THEY STUCK YOU WITH AN AIDE?

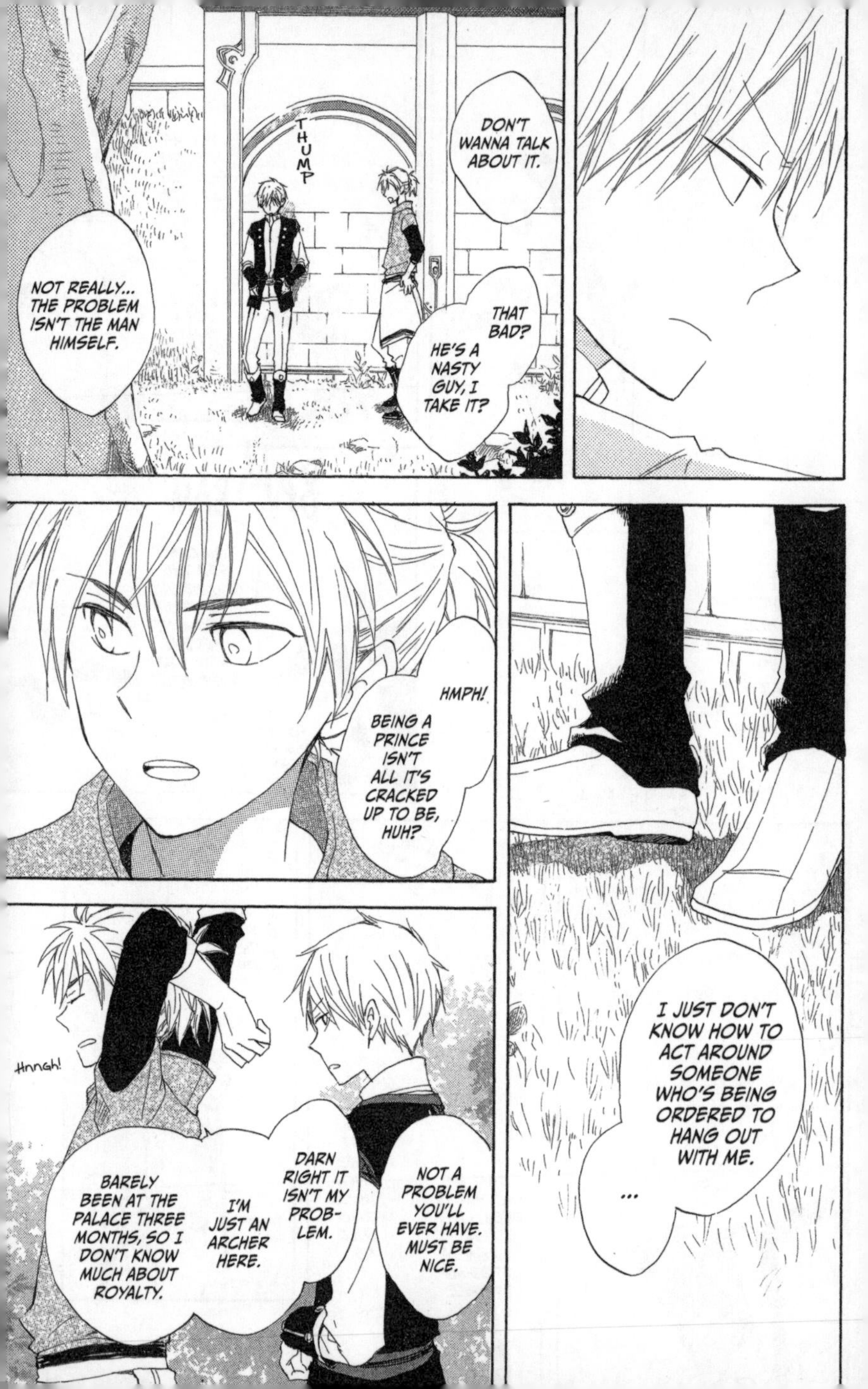

DON'T WANNA TALK ABOUT IT.
THUMP
THAT BAD?
HE'S A NASTY GUY, I TAKE IT?
NOT REALLY... THE PROBLEM ISN'T THE MAN HIMSELF.
I JUST DON'T KNOW HOW TO ACT AROUND SOMEONE WHO'S BEING ORDERED TO HANG OUT WITH ME.
...
HMPH!
BEING A PRINCE ISN'T ALL IT'S CRACKED UP TO BE, HUH?
NOT A PROBLEM YOU'LL EVER HAVE. MUST BE NICE.
DARN RIGHT IT ISN'T MY PROB-LEM.
I'M JUST AN ARCHER HERE.
BARELY BEEN AT THE PALACE THREE MONTHS, SO I DON'T KNOW MUCH ABOUT ROYALTY.
Hnngh!

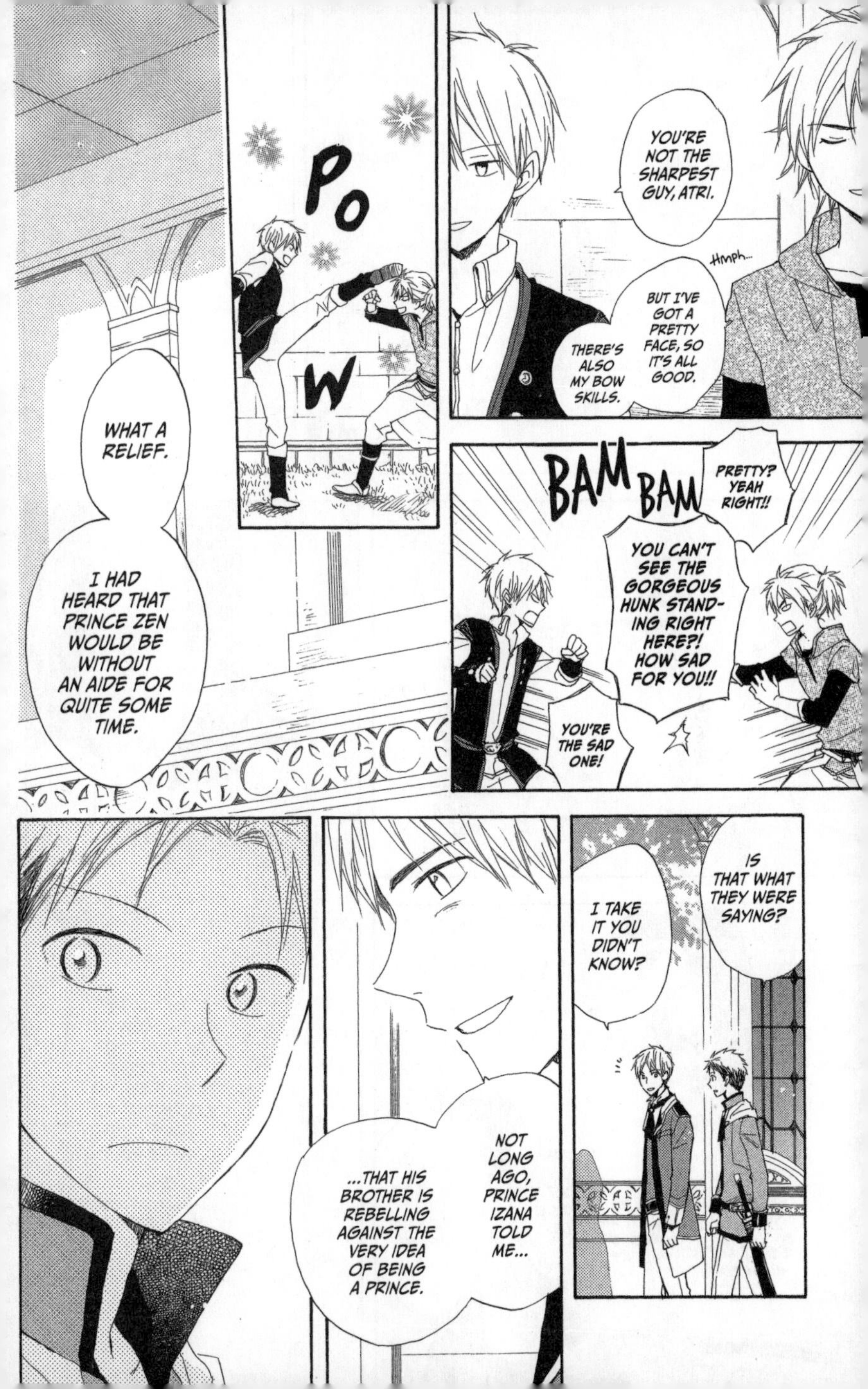
YOU'RE NOT THE SHARPEST GUY, ATRI.
Hmph...
BUT I'VE GOT A PRETTY FACE, SO IT'S ALL GOOD.
THERE'S ALSO MY BOW SKILLS.
BAM
BAM
PRETTY? YEAH RIGHT!!
YOU CAN'T SEE THE GORGEOUS HUNK STANDING RIGHT HERE?! HOW SAD FOR YOU!!
YOU'RE THE SAD ONE!
POW
WHAT A RELIEF.
I HAD HEARD THAT PRINCE ZEN WOULD BE WITHOUT AN AIDE FOR QUITE SOME TIME.
IS THAT WHAT THEY WERE SAYING?
I TAKE IT YOU DIDN'T KNOW?
NOT LONG AGO, PRINCE IZANA TOLD ME...
...THAT HIS BROTHER IS REBELLING AGAINST THE VERY IDEA OF BEING A PRINCE.

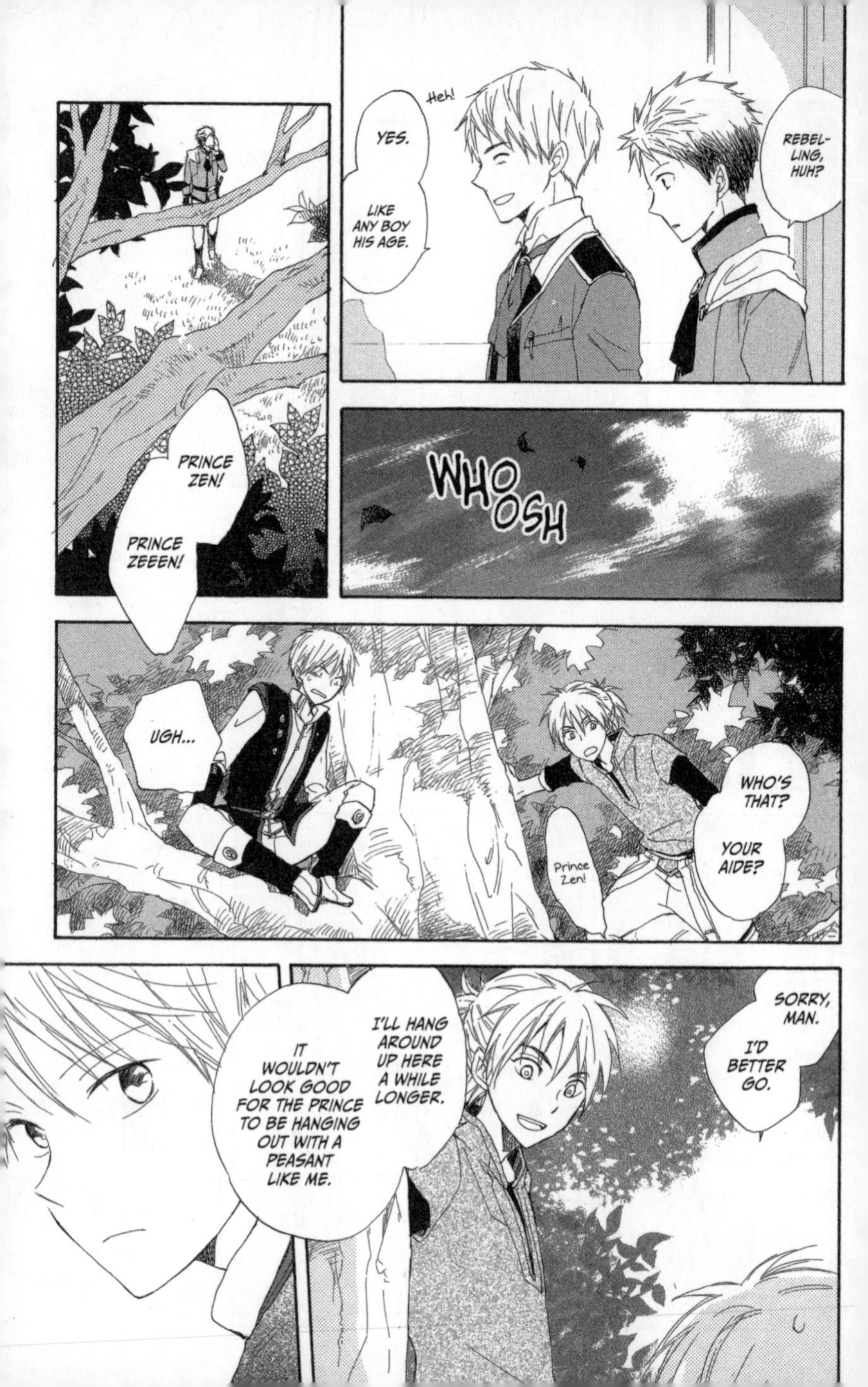
REBELLING, HUH?
Heh!
YES.
LIKE ANY BOY HIS AGE.
WHOOSH
PRINCE ZEN!
PRINCE ZEEEN!
WHO'S THAT?
YOUR AIDE?
Prince Zen!
UGH...
SORRY, MAN.
I'D BETTER GO.
I'LL HANG AROUND UP HERE A WHILE LONGER.
IT WOULDN'T LOOK GOOD FOR THE PRINCE TO BE HANGING OUT WITH A PEASANT LIKE ME.

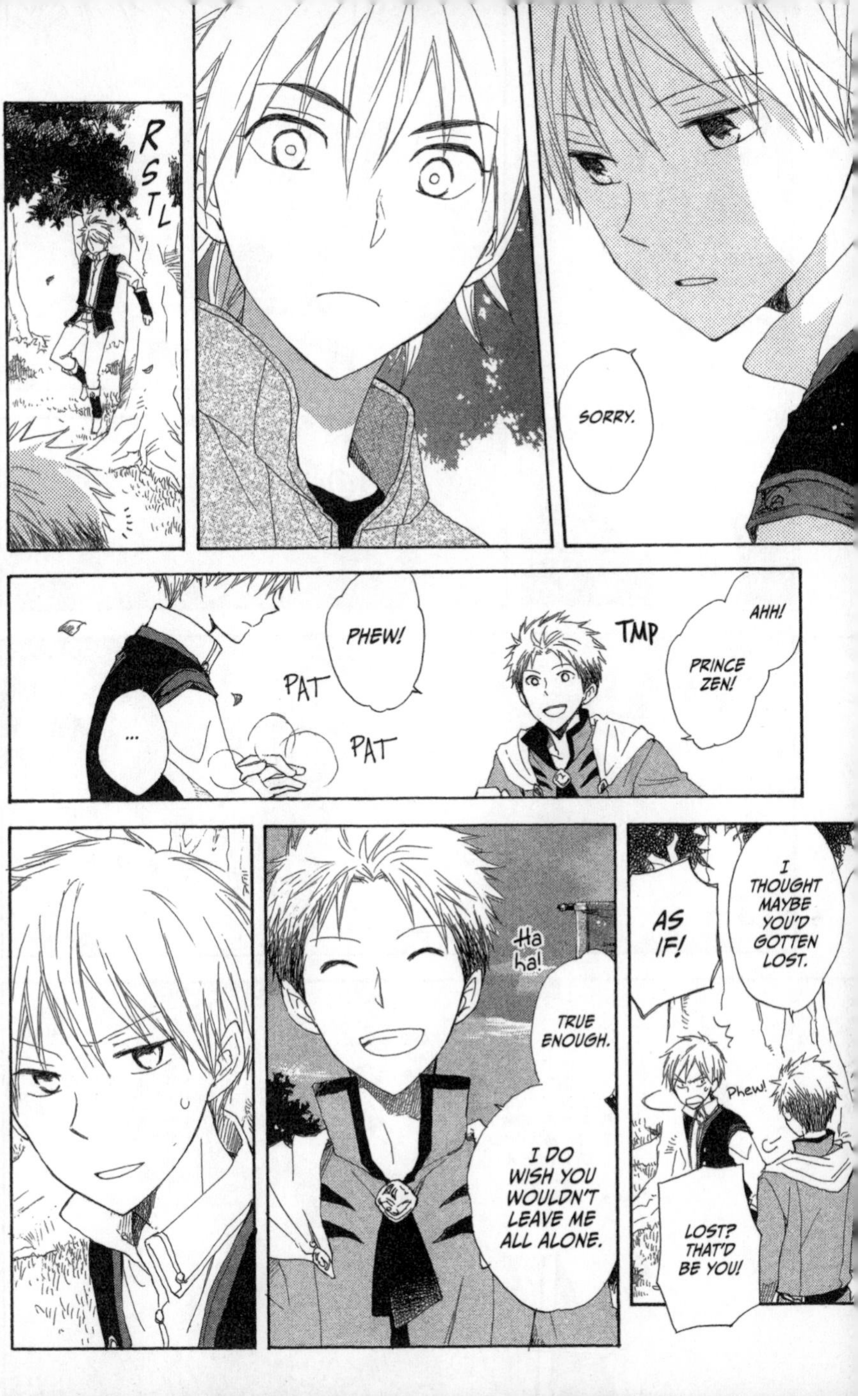
SORRY.
RSTL
AHH! PRINCE ZEN!
TMP
PHEW!
PAT
PAT
...
I THOUGHT MAYBE YOU'D GOTTEN LOST.
AS IF!
Phew!
LOST? THAT'D BE YOU!
Ha ha!
TRUE ENOUGH.
I DO WISH YOU WOULDN'T LEAVE ME ALL ALONE.

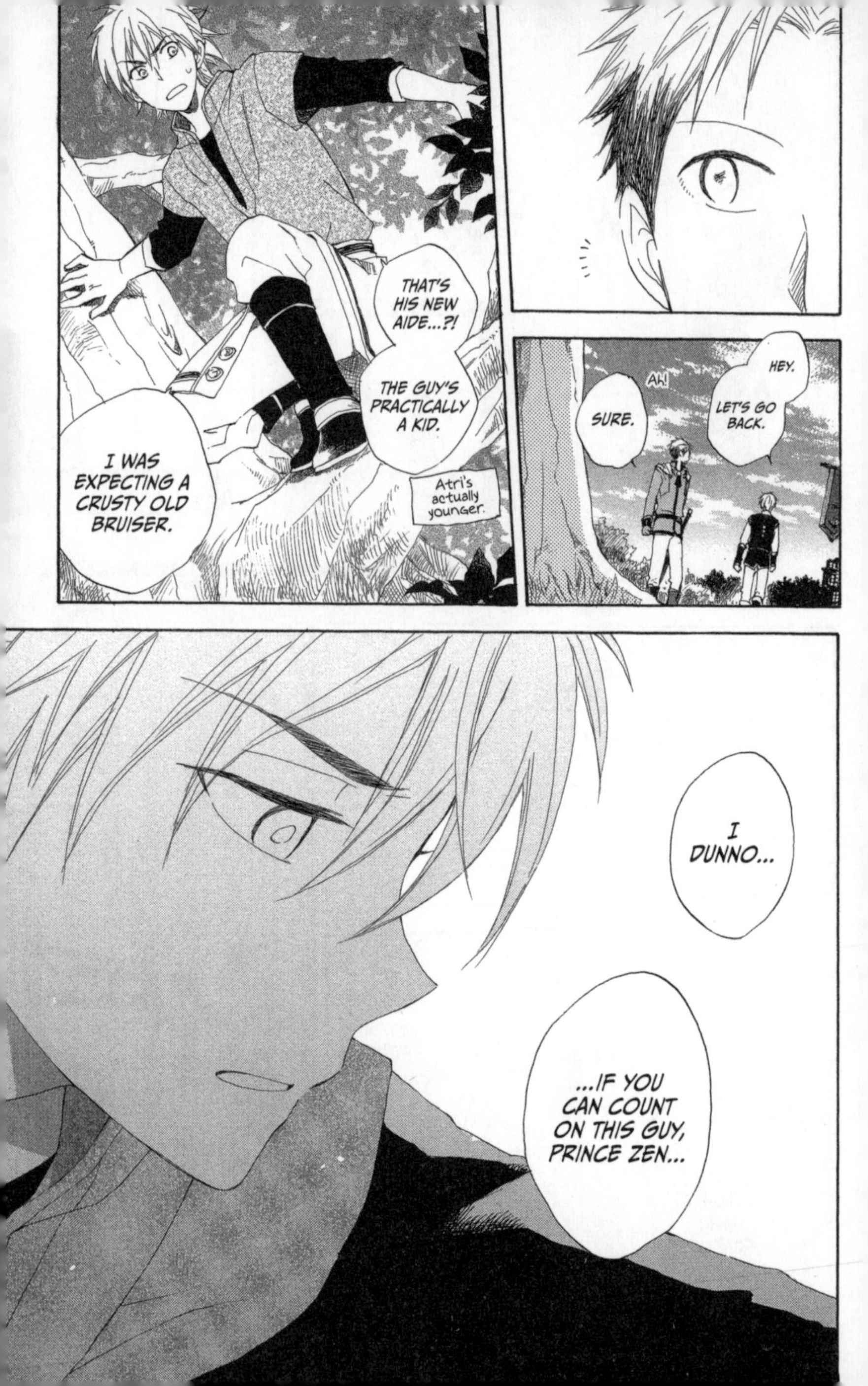
HEY. LET'S GO BACK.
AH!
SURE.
THAT'S HIS NEW AIDE...?!
THE GUY'S PRACTICALLY A KID.
Atri's actually younger.
I WAS EXPECTING A CRUSTY OLD BRUISER.
I DUNNO...
...IF YOU CAN COUNT ON THIS GUY, PRINCE ZEN...

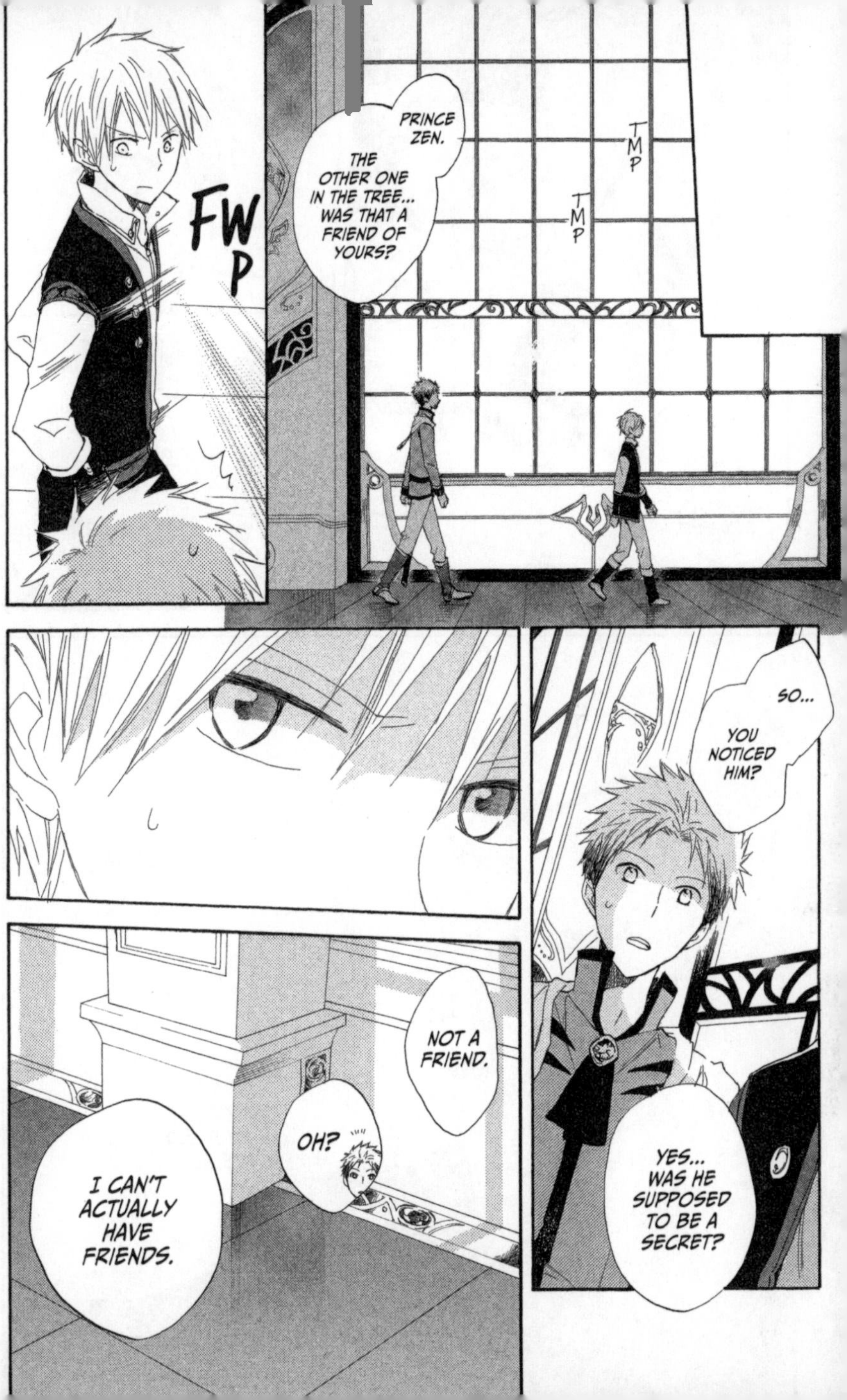
TMP
TMP
PRINCE ZEN.
THE OTHER ONE IN THE TREE... WAS THAT A FRIEND OF YOURS?
FWP
SO...
YOU NOTICED HIM?
YES... WAS HE SUPPOSED TO BE A SECRET?
NOT A FRIEND.
OH?
I CAN'T ACTUALLY HAVE FRIENDS.

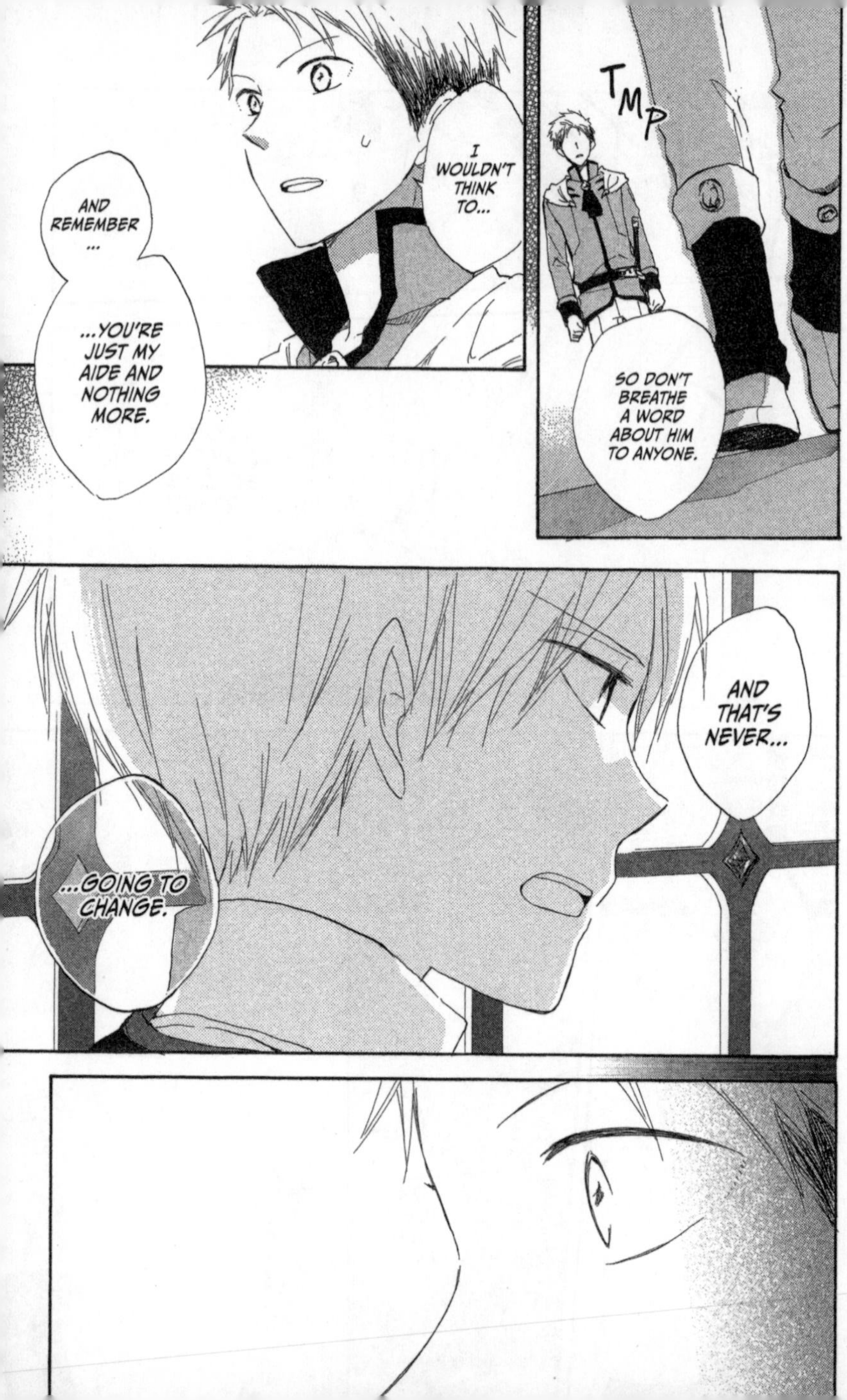
TMP
SO DON'T BREATHE A WORD ABOUT HIM TO ANYONE.
I WOULDN'T THINK TO...
AND REMEMBER...
...YOU'RE JUST MY AIDE AND NOTHING MORE.
AND THAT'S NEVER...
...GOING TO CHANGE.

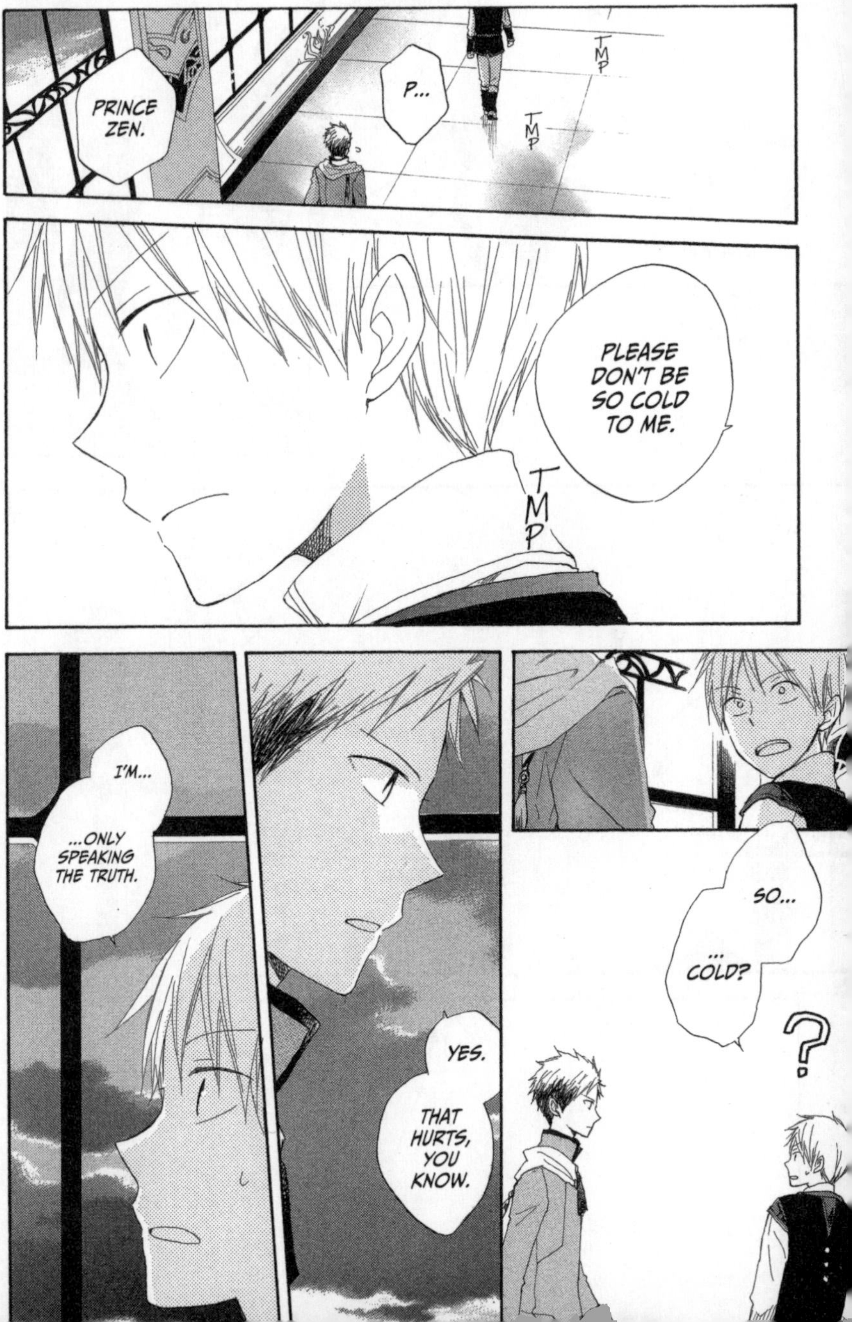
TMP
P...
TMP
PRINCE ZEN.
PLEASE DON'T BE SO COLD TO ME.
TMP
SO...
...COLD?
?
YES.
THAT HURTS, YOU KNOW.
I'M...
...ONLY SPEAKING THE TRUTH.

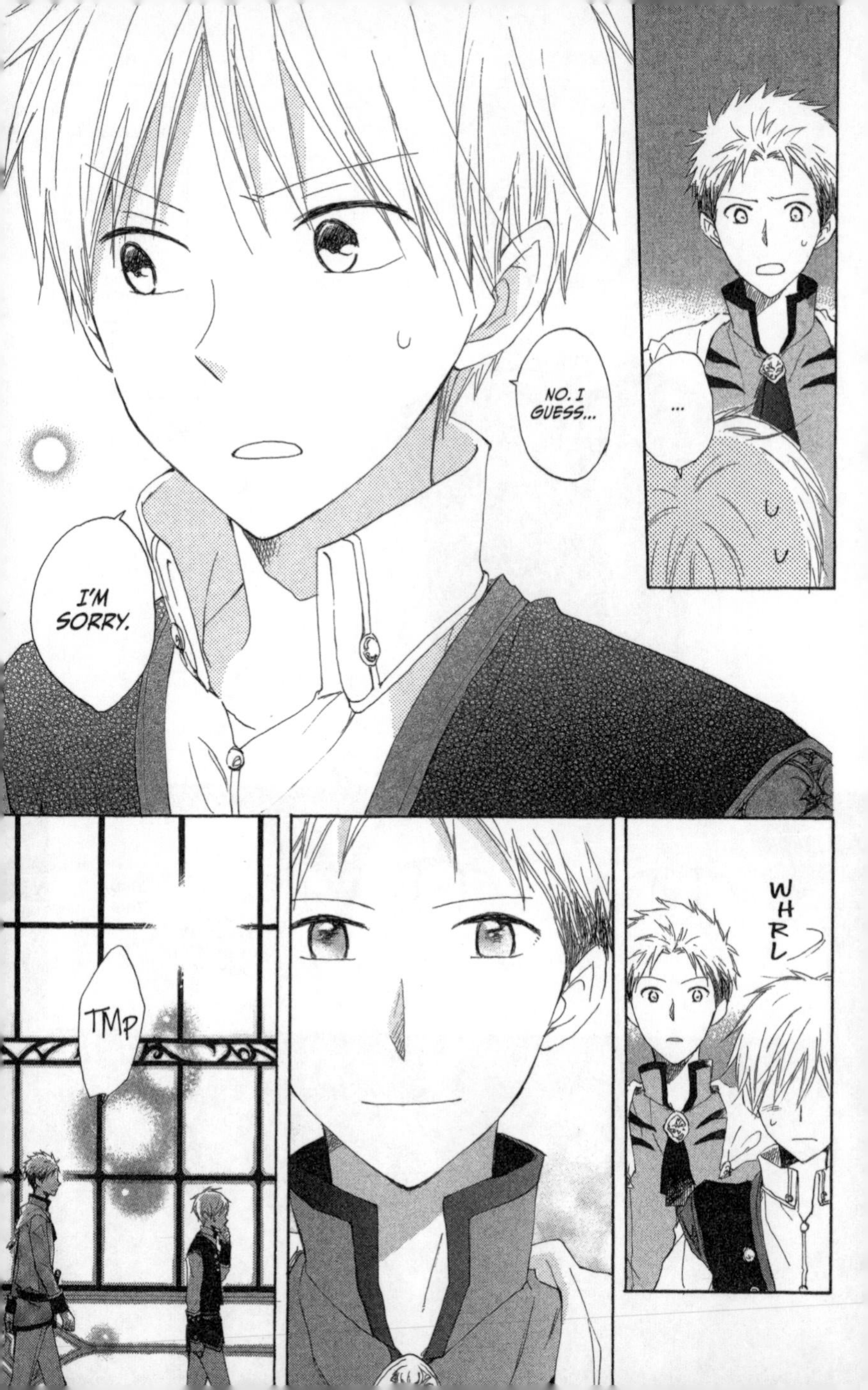
...
NO. I GUESS...
I'M SORRY.
WHRL
TMP

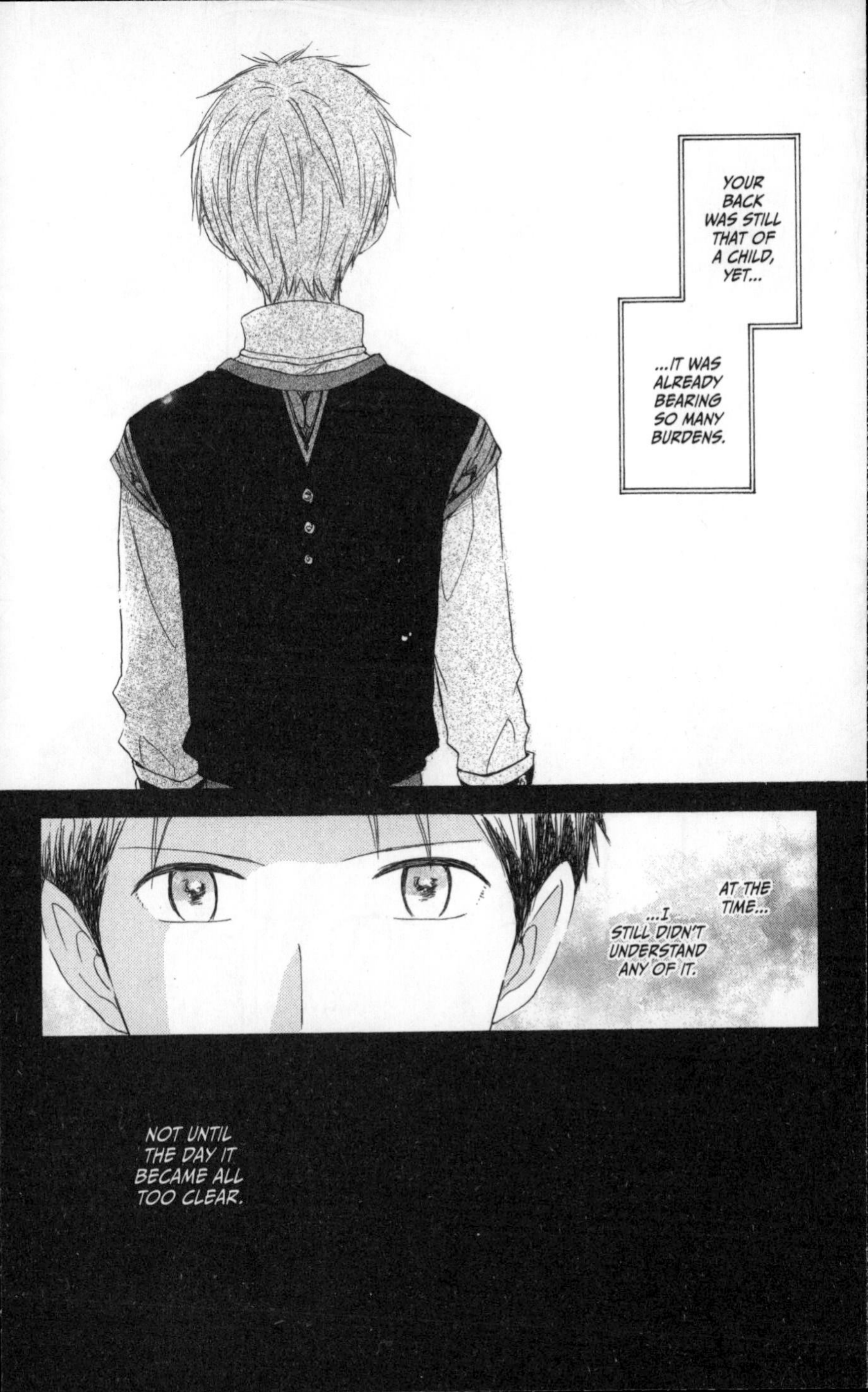
YOUR BACK WAS STILL THAT OF A CHILD, YET...
...IT WAS ALREADY BEARING SO MANY BURDENS.
AT THE TIME...
...I STILL DIDN'T UNDERSTAND ANY OF IT.
NOT UNTIL THE DAY IT BECAME ALL TOO CLEAR.

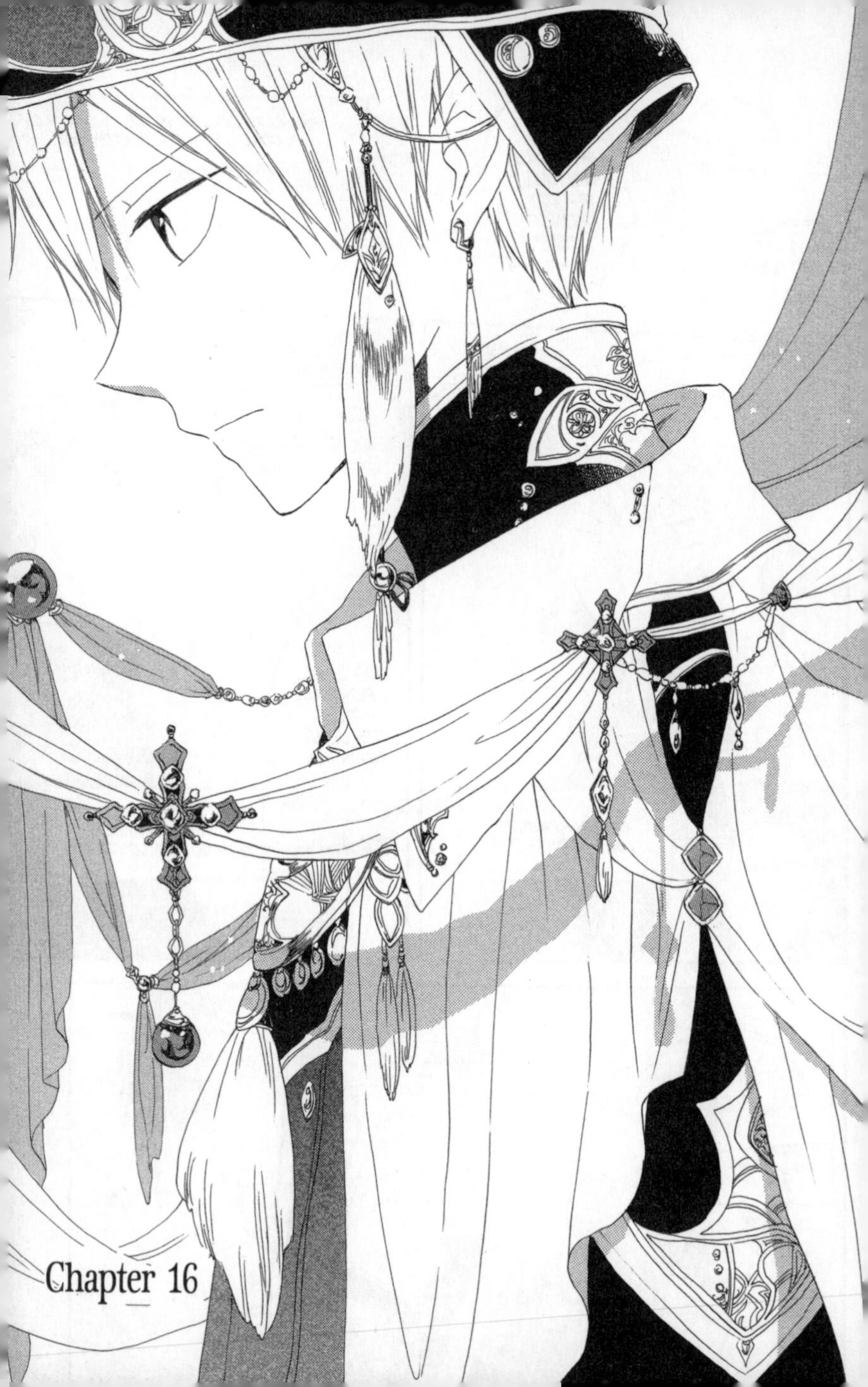
Chapter 16

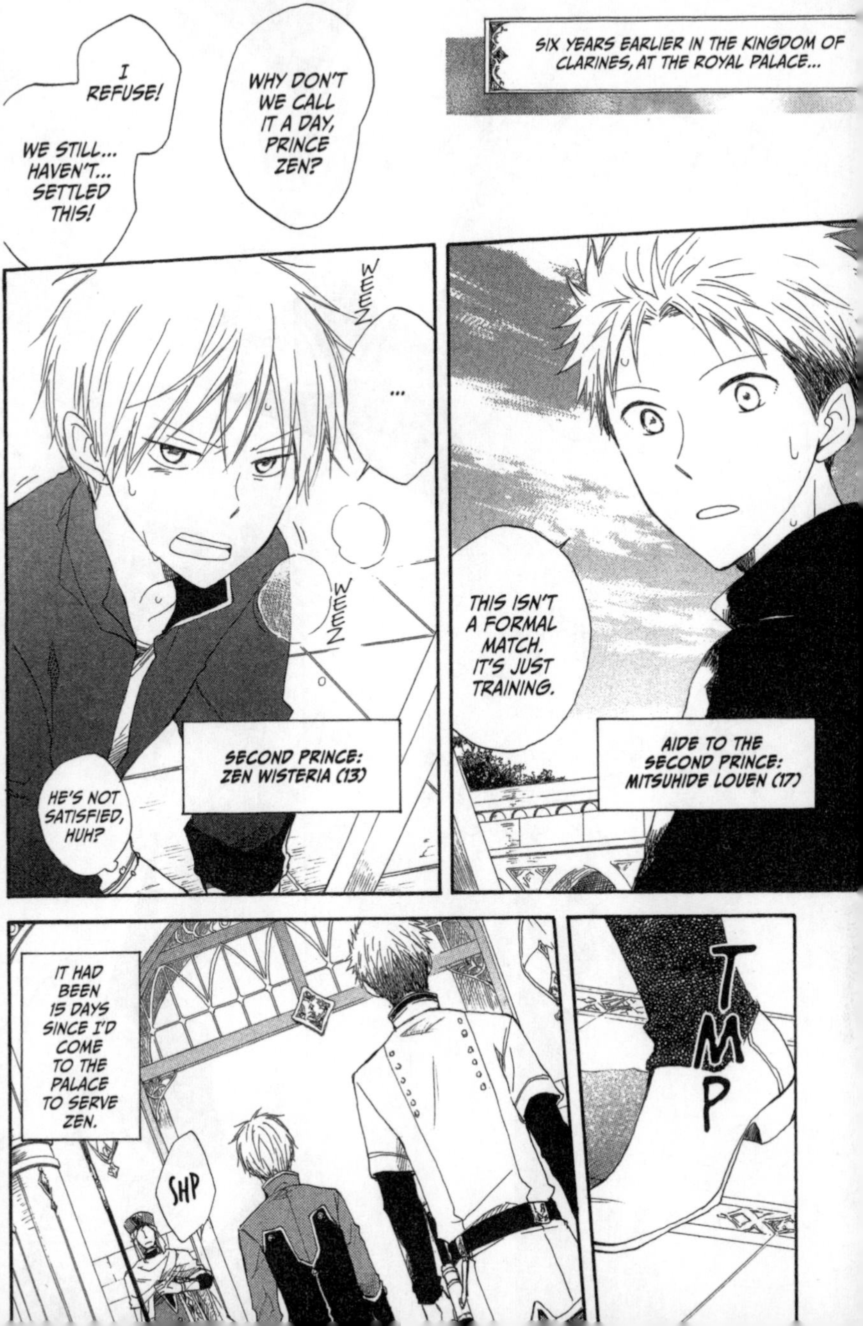
SIX YEARS EARLIER IN THE KINGDOM OF CLARINES, AT THE ROYAL PALACE...
WHY DON'T WE CALL IT A DAY, PRINCE ZEN?
I REFUSE!
WE STILL... HAVEN'T... SETTLED THIS!
THIS ISN'T A FORMAL MATCH. IT'S JUST TRAINING.
AIDE TO THE SECOND PRINCE: MITSUHIDE LOUEN (17)
WEEZ
...
WEEZ
SECOND PRINCE: ZEN WISTERIA (13)
HE'S NOT SATISFIED, HUH?
TMP
IT HAD BEEN 15 DAYS SINCE I'D COME TO THE PALACE TO SERVE ZEN.
SHP

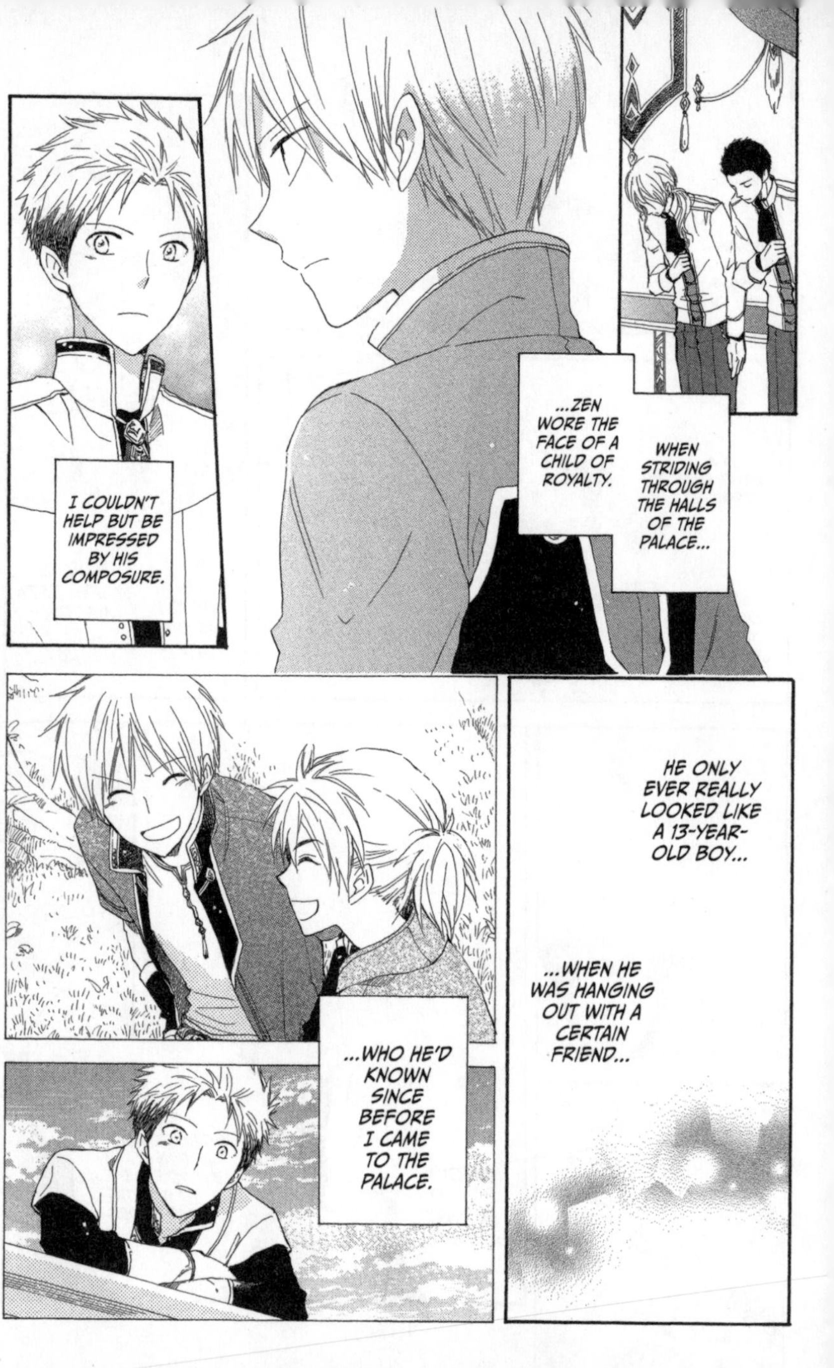
WHEN STRIDING THROUGH THE HALLS OF THE PALACE...
...ZEN WORE THE FACE OF A CHILD OF ROYALTY.
I COULDN'T HELP BUT BE IMPRESSED BY HIS COMPOSURE.
HE ONLY EVER REALLY LOOKED LIKE A 13-YEAR-OLD BOY...
...WHEN HE WAS HANGING OUT WITH A CERTAIN FRIEND...
...WHO HE'D KNOWN SINCE BEFORE I CAME TO THE PALACE.

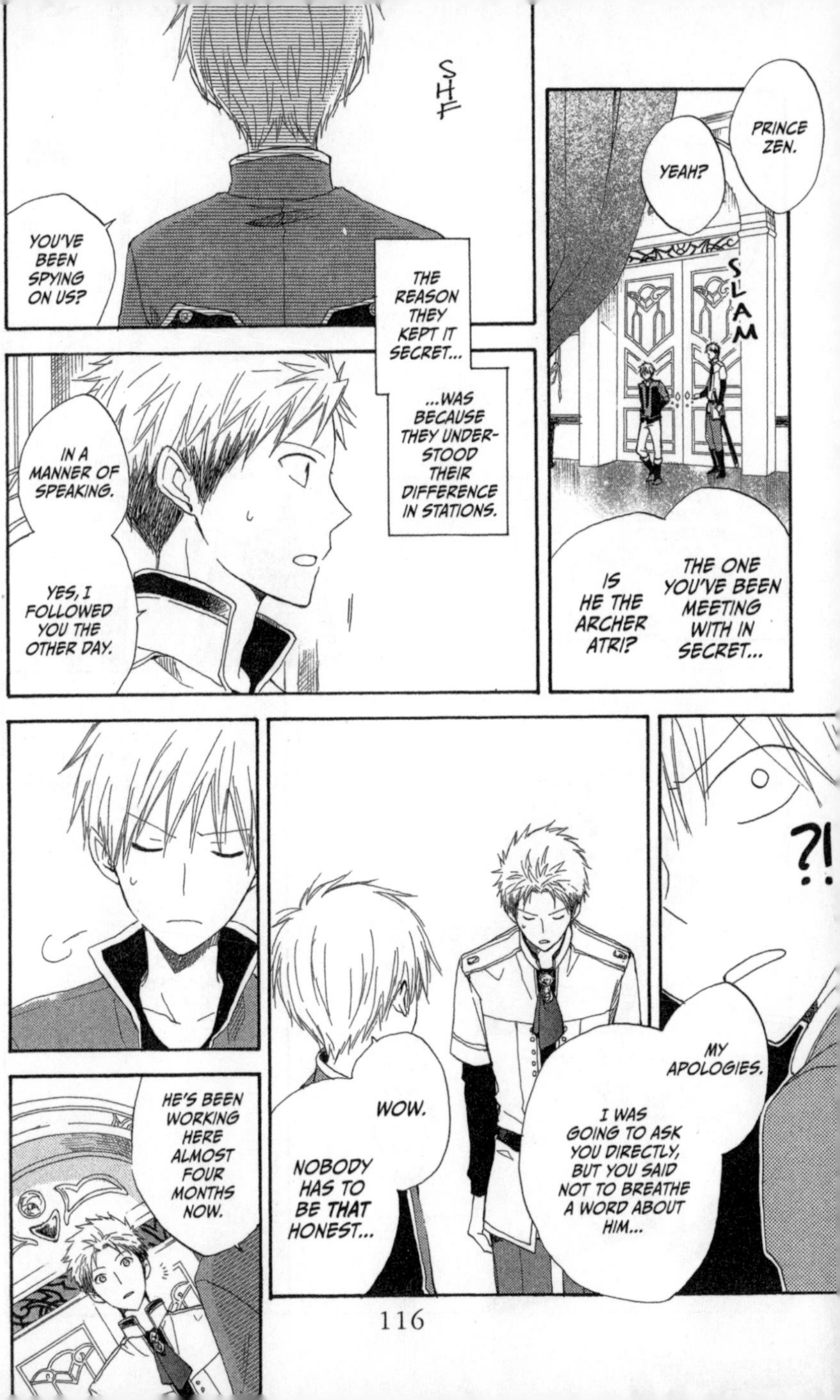
PRINCE ZEN.
YEAH?
SLAM
THE ONE YOU'VE BEEN MEETING WITH IN SECRET...
IS HE THE ARCHER ATRI?
SHF
YOU'VE BEEN SPYING ON US?
THE REASON THEY KEPT IT SECRET...
...WAS BECAUSE THEY UNDERSTOOD THEIR DIFFERENCE IN STATIONS.
IN A MANNER OF SPEAKING.
YES, I FOLLOWED YOU THE OTHER DAY.
?!
MY APOLOGIES.
I WAS GOING TO ASK YOU DIRECTLY, BUT YOU SAID NOT TO BREATHE A WORD ABOUT HIM...
WOW.
NOBODY HAS TO BE THAT HONEST...
HE'S BEEN WORKING HERE ALMOST FOUR MONTHS NOW.

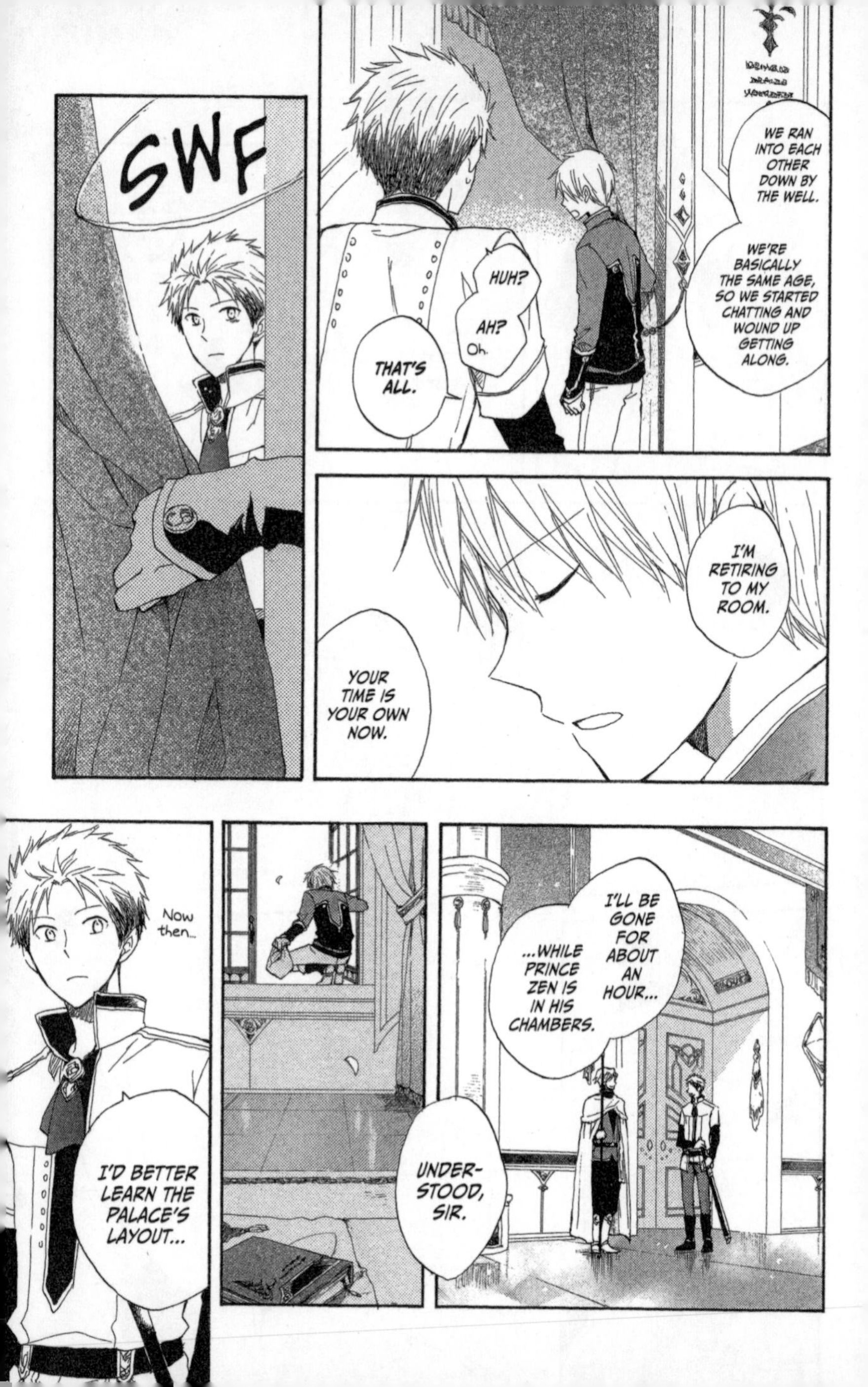
WE RAN INTO EACH OTHER DOWN BY THE WELL.
WE'RE BASICALLY THE SAME AGE, SO WE STARTED CHATTING AND WOUND UP GETTING ALONG.
HUH?
AH?
Oh.
THAT'S ALL.
I'M RETIRING TO MY ROOM.
YOUR TIME IS YOUR OWN NOW.
SWF
I'LL BE GONE FOR ABOUT AN HOUR...
...WHILE PRINCE ZEN IS IN HIS CHAMBERS.
UNDER-STOOD, SIR.
Now then...
I'D BETTER LEARN THE PALACE'S LAYOUT...

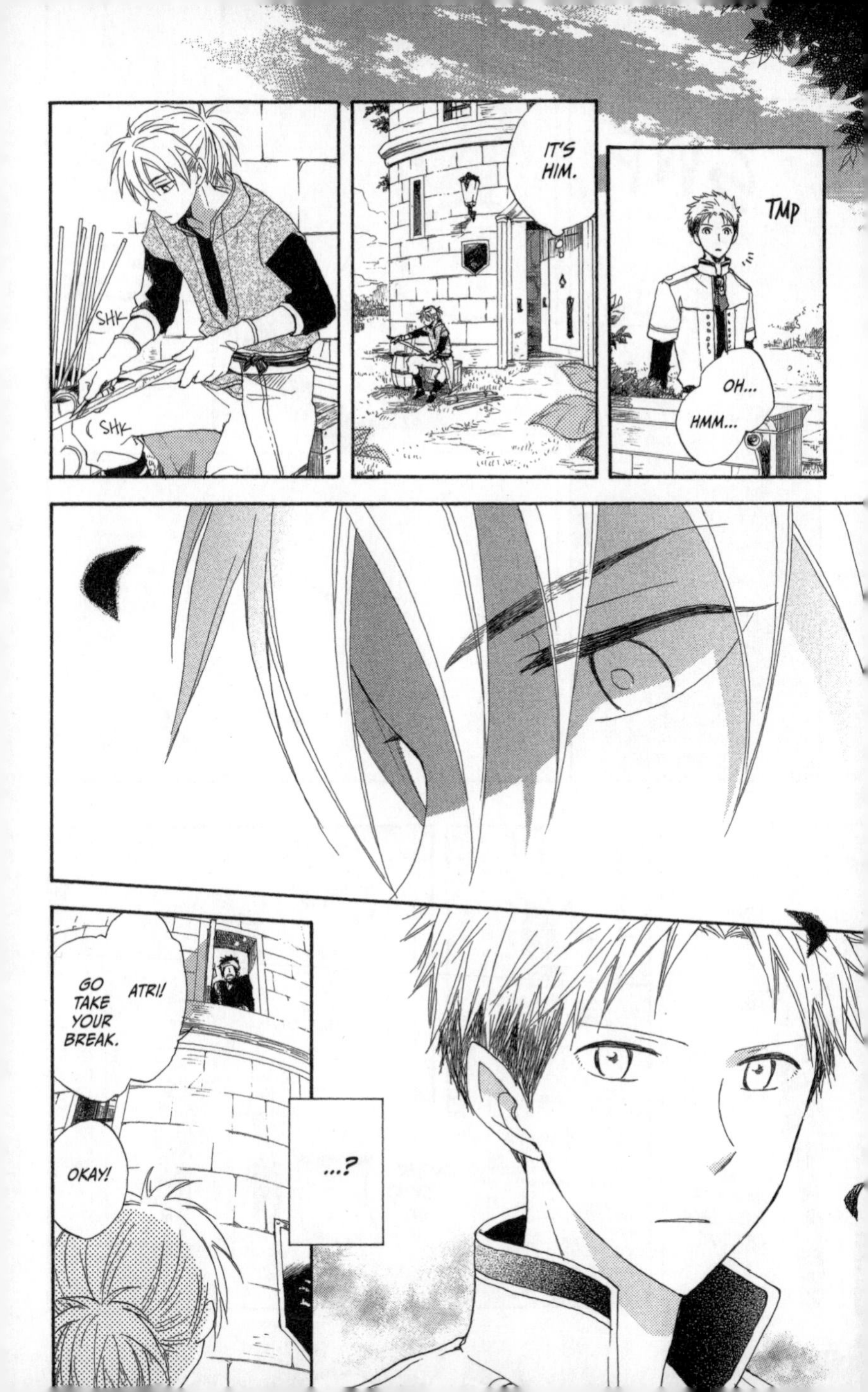
TMP
OH... HMM...
IT'S HIM.
SHK
SHK
ATRI!
GO TAKE YOUR BREAK.
OKAY!
...?

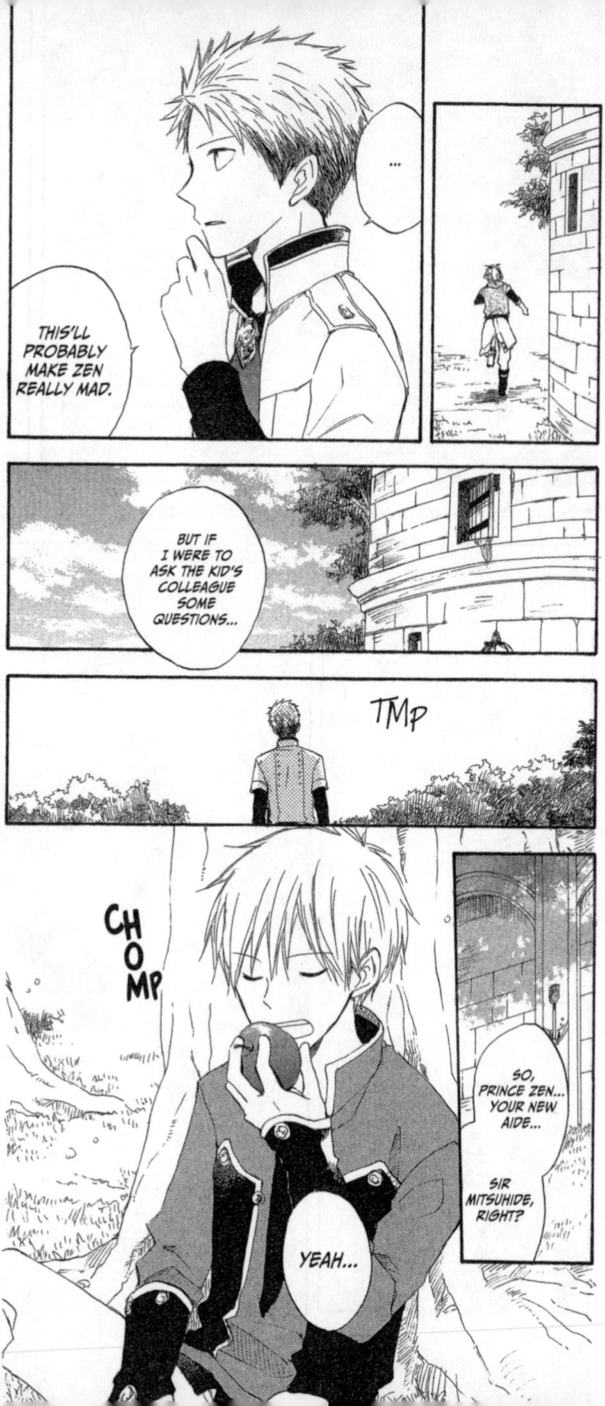
...
THIS'LL PROBABLY MAKE ZEN REALLY MAD.
BUT IF I WERE TO ASK THE KID'S COLLEAGUE SOME QUESTIONS...
TMP
SO, PRINCE ZEN... YOUR NEW AIDE...
SIR MITSUHIDE, RIGHT?
CHOMP
YEAH...

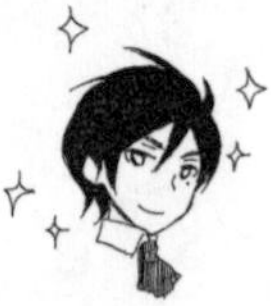

Raj

Likes

- Wine
- Gaudy things, bundled together

Can't handle

- Fresh veggies
- Milk (cold)
- Red things
- Cold places

Basically lacks life skills. Hates simple flower arrangements with a single flower.

That's all there is to know about Prince Raj.

8

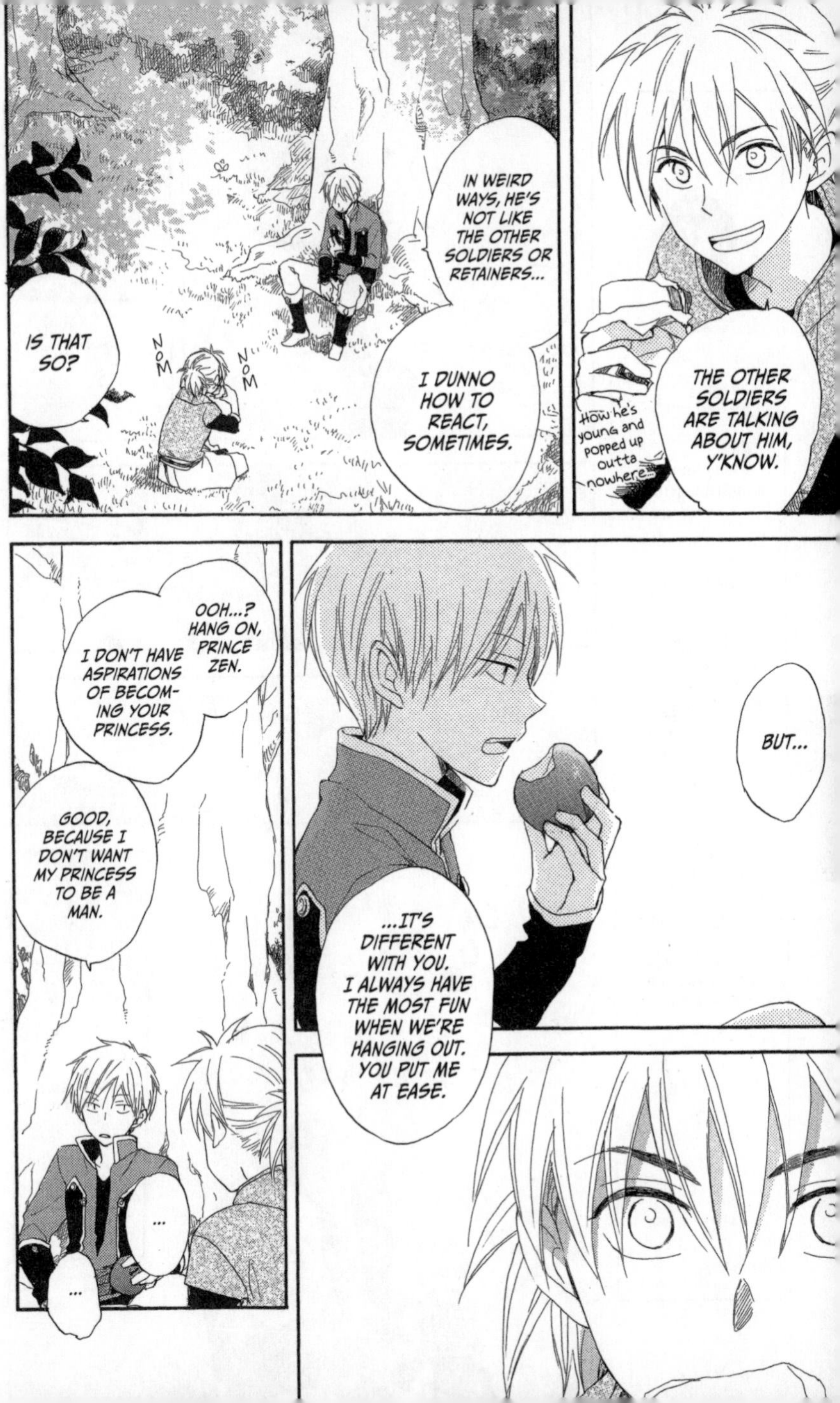
THE OTHER SOLDIERS ARE TALKING ABOUT HIM, Y'KNOW.
How he's young and popped up outta nowhere...
IN WEIRD WAYS, HE'S NOT LIKE THE OTHER SOLDIERS OR RETAINERS...
I DUNNO HOW TO REACT, SOMETIMES.
NOM NOM
IS THAT SO?
BUT...
...IT'S DIFFERENT WITH YOU. I ALWAYS HAVE THE MOST FUN WHEN WE'RE HANGING OUT. YOU PUT ME AT EASE.
OOH...? HANG ON, PRINCE ZEN.
I DON'T HAVE ASPIRATIONS OF BECOMING YOUR PRINCESS.
GOOD, BECAUSE I DON'T WANT MY PRINCESS TO BE A MAN.
...
...

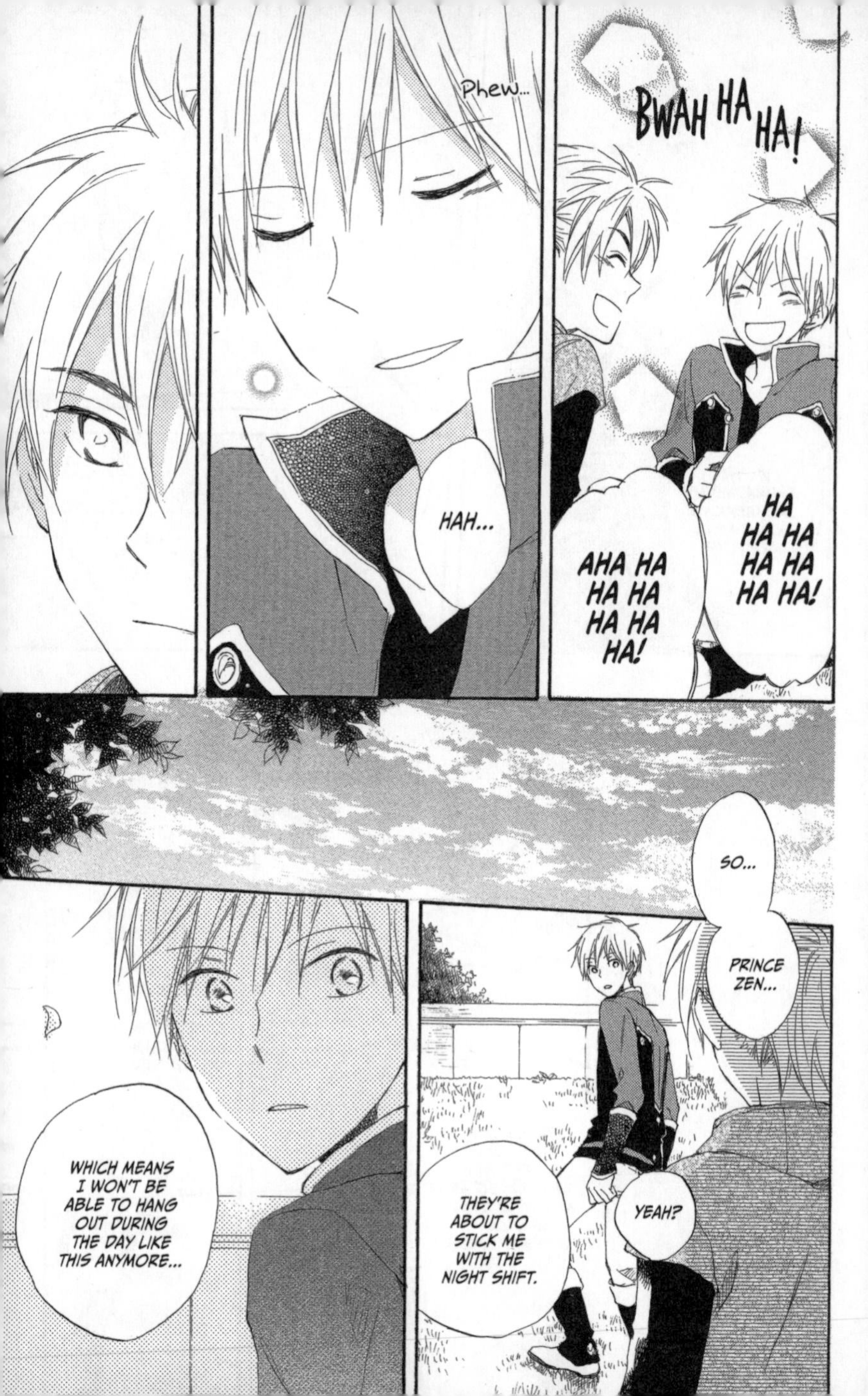
BWAH HA HA!
HA HA HA HA HA HA HA!
AHA HA HA HA HA HA HA!
Phew...
HAH...
SO...
PRINCE ZEN...
YEAH?
THEY'RE ABOUT TO STICK ME WITH THE NIGHT SHIFT.
WHICH MEANS I WON'T BE ABLE TO HANG OUT DURING THE DAY LIKE THIS ANYMORE...

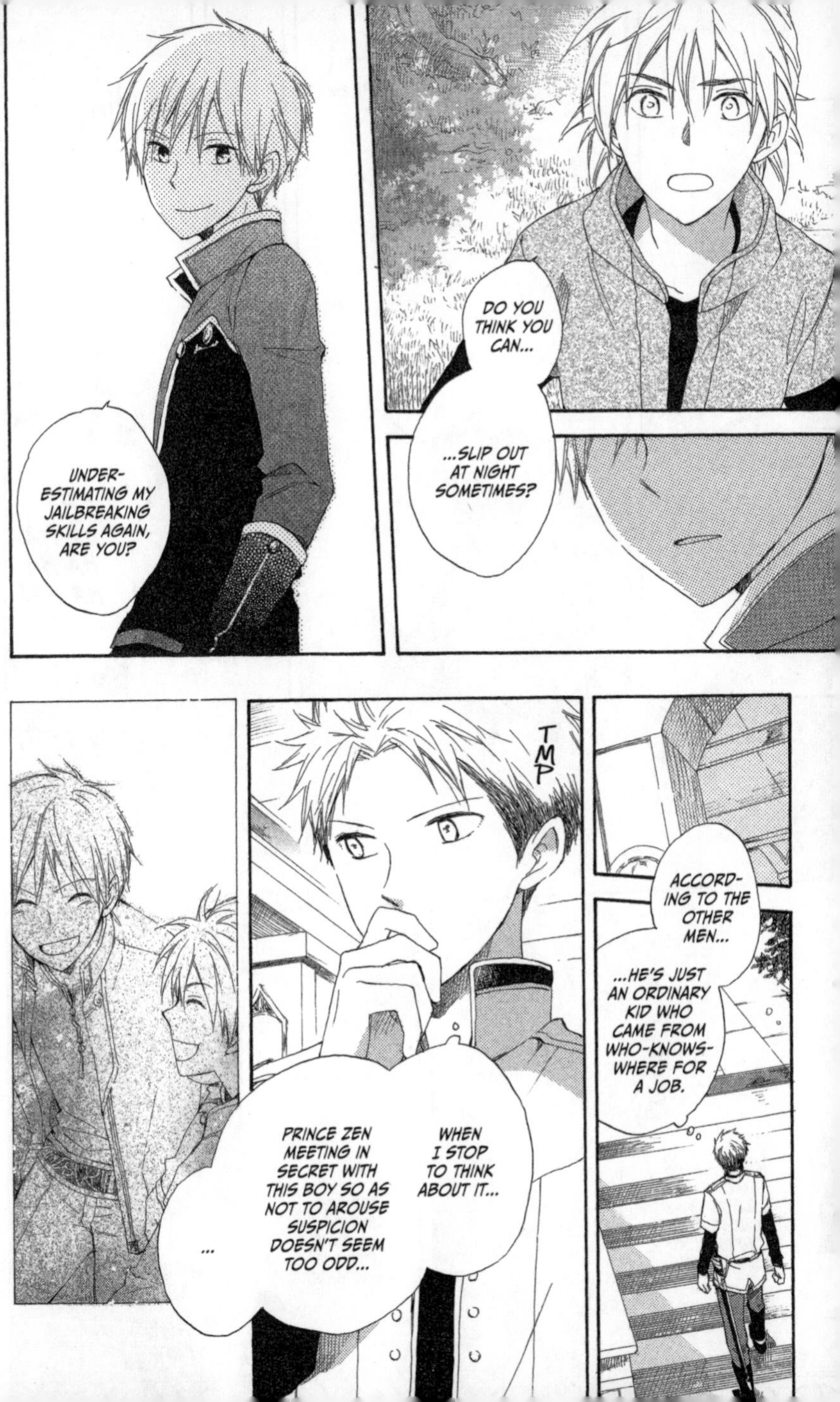
DO YOU THINK YOU CAN...
...SLIP OUT AT NIGHT SOMETIMES?
UNDER-ESTIMATING MY JAILBREAKING SKILLS AGAIN, ARE YOU?
ACCORDING TO THE OTHER MEN...
...HE'S JUST AN ORDINARY KID WHO CAME FROM WHO-KNOWS-WHERE FOR A JOB.
TMP
WHEN I STOP TO THINK ABOUT IT...
PRINCE ZEN MEETING IN SECRET WITH THIS BOY SO AS NOT TO AROUSE SUSPICION DOESN'T SEEM TOO ODD...
...

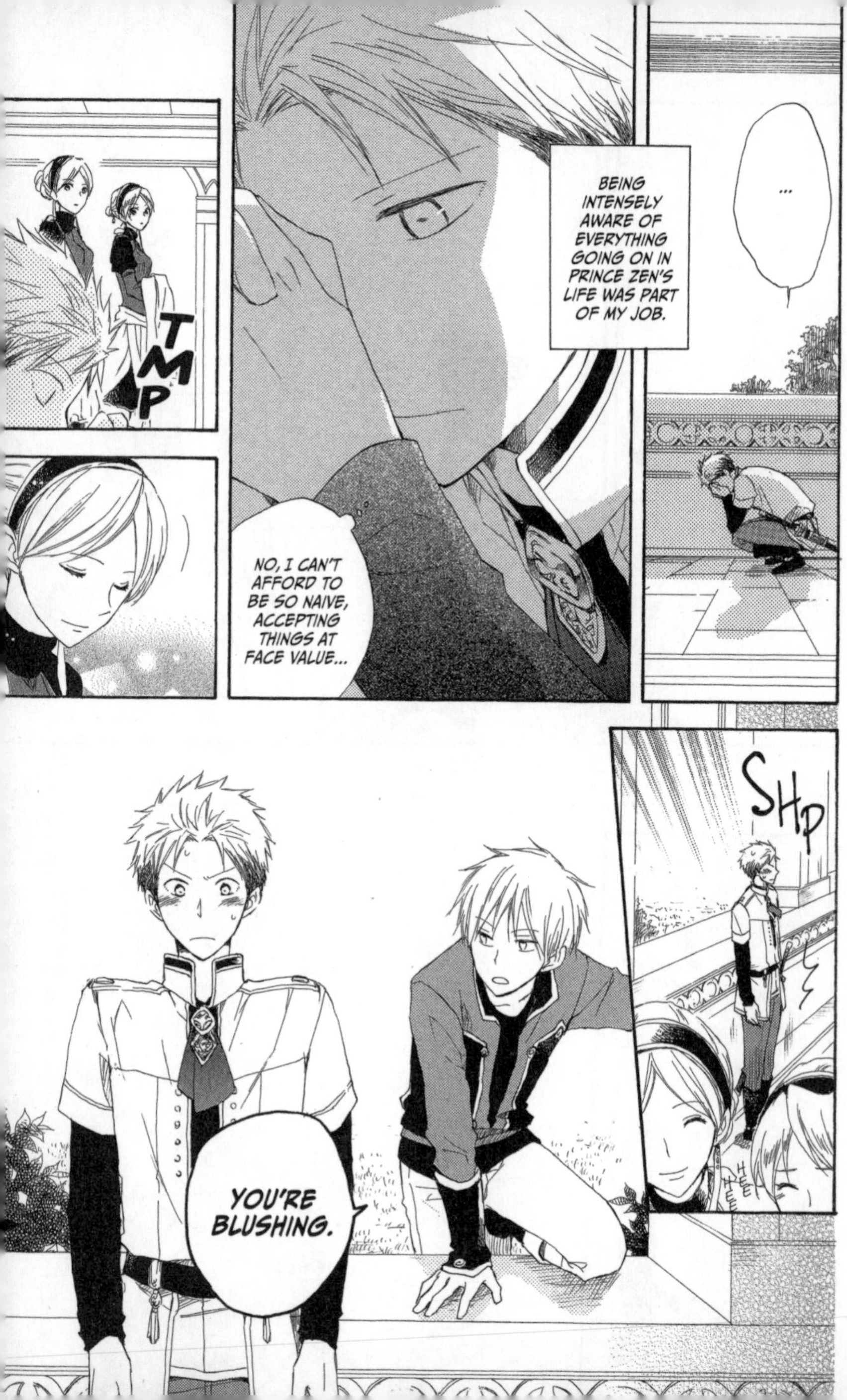
...
BEING INTENSELY AWARE OF EVERYTHING GOING ON IN PRINCE ZEN'S LIFE WAS PART OF MY JOB.
NO, I CAN'T AFFORD TO BE SO NAIVE, ACCEPTING THINGS AT FACE VALUE...
TMP
SHP
HEE HEE
YOU'RE BLUSHING.

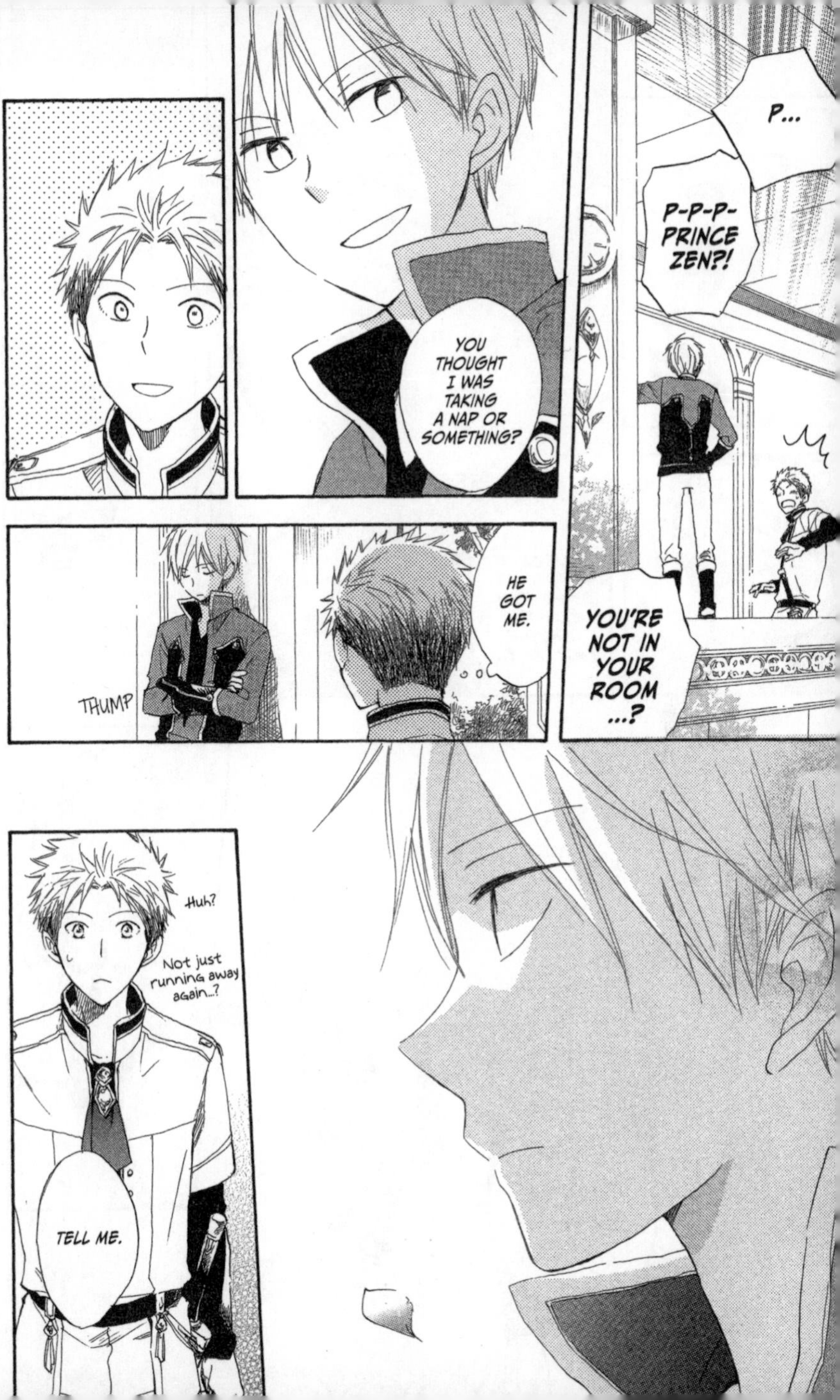
P...
P-P-P-PRINCE ZEN?!
YOU'RE NOT IN YOUR ROOM ...?
YOU THOUGHT I WAS TAKING A NAP OR SOMETHING?
HE GOT ME.
THUMP
Huh?
Not just running away again...?
TELL ME.

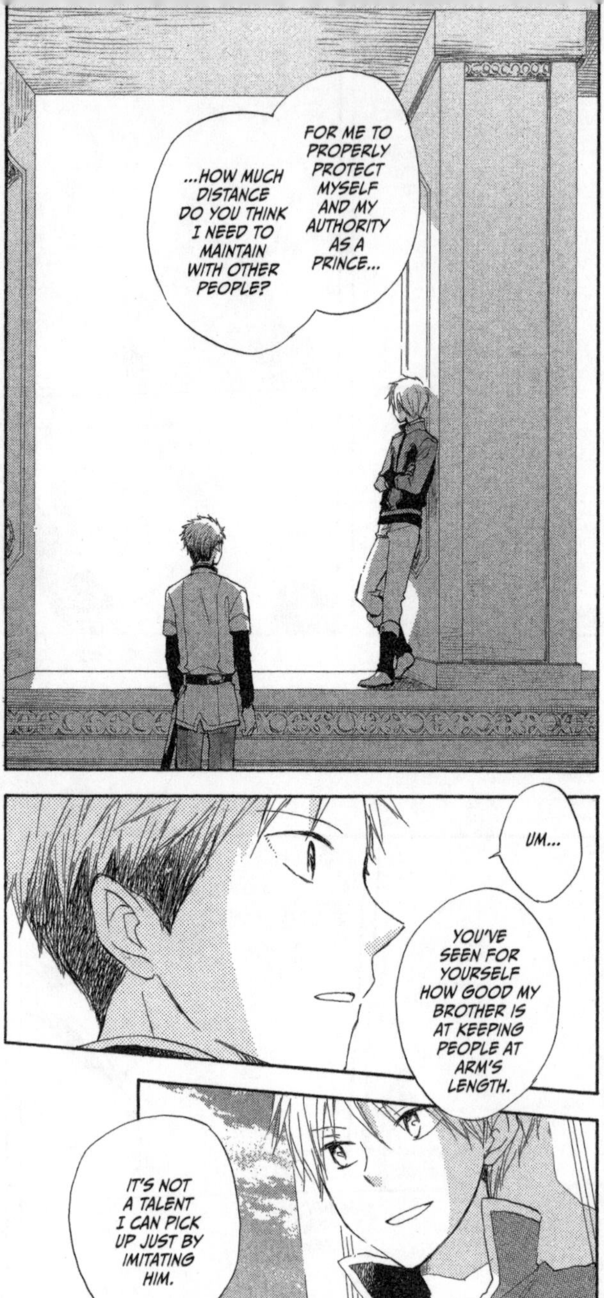
FOR ME TO PROPERLY PROTECT MYSELF AND MY AUTHORITY AS A PRINCE...
...HOW MUCH DISTANCE DO YOU THINK I NEED TO MAINTAIN WITH OTHER PEOPLE?
UM...
YOU'VE SEEN FOR YOURSELF HOW GOOD MY BROTHER IS AT KEEPING PEOPLE AT ARM'S LENGTH.
IT'S NOT A TALENT I CAN PICK UP JUST BY IMITATING HIM.

Going back and reading chapter 1, I realized how lacking in charm Shirayuki and Zen's first encounter is. What a rush of nostalgia.

Like when he smiles and rejects her offer of medicine?

What an attitude!

When I mentioned how Shirayuki's been blushing a lot more lately, my big sister quipped back with,

"It's fine. I bet she'll be plenty pale in the days to come."

How is that fine?

9

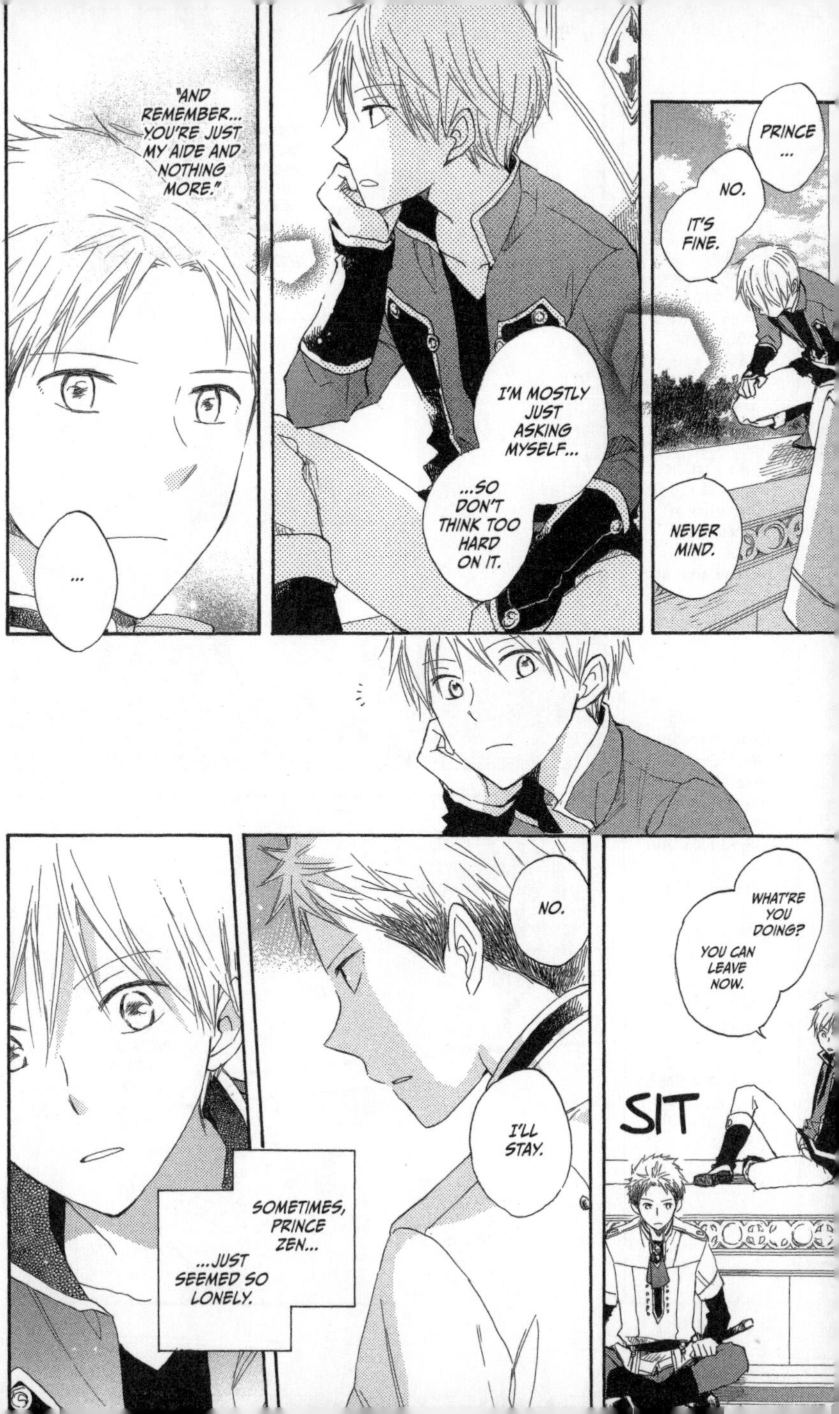
PRINCE...
NO.
IT'S FINE.
NEVER MIND.
I'M MOSTLY JUST ASKING MYSELF...
...SO DON'T THINK TOO HARD ON IT.
"AND REMEMBER... YOU'RE JUST MY AIDE AND NOTHING MORE."
...
WHAT'RE YOU DOING?
YOU CAN LEAVE NOW.
SIT
NO.
I'LL STAY.
SOMETIMES, PRINCE ZEN...
...JUST SEEMED SO LONELY.

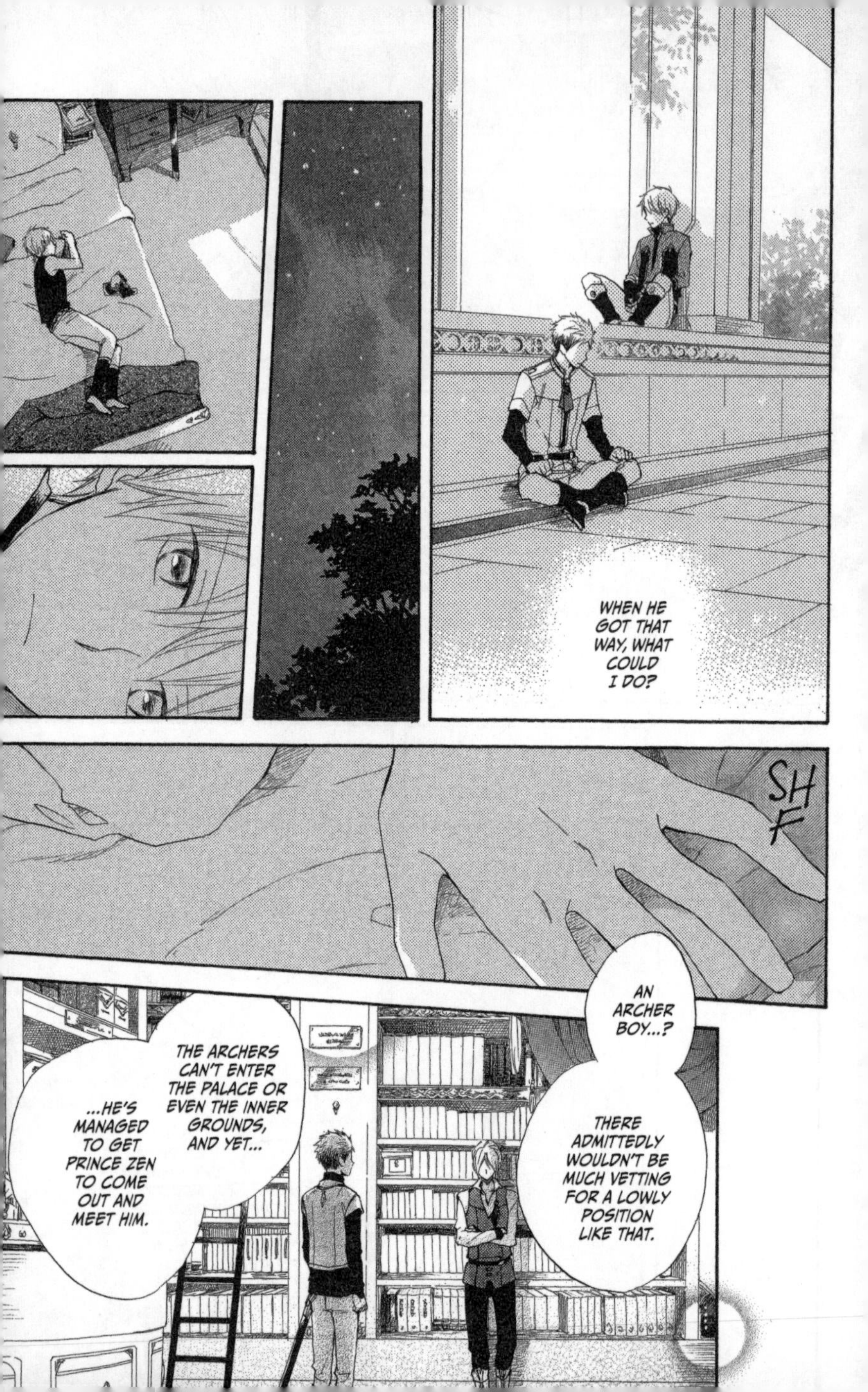
WHEN HE GOT THAT WAY, WHAT COULD I DO?
SHF
AN ARCHER BOY...?
THERE ADMITTEDLY WOULDN'T BE MUCH VETTING FOR A LOWLY POSITION LIKE THAT.
THE ARCHERS CAN'T ENTER THE PALACE OR EVEN THE INNER GROUNDS, AND YET...
...HE'S MANAGED TO GET PRINCE ZEN TO COME OUT AND MEET HIM.

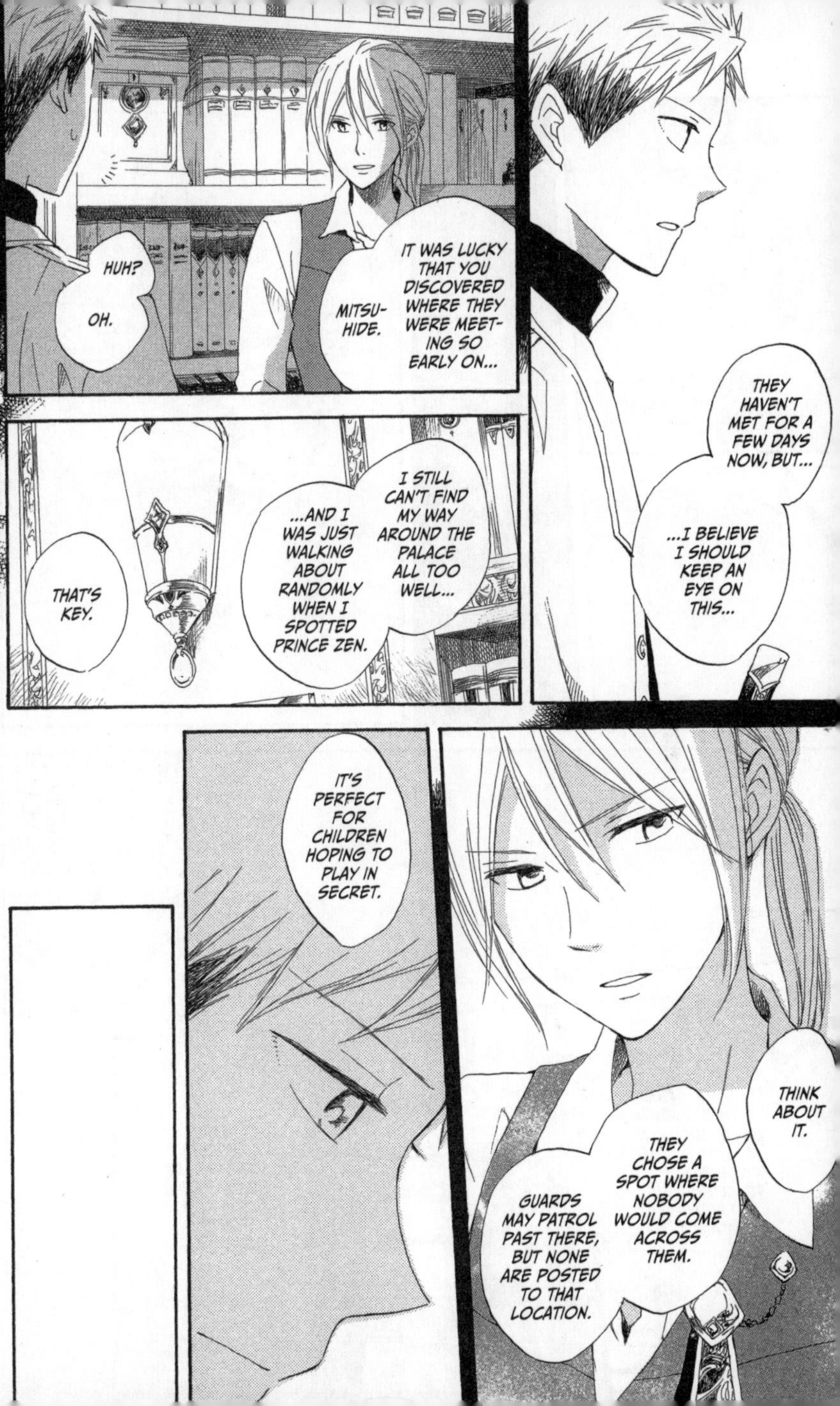
THEY HAVEN'T MET FOR A FEW DAYS NOW, BUT...
...I BELIEVE I SHOULD KEEP AN EYE ON THIS...
IT WAS LUCKY THAT YOU DISCOVERED WHERE THEY WERE MEET-ING SO EARLY ON...
MITSU-HIDE.
HUH?
OH.
I STILL CAN'T FIND MY WAY AROUND THE PALACE ALL TOO WELL...
...AND I WAS JUST WALKING ABOUT RANDOMLY WHEN I SPOTTED PRINCE ZEN.
THAT'S KEY.
THINK ABOUT IT.
THEY CHOSE A SPOT WHERE NOBODY WOULD COME ACROSS THEM.
GUARDS MAY PATROL PAST THERE, BUT NONE ARE POSTED TO THAT LOCATION.
IT'S PERFECT FOR CHILDREN HOPING TO PLAY IN SECRET.

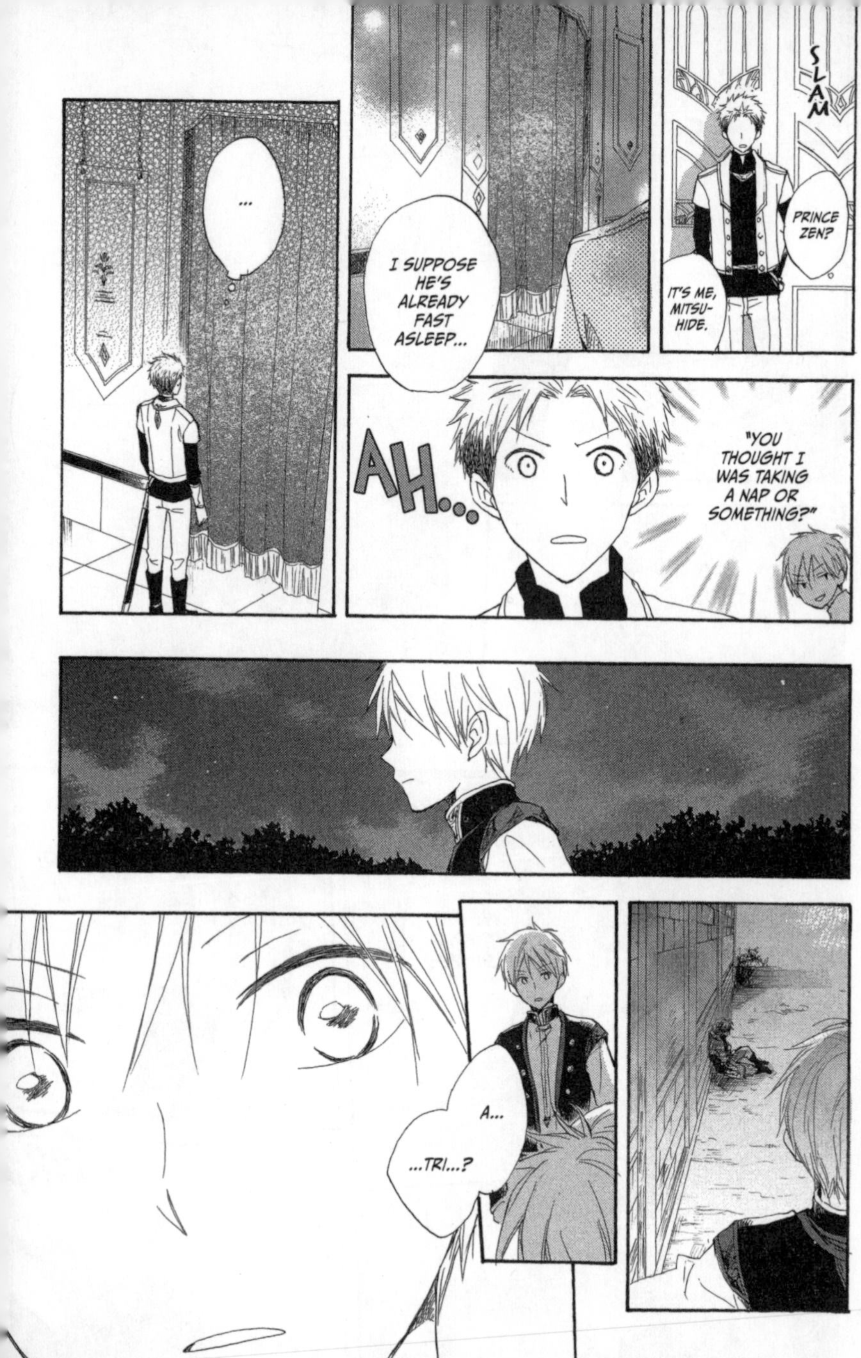
SLAM
PRINCE ZEN?
IT'S ME, MITSUHIDE.
I SUPPOSE HE'S ALREADY FAST ASLEEP...
"YOU THOUGHT I WAS TAKING A NAP OR SOMETHING?"
AH...
...
A...
...TRI...?

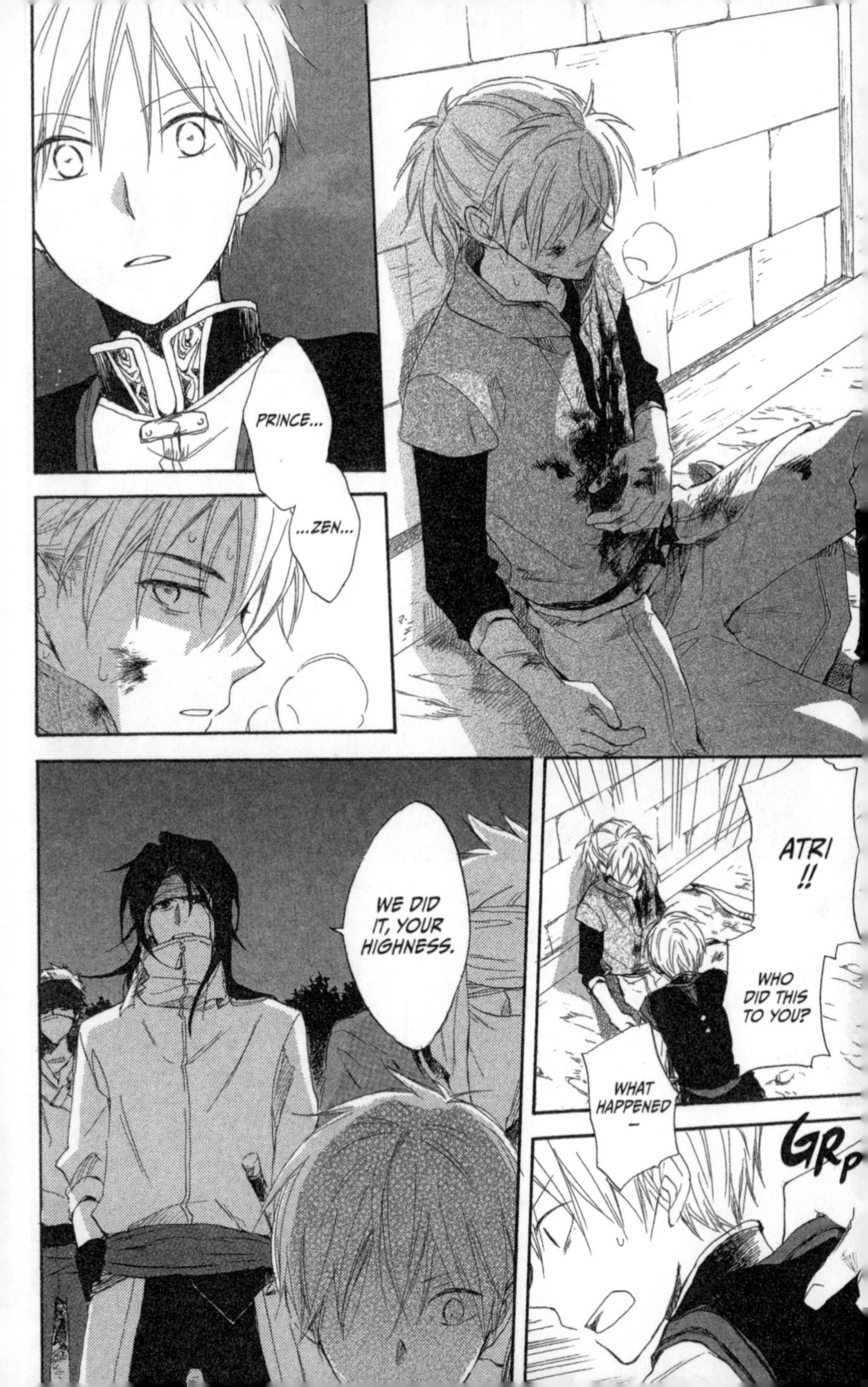
PRINCE...
...ZEN...
ATRI !!
WHO DID THIS TO YOU?
WHAT HAPPENED —
GRP
WE DID IT, YOUR HIGHNESS.

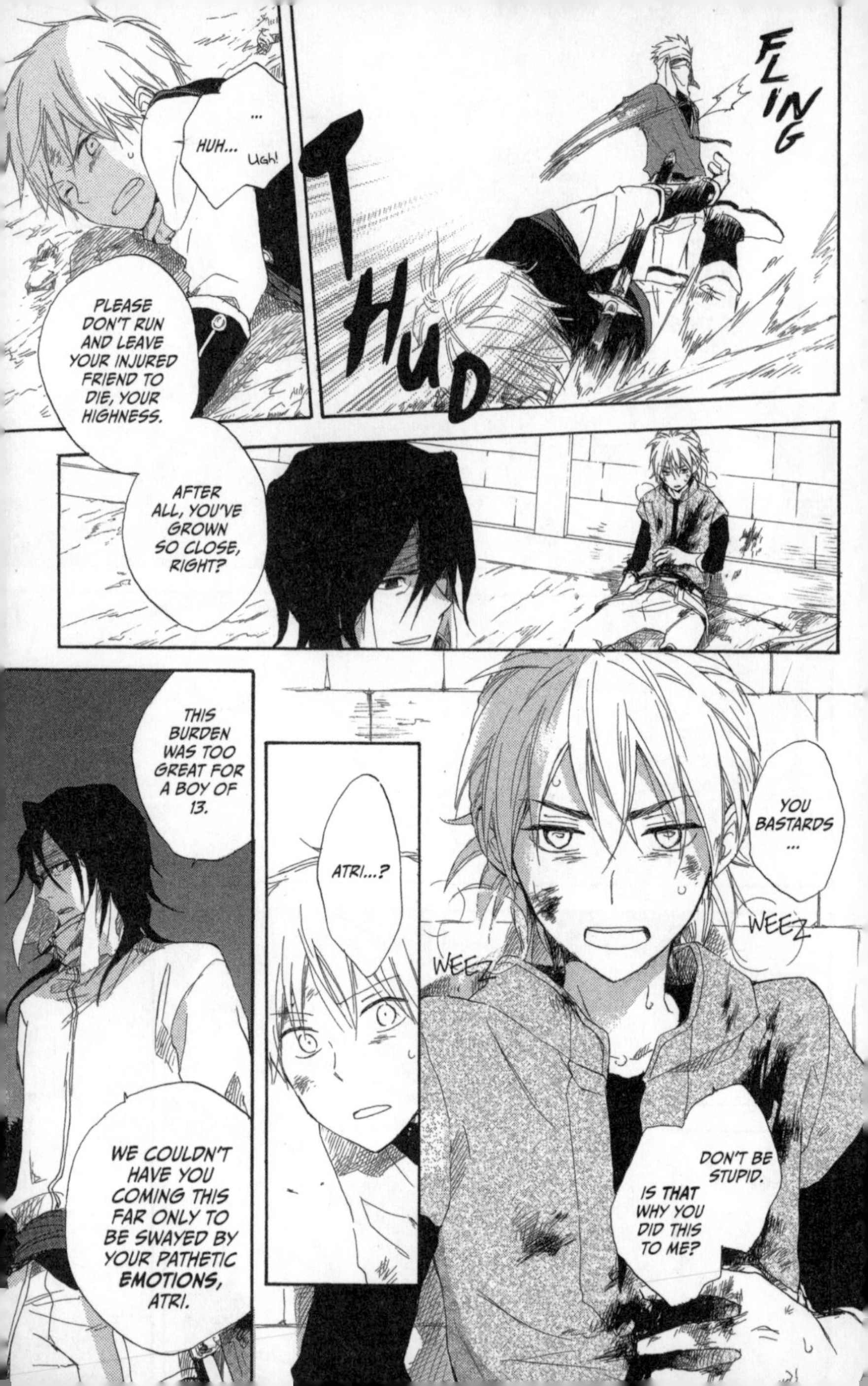
FLING
THUD
...
HUH...
Ugh!
PLEASE DON'T RUN AND LEAVE YOUR INJURED FRIEND TO DIE, YOUR HIGHNESS.
AFTER ALL, YOU'VE GROWN SO CLOSE, RIGHT?
YOU BASTARDS ...
WEEZ
WEEZ
DON'T BE STUPID.
IS THAT WHY YOU DID THIS TO ME?
ATRI...?
THIS BURDEN WAS TOO GREAT FOR A BOY OF 13.
WE COULDN'T HAVE YOU COMING THIS FAR ONLY TO BE SWAYED BY YOUR PATHETIC EMOTIONS, ATRI.

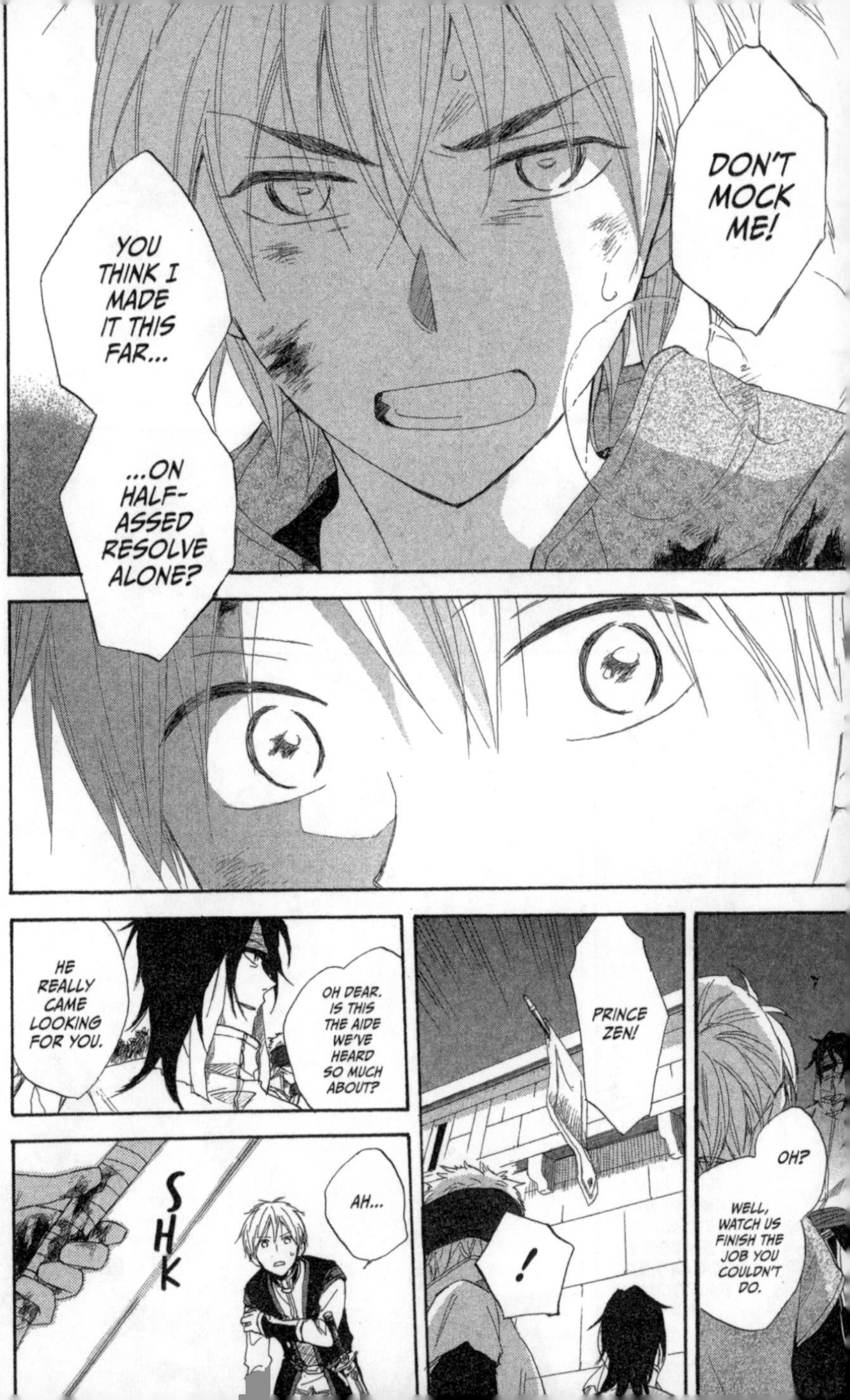
DON'T MOCK ME!
YOU THINK I MADE IT THIS FAR...
...ON HALF-ASSED RESOLVE ALONE?
OH?
WELL, WATCH US FINISH THE JOB YOU COULDN'T DO.
PRINCE ZEN!
!
OH DEAR. IS THIS THE AIDE WE'VE HEARD SO MUCH ABOUT?
HE REALLY CAME LOOKING FOR YOU.
AH...
SHK

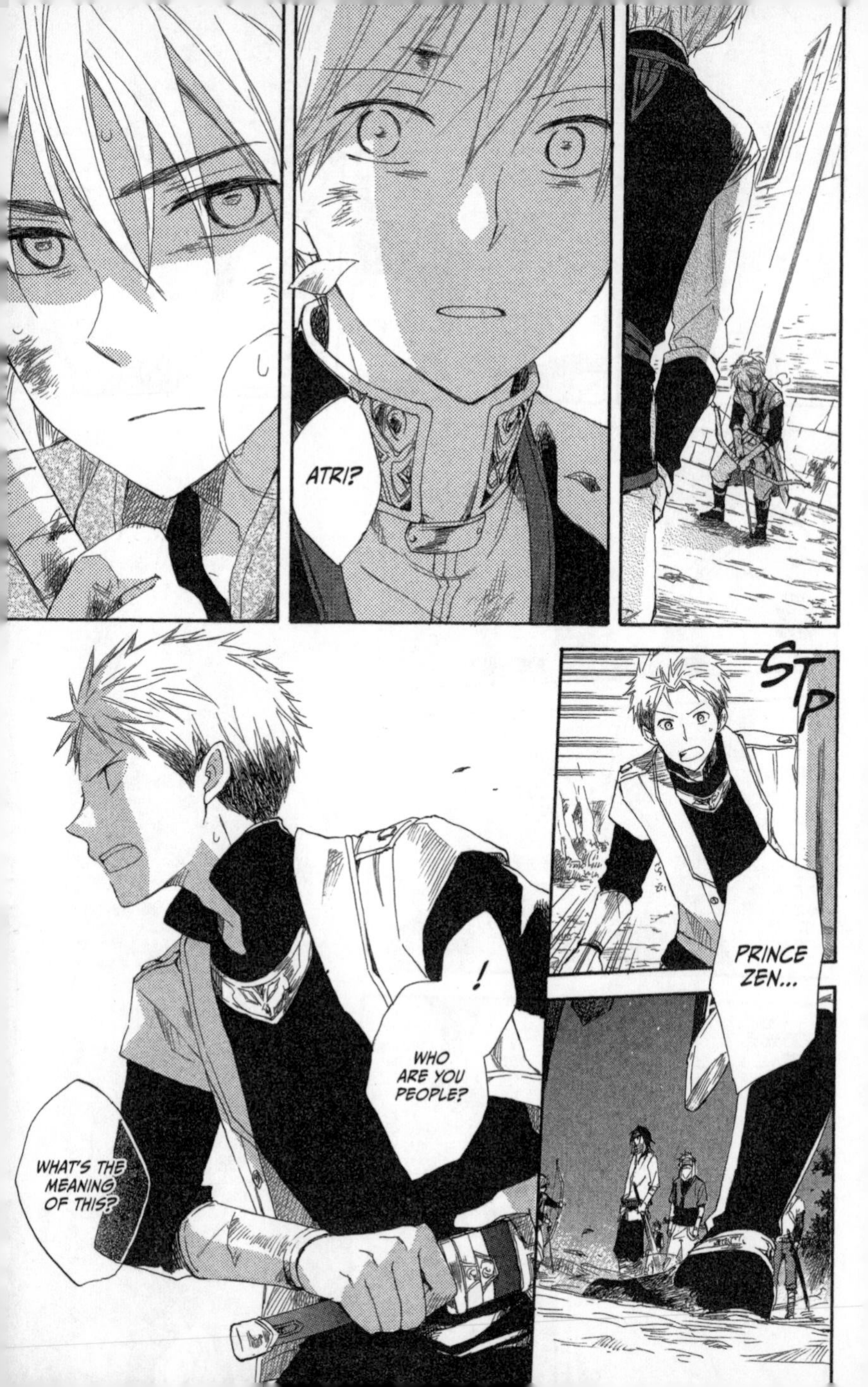
ATRI?
STP
PRINCE ZEN...
!
WHO ARE YOU PEOPLE?
WHAT'S THE MEANING OF THIS?

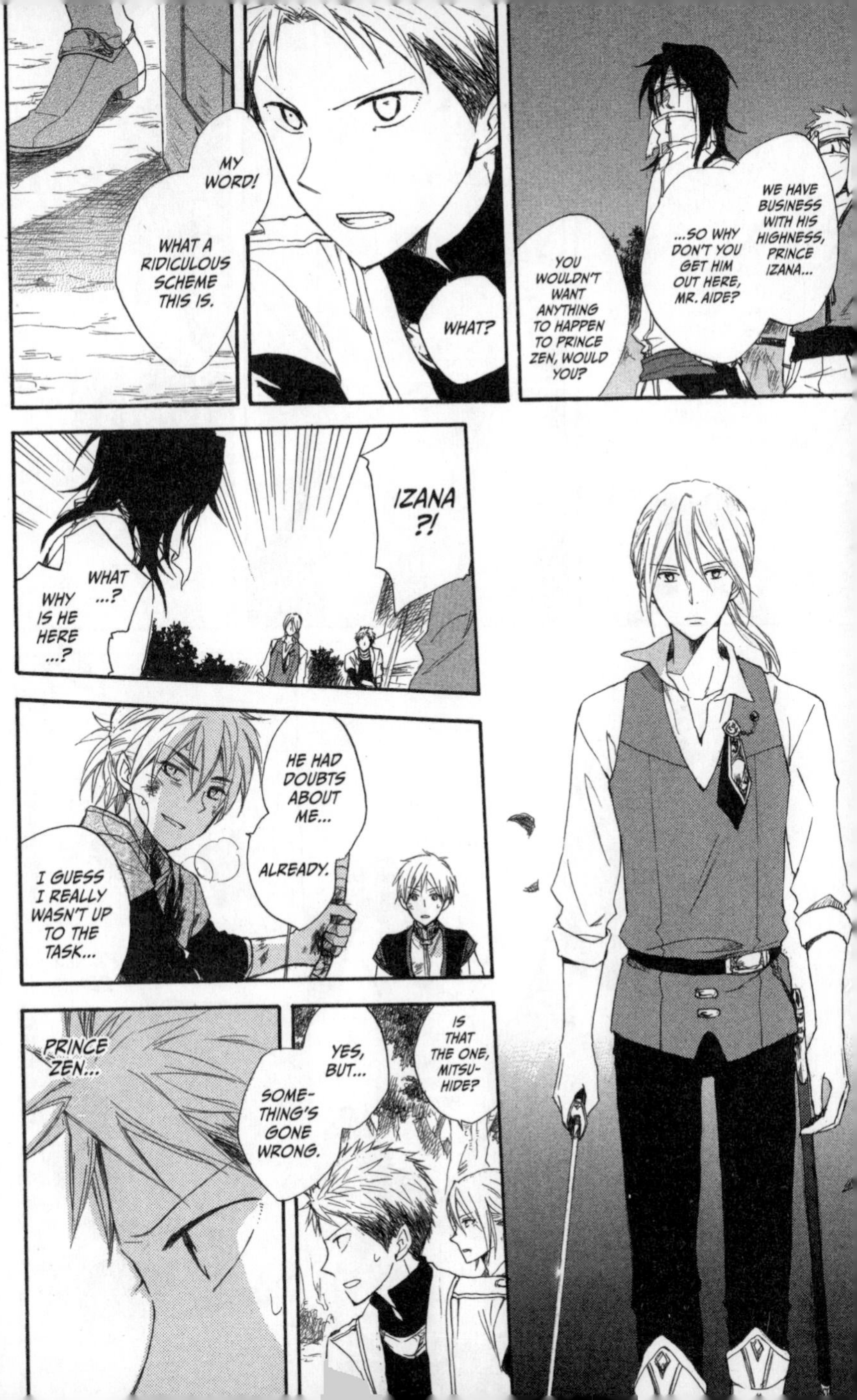
WE HAVE BUSINESS WITH HIS HIGHNESS, PRINCE IZANA...
...SO WHY DON'T YOU GET HIM OUT HERE, MR. AIDE?
YOU WOULDN'T WANT ANYTHING TO HAPPEN TO PRINCE ZEN, WOULD YOU?
WHAT?
MY WORD!
WHAT A RIDICULOUS SCHEME THIS IS.
IZANA ?!
WHAT ...?
WHY IS HE HERE ...?
HE HAD DOUBTS ABOUT ME...
ALREADY.
I GUESS I REALLY WASN'T UP TO THE TASK...
IS THAT THE ONE, MITSU-HIDE?
YES, BUT...
SOME-THING'S GONE WRONG.
PRINCE ZEN...

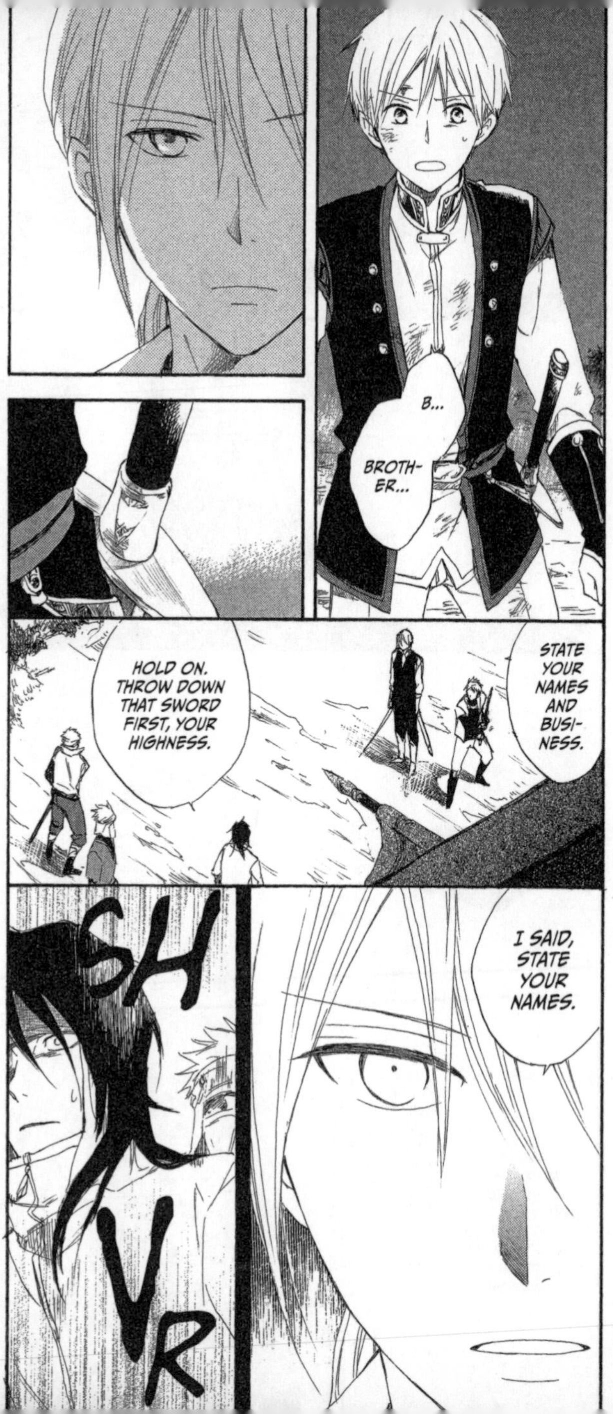
B...
BROTHER-ER...
STATE YOUR NAMES AND BUSI-NESS.
HOLD ON. THROW DOWN THAT SWORD FIRST, YOUR HIGHNESS.
I SAID, STATE YOUR NAMES.
SHVR

I got a fan letter asking, "Will there be a character with glasses in *Snow White with the Red Hair?*" and it got me thinking...

Maybe they don't have glasses in this world? No, wait, they totally do!

In fantasy settings, characters who wear glasses always have a hidden side to them. They may look friendly, but don't be fooled... Or something like that.

Does that mean I'm bound to have a character like that eventually, with a hidden dark side?! Seems likely.

But now I'm in a bind.

Fine, if I do have a character with glasses, they'll actually be good!

But still, don't be fooled!

Now I'm just confusing myself.

10

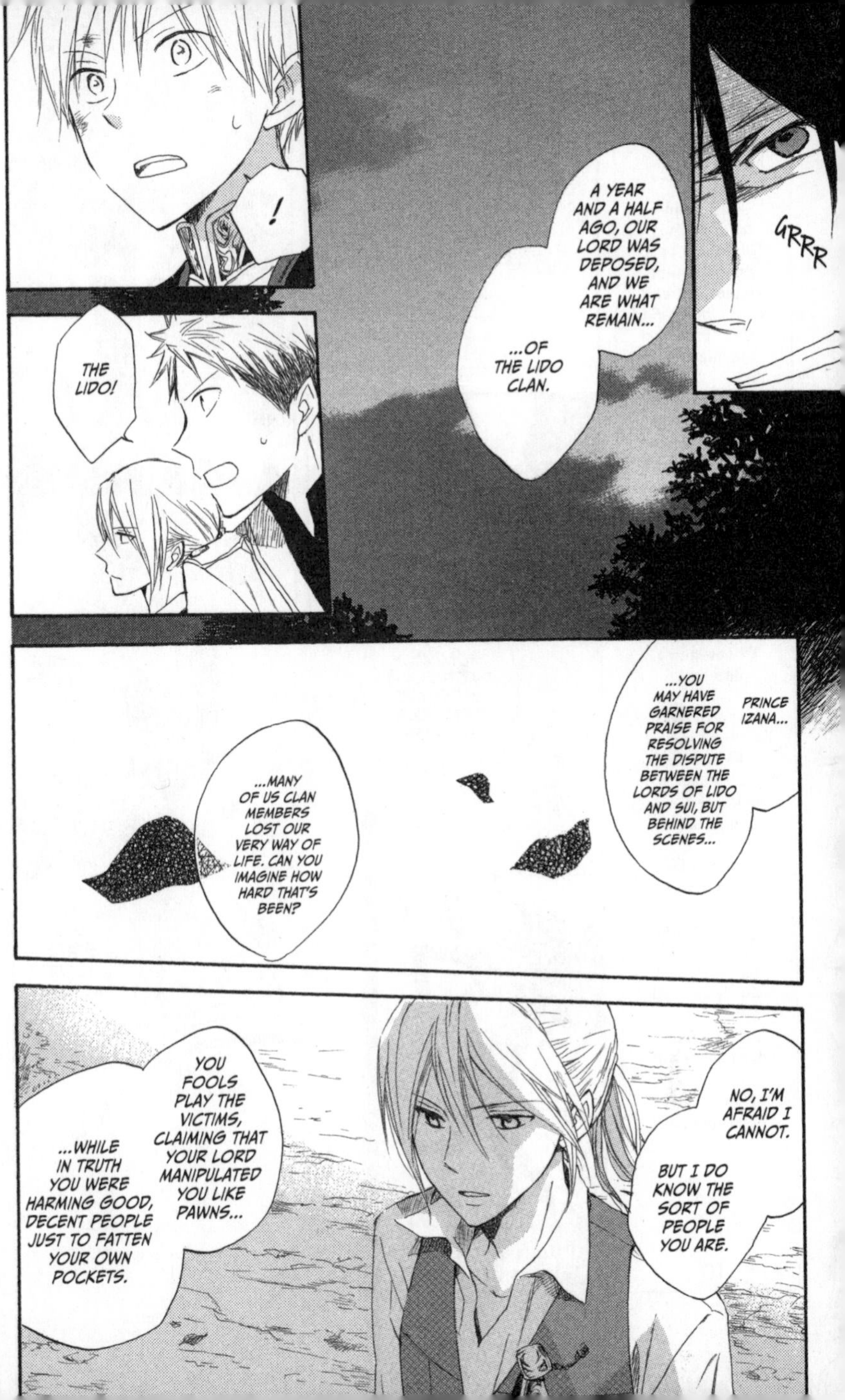
GRRR
A YEAR AND A HALF AGO, OUR LORD WAS DEPOSED, AND WE ARE WHAT REMAIN...
...OF THE LIDO CLAN.
!
THE LIDO!
PRINCE IZANA...
...YOU MAY HAVE GARNERED PRAISE FOR RESOLVING THE DISPUTE BETWEEN THE LORDS OF LIDO AND SUI, BUT BEHIND THE SCENES...
...MANY OF US CLAN MEMBERS LOST OUR VERY WAY OF LIFE. CAN YOU IMAGINE HOW HARD THAT'S BEEN?
NO, I'M AFRAID I CANNOT.
BUT I DO KNOW THE SORT OF PEOPLE YOU ARE.
YOU FOOLS PLAY THE VICTIMS, CLAIMING THAT YOUR LORD MANIPULATED YOU LIKE PAWNS...
...WHILE IN TRUTH YOU WERE HARMING GOOD, DECENT PEOPLE JUST TO FATTEN YOUR OWN POCKETS.

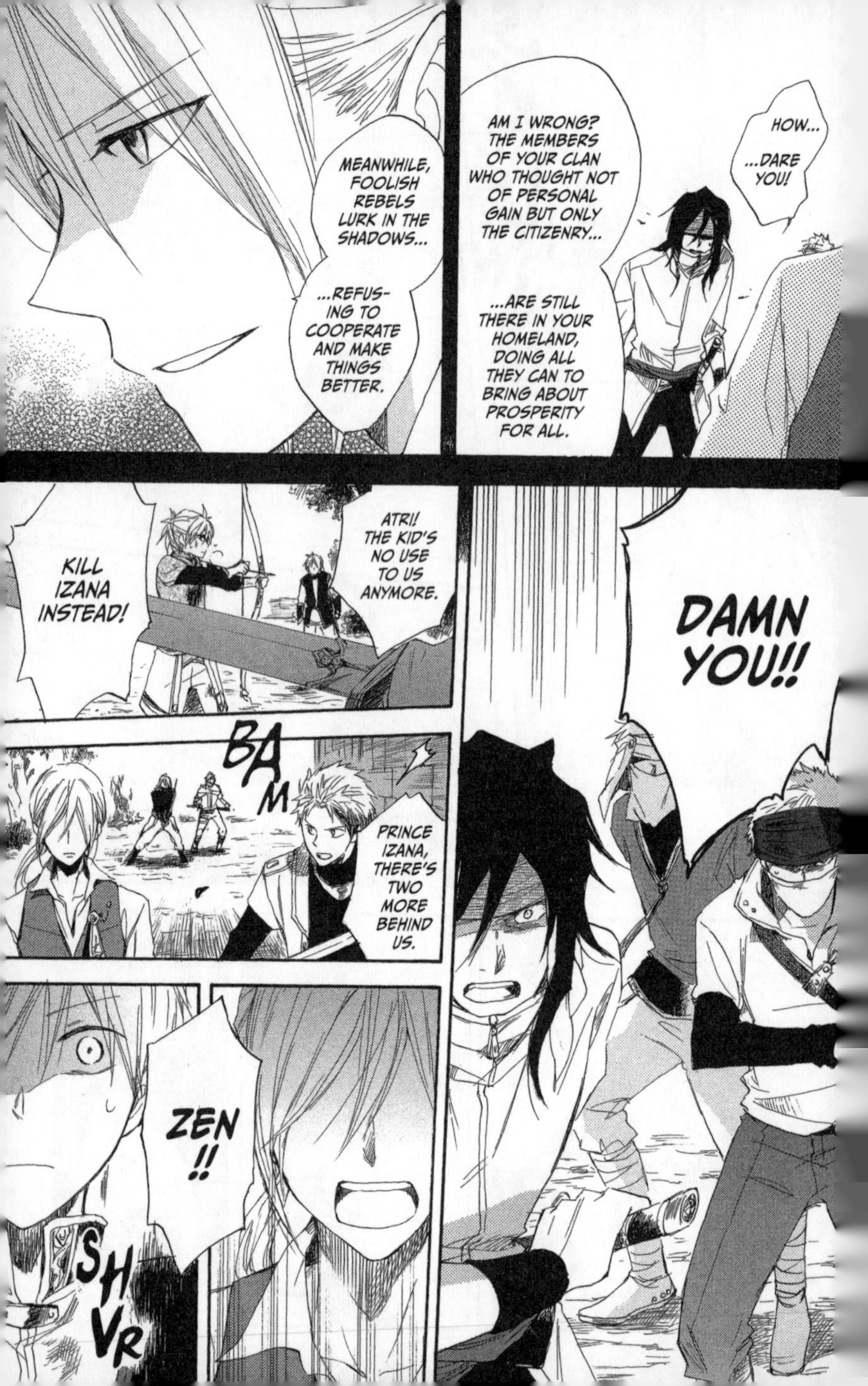
HOW...
...DARE YOU!
AM I WRONG? THE MEMBERS OF YOUR CLAN WHO THOUGHT NOT OF PERSONAL GAIN BUT ONLY THE CITIZENRY...
...ARE STILL THERE IN YOUR HOMELAND, DOING ALL THEY CAN TO BRING ABOUT PROSPERITY FOR ALL.
MEANWHILE, FOOLISH REBELS LURK IN THE SHADOWS...
...REFUS-ING TO COOPERATE AND MAKE THINGS BETTER.
DAMN YOU!!
ATRI! THE KID'S NO USE TO US ANYMORE.
KILL IZANA INSTEAD!
BAM
PRINCE IZANA, THERE'S TWO MORE BEHIND US.
ZEN!!
SHVR

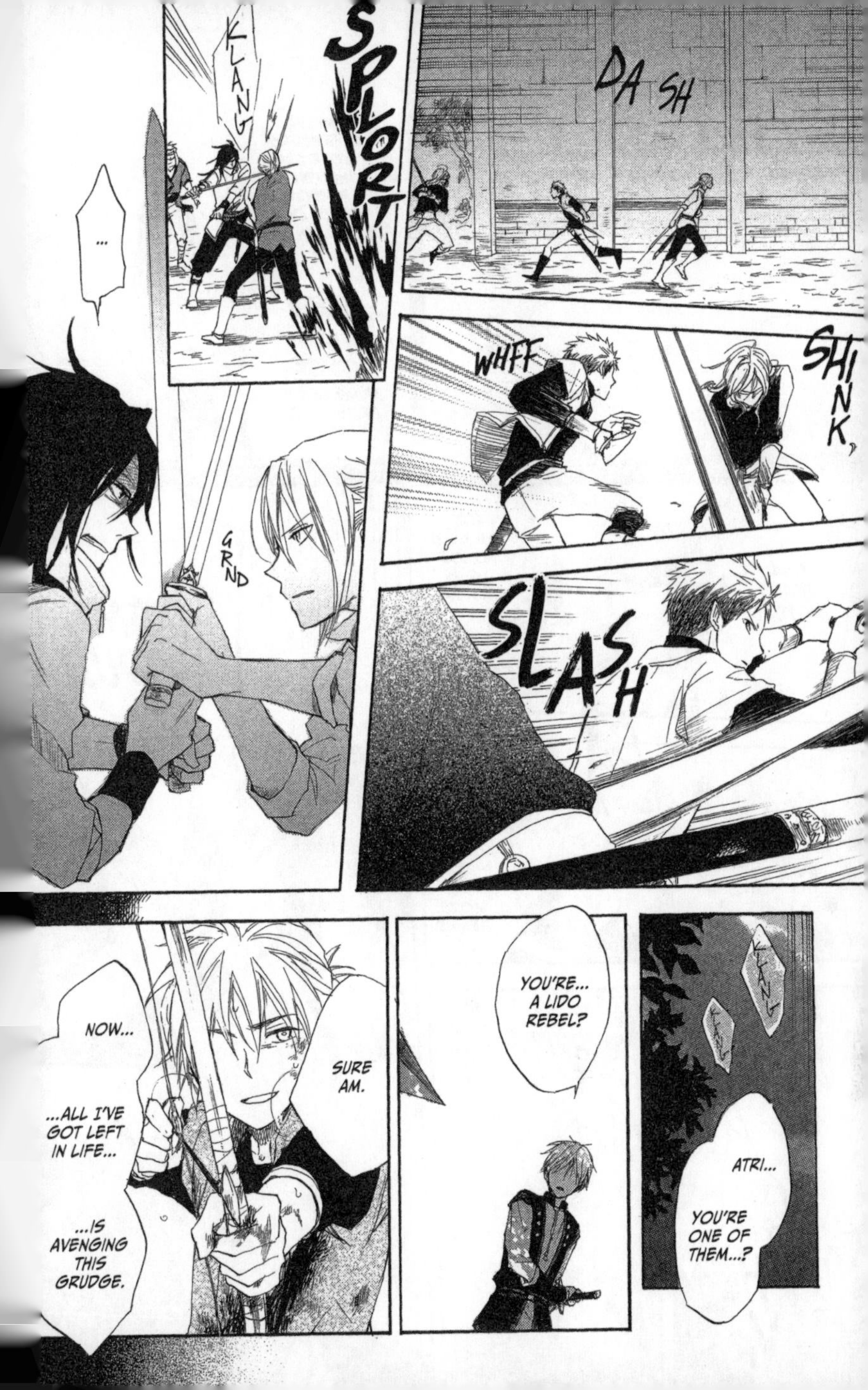
DASH
SPLORT
KLANG
SHINK,
WHFF
SLASH
...
GRND
KLANG
KLANG
ATRI...
YOU'RE ONE OF THEM...?
YOU'RE... A LIDO REBEL?
SURE AM.
NOW...
...ALL I'VE GOT LEFT IN LIFE...
...IS AVENGING THIS GRUDGE.

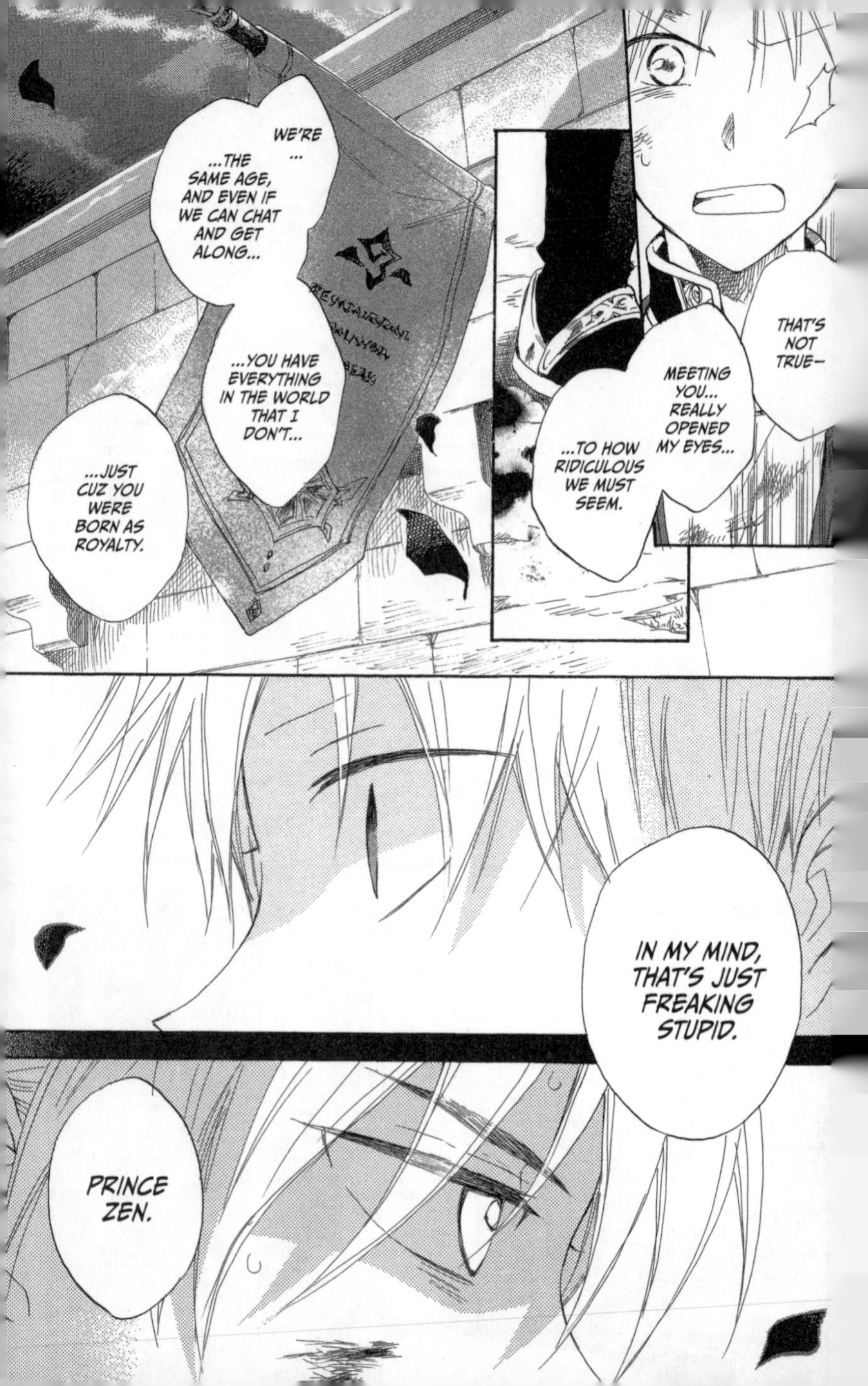
THAT'S NOT TRUE—
MEETING YOU... REALLY OPENED MY EYES...
...TO HOW RIDICULOUS WE MUST SEEM.
WE'RE...
...THE SAME AGE, AND EVEN IF WE CAN CHAT AND GET ALONG...
...YOU HAVE EVERYTHING IN THE WORLD THAT I DON'T...
...JUST CUZ YOU WERE BORN AS ROYALTY.
IN MY MIND, THAT'S JUST FREAKING STUPID.
PRINCE ZEN.

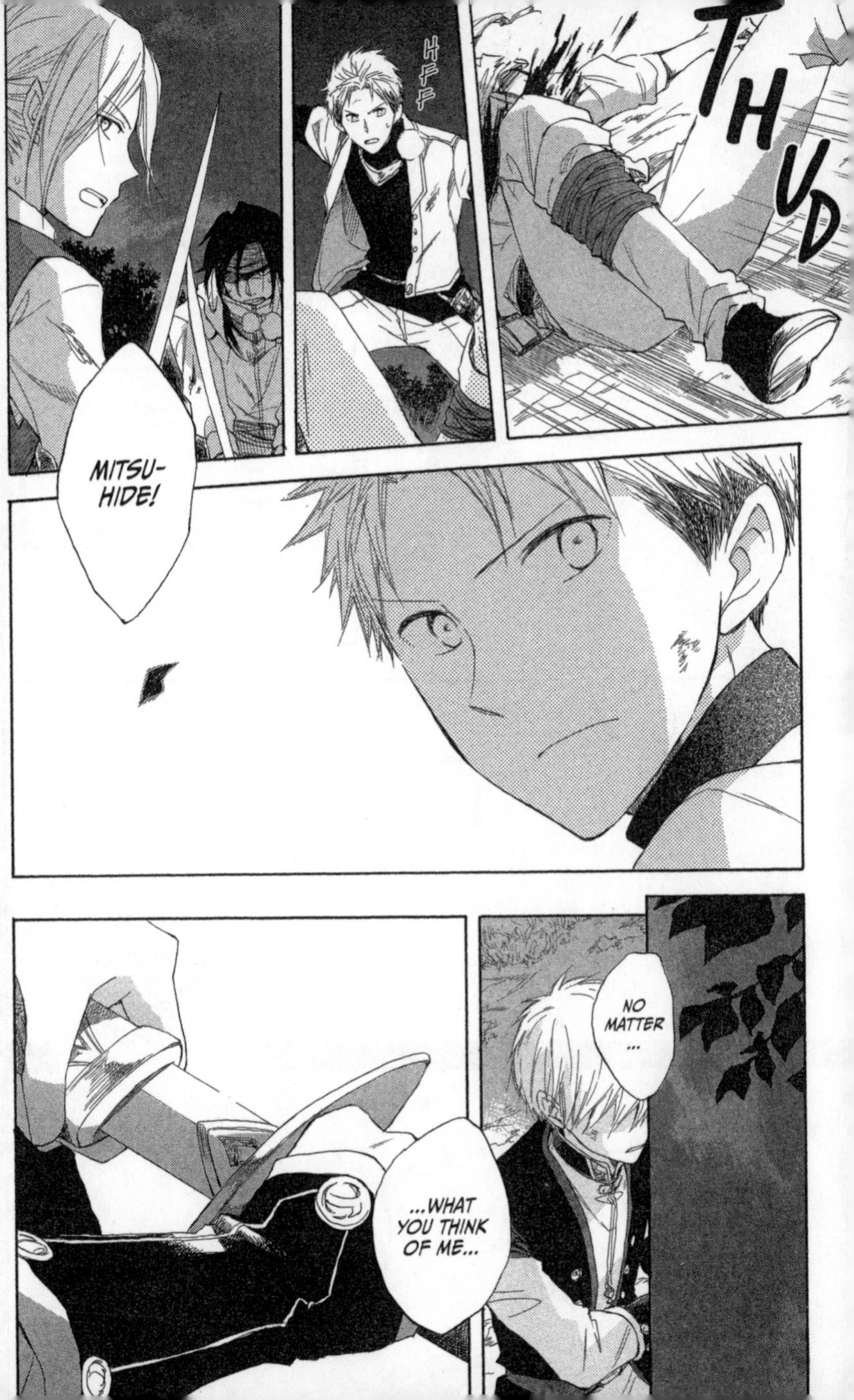
THUD
HFF
MITSU-HIDE!
NO MATTER...
...WHAT YOU THINK OF ME...

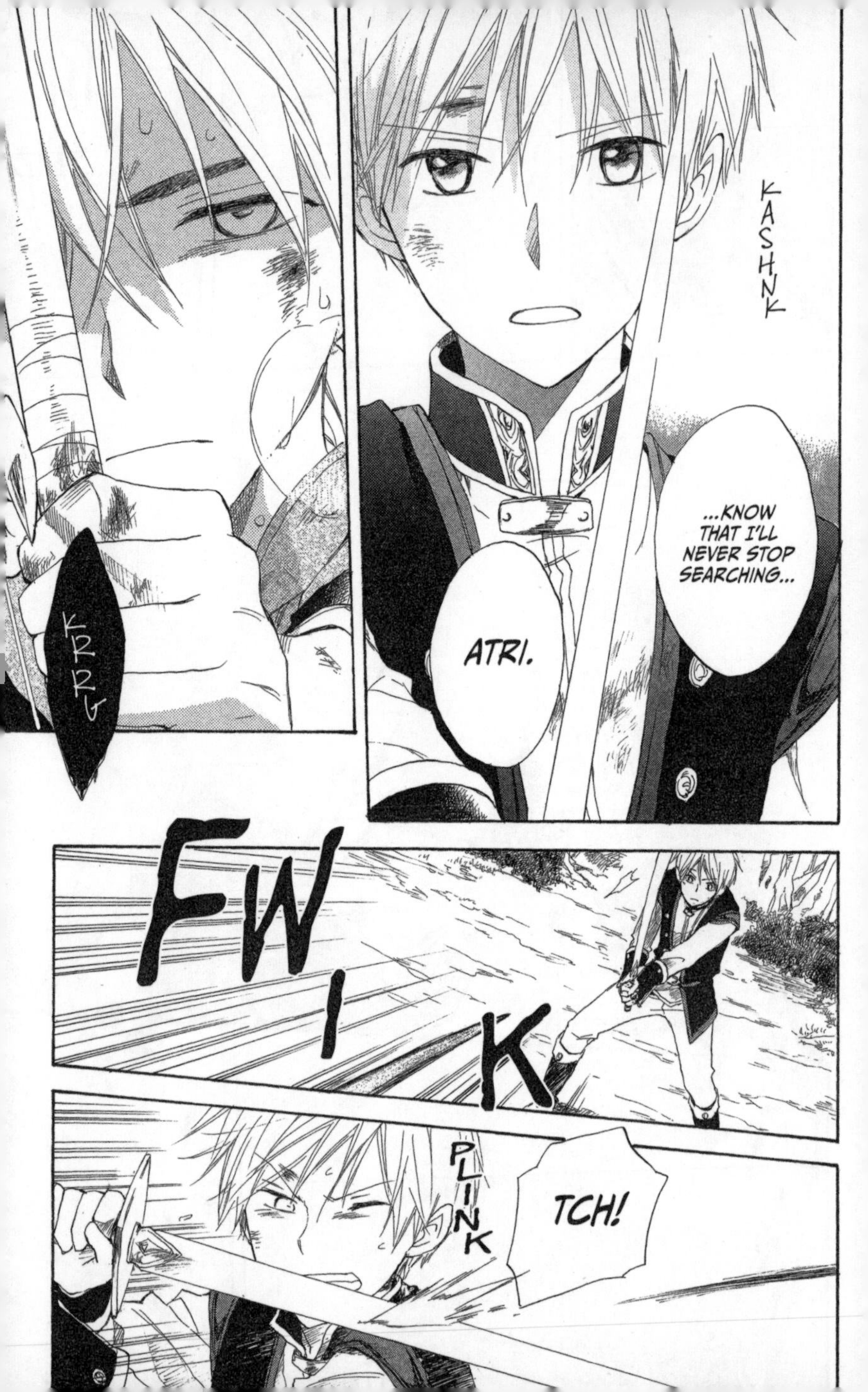
KASHNK
...KNOW THAT I'LL NEVER STOP SEARCHING...
ATRI.
KRRU
FWIK
PLINK
TCH!

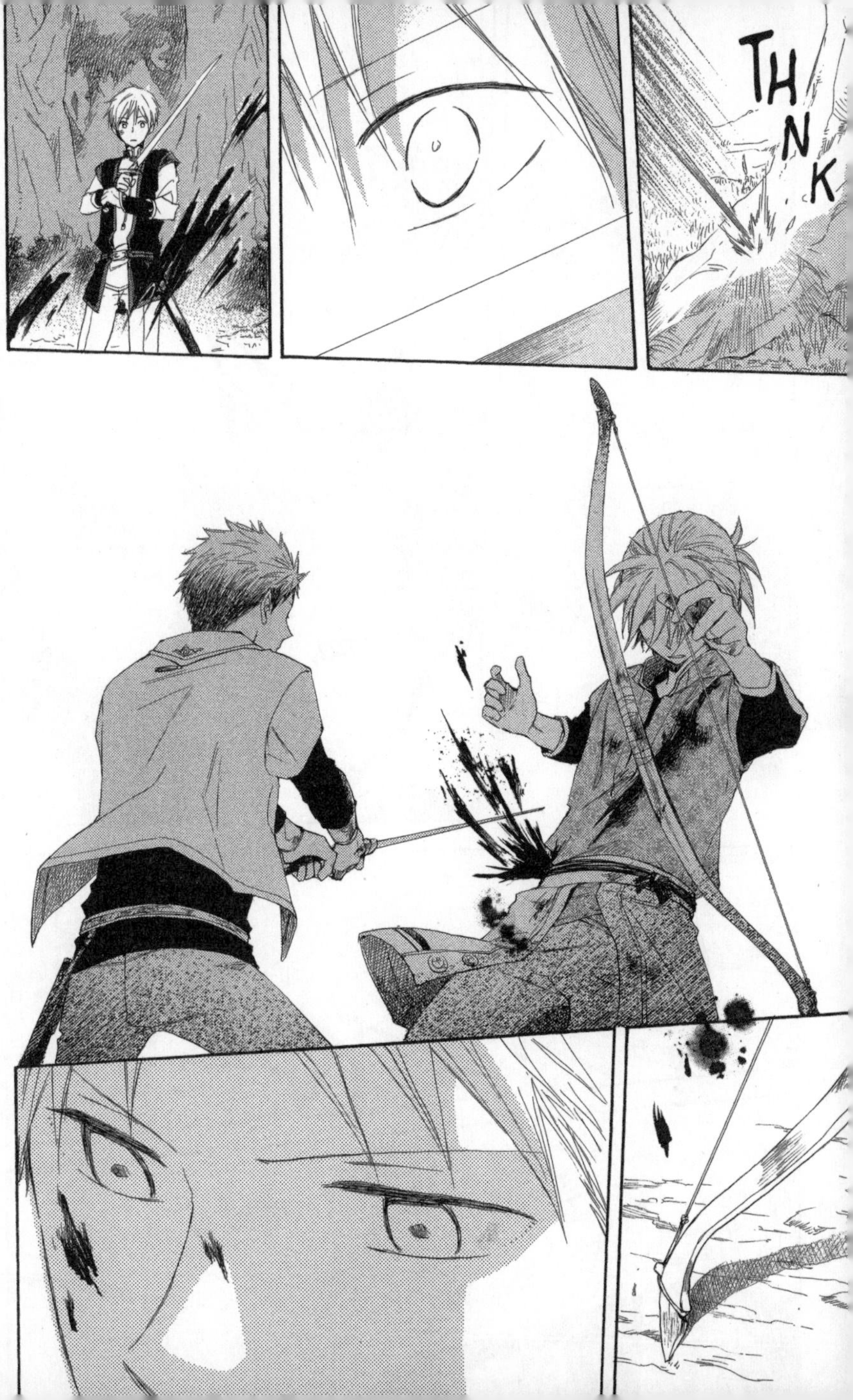
THNK

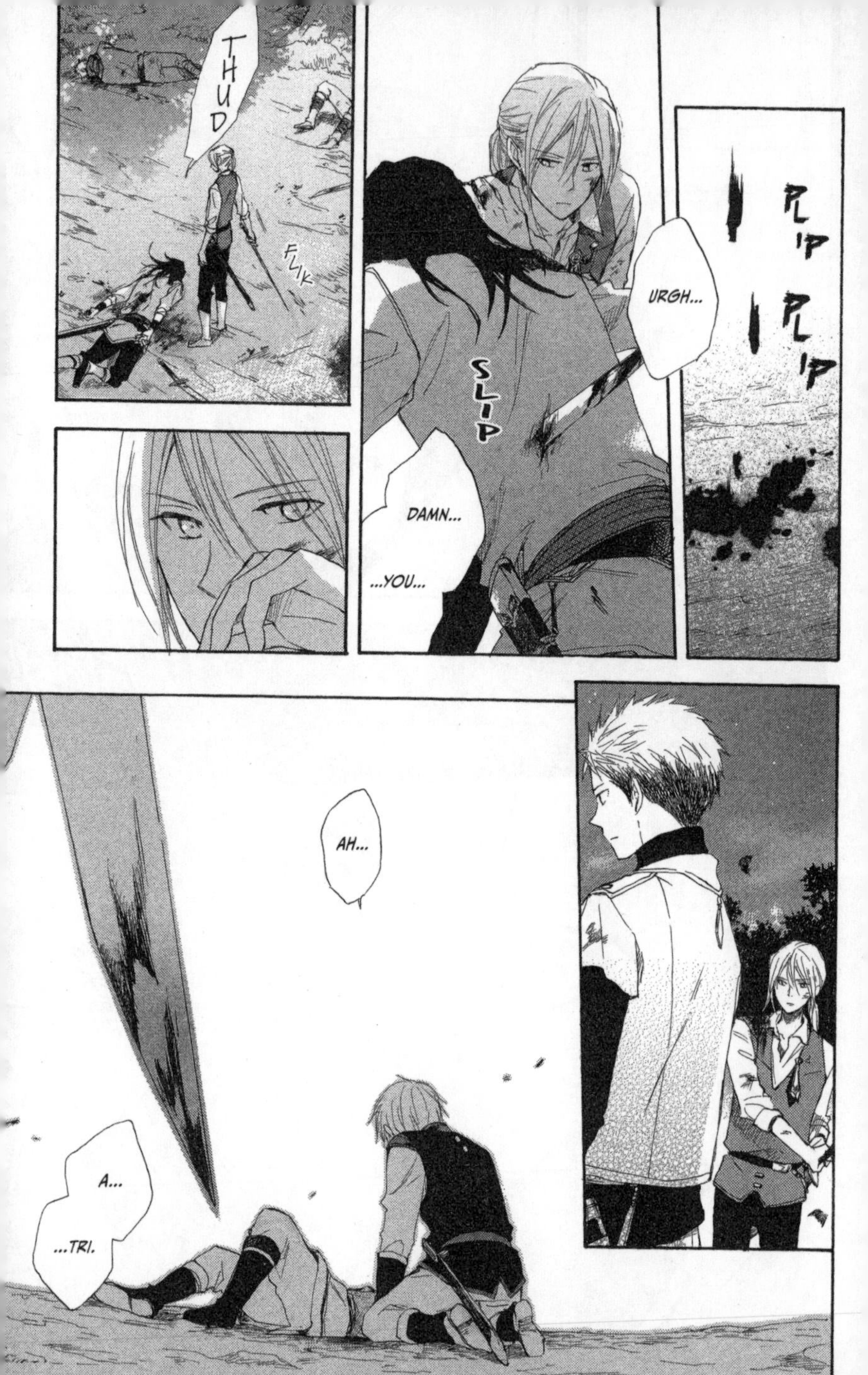
PLIP
PLIP
URGH...
SLIP
DAMN...
...YOU...
THUD
FLIK
AH...
A...
...TRI.

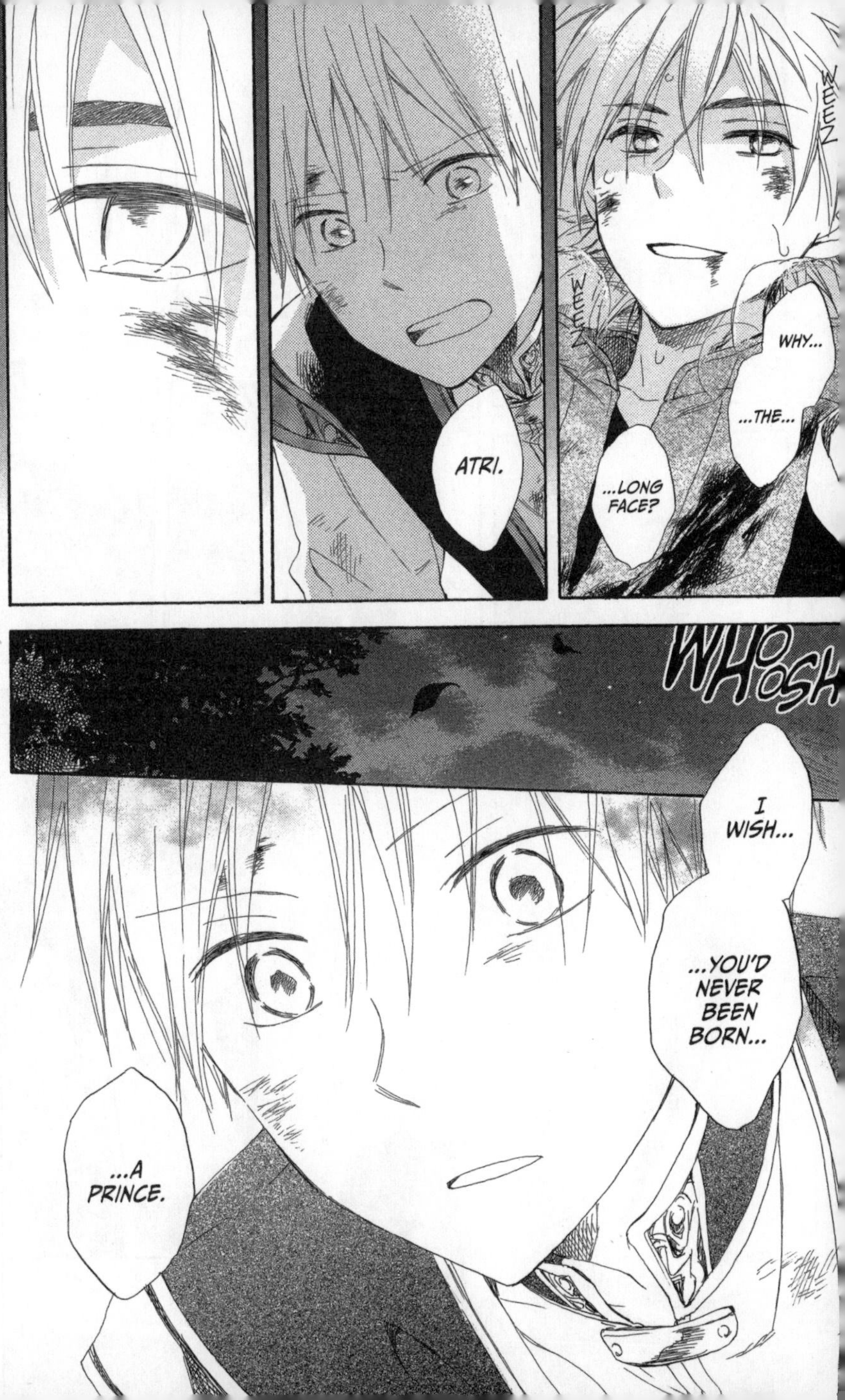
WEEZ
WEEZ
WHY...
...THE...
...LONG FACE?
ATRI.
WHOOSH
I WISH...
...YOU'D NEVER BEEN BORN...
...A PRINCE.

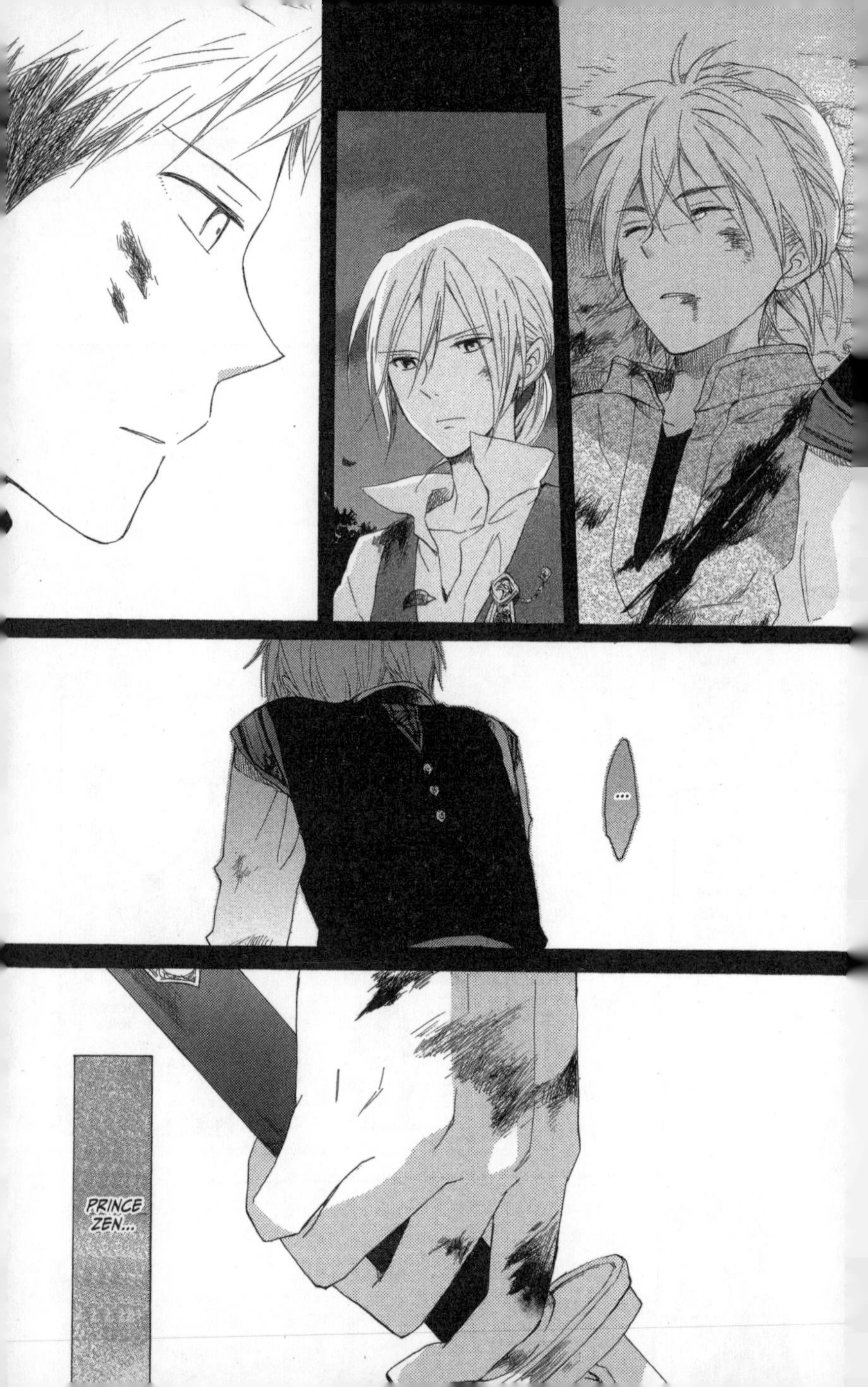
...
PRINCE ZEN...

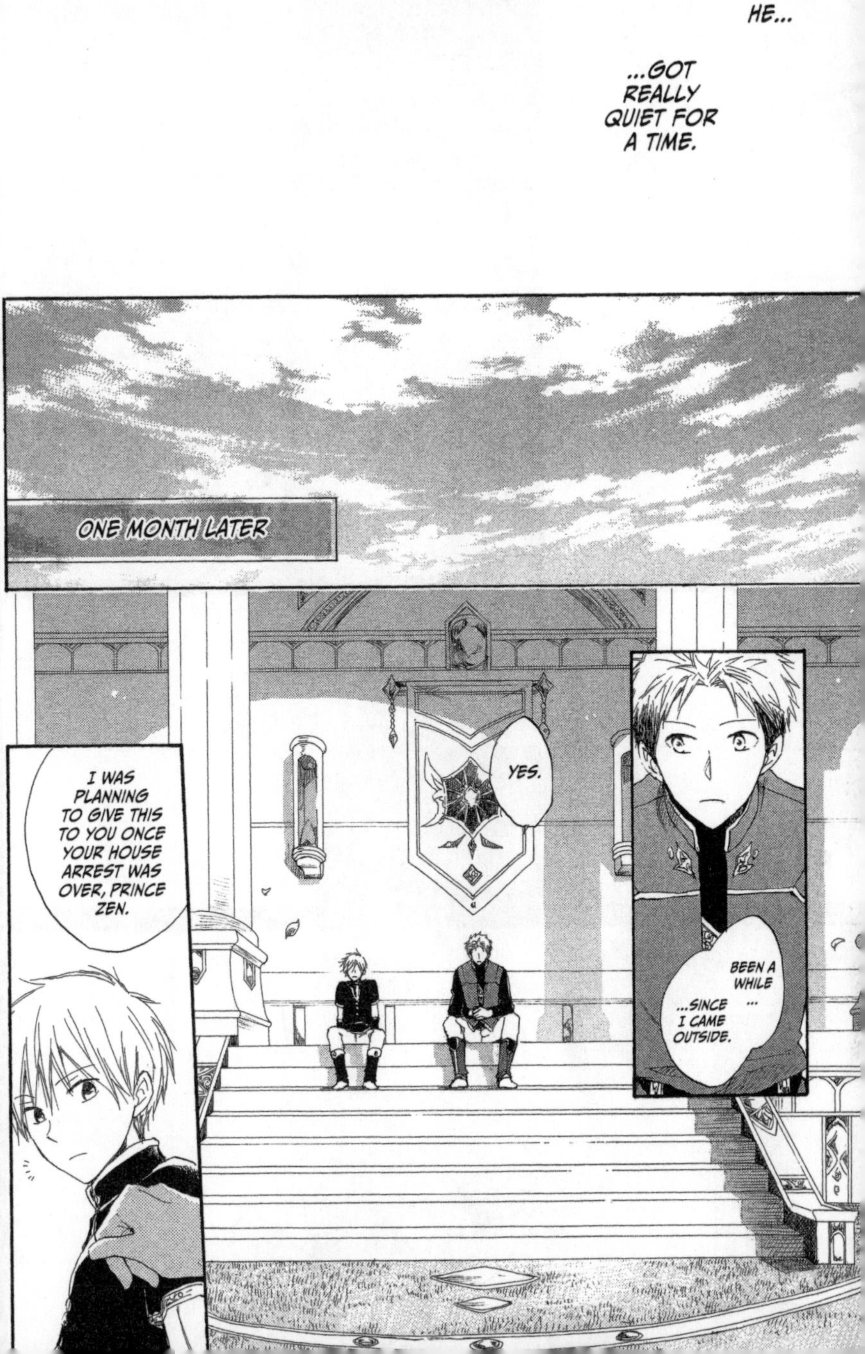
HE...
...GOT REALLY QUIET FOR A TIME.
ONE MONTH LATER
BEEN A WHILE ... ...SINCE I CAME OUTSIDE.
YES.
I WAS PLANNING TO GIVE THIS TO YOU ONCE YOUR HOUSE ARREST WAS OVER, PRINCE ZEN.

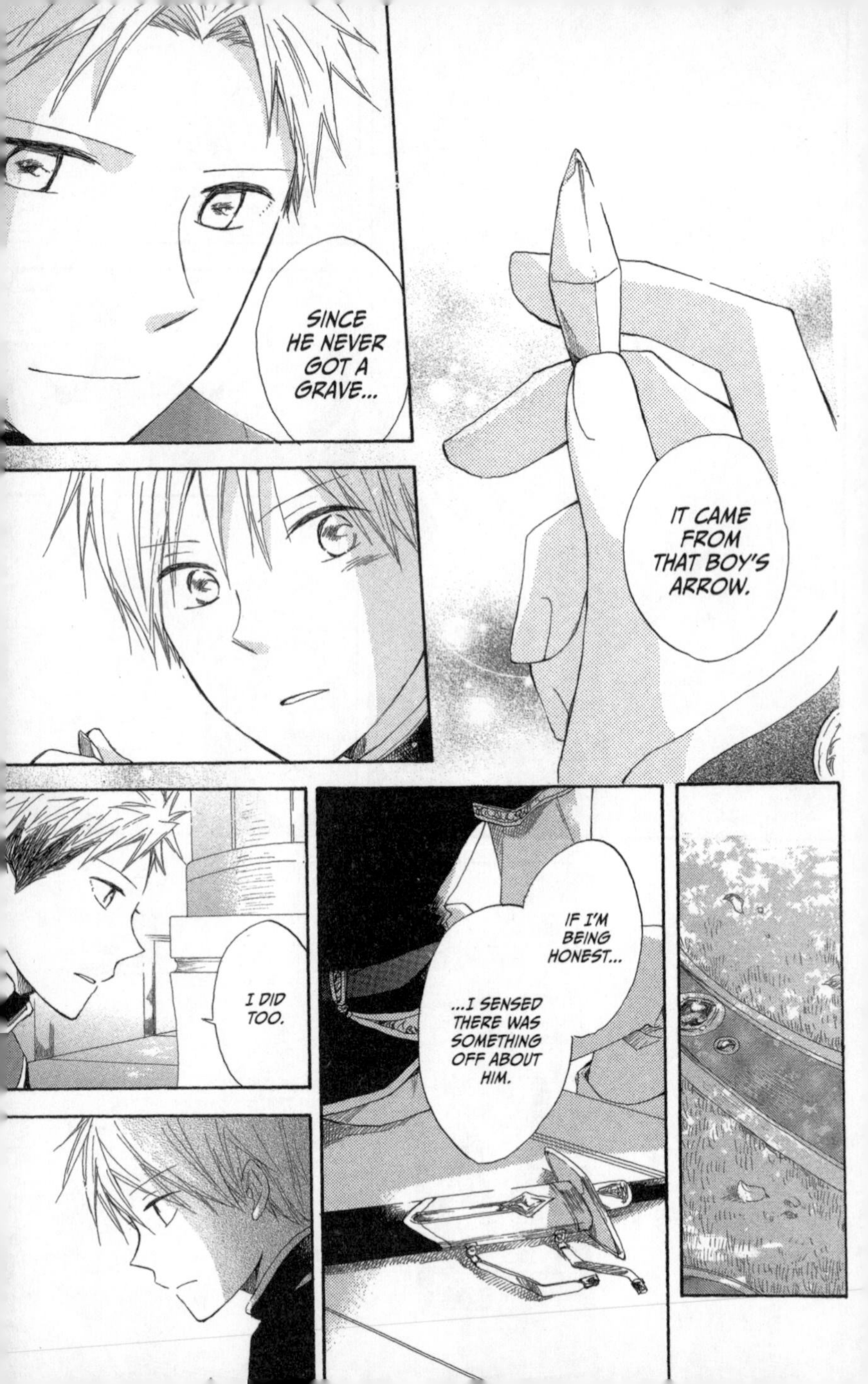
IT CAME FROM THAT BOY'S ARROW.
SINCE HE NEVER GOT A GRAVE...
IF I'M BEING HONEST...
...I SENSED THERE WAS SOMETHING OFF ABOUT HIM.
I DID TOO.

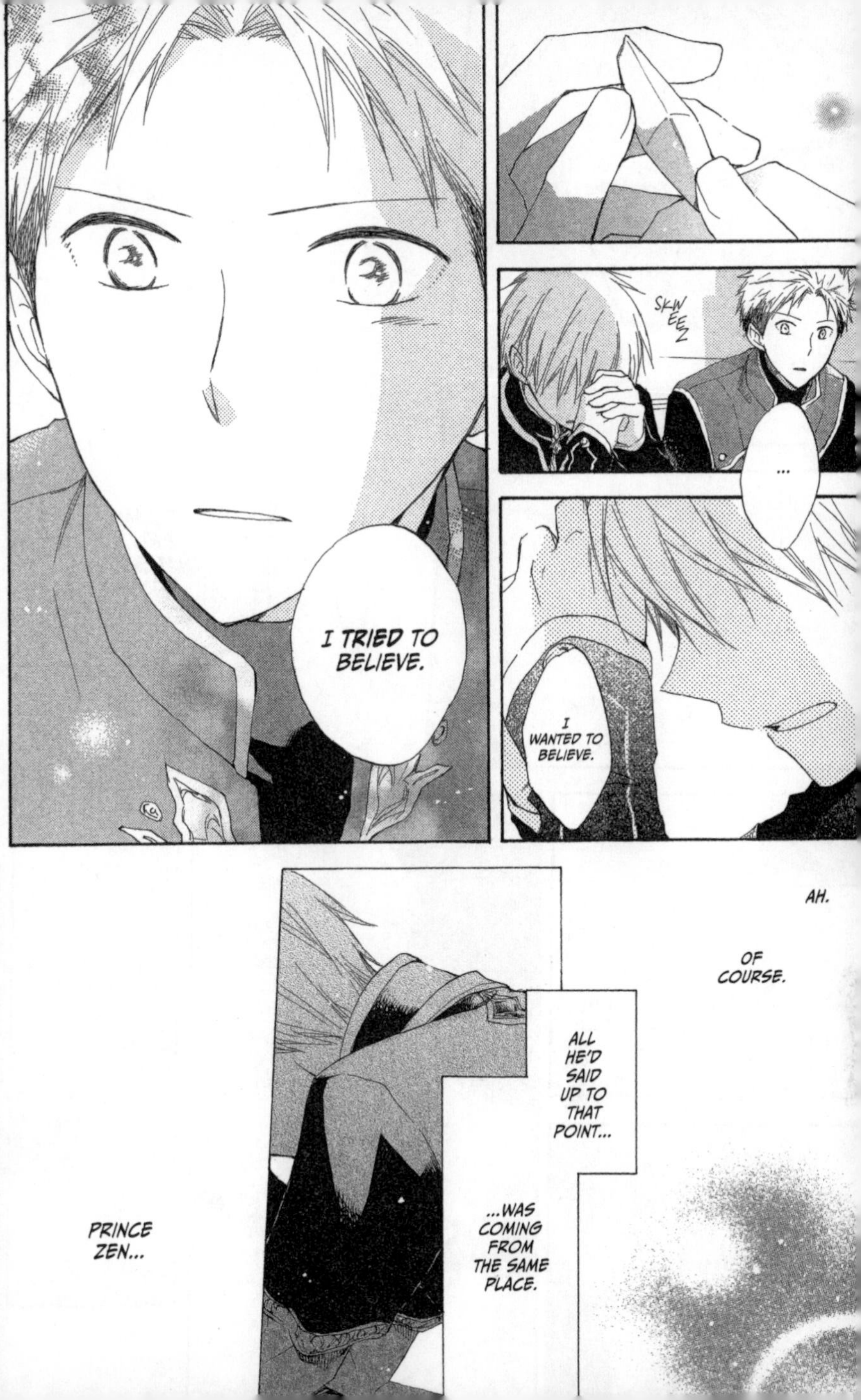
SKWEEZ
...
I WANTED TO BELIEVE.
I TRIED TO BELIEVE.
AH.
OF COURSE.
ALL HE'D SAID UP TO THAT POINT...
...WAS COMING FROM THE SAME PLACE.
PRINCE ZEN...

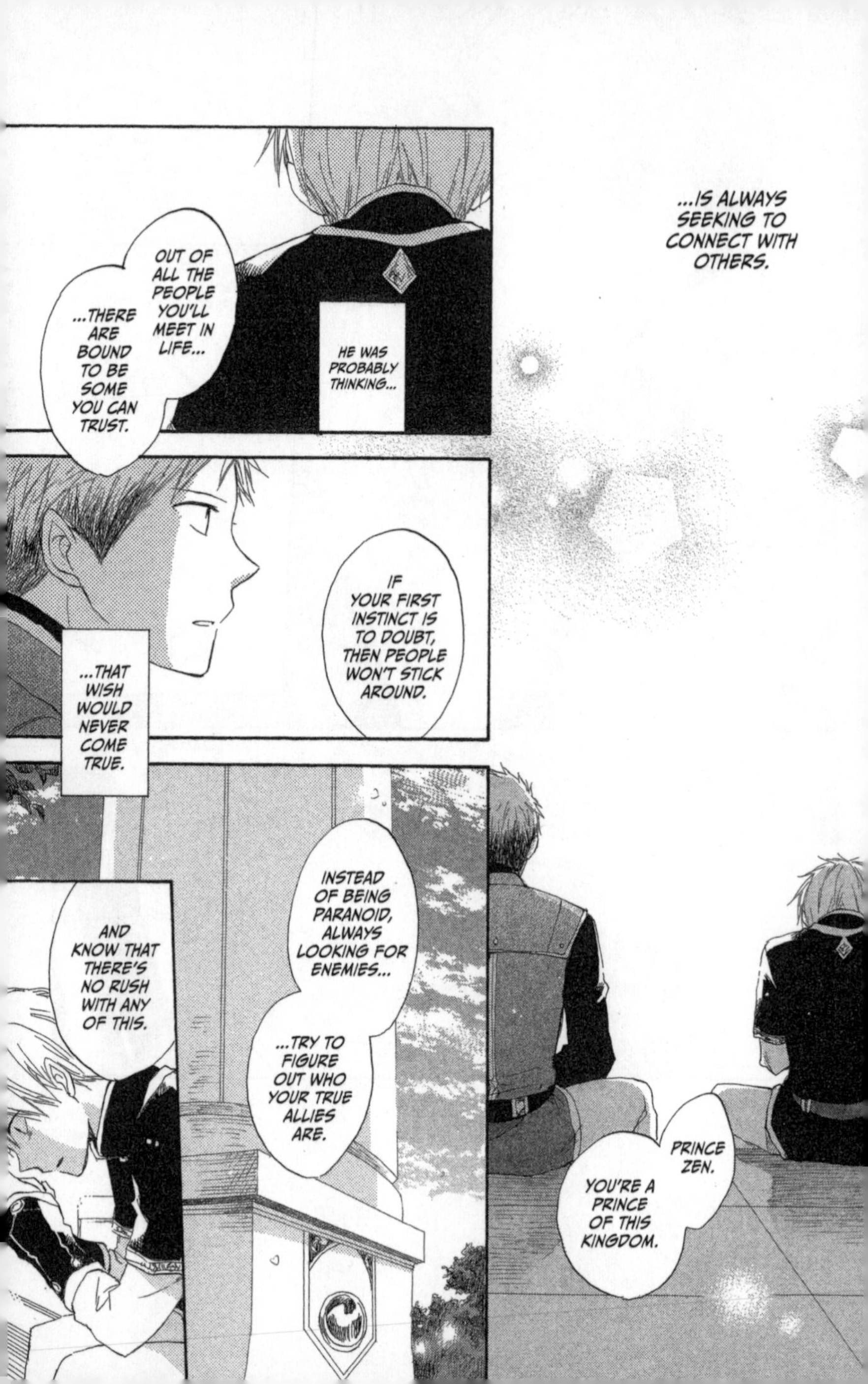
...IS ALWAYS SEEKING TO CONNECT WITH OTHERS.
PRINCE ZEN.
YOU'RE A PRINCE OF THIS KINGDOM.
HE WAS PROBABLY THINKING...
OUT OF ALL THE PEOPLE YOU'LL MEET IN LIFE...
...THERE ARE BOUND TO BE SOME YOU CAN TRUST.
IF YOUR FIRST INSTINCT IS TO DOUBT, THEN PEOPLE WON'T STICK AROUND.
...THAT WISH WOULD NEVER COME TRUE.
INSTEAD OF BEING PARANOID, ALWAYS LOOKING FOR ENEMIES...
...TRY TO FIGURE OUT WHO YOUR TRUE ALLIES ARE.
AND KNOW THAT THERE'S NO RUSH WITH ANY OF THIS.

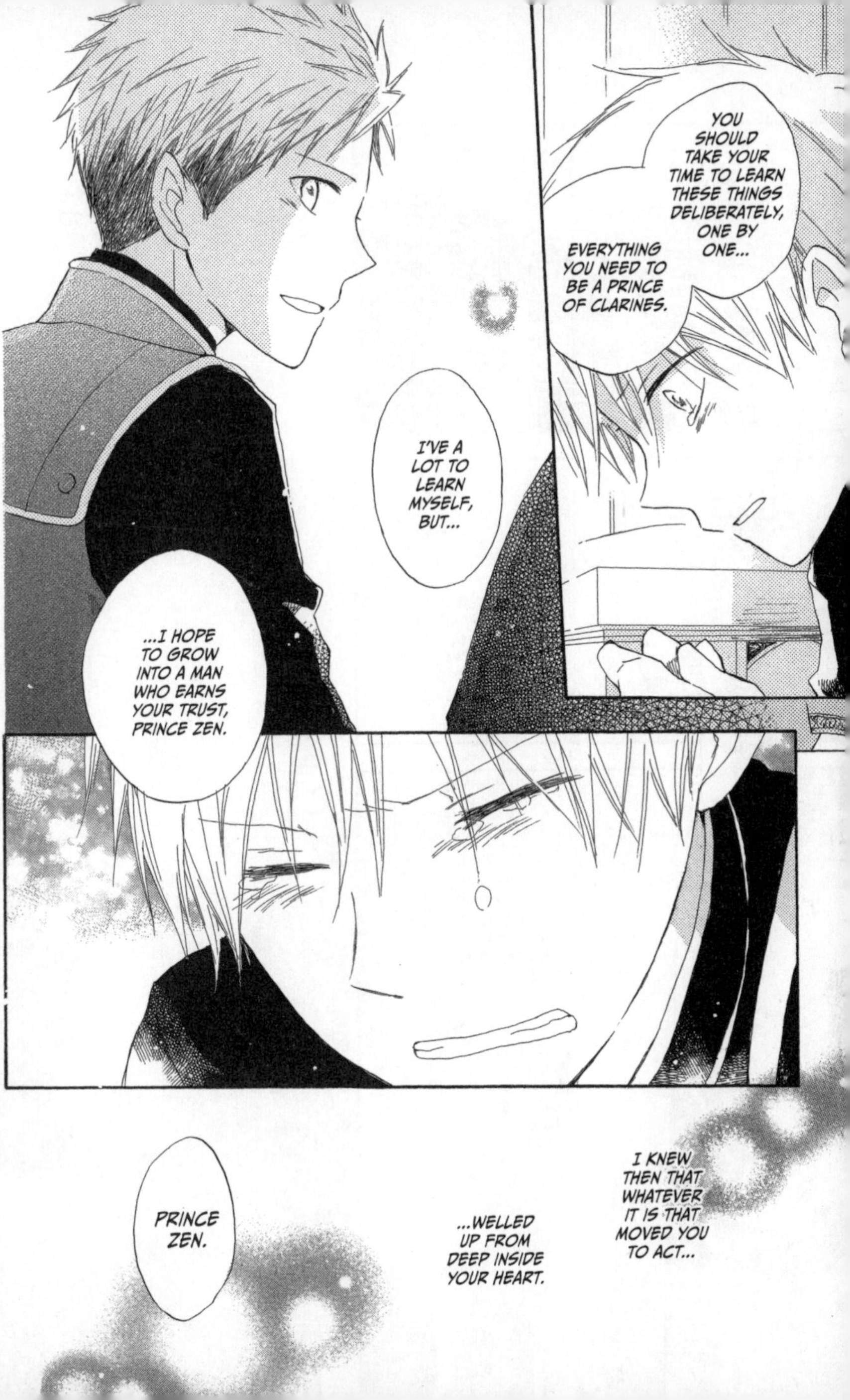
YOU SHOULD TAKE YOUR TIME TO LEARN THESE THINGS DELIBERATELY, ONE BY ONE...
EVERYTHING YOU NEED TO BE A PRINCE OF CLARINES.
I'VE A LOT TO LEARN MYSELF, BUT...
...I HOPE TO GROW INTO A MAN WHO EARNS YOUR TRUST, PRINCE ZEN.
I KNEW THEN THAT WHATEVER IT IS THAT MOVED YOU TO ACT...
...WELLED UP FROM DEEP INSIDE YOUR HEART.
PRINCE ZEN.

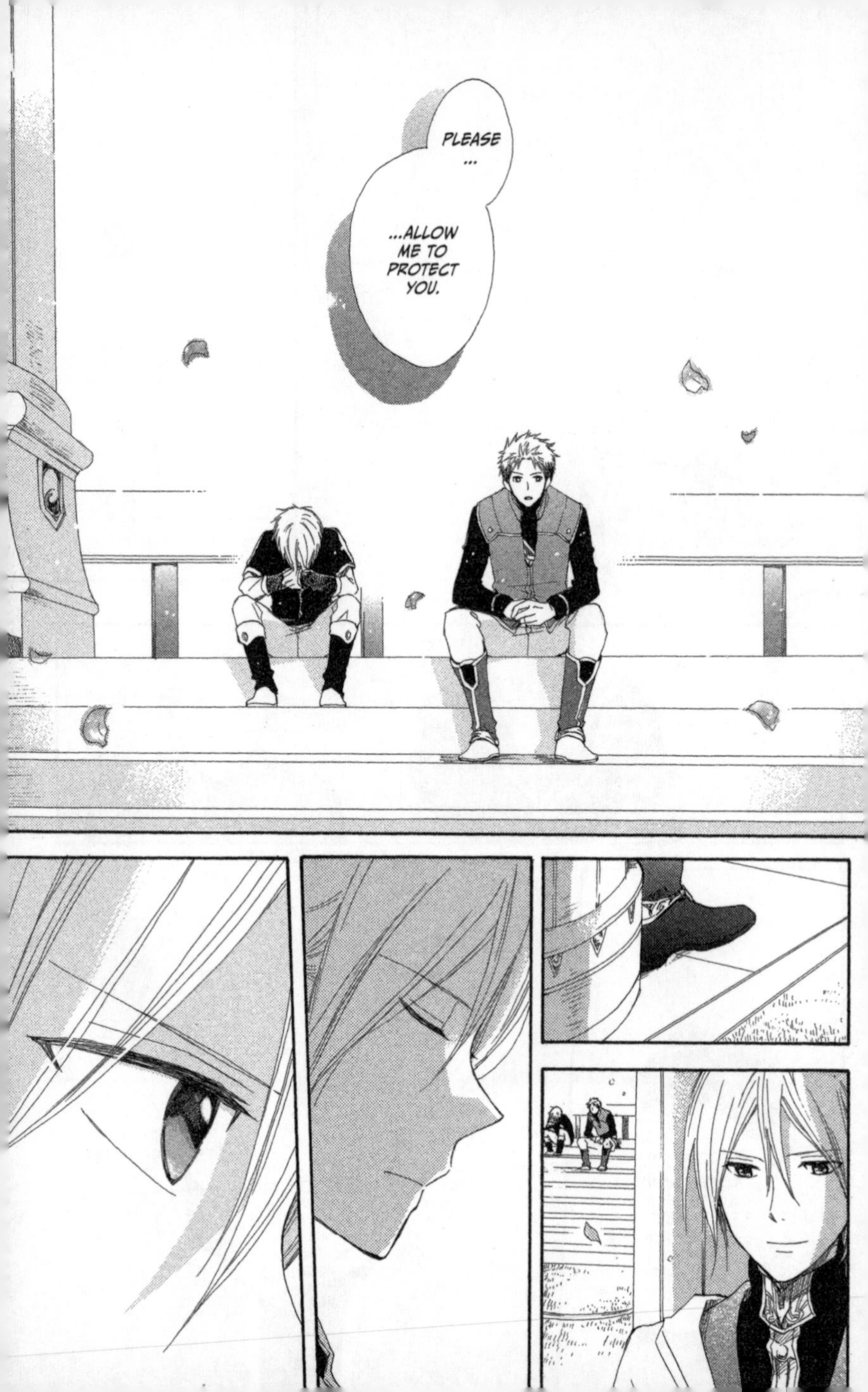
PLEASE ...
...ALLOW ME TO PROTECT YOU.

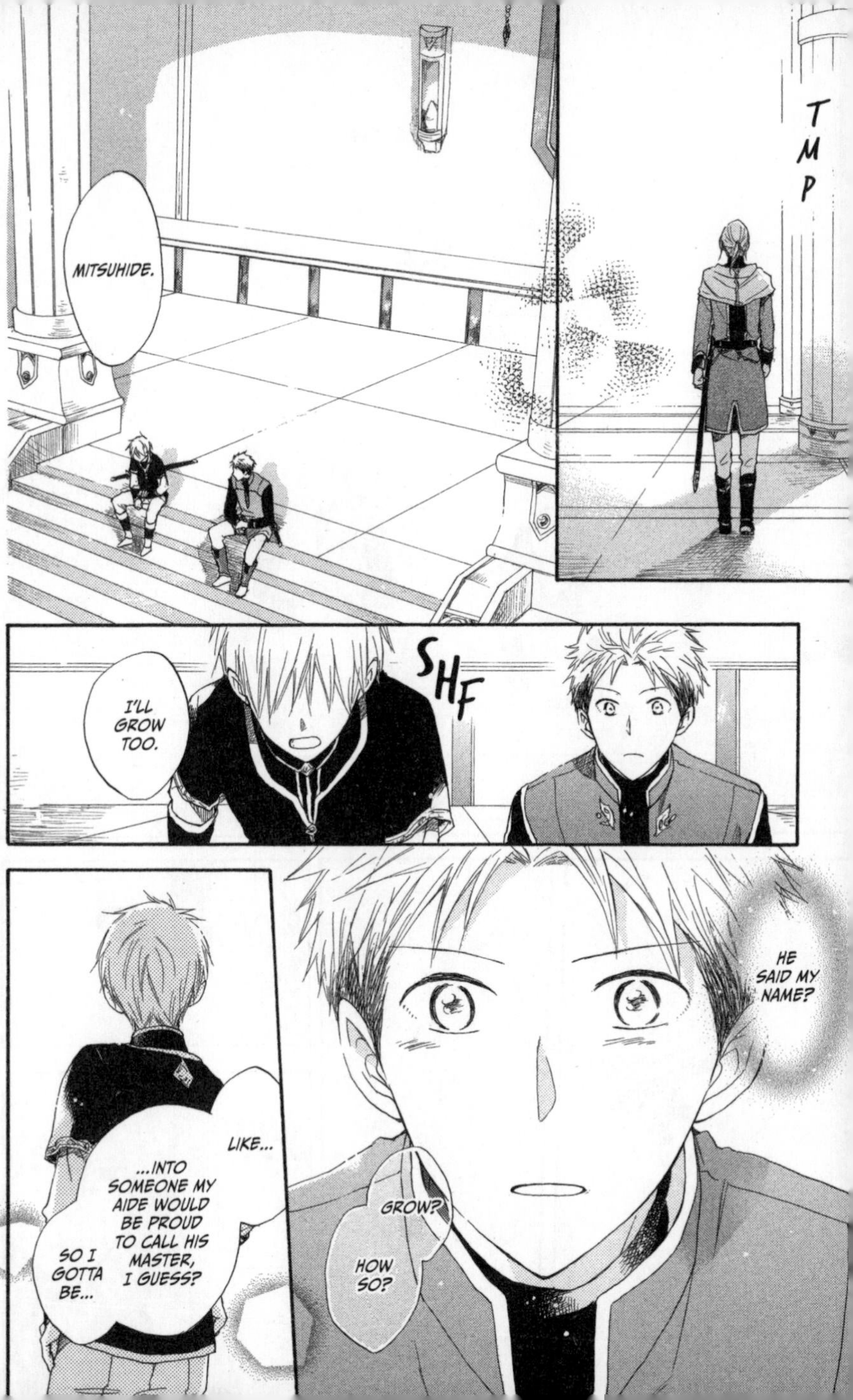
TMP
MITSUHIDE.
SHF
I'LL GROW TOO.
HE SAID MY NAME?
GROW?
HOW SO?
LIKE...
...INTO SOMEONE MY AIDE WOULD BE PROUD TO CALL HIS MASTER, I GUESS?
SO I GOTTA BE...

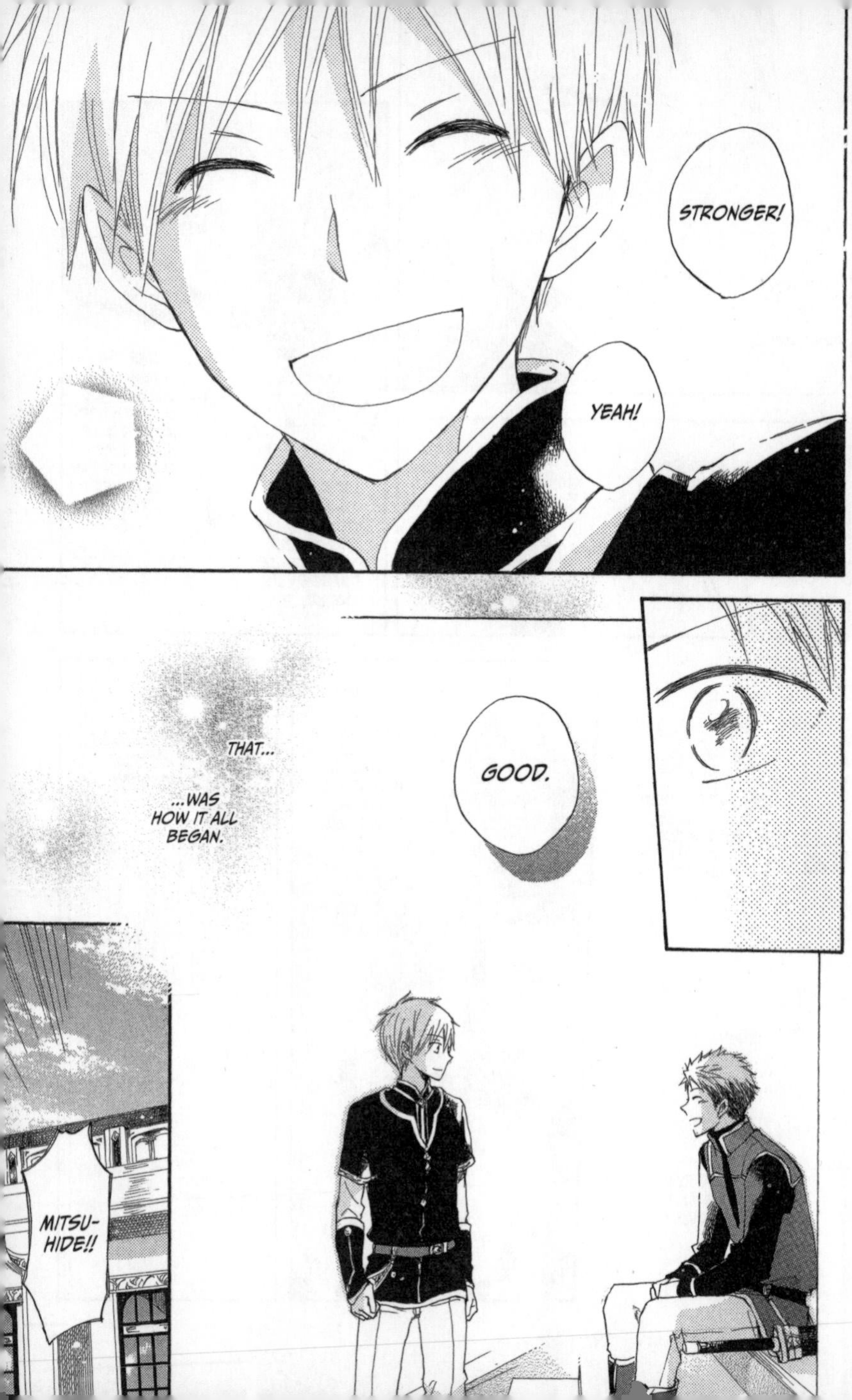
STRONGER!
YEAH!
GOOD.
THAT...
...WAS HOW IT ALL BEGAN.
MITSU-HIDE!!

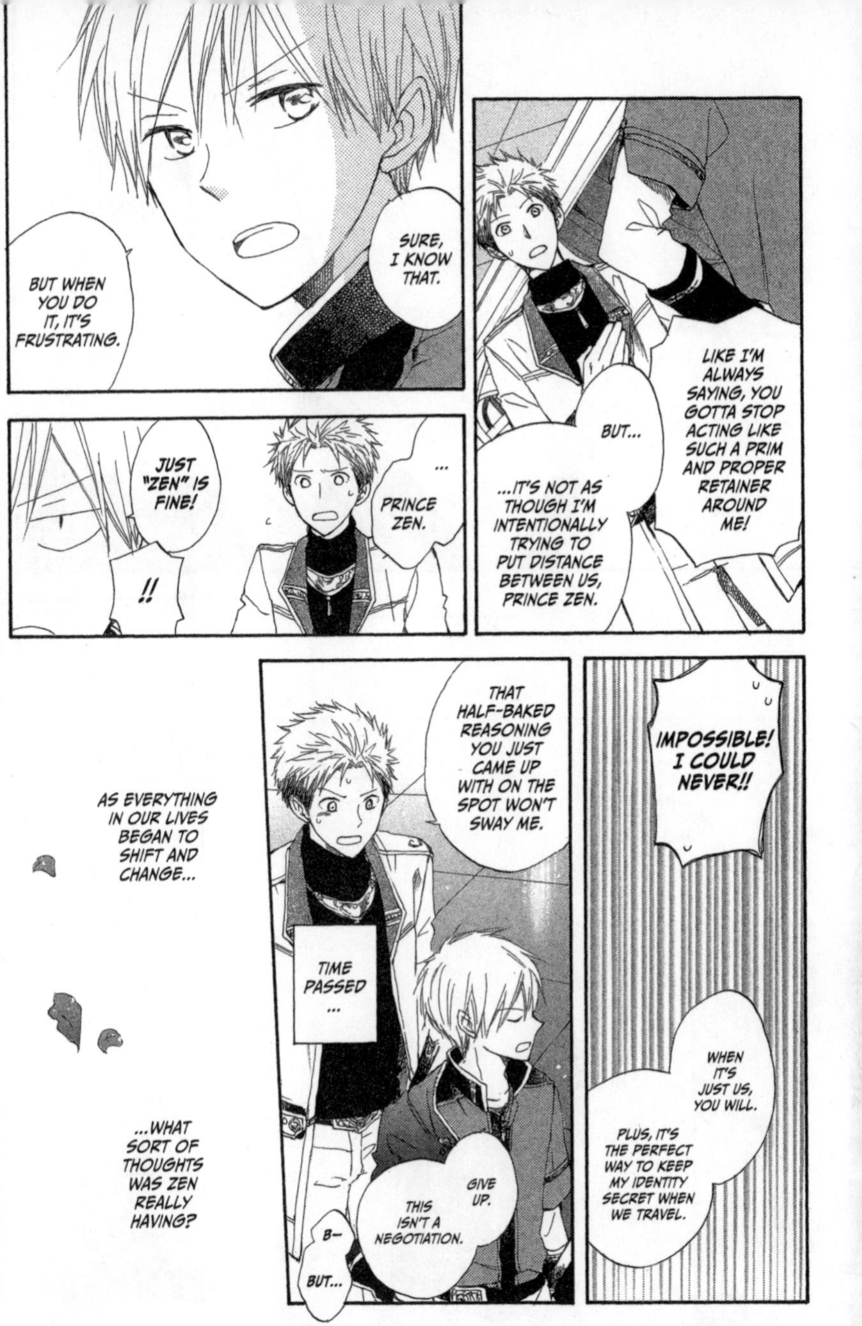

LIKE I'M ALWAYS SAYING, YOU GOTTA STOP ACTING LIKE SUCH A PRIM AND PROPER RETAINER AROUND ME!
BUT...
...IT'S NOT AS THOUGH I'M INTENTIONALLY TRYING TO PUT DISTANCE BETWEEN US, PRINCE ZEN.
SURE, I KNOW THAT.
BUT WHEN YOU DO IT, IT'S FRUSTRATING.
... PRINCE ZEN.
JUST "ZEN" IS FINE!
!!
IMPOSSIBLE! I COULD NEVER!!
WHEN IT'S JUST US, YOU WILL.
PLUS, IT'S THE PERFECT WAY TO KEEP MY IDENTITY SECRET WHEN WE TRAVEL.
THAT HALF-BAKED REASONING YOU JUST CAME UP WITH ON THE SPOT WON'T SWAY ME.
TIME PASSED ...
GIVE UP.
THIS ISN'T A NEGOTIATION.
B— BUT...
AS EVERYTHING IN OUR LIVES BEGAN TO SHIFT AND CHANGE...
...WHAT SORT OF THOUGHTS WAS ZEN REALLY HAVING?

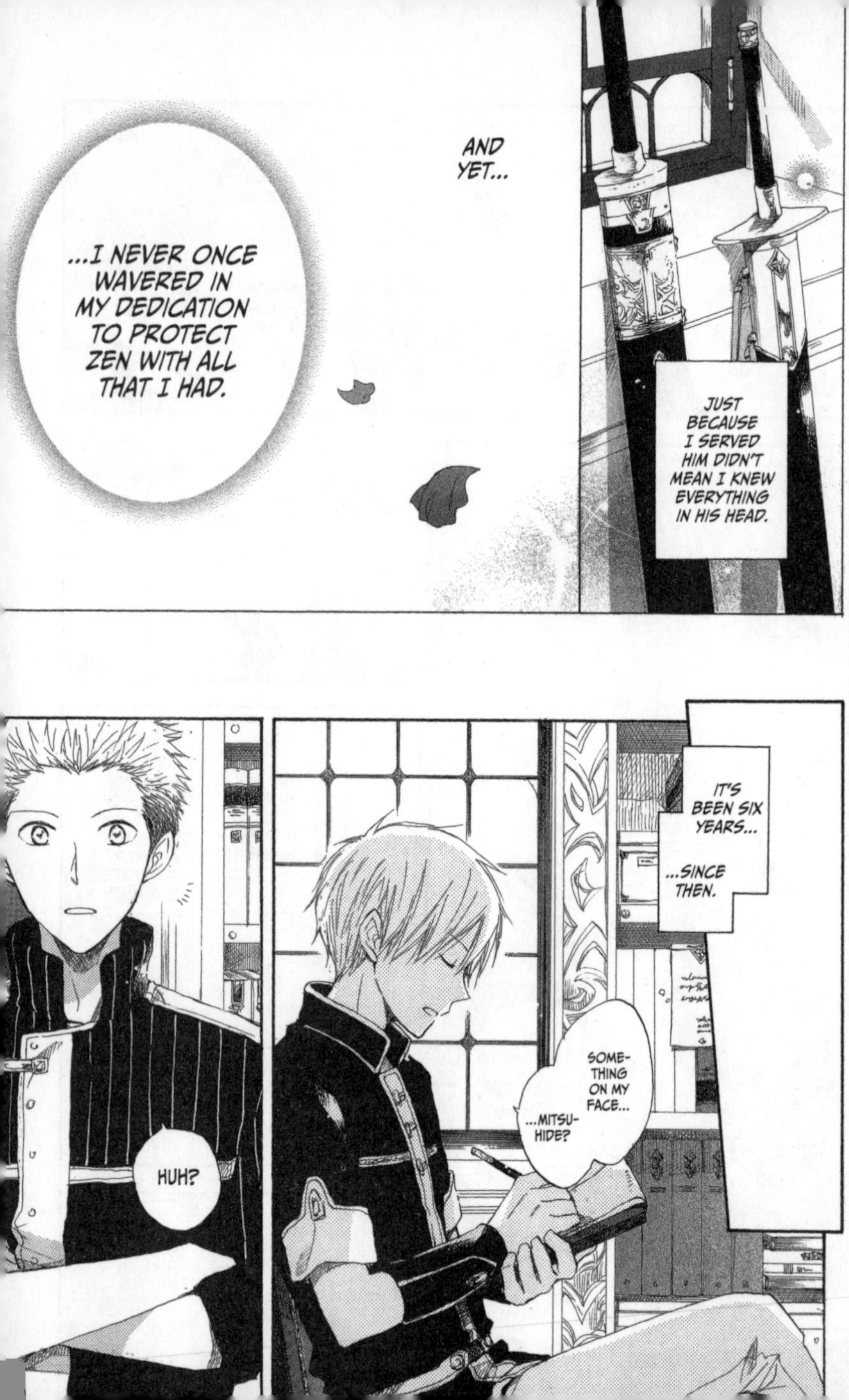

JUST BECAUSE I SERVED HIM DIDN'T MEAN I KNEW EVERYTHING IN HIS HEAD.
AND YET...
...I NEVER ONCE WAVERED IN MY DEDICATION TO PROTECT ZEN WITH ALL THAT I HAD.
IT'S BEEN SIX YEARS...
...SINCE THEN.
SOME-THING ON MY FACE...
...MITSU-HIDE?
HUH?

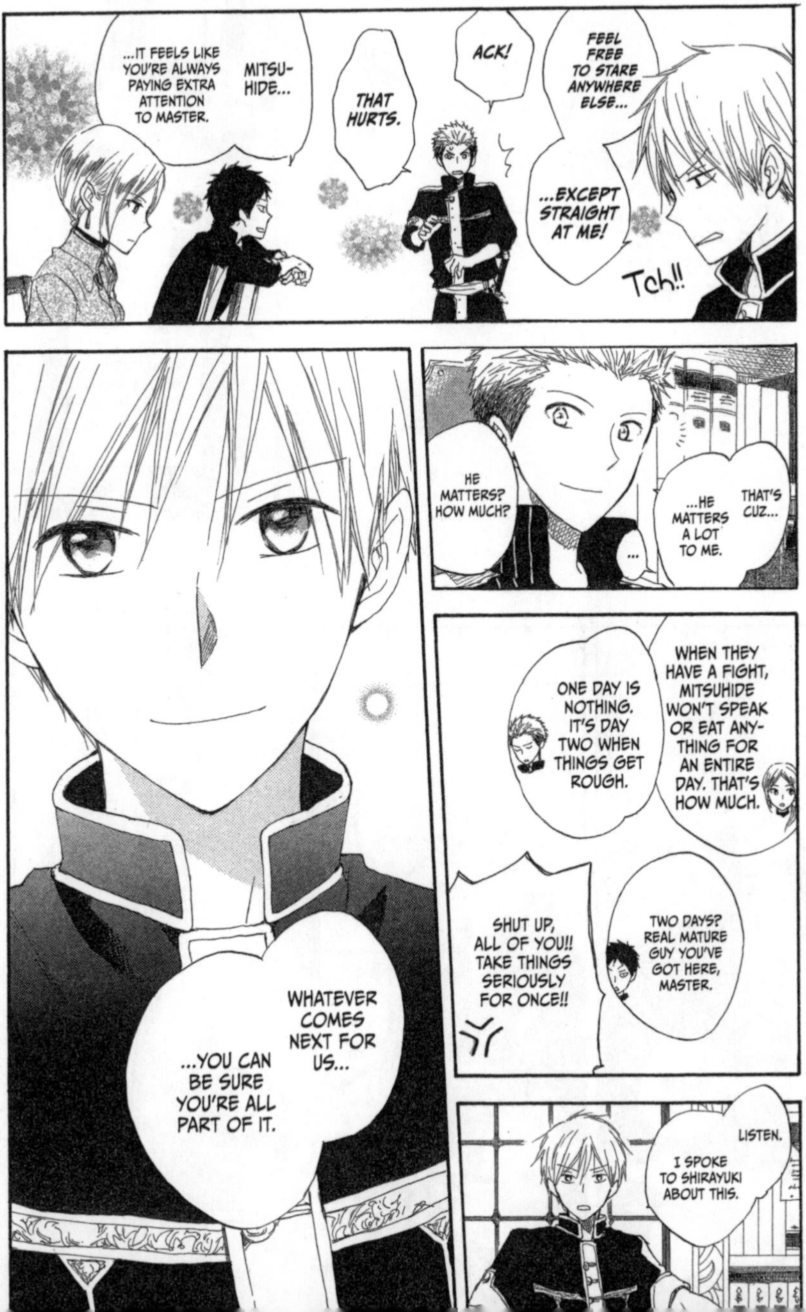
FEEL FREE TO STARE ANYWHERE ELSE...
...EXCEPT STRAIGHT AT ME!
Tch!!
ACK!
THAT HURTS.
MITSU-HIDE...
...IT FEELS LIKE YOU'RE ALWAYS PAYING EXTRA ATTENTION TO MASTER.
THAT'S CUZ...
...HE MATTERS A LOT TO ME.
...
HE MATTERS? HOW MUCH?
WHEN THEY HAVE A FIGHT, MITSUHIDE WON'T SPEAK OR EAT ANY-THING FOR AN ENTIRE DAY. THAT'S HOW MUCH.
ONE DAY IS NOTHING. IT'S DAY TWO WHEN THINGS GET ROUGH.
TWO DAYS? REAL MATURE GUY YOU'VE GOT HERE, MASTER.
SHUT UP, ALL OF YOU!! TAKE THINGS SERIOUSLY FOR ONCE!!
LISTEN.
I SPOKE TO SHIRAYUKI ABOUT THIS.
WHATEVER COMES NEXT FOR US...
...YOU CAN BE SURE YOU'RE ALL PART OF IT.

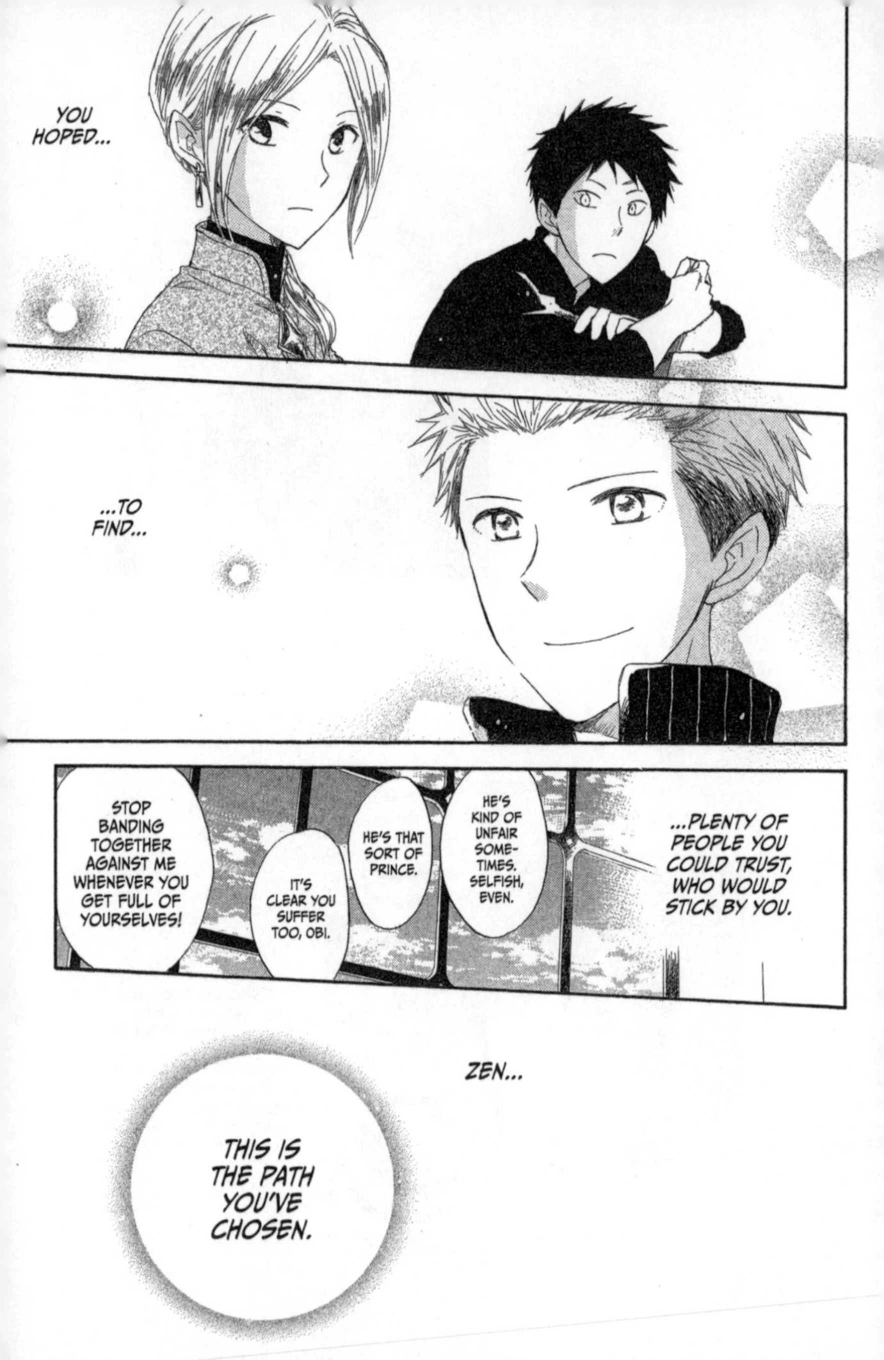
YOU HOPED...
...TO FIND...
...PLENTY OF PEOPLE YOU COULD TRUST, WHO WOULD STICK BY YOU.
HE'S KIND OF UNFAIR SOME-TIMES. SELFISH, EVEN.
HE'S THAT SORT OF PRINCE.
IT'S CLEAR YOU SUFFER TOO, OBI.
STOP BANDING TOGETHER AGAINST ME WHENEVER YOU GET FULL OF YOURSELVES!
ZEN...
THIS IS THE PATH YOU'VE CHOSEN.

Excerpts from ads
for chapter 16 (above)
and chapter 17 (left)

Placing them together
like this, it almost looks like
Mitsuhide is off fighting a
war and thinking of his
sweetheart back at home.

Chapter 17

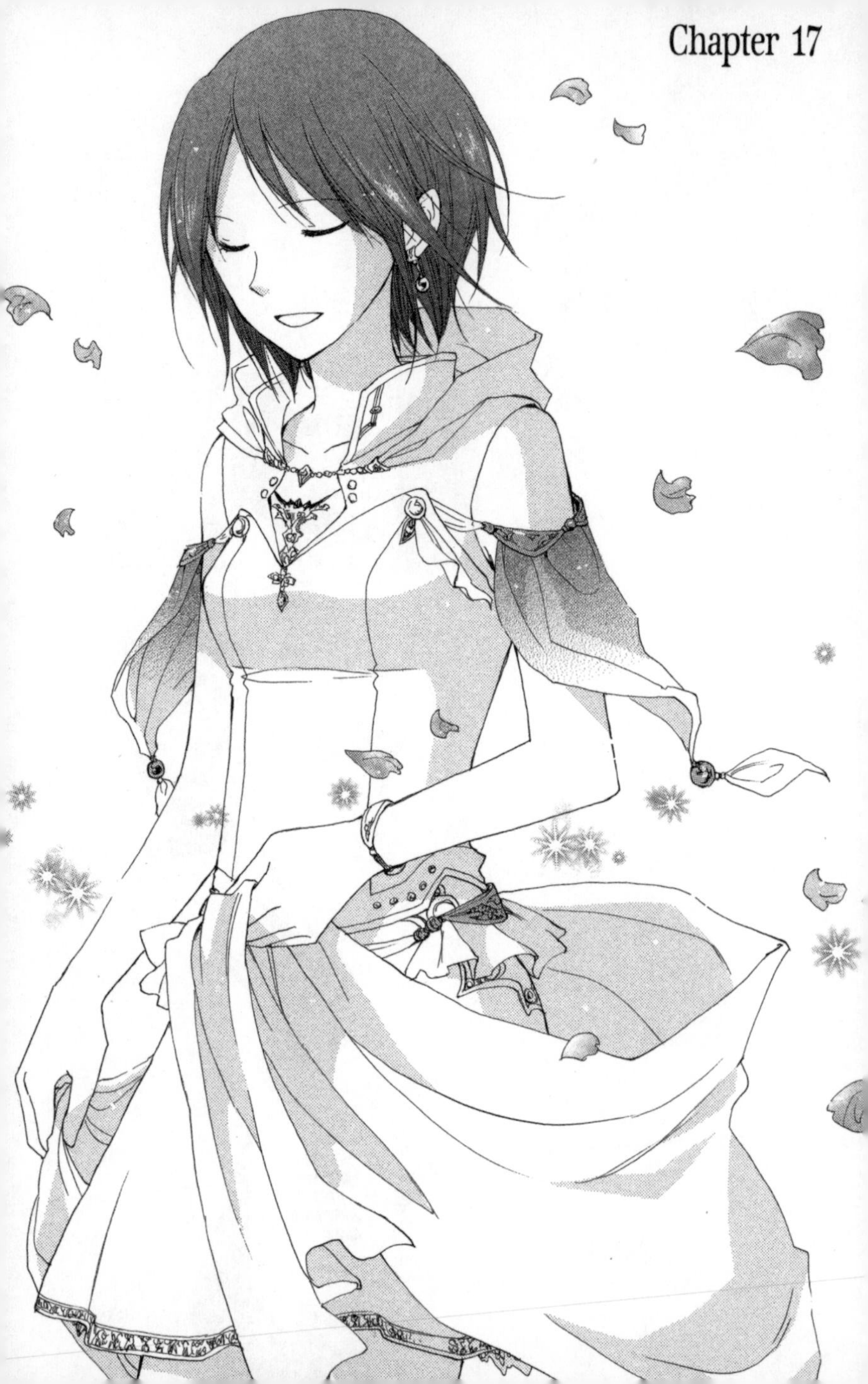

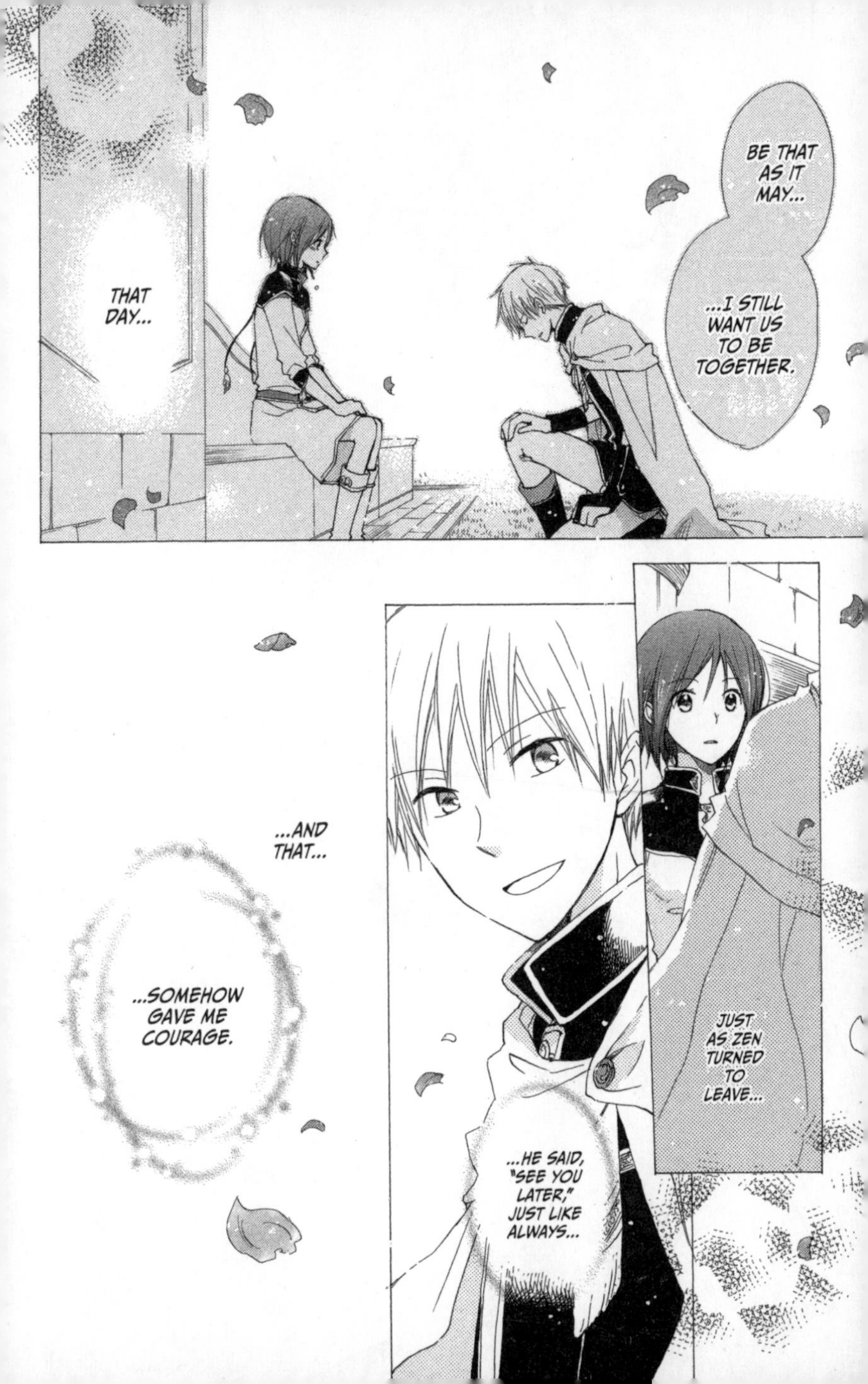
BE THAT AS IT MAY...
...I STILL WANT US TO BE TOGETHER.
THAT DAY...
JUST AS ZEN TURNED TO LEAVE...
...HE SAID, "SEE YOU LATER," JUST LIKE ALWAYS...
...AND THAT...
...SOMEHOW GAVE ME COURAGE.

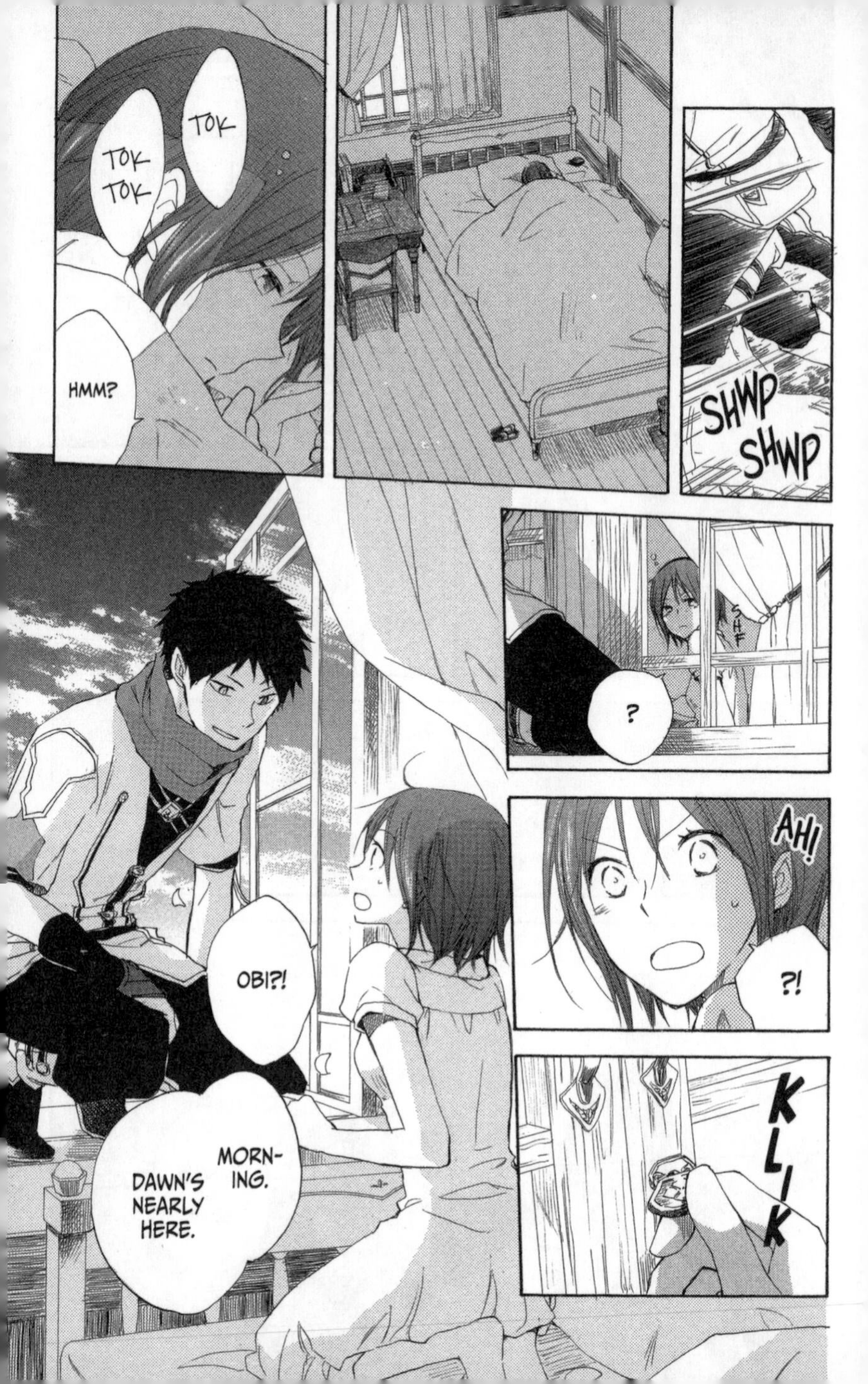
SHWP
SHWP
TOK
TOK
TOK
HMM?
SHF
?
AH!
?!
KLIK
OBI?!
MORN-
ING.
DAWN'S
NEARLY
HERE.

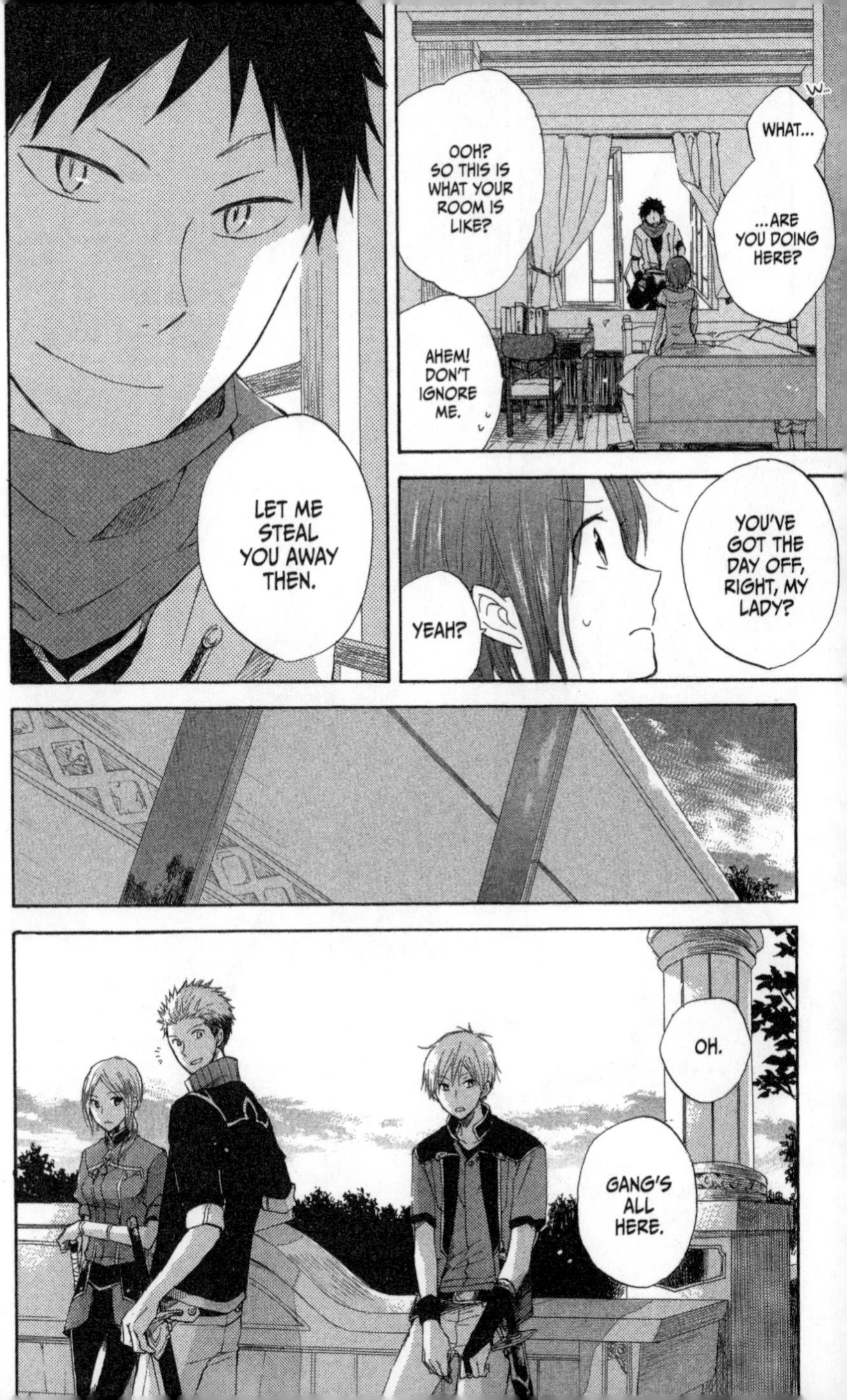
W...
WHAT...
...ARE YOU DOING HERE?
OOH? SO THIS IS WHAT YOUR ROOM IS LIKE?
AHEM! DON'T IGNORE ME.
YOU'VE GOT THE DAY OFF, RIGHT, MY LADY?
YEAH?
LET ME STEAL YOU AWAY THEN.
OH.
GANG'S ALL HERE.

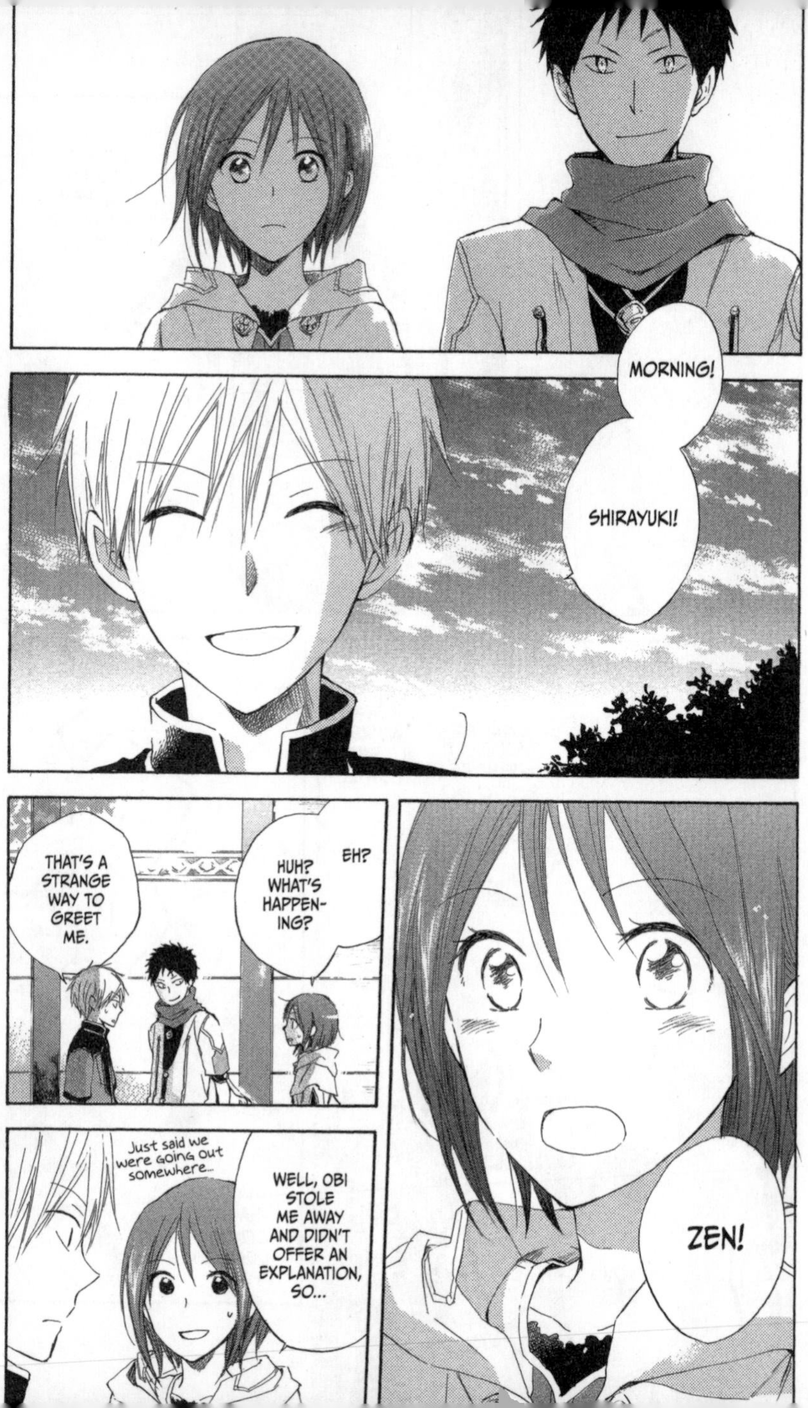
MORNING!
SHIRAYUKI!
ZEN!
EH?
HUH? WHAT'S HAPPEN-ING?
THAT'S A STRANGE WAY TO GREET ME.
WELL, OBI STOLE ME AWAY AND DIDN'T OFFER AN EXPLANATION, SO...
Just said we were going out somewhere...

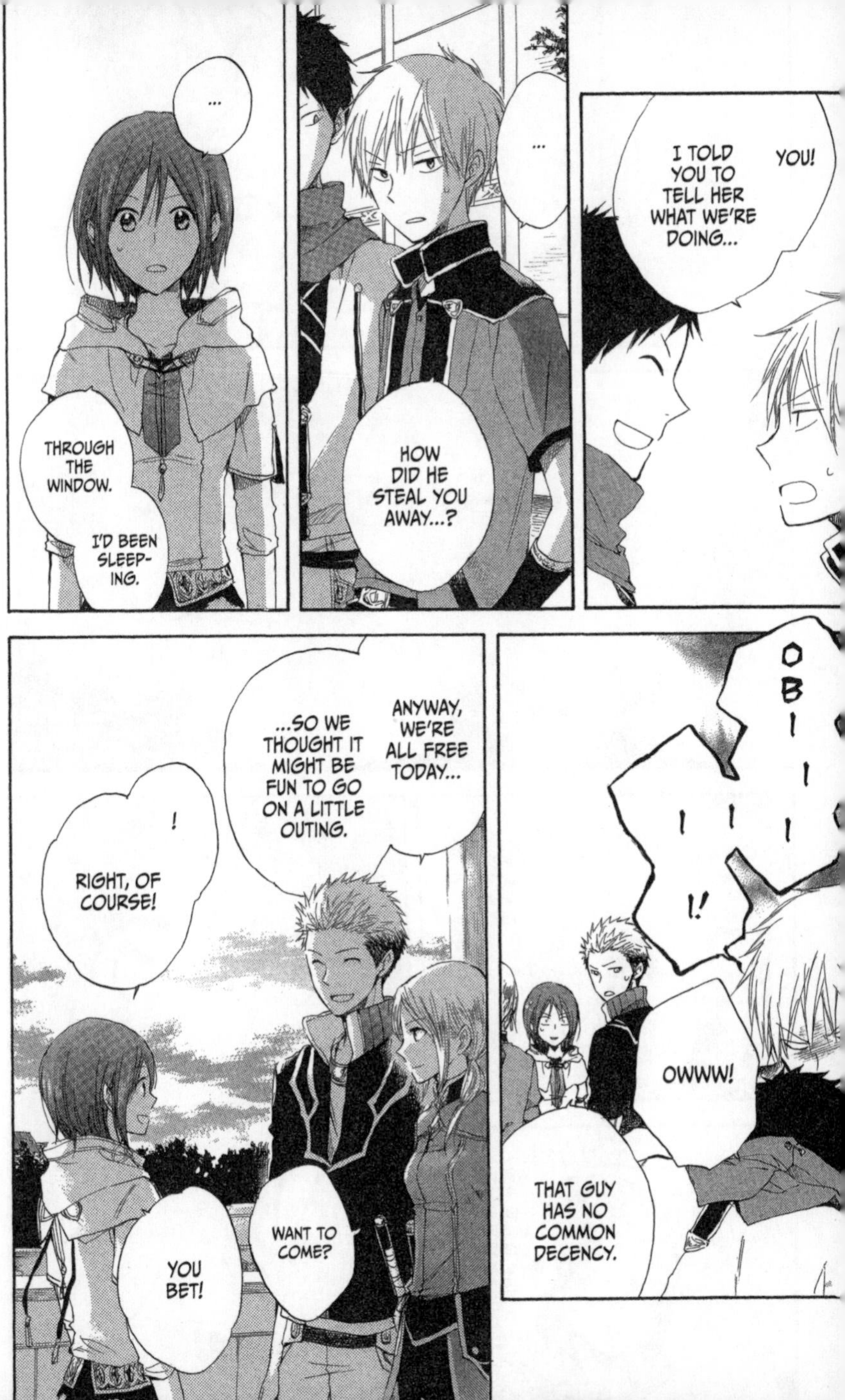
I TOLD YOU TO TELL HER WHAT WE'RE DOING... YOU!
...
HOW DID HE STEAL YOU AWAY...?
...
THROUGH THE WINDOW.
I'D BEEN SLEEP-ING.
OBIIIIII!!
OWWW!
THAT GUY HAS NO COMMON DECENCY.
ANYWAY, WE'RE ALL FREE TODAY...
...SO WE THOUGHT IT MIGHT BE FUN TO GO ON A LITTLE OUTING.
!
RIGHT, OF COURSE!
WANT TO COME?
YOU BET!

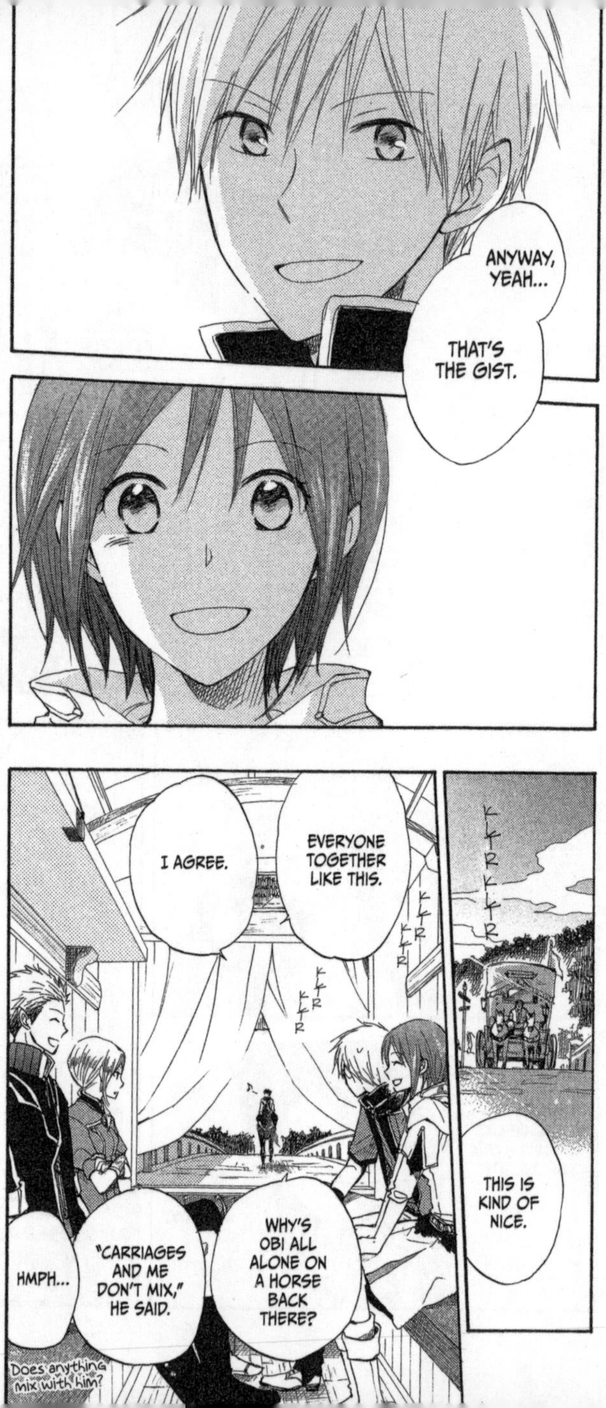
ANYWAY, YEAH...
THAT'S THE GIST.
THIS IS KIND OF NICE.
EVERYONE TOGETHER LIKE THIS.
I AGREE.
WHY'S OBI ALL ALONE ON A HORSE BACK THERE?
"CARRIAGES AND ME DON'T MIX," HE SAID.
HMPH...
Does anything mix with him?

Regarding the Characters' Ages

In chapter 15's flashback, we get Zen's and Mitsuhide's ages.

That's right. Finally revealed.

The flashback took place six years earlier, so...

-Zen is now 19

-Mitsuhide is now 23

-And Shirayuki is one year younger than Zen, which makes her 18

While we're at it, might as well reveal the ages of the other two!

-Kiki is 20

-Obi is 21 (probably?)

I tend to place more of an emphasis on the age gaps between the characters than on their actual ages.

As for Raj...?

Raj is...

11

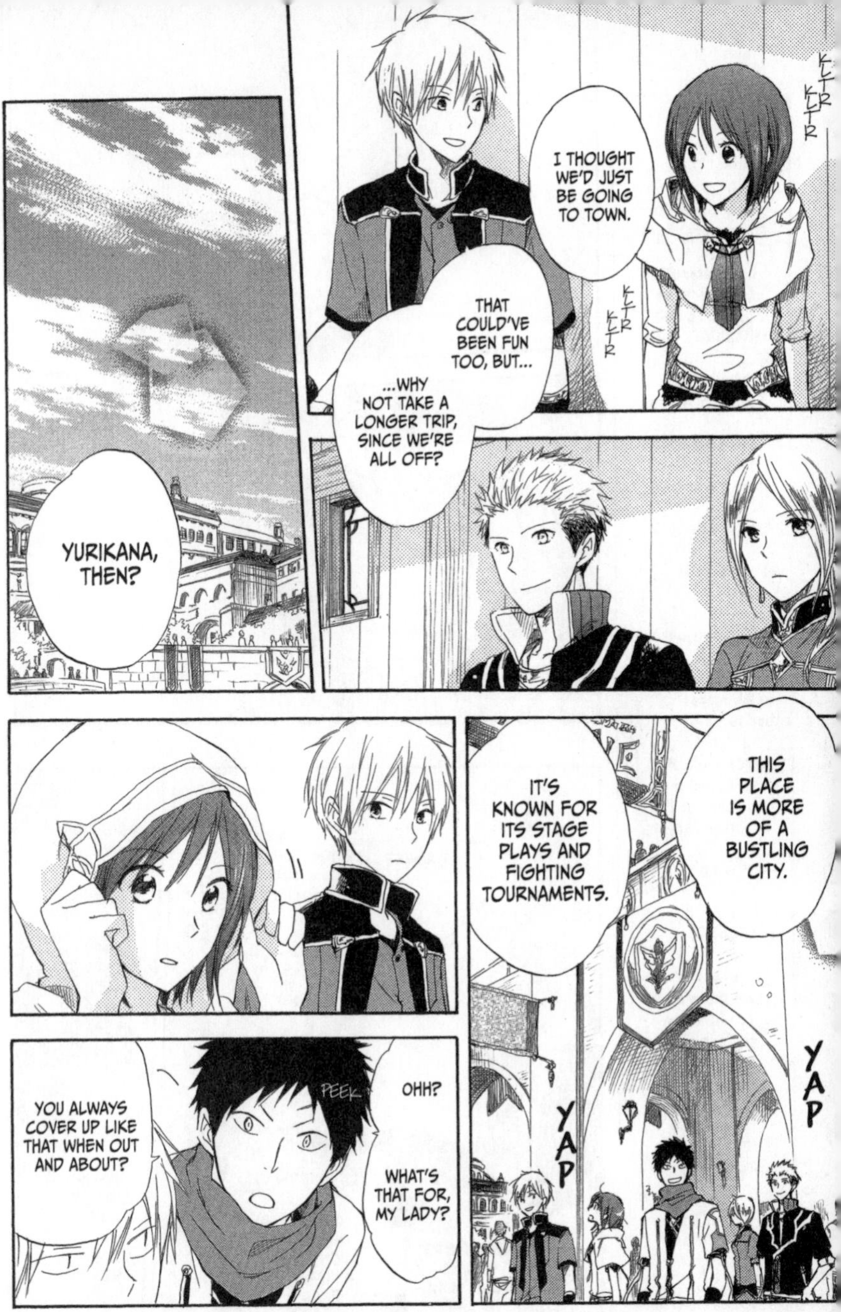

KLTR KLTR
I THOUGHT WE'D JUST BE GOING TO TOWN.
THAT COULD'VE BEEN FUN TOO, BUT...
KLTR KLTR
...WHY NOT TAKE A LONGER TRIP, SINCE WE'RE ALL OFF?
YURIKANA, THEN?
THIS PLACE IS MORE OF A BUSTLING CITY.
IT'S KNOWN FOR ITS STAGE PLAYS AND FIGHTING TOURNAMENTS.
YAP YAP
YAP YAP
PEEK
OHH?
WHAT'S THAT FOR, MY LADY?
YOU ALWAYS COVER UP LIKE THAT WHEN OUT AND ABOUT?

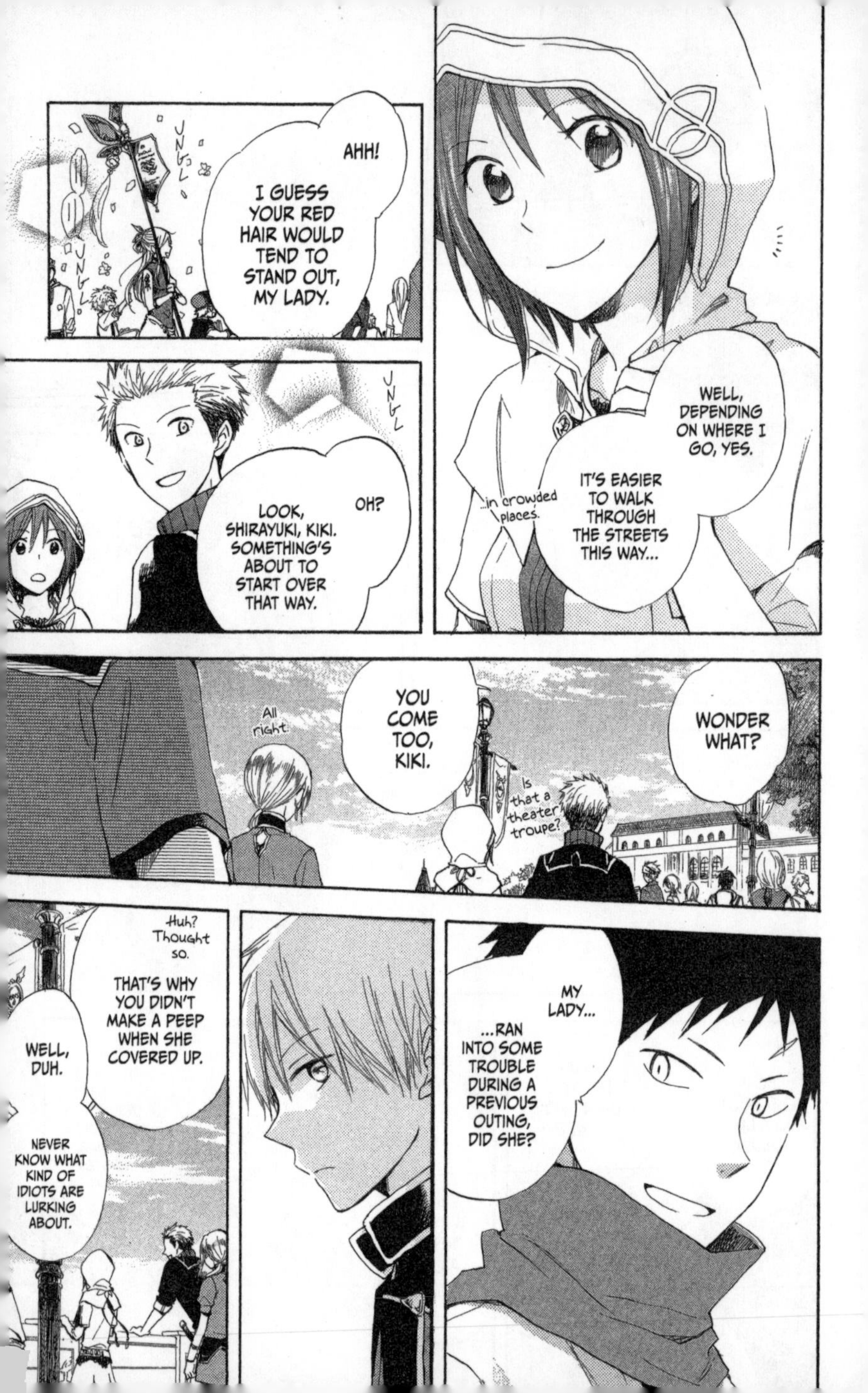
WELL, DEPENDING ON WHERE I GO, YES.
IT'S EASIER TO WALK THROUGH THE STREETS THIS WAY...
...in crowded places.
AHH!
I GUESS YOUR RED HAIR WOULD TEND TO STAND OUT, MY LADY.
OH?
LOOK, SHIRAYUKI, KIKI. SOMETHING'S ABOUT TO START OVER THAT WAY.
WONDER WHAT?
Is that a theater troupe?
YOU COME TOO, KIKI.
All right.
MY LADY...
...RAN INTO SOME TROUBLE DURING A PREVIOUS OUTING, DID SHE?
Huh? Thought so.
THAT'S WHY YOU DIDN'T MAKE A PEEP WHEN SHE COVERED UP.
WELL, DUH.
NEVER KNOW WHAT KIND OF IDIOTS ARE LURKING ABOUT.

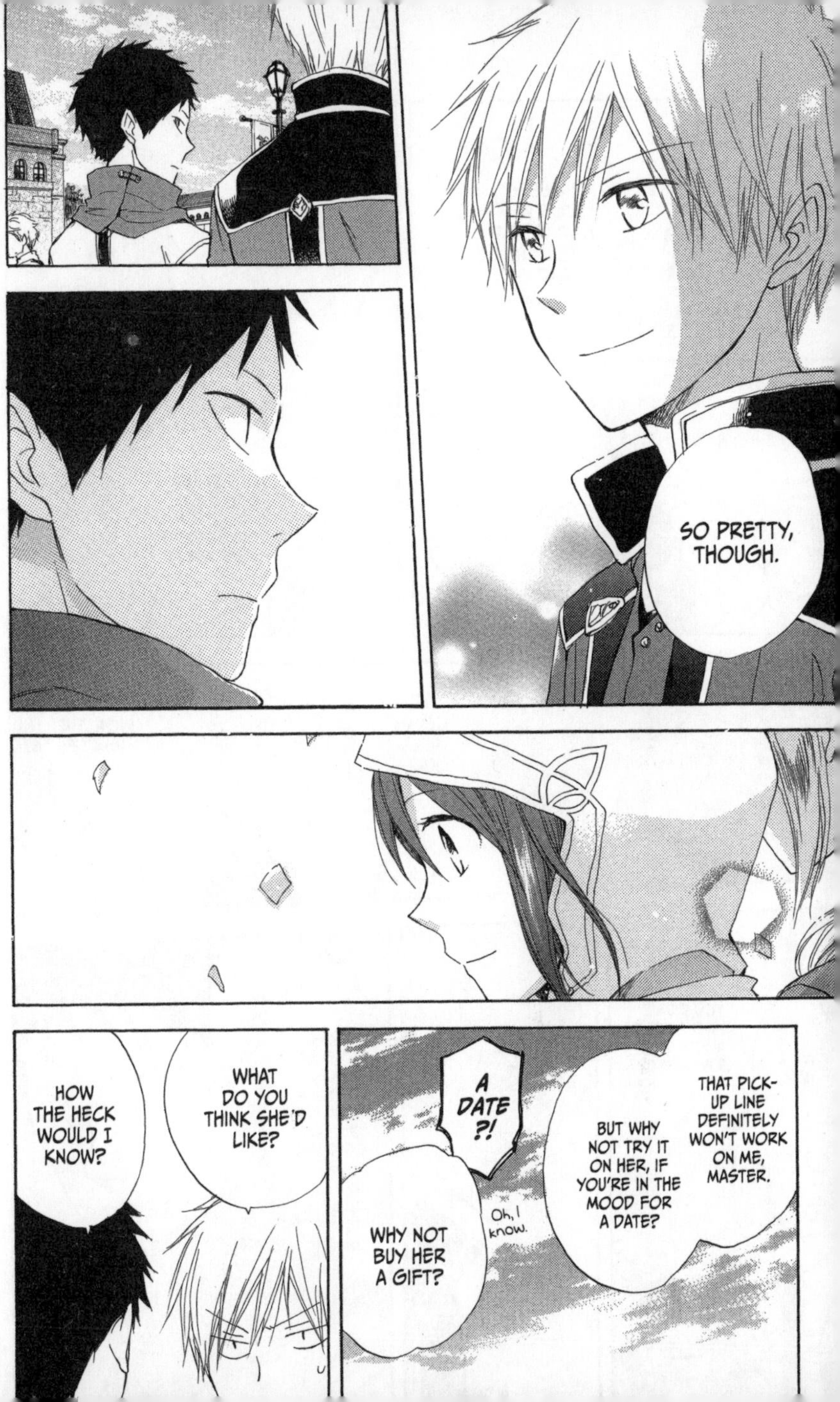
SO PRETTY, THOUGH.
THAT PICK-UP LINE DEFINITELY WON'T WORK ON ME, MASTER.
BUT WHY NOT TRY IT ON HER, IF YOU'RE IN THE MOOD FOR A DATE?
A DATE?!
Oh, I know.
WHY NOT BUY HER A GIFT?
WHAT DO YOU THINK SHE'D LIKE?
HOW THE HECK WOULD I KNOW?

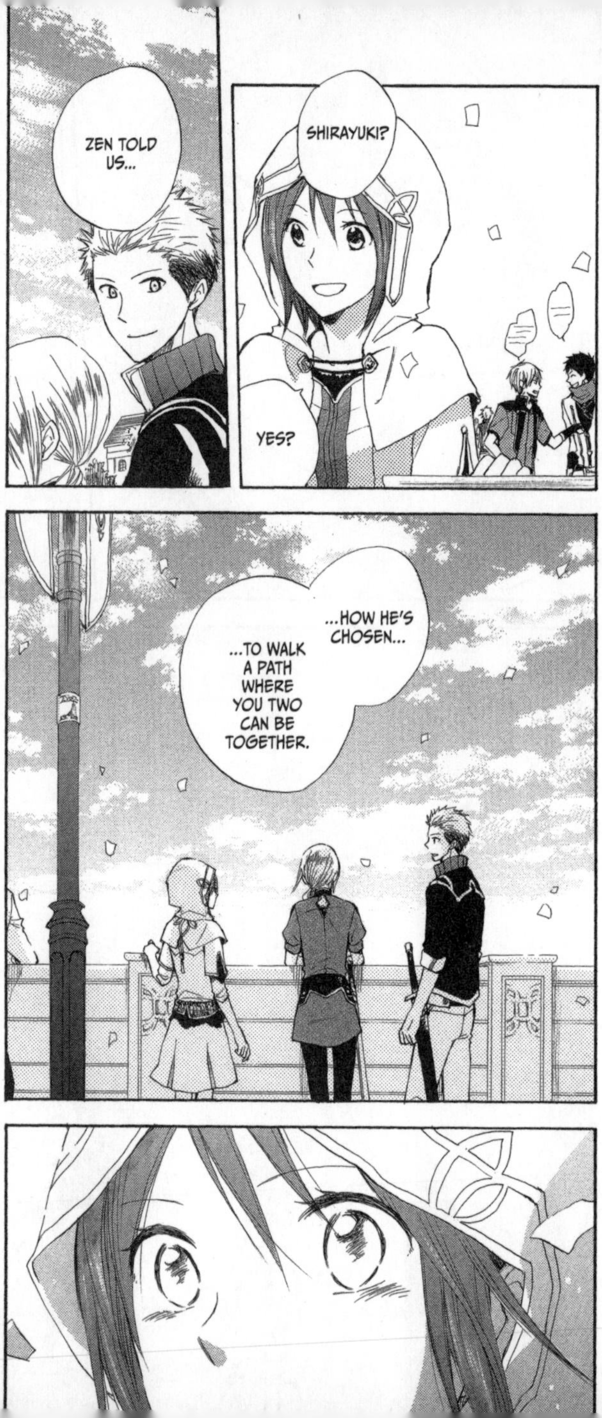

SHIRAYUKI?
YES?
ZEN TOLD US...
...HOW HE'S CHOSEN...
...TO WALK A PATH WHERE YOU TWO CAN BE TOGETHER.

In September of 2009, I went to France with my friend Toki Yajima. It was my first trip abroad!

We went on a tour of old castles—Mont Saint Michel, the Louvre and so on. Everyone in our tour group had a grand old time, and me and Yajima were going nuts and having fun here, there and everywhere... It felt like a dream.

*The "going nuts" mostly happened at those old castles.

I took plenty of pictures, of course, and I had my older sister pick the prints up after getting them developed. The guy at the shop asked her, "Was this really a vacation?"

So many weird pictures... (About 90 percent were basically reference shots for my art.)

I remember our tour guide being really cute.

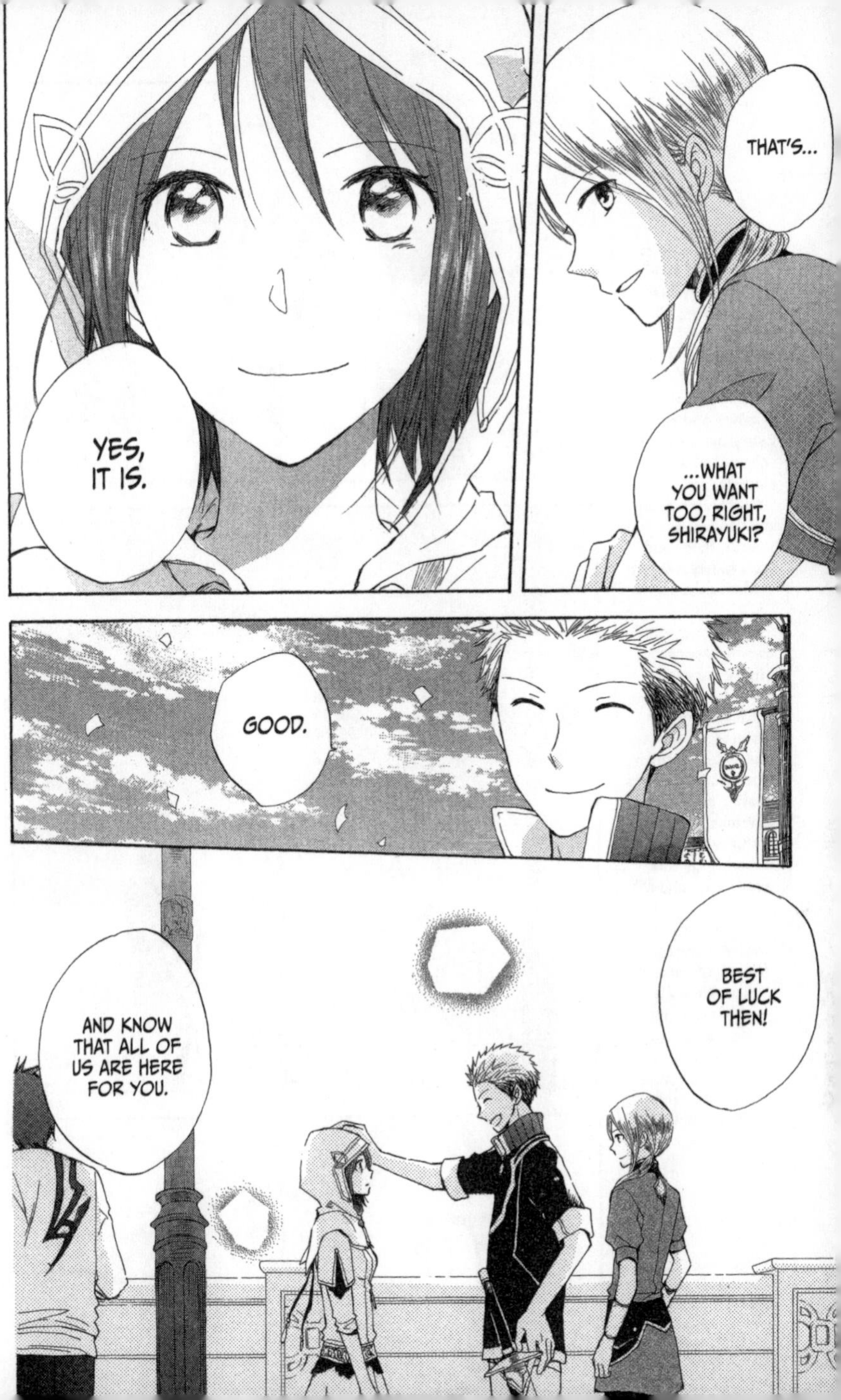
THAT'S...
...WHAT YOU WANT TOO, RIGHT, SHIRAYUKI?
YES, IT IS.
GOOD.
BEST OF LUCK THEN!
AND KNOW THAT ALL OF US ARE HERE FOR YOU.

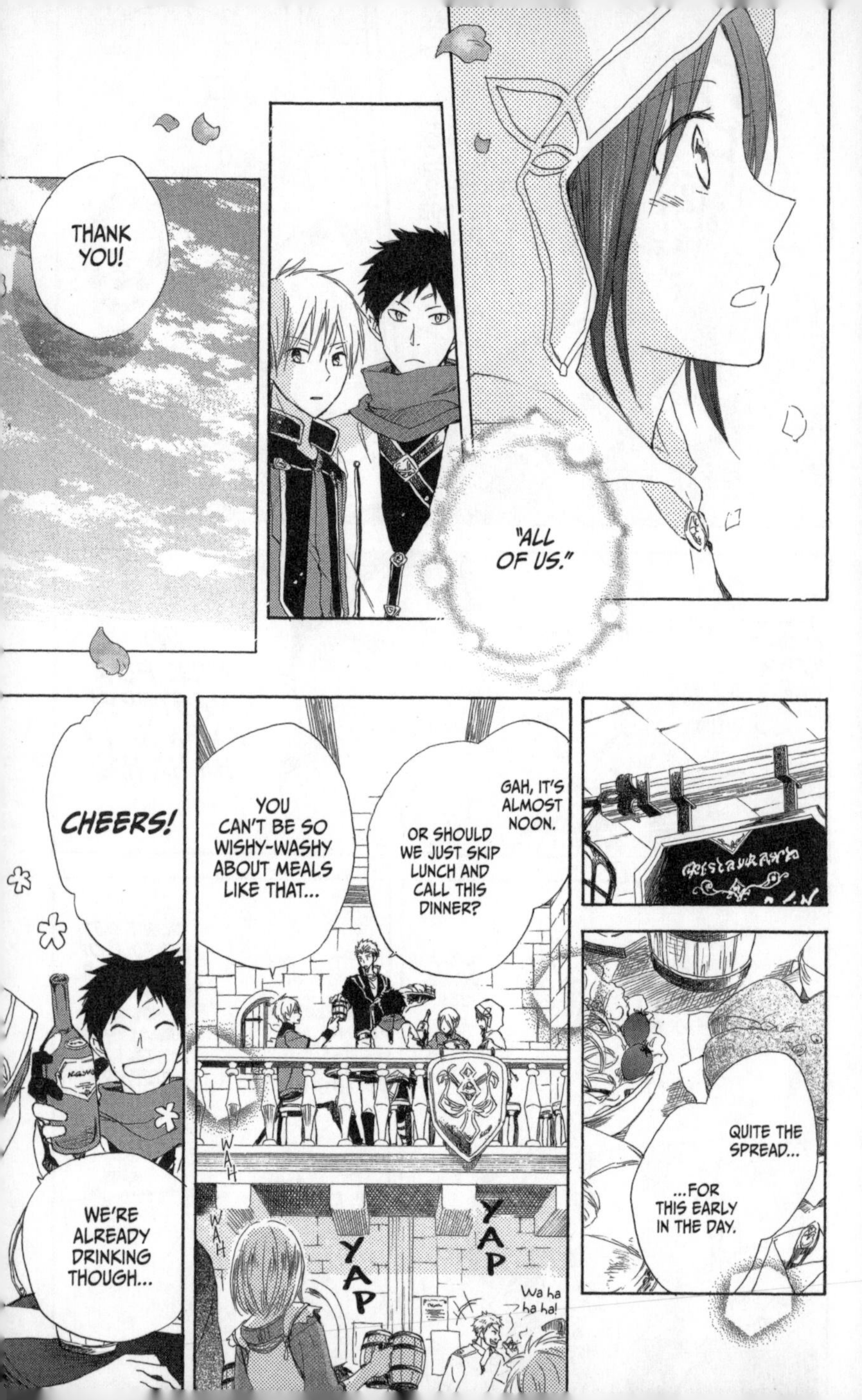
"ALL OF US."
THANK YOU!
QUITE THE SPREAD...
...FOR THIS EARLY IN THE DAY.
GAH, IT'S ALMOST NOON.
OR SHOULD WE JUST SKIP LUNCH AND CALL THIS DINNER?
YOU CAN'T BE SO WISHY-WASHY ABOUT MEALS LIKE THAT...
WAH
WAH
YAP
YAP
Wa ha ha ha!
CHEERS!
WE'RE ALREADY DRINKING THOUGH...

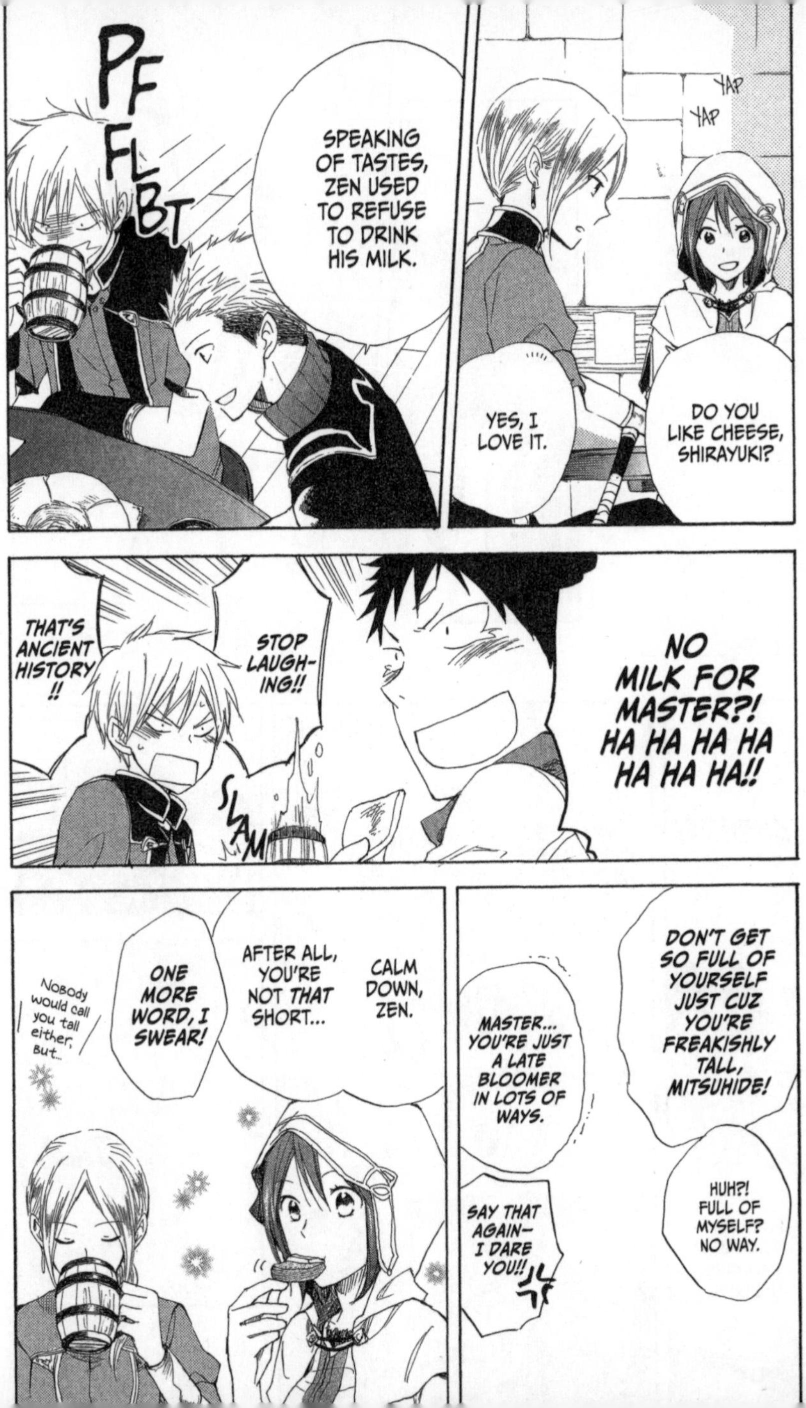
YAP
YAP
DO YOU LIKE CHEESE, SHIRAYUKI?
YES, I LOVE IT.
SPEAKING OF TASTES, ZEN USED TO REFUSE TO DRINK HIS MILK.
PFFLBT
NO MILK FOR MASTER?! HA HA HA HA HA HA HA!!
STOP LAUGHING!!
THAT'S ANCIENT HISTORY!!
SLAM
DON'T GET SO FULL OF YOURSELF JUST CUZ YOU'RE FREAKISHLY TALL, MITSUHIDE!
MASTER... YOU'RE JUST A LATE BLOOMER IN LOTS OF WAYS.
HUH?! FULL OF MYSELF? NO WAY.
SAY THAT AGAIN— I DARE YOU!!
CALM DOWN, ZEN.
AFTER ALL, YOU'RE NOT THAT SHORT...
ONE MORE WORD, I SWEAR!
Nobody would call you tall either, but...

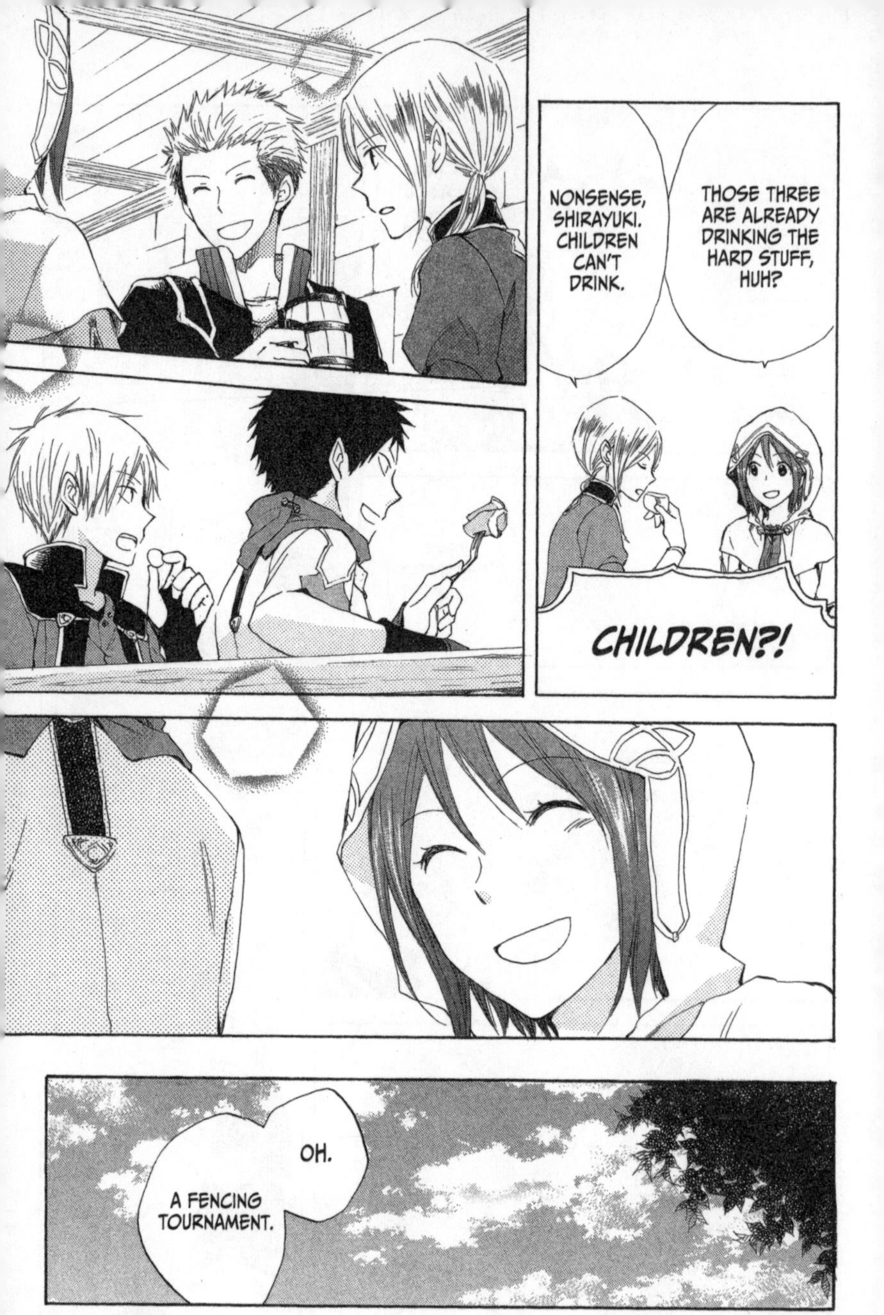
THOSE THREE ARE ALREADY DRINKING THE HARD STUFF, HUH?
NONSENSE, SHIRAYUKI. CHILDREN CAN'T DRINK.
CHILDREN?!
OH.
A FENCING TOURNAMENT.

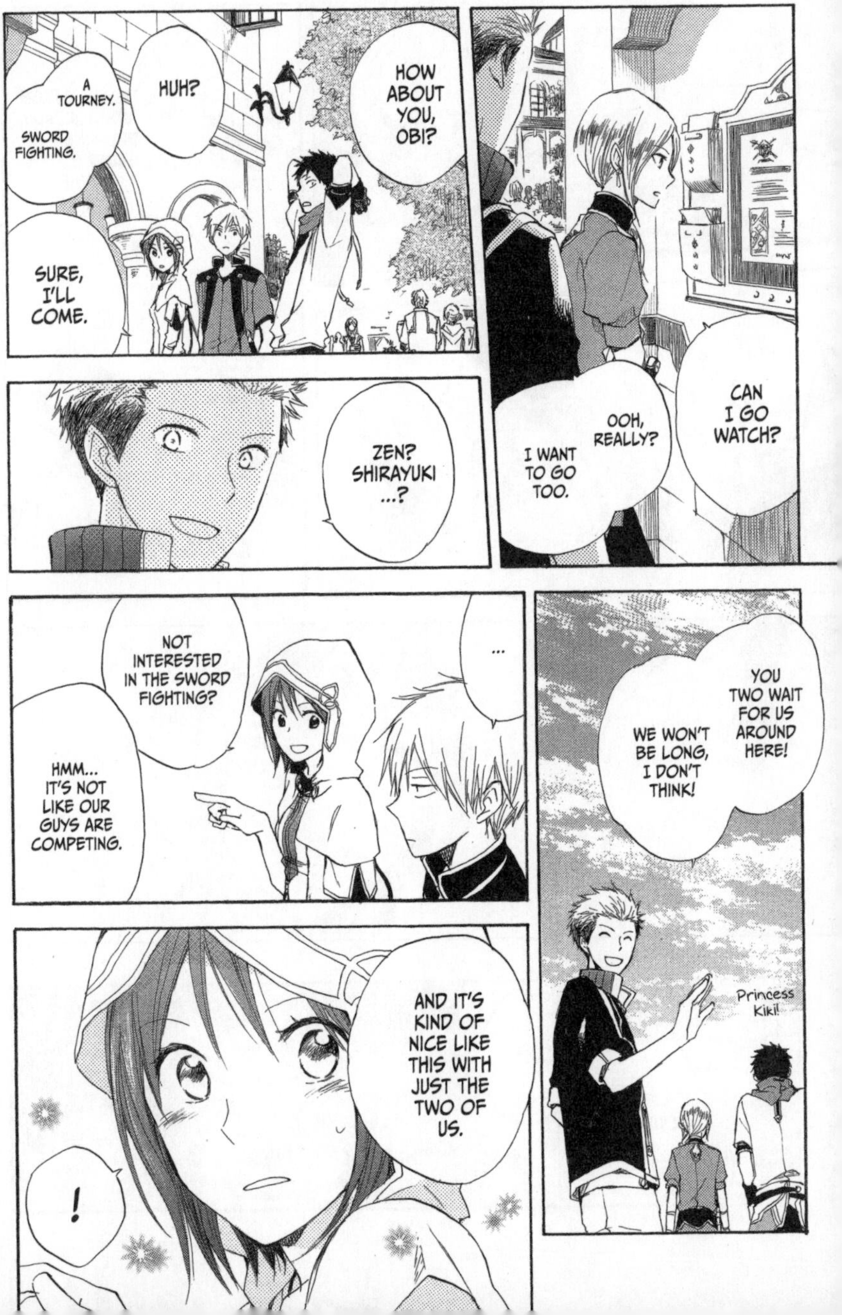
CAN I GO WATCH?
OOH, REALLY?
I WANT TO GO TOO.
HOW ABOUT YOU, OBI?
HUH?
A TOURNEY.
SWORD FIGHTING.
SURE, I'LL COME.
ZEN? SHIRAYUKI ...?
YOU TWO WAIT FOR US AROUND HERE!
WE WON'T BE LONG, I DON'T THINK!
Princess Kiki!
...
NOT INTERESTED IN THE SWORD FIGHTING?
HMM... IT'S NOT LIKE OUR GUYS ARE COMPETING.
AND IT'S KIND OF NICE LIKE THIS WITH JUST THE TWO OF US.
!

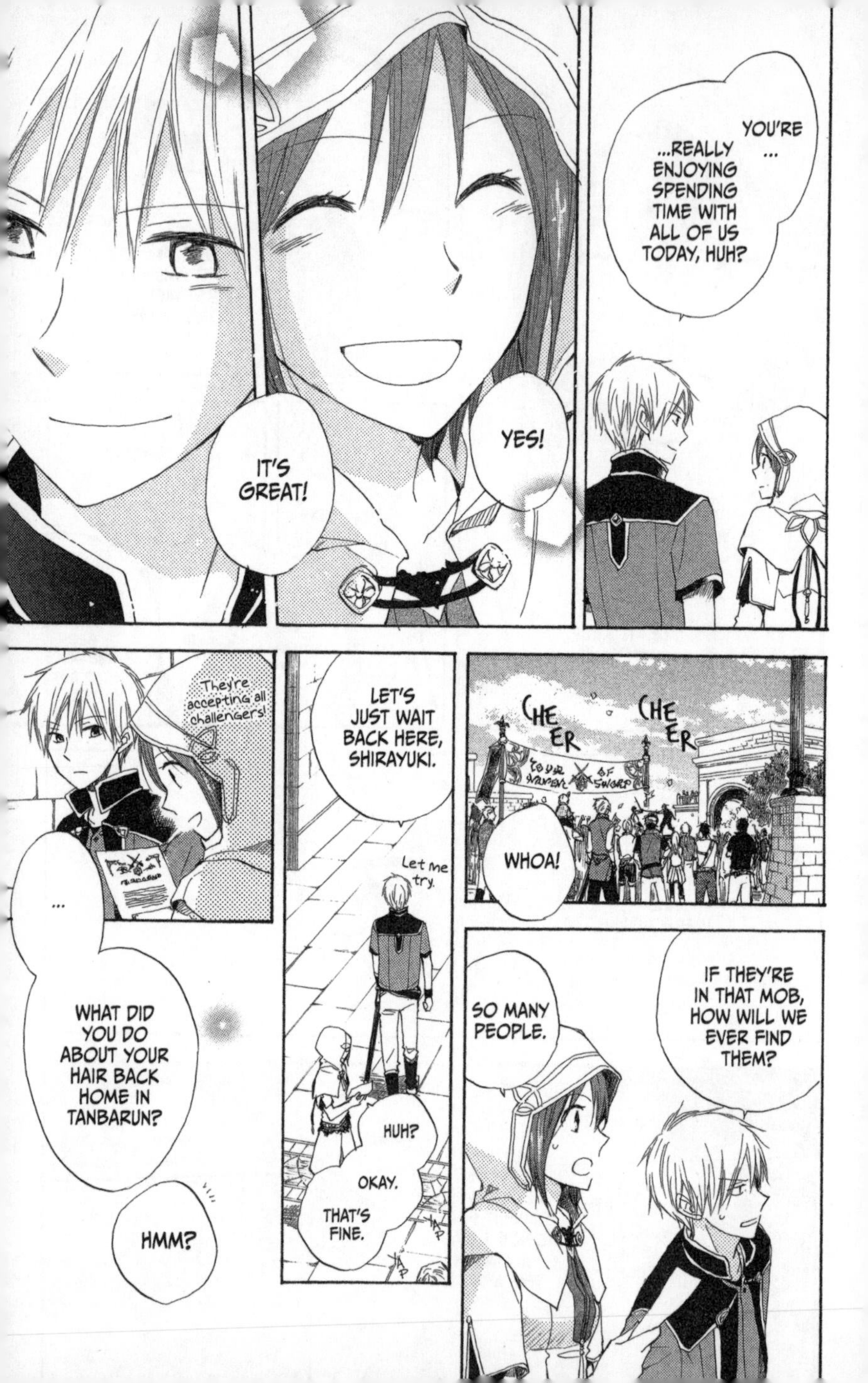
YOU'RE ...
...REALLY ENJOYING SPENDING TIME WITH ALL OF US TODAY, HUH?
YES!
IT'S GREAT!
CHEER
CHEER
WHOA!
IF THEY'RE IN THAT MOB, HOW WILL WE EVER FIND THEM?
SO MANY PEOPLE.
LET'S JUST WAIT BACK HERE, SHIRAYUKI.
Let me try.
HUH?
OKAY.
THAT'S FINE.
YAP
YAP
They're accepting all challengers!
...
WHAT DID YOU DO ABOUT YOUR HAIR BACK HOME IN TANBARUN?
HMM?

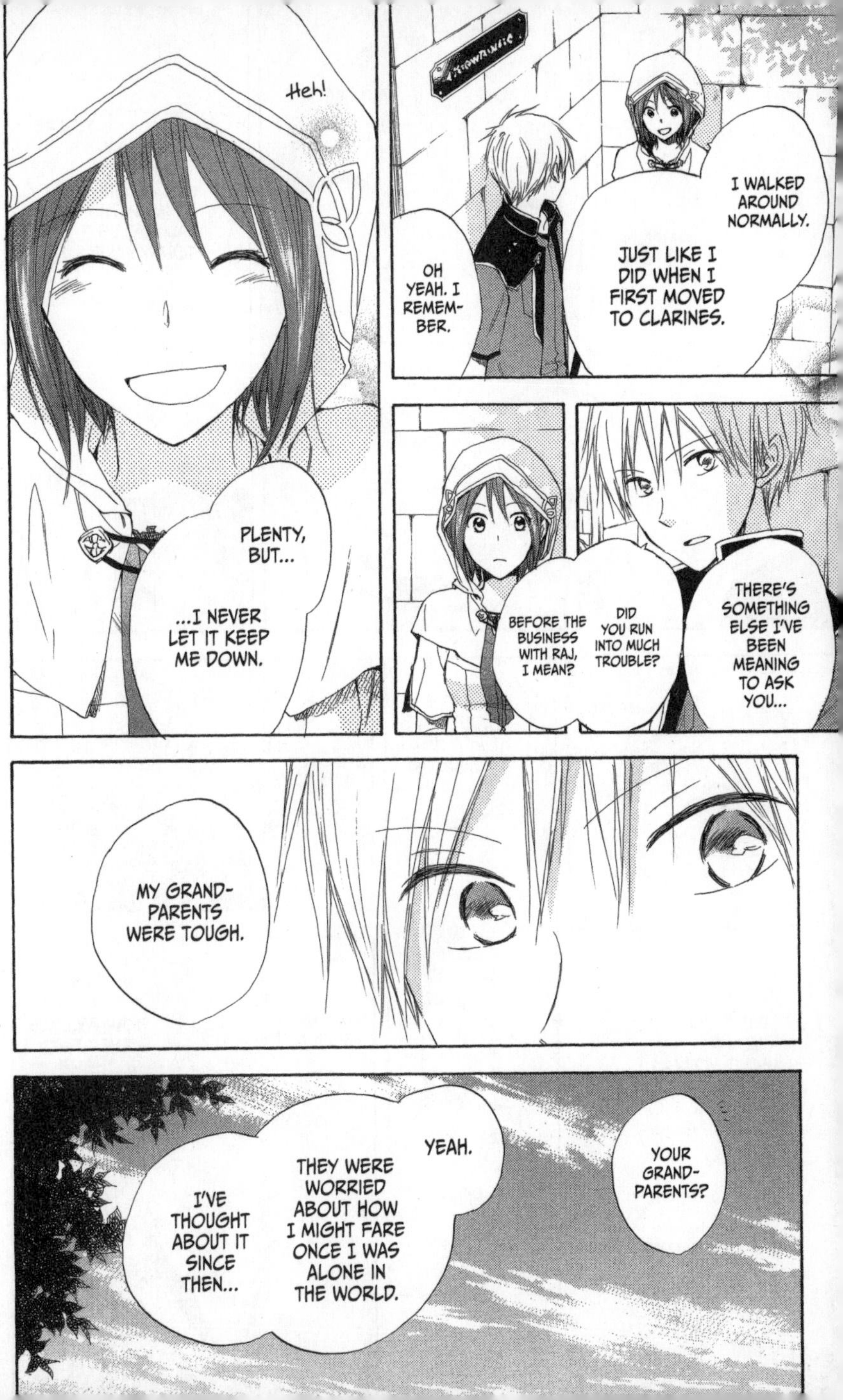
I WALKED AROUND NORMALLY.
JUST LIKE I DID WHEN I FIRST MOVED TO CLARINES.
OH YEAH. I REMEMBER.
THERE'S SOMETHING ELSE I'VE BEEN MEANING TO ASK YOU...
DID YOU RUN INTO MUCH TROUBLE?
BEFORE THE BUSINESS WITH RAJ, I MEAN?
Heh!
PLENTY, BUT...
...I NEVER LET IT KEEP ME DOWN.
MY GRAND-PARENTS WERE TOUGH.
YOUR GRAND-PARENTS?
YEAH.
THEY WERE WORRIED ABOUT HOW I MIGHT FARE ONCE I WAS ALONE IN THE WORLD.
I'VE THOUGHT ABOUT IT SINCE THEN...

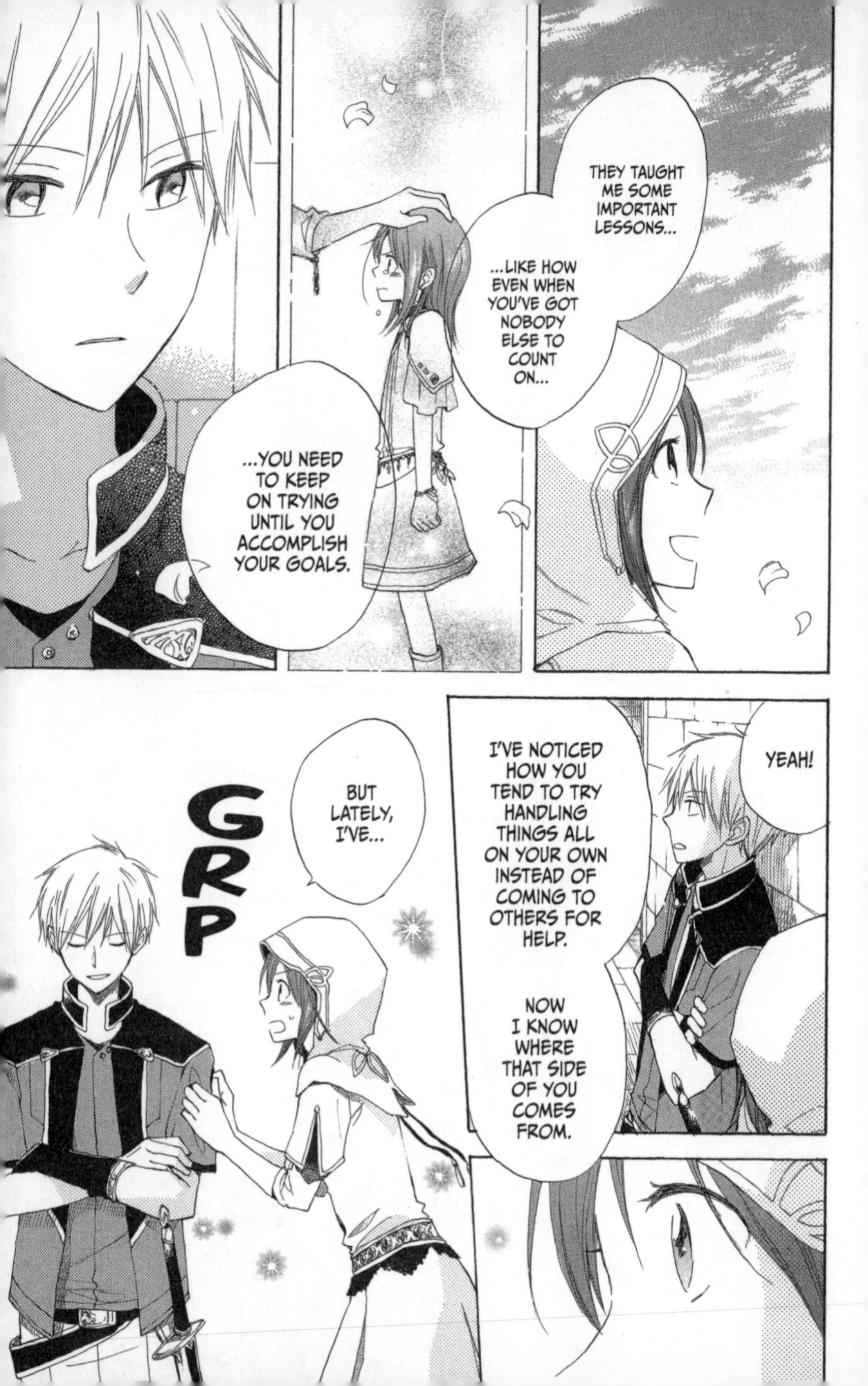
THEY TAUGHT ME SOME IMPORTANT LESSONS...
...LIKE HOW EVEN WHEN YOU'VE GOT NOBODY ELSE TO COUNT ON...
...YOU NEED TO KEEP ON TRYING UNTIL YOU ACCOMPLISH YOUR GOALS.
YEAH!
I'VE NOTICED HOW YOU TEND TO TRY HANDLING THINGS ALL ON YOUR OWN INSTEAD OF COMING TO OTHERS FOR HELP.
NOW I KNOW WHERE THAT SIDE OF YOU COMES FROM.
GRP
BUT LATELY, I'VE...

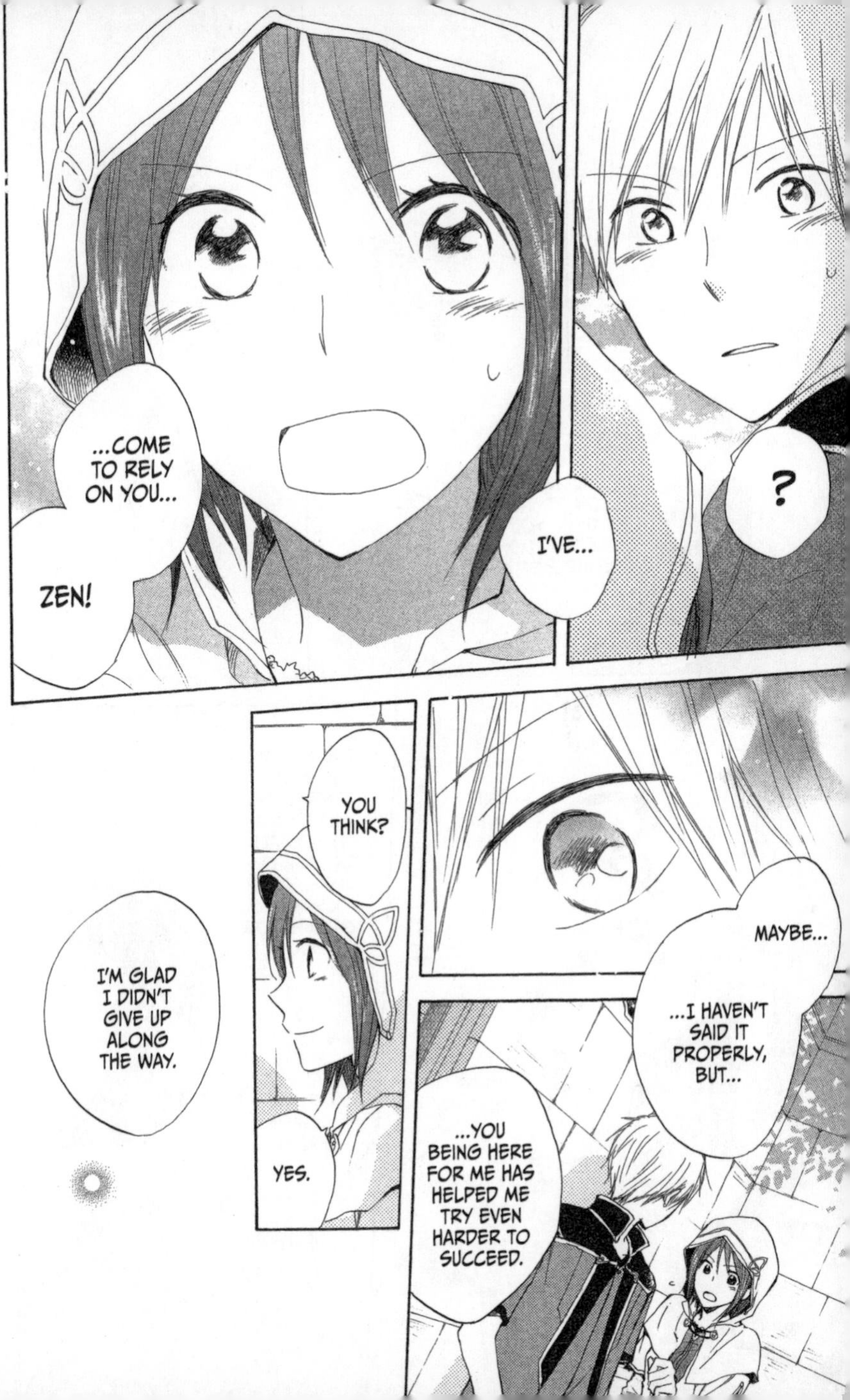
?
I'VE...
...COME TO RELY ON YOU...
ZEN!
MAYBE...
...I HAVEN'T SAID IT PROPERLY, BUT...
...YOU BEING HERE FOR ME HAS HELPED ME TRY EVEN HARDER TO SUCCEED.
YOU THINK?
YES.
I'M GLAD I DIDN'T GIVE UP ALONG THE WAY.

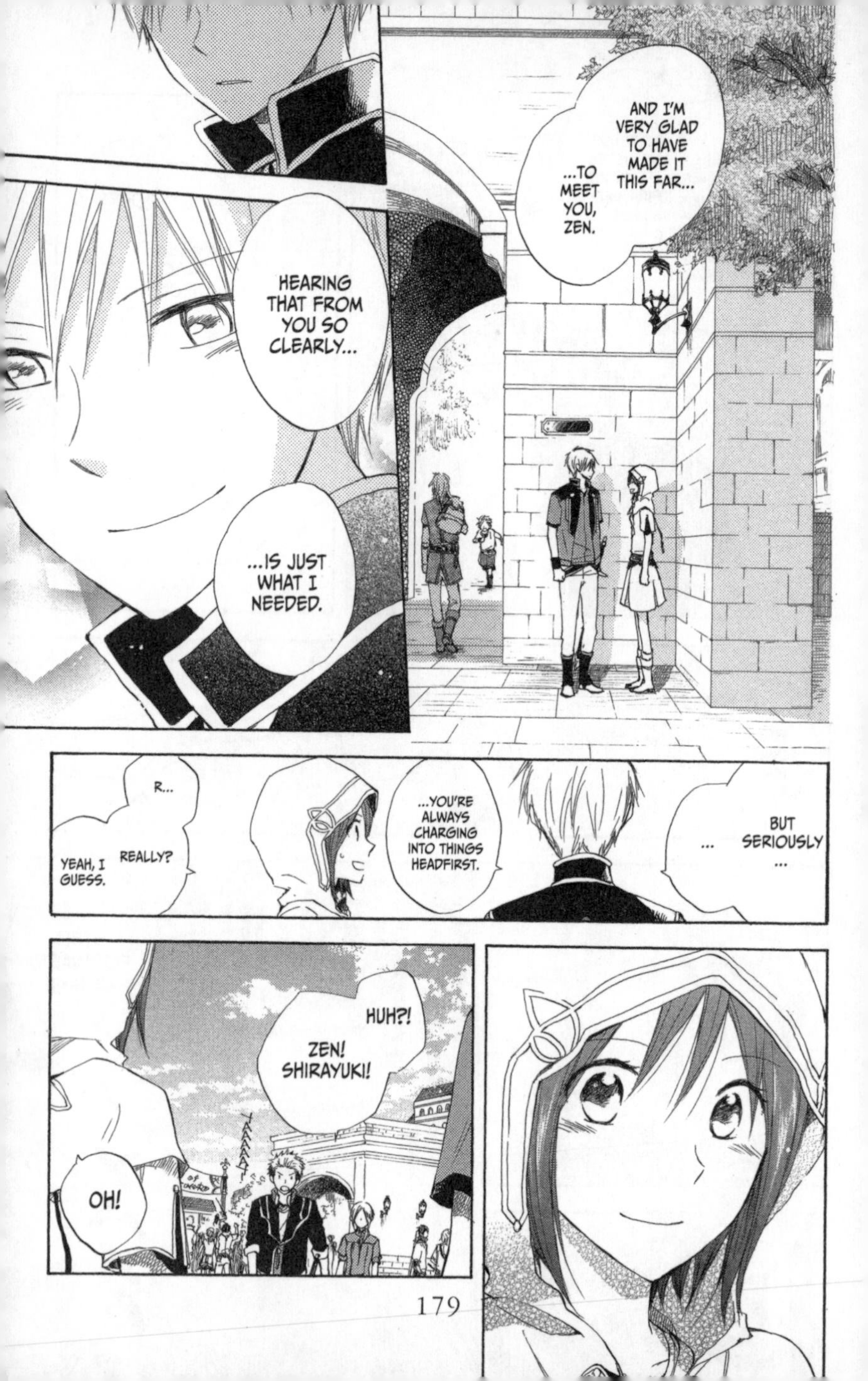
AND I'M VERY GLAD TO HAVE MADE IT THIS FAR...
...TO MEET YOU, ZEN.
HEARING THAT FROM YOU SO CLEARLY...
...IS JUST WHAT I NEEDED.
... BUT SERIOUSLY ...
...YOU'RE ALWAYS CHARGING INTO THINGS HEADFIRST.
R... REALLY?
YEAH, I GUESS.
HUH?!
ZEN! SHIRAYUKI!
OH!

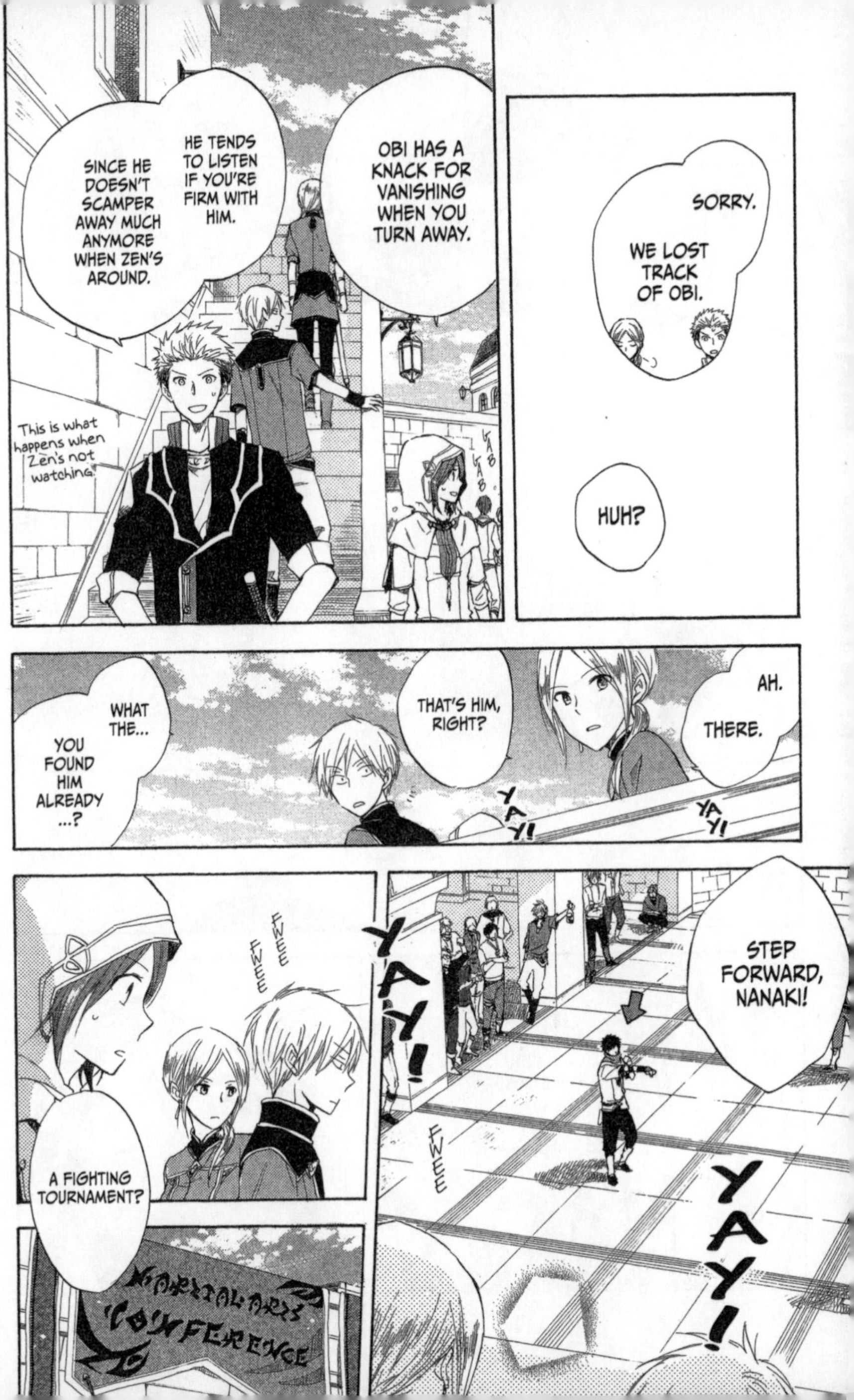
SORRY.
WE LOST TRACK OF OBI.
HUH?
OBI HAS A KNACK FOR VANISHING WHEN YOU TURN AWAY.
HE TENDS TO LISTEN IF YOU'RE FIRM WITH HIM.
SINCE HE DOESN'T SCAMPER AWAY MUCH ANYMORE WHEN ZEN'S AROUND.
GAB GAB
This is what happens when Zen's not watching!
AH.
THERE.
THAT'S HIM, RIGHT?
WHAT THE...
YOU FOUND HIM ALREADY ...?
YAY!
YAY!
STEP FORWARD, NANAKI!
YAY!
YAY!
FWEE
FWEE
FWEE
A FIGHTING TOURNAMENT?
MARTIAL ARTS CONFERENCE

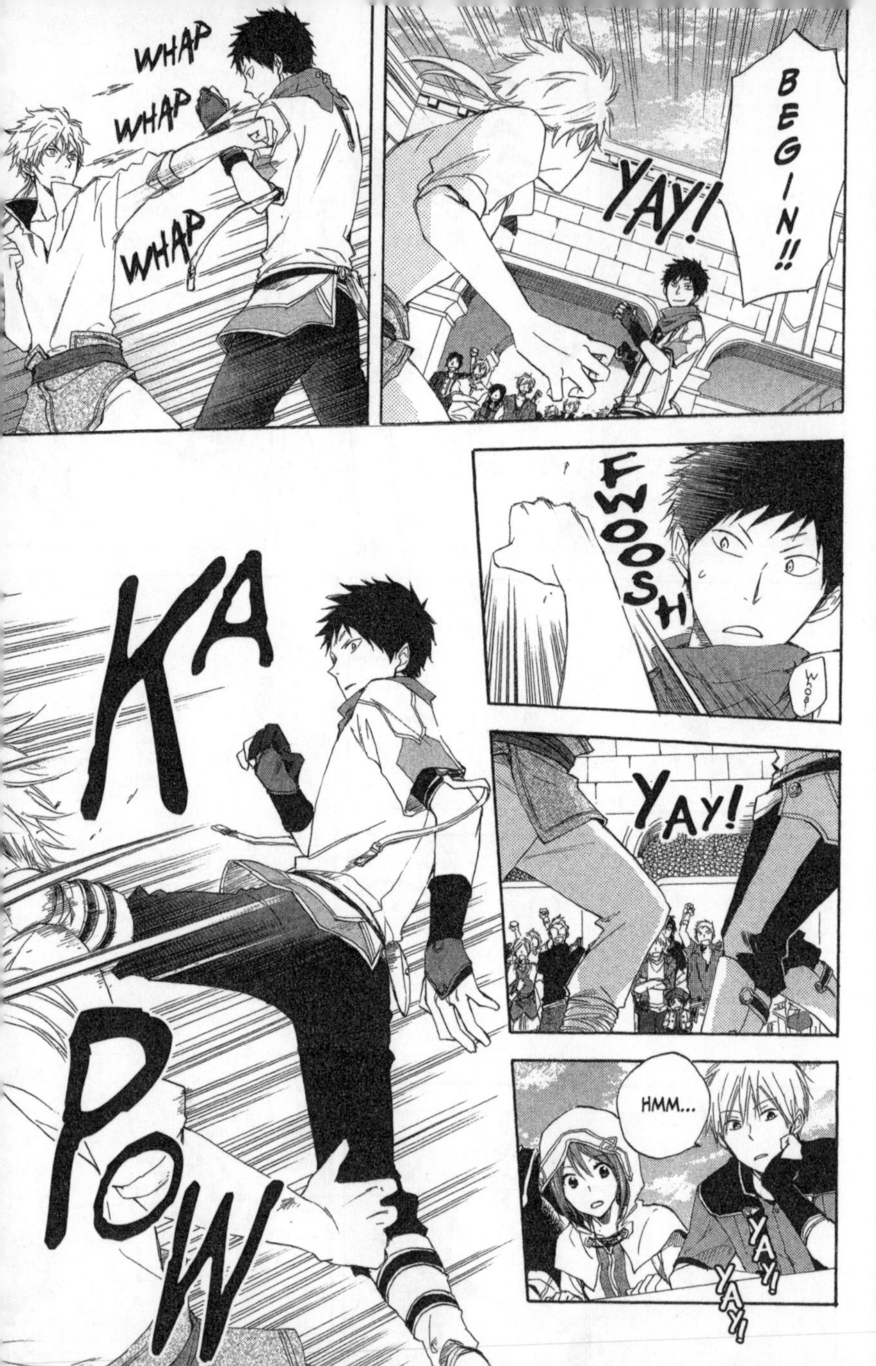
BEGIN!!
YAY!
WHAP
WHAP
WHAP
FWOOSH
whoop!
YAY!
HMM...
YAY!
YAY!
YAY!
KA
POW

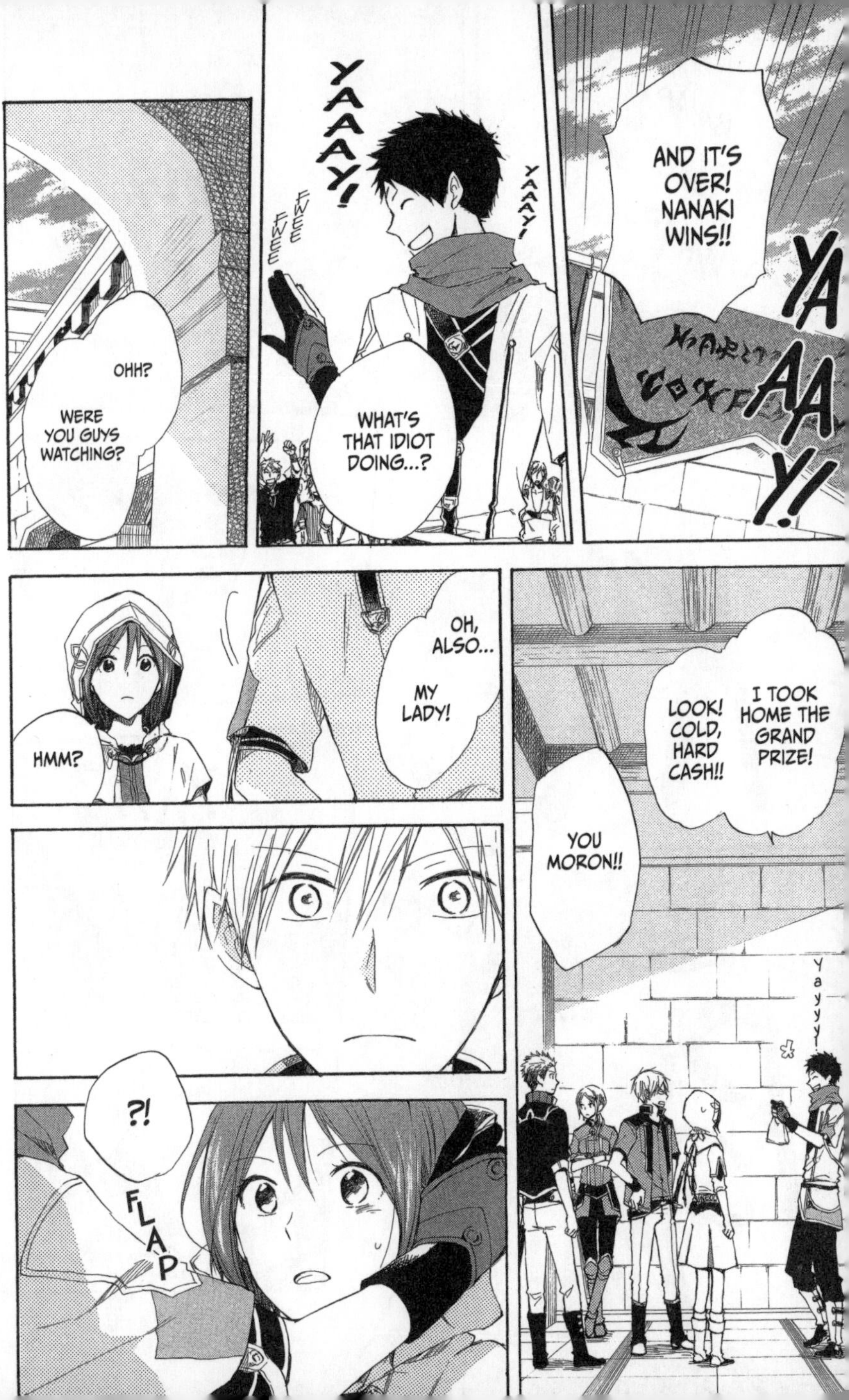
AND IT'S OVER! NANAKI WINS!!
YAAAAY!
YAAAY!
YAAAAY!
FWEE FWEE
WHAT'S THAT IDIOT DOING...?
OHH?
WERE YOU GUYS WATCHING?
I TOOK HOME THE GRAND PRIZE!
LOOK! COLD, HARD CASH!!
YOU MORON!!
Yayyy!
OH, ALSO...
MY LADY!
HMM?
?!
FLAP

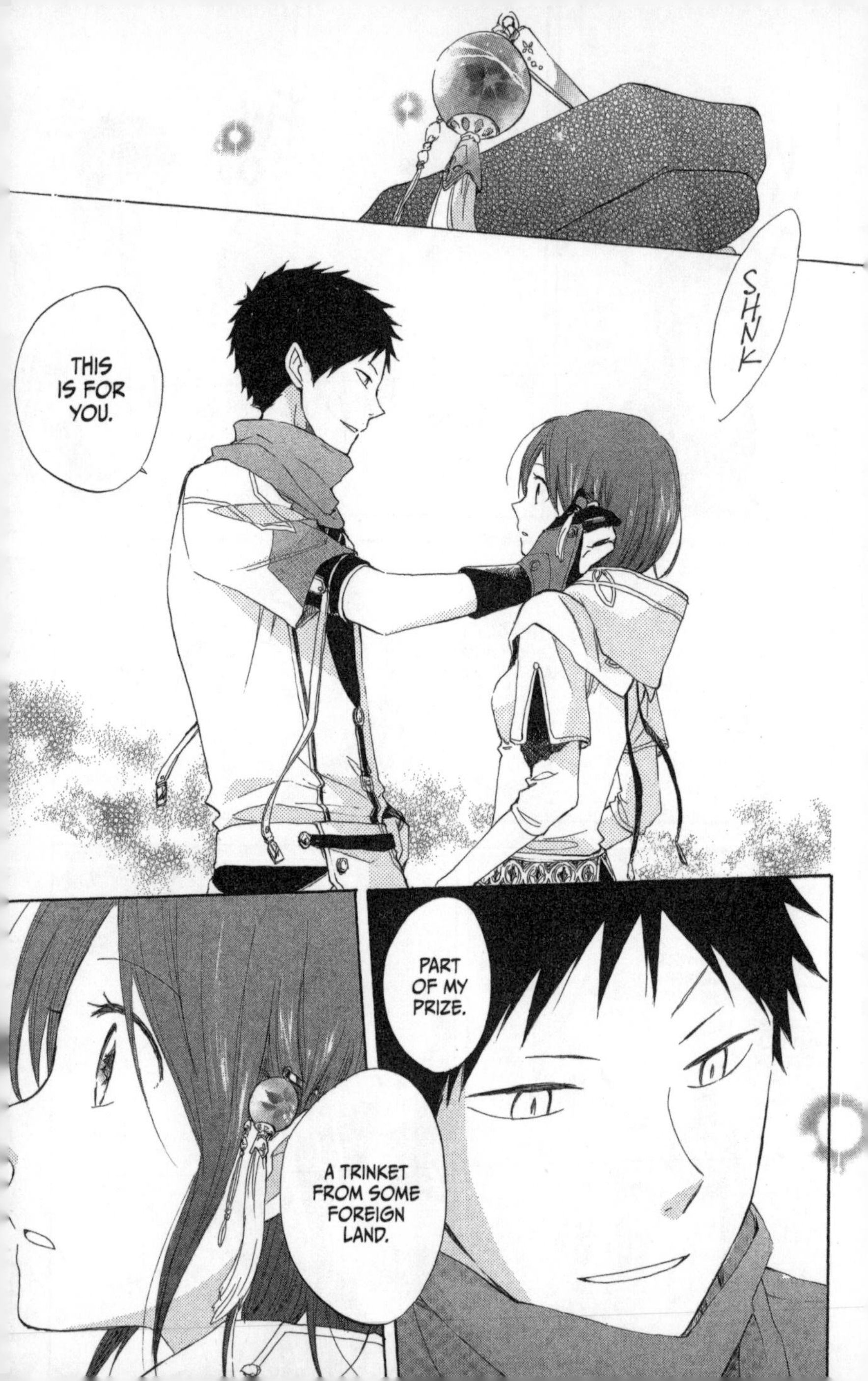
SHNK
THIS IS FOR YOU.
PART OF MY PRIZE.
A TRINKET FROM SOME FOREIGN LAND.

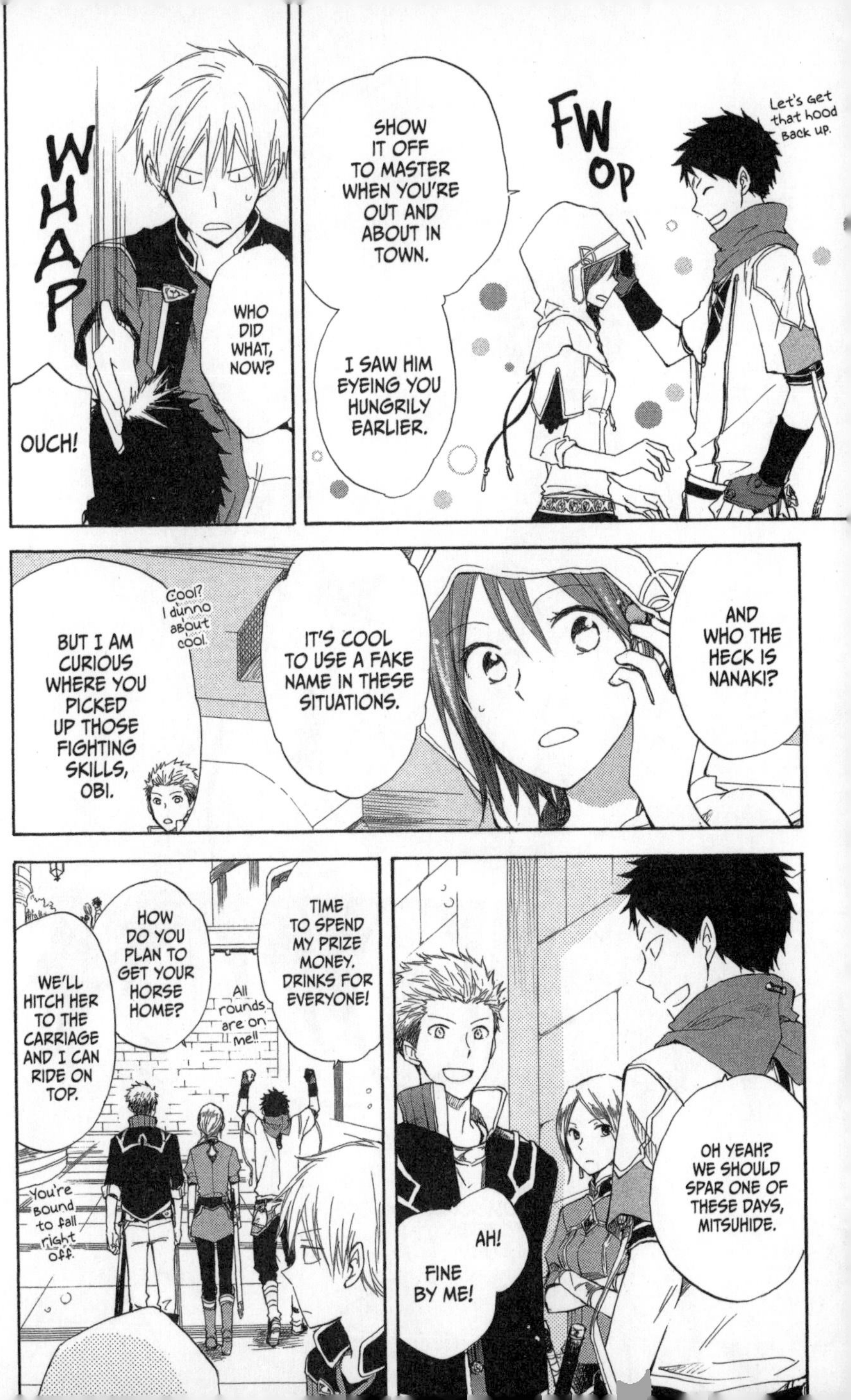
Let's get that hood back up.
FWOP
SHOW IT OFF TO MASTER WHEN YOU'RE OUT AND ABOUT IN TOWN.
I SAW HIM EYEING YOU HUNGRILY EARLIER.
WHAP
WHO DID WHAT, NOW?
OUCH!
AND WHO THE HECK IS NANAKI?
IT'S COOL TO USE A FAKE NAME IN THESE SITUATIONS.
Cool? I dunno about cool.
BUT I AM CURIOUS WHERE YOU PICKED UP THOSE FIGHTING SKILLS, OBI.
OH YEAH? WE SHOULD SPAR ONE OF THESE DAYS, MITSUHIDE.
AH!
FINE BY ME!
TIME TO SPEND MY PRIZE MONEY. DRINKS FOR EVERYONE!
All rounds are on me!!
HOW DO YOU PLAN TO GET YOUR HORSE HOME?
WE'LL HITCH HER TO THE CARRIAGE AND I CAN RIDE ON TOP.
You're bound to fall right off.

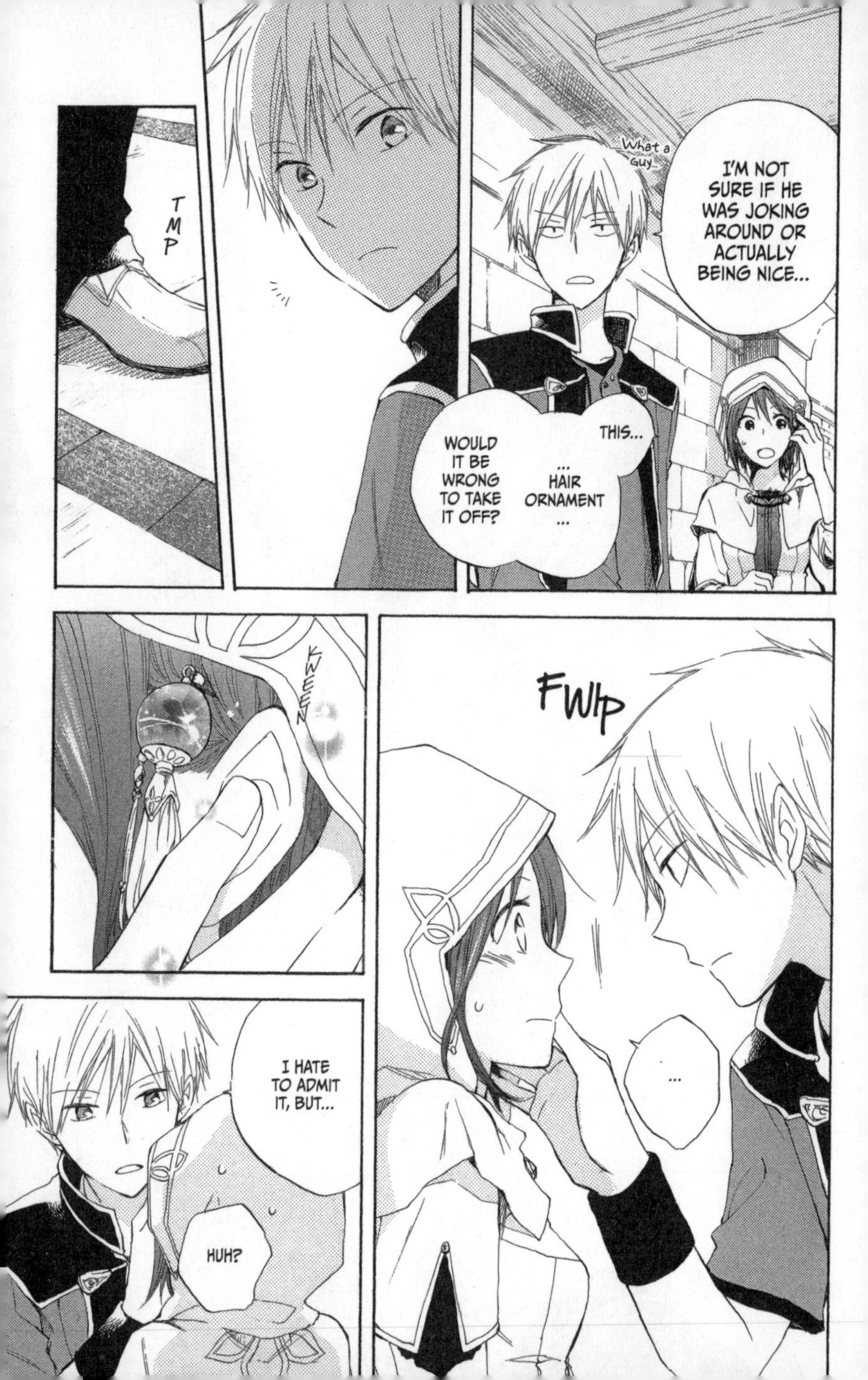
What a Guy...
I'M NOT SURE IF HE WAS JOKING AROUND OR ACTUALLY BEING NICE...
THIS...
... HAIR ORNAMENT ...
WOULD IT BE WRONG TO TAKE IT OFF?
TMP
FWIP
...
KWEEN
I HATE TO ADMIT IT, BUT...
HUH?

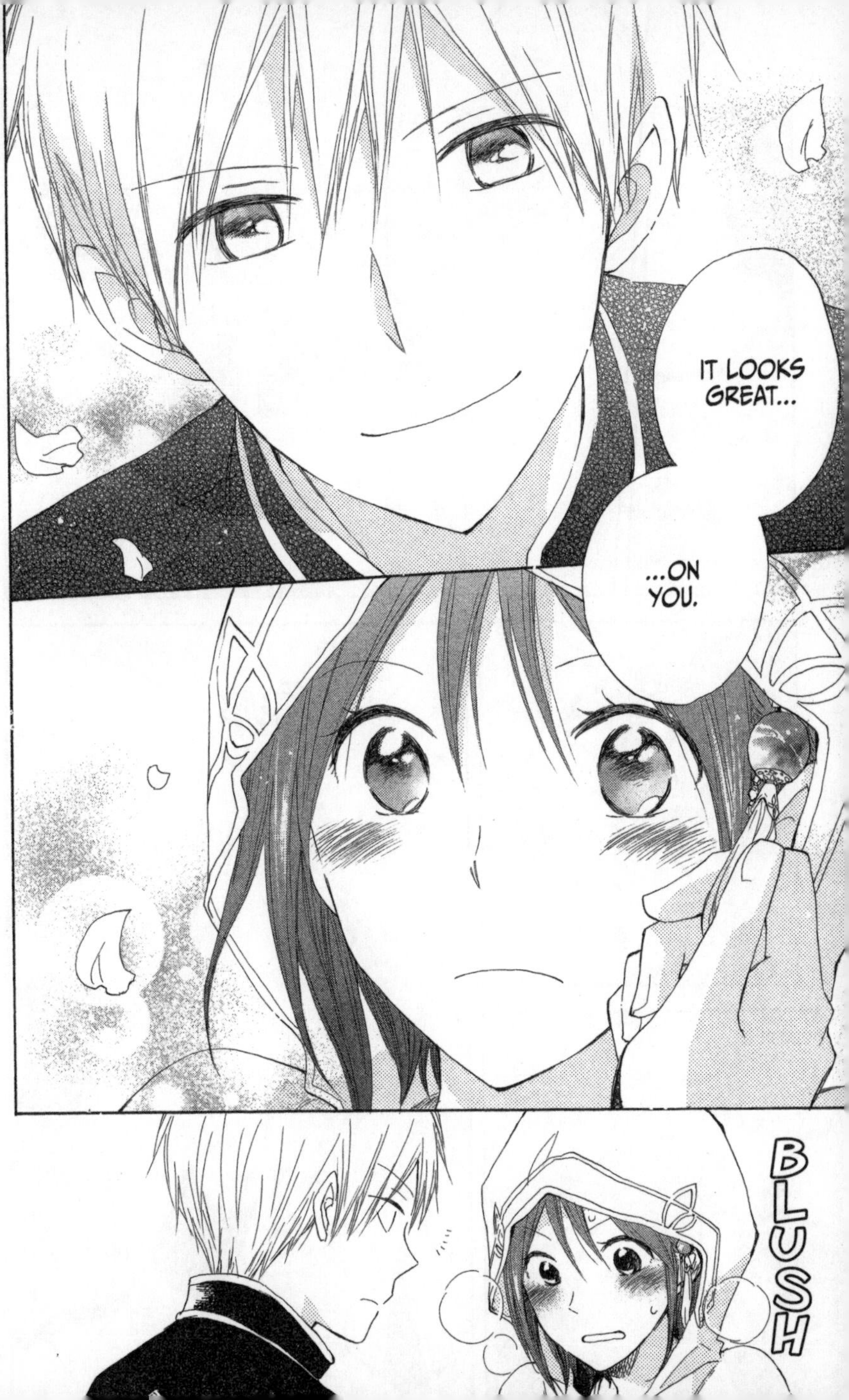
IT LOOKS GREAT...
...ON YOU.
BLUSH

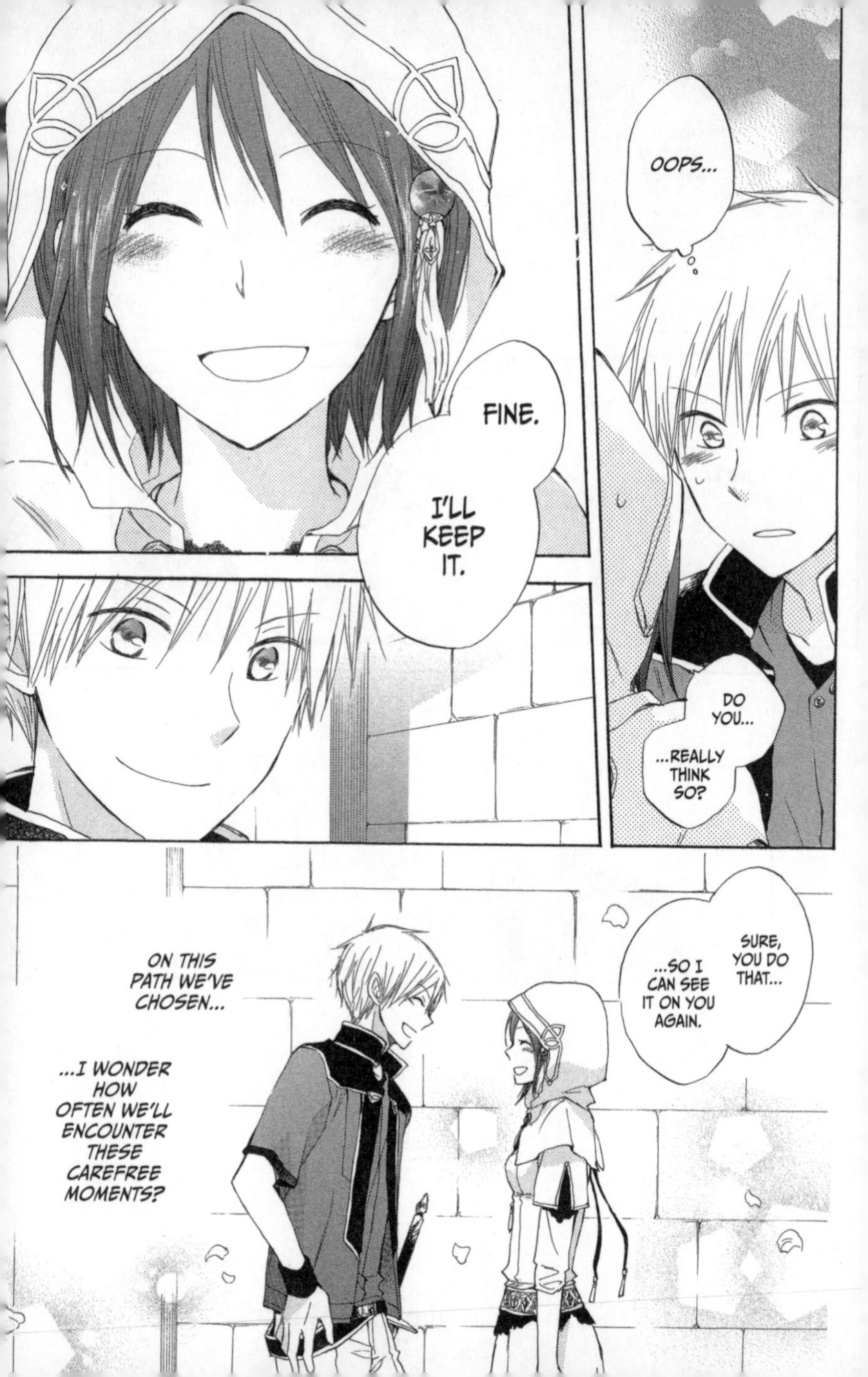
OOPS...
DO YOU...
...REALLY THINK SO?
FINE.
I'LL KEEP IT.
SURE, YOU DO THAT...
...SO I CAN SEE IT ON YOU AGAIN.
ON THIS PATH WE'VE CHOSEN...
...I WONDER HOW OFTEN WE'LL ENCOUNTER THESE CAREFREE MOMENTS?

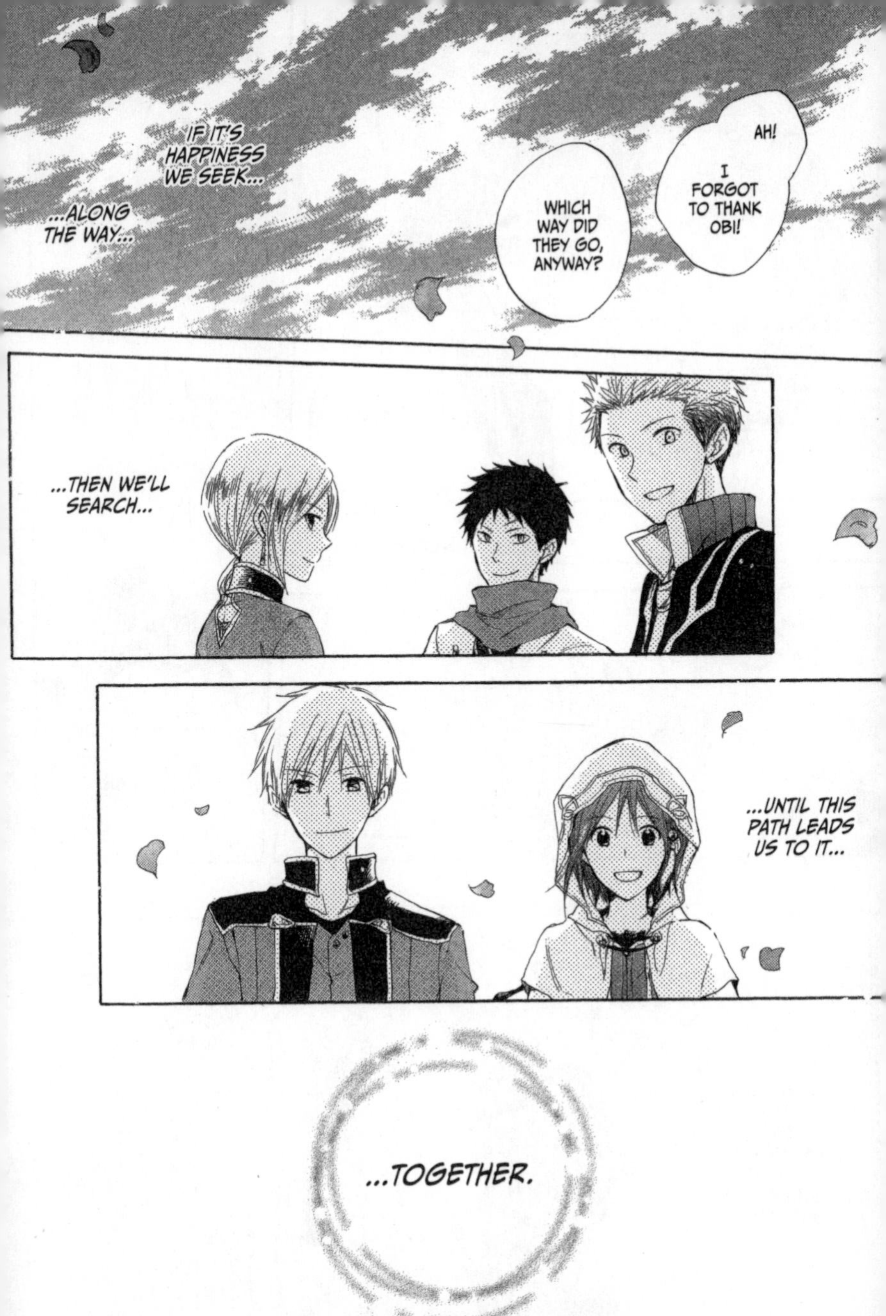
AH!
I FORGOT TO THANK OBI!
WHICH WAY DID THEY GO, ANYWAY?
IF IT'S HAPPINESS WE SEEK...
...ALONG THE WAY...
...THEN WE'LL SEARCH...
...UNTIL THIS PATH LEADS US TO IT...
...TOGETHER.

Snow White with the Red Hair
Vol. 4: End

BONUS PAGE

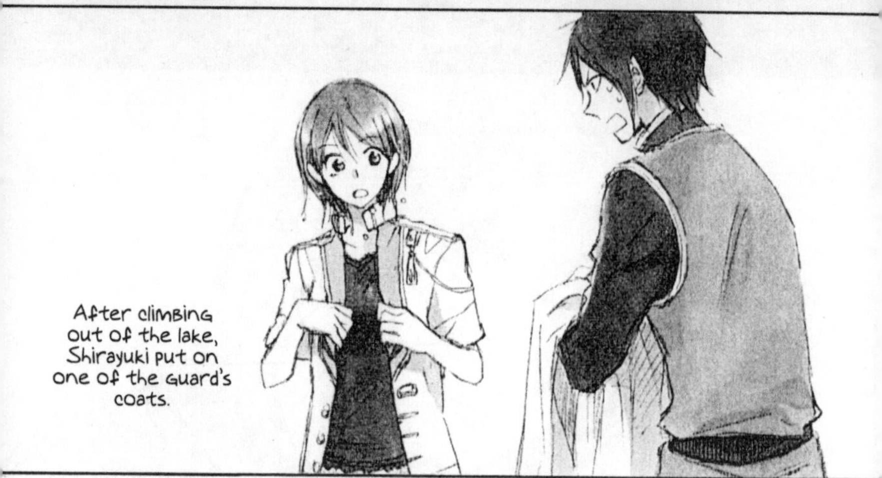
After climbing out of the lake, Shirayuki put on one of the guard's coats.

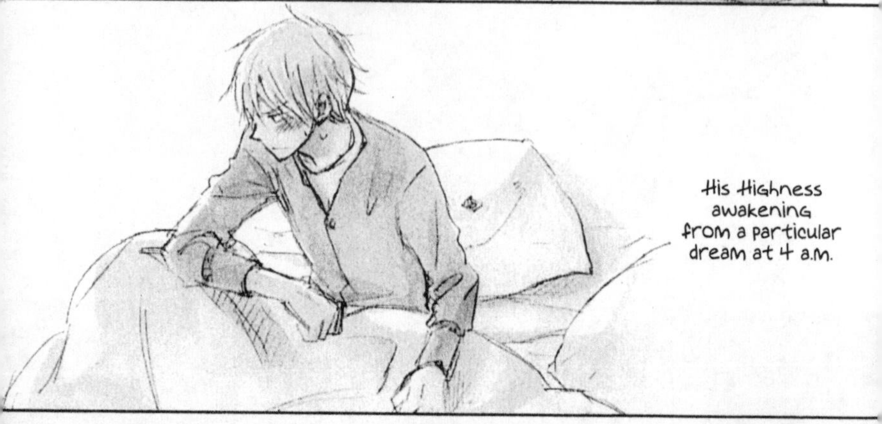
His Highness awakening from a particular dream at 4 a.m.

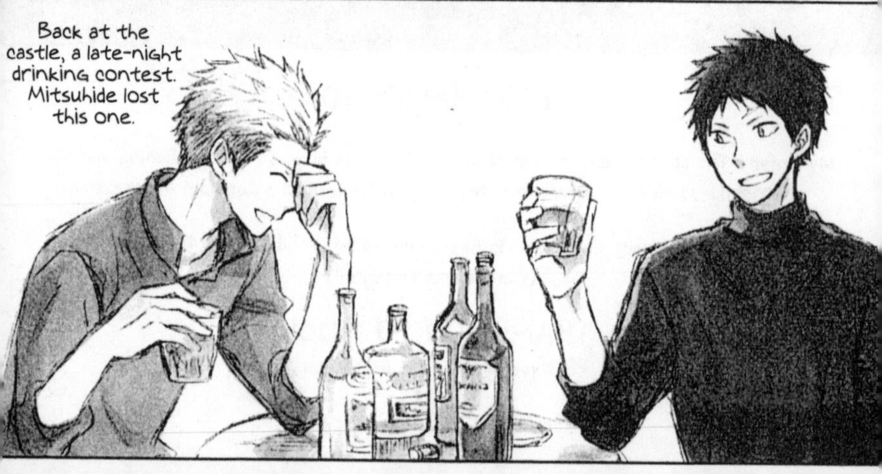
Back at the castle, a late-night drinking contest. Mitsuhide lost this one.

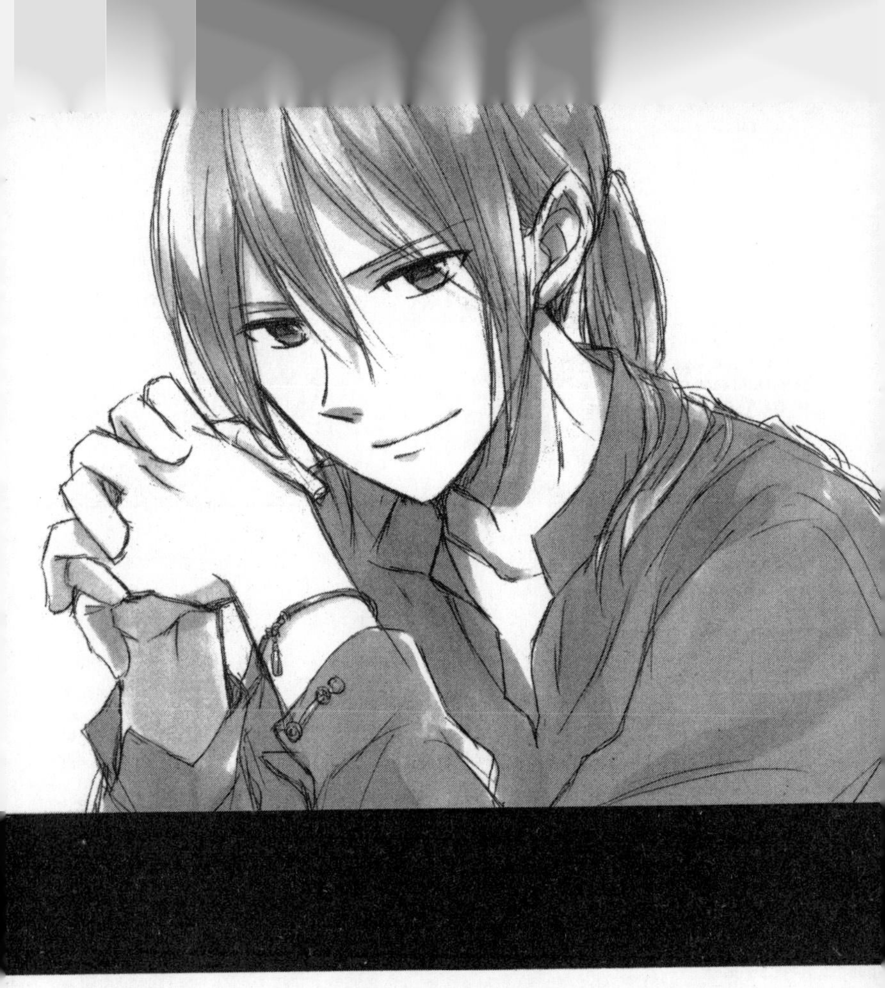

[redacted]

BIG THANKS TO:

My editor • The editorial department at *LaLa* • Everyone involved with publishing and sales
Yamashita-sama • Fellow warriors: My big sister and Mom • Constant backup: Dad

And everyone who supports this series and/or sends me fan letters!
(You give me strength!!)

THANK YOU SO MUCH!

See you again in the next volume.

-Sorata Akiduki, November 2009